I AM

SOLDIER OF FORTUNE

U.S.ARMY

I AM SOLDIER OF FORTUNE

Dancing with Devils

"I'm not going to tip-toe through life so I can face death safely."
— *anonymous*

LT COL ROBERT K. BROWN, USAR, (RET.)
WITH VANN SPENCER

CASEMATE
Philadelphia & Oxford

Published in the United States of America and Great Britain in 2013 by
CASEMATE PUBLISHERS
908 Darby Road, Havertown, PA 19083
and
10 Hythe Bridge Street, Oxford, OX1 2EW

ISBN 978-1-61200-193-7
Digital Edition: ISBN 978-1-61200-194-4

Cataloging-in-publication data is available from the Library of Congress and the British Library.

10 9 8 7 6 5 4 3 2

Printed and bound in the United States of America.

For a complete list of Casemate titles please contact:

CASEMATE PUBLISHERS (US)
Telephone (610) 853-9131, Fax (610) 853-9146
E-mail: casemate@casematepublishing.com

CASEMATE PUBLISHERS (UK)
Telephone (01865) 241249, Fax (01865) 794449
E-mail: casemate-uk@casematepublishing.co.uk

CONTENTS

PROLOGUE

Most of the artillery explosions and white-hot arcs of large-caliber tracer bullets were a few kilometers behind us on the Sarajevo skyline. We had been cramped in the truck bed for hours that seemed like days, stuck in the suburbs of the city. We were miserably bound in flak jackets, in a sandbagged truck bed and were numb to the much closer AK-47 fire.

As long as no bullets pinged through the steel of our truck, no one in our party seemed too concerned about the random rounds. All 12 of us in the truck were exhausted and wet enough that we could give a damn about who got greased as long as it wasn't us. Then suddenly, a Serbian 12.7mm heavy machine gun opened up on us, coming at us in what seemed like football-sized orange tracers.

The hot rounds came screaming toward our soft-skinned truck and softer-skinned bodies. Silently, and instinctively, we scrambled to shove ourselves deeper into the truck bed to protect our heads and arms from the killer rounds. Moments earlier, I'd been amusing myself by dictating a play by play of the action into a tape recorder. I have been told that I record everything and that my tapes could fill dump trucks. But now we had nothing to do but count the malevolent tracers swishing overhead as the heavy machine gun roared in the background. My tape recorder was a welcome distraction.

"I figure that the gun position is about 500 meters out and the only reason we aren't exposed is because we are hidden by that ridge of dirt," John Jordan, a big, blustery, hot-headed Marine vet said.

He had left his Springfield Armory Super Match MIA behind in Sarajevo or we might have gone into the night looking for the Russian machine gun. Jordan let out one of his booming laughs of nervous relief that shattered our silence, "The SOB knows we are here but he can't quite get low enough to get us. His gun is mounted in a concrete bunker and unless he takes it off the mount and moves out of the bunker, he can't get to us."

I glanced at the pack of trucks in the rain. Who knows what the Serb was thinking as he glared at our white United Nations truck. We seriously doubted that he knew that the 12 men in the truck were Americans and Canadians who had just smuggled in some critical items right under his very nose, or worse yet, that John Jordan, who had killed some Serbs, was in our group. At that moment, Jordan was no more popular with us than he was with the Serbs. He was the one who had gotten us into this deadly mess that had reduced us to sitting ducks at the base of Mount Igman, some 10 klicks from Sarajevo.

What the hell was I doing here, anyhow? I had long lost count of the times I had asked my self that question when caught in some hotspot with no escape hatch in sight, vowing that I was done with jumping into the heat of hostilities between some vindictive ethnic groups or hashish crazed warring tribes. Again as the tracers screamed overhead, I tried to convince myself that it was all for the sake of the readers of my adventure magazine, *Soldier of Fortune*, but who was I kidding? Mama Brown's boy hadn't changed much since those wild college days when Fidel Castro's Cuban revolution came calling.

INTRODUCTION *BY VANN SPENCER*

FLAMING LIBERAL TOWN HOSTS A SHADY "HOTEL"

I have long been planning to write a book on what went on behind the scenes of *Soldier of Fortune* magazine, which would, without a doubt, be a bestseller. This thriller would provide any adventurer, scam artist, drama queen, scandal addict or madman the read of their lives, and I could retire in comfort. But first, the long awaited story of the magazine's daring, maverick publisher himself must be told.

Before we jump into the action that takes place in many of the most treacherous battlefields in the world, I will expose the most tempestuous and threatening fight that *Soldier of Fortune* and its notorious publisher faced. A nightmare with Orwellian twists, the battle dealt a near death knell to *SOF* and dragged me against my will and better judgment into that bizarre world.

I was in my first year of law school. In my serene neighborhood set in the spectacular Rocky Mountain foothills, I could hear—far more often than any civilized neighbor or student seeking refuge should ever have to bear—earsplitting "music," boisterous thundering voices engaged in a contest to out-bellow each other, drunken howls, hilarity and madness that went on for hours, shattering the night air and any existing peace.

I soon learned that the publisher of *Soldier of Fortune* magazine, Lieutenant Colonel Robert K. Brown USAR (Ret.), aka "Uncle Bob," "RKB," or "The Colonel," had established the "Brown Hotel" which the neighborhood dubbed the "House of Madness," two houses down from mine. Without a doubt in violation of all zoning laws and noise ordnances, the

"Brown Hotel" hosted an unending stream of action-seeking famous and infamous mercenaries and former Special Operations Forces-types. Scores of Viking or pirate-looking men, bearded or closely shaven, buzzed or with ponytails and tattoos, dressed in camouflage or black leather biker gear, met there to conspire not so stealthily for their next missions to Africa, Asia or Latin America. Myriad guests who roared in and out of the quarters on deafeningly loud motorcycles, chauffeured cars, macho trucks or revved-up autos often joined them. All came to visit the notorious Brown Hotel set in the unlikely locale of the flamingly liberal People's Republic of Boulder, Colorado.

One of the countless rumors that made the rounds of the neighborhood had it that on one occasion an entire busload of Special Forces operators dressed in camouflage and berets drove into the driveway of the "Brown Hotel" and stormed in. The raucousness that night was beyond description, as the story goes. I found the outrageous tale far-fetched, as the neighbors warned that the squad was preparing to overthrow some dictator or even take over the Flaming Liberal Republic of Boulder. I found out that the incident was indeed true, except for the juicy part about overthrowing some dictator, but only for THAT busload. A U.S. Army Master Sergeant had called the Colonel and told him he was bringing 30 of his Green Berets out for mountain climbing training in the rugged Rockies. The Colonel flew into action, even providing rock-climbing instructors. That night *SOF* threw a Fourth of July-ish bash, the likes of which the neighborhood had never seen nor heard. It was not July, let alone the 4th.

Lest the reader believe that I exaggerate, here is how one partygoer in the "Brown Hotel" recalled one rowdy night:

> It was sometime back in the early 80s after some gun show, a bunch of us would show up at your place to do some serious "partying." I was there with my dog "Smokey" and my wife at the time, Lorraine. The only other name that I can remember was Chuck Taylor, who had been teaching at Cooper's "Gunsite Training Academy." The reason I remember Taylor is that when I woke up from sleeping (passed out) on the floor and took my dog out for his morning walk, I found a .45 caliber grease gun with a 30-round loaded magazine on the hood of his car out in front—covered with

dew, as it had been out all night! Yes, sir! Those were some wild times . . .

Soldier of Fortune and its master-of-intrigue founder captured worldwide attention. Every fall, TV screens, air waves and journals would become filled with highly entertaining tales, not to mention rumors and flat out lies, about the scandalous *Soldier of Fortune* conventions held in Missouri and later in Las Vegas, where the mayor declared a "*Soldier of Fortune Day.*"

One far-fetched account of the first *SOF* "Congress" appeared in the Russian wire service, TASS, in September 1980:

> In shirts with inscriptions like "Worship War" and "Happiness is in Murder," with hands clutching at guns and rifles—this is how the U.S. press depicts today the professional gangsters and mercenaries ready at a moment's notice to rush to far-flung areas in order to kill and hang people, and overthrow legitimate governments. These people have converged on the town of Columbia, Missouri to take part in the first "Congress" organized by the magazine called *Soldier of Fortune*, which specializes in providing publicity for mercenaries. Henceforward, such gatherings are to be held on an annual basis.
>
> For three days in a row, hundreds of professional assassins competed in shooting and in the art of using knives and daggers. In the breaks between shooting competitions they boasted of their feats during their foreign trips, and unblushingly named the number of "communists" killed by them. Discussions in the conference halls centered on plans to give assistance to gangs that are now responsible for bloody atrocities committed in Afghanistan, Zimbabwe and other countries. . . . The magazine *Soldier of Fortune* has published a large-circulation booklet specifically for the gathering of the assassins. The booklet has a characteristic title, "The Technique of Intimidation."

Yet no one, certainly not the local or other law enforcement or CIA personnel who religiously picked up the magazine (whether they admitted it or not, mainly not), dared disturb the goings-on at the "Brown Hotel." Many showed up at the *SOF* conventions, not wanting to miss out on the action.

Newsweek magazine's Periscope section in September 1981 outed the CIA's obsession with its nemesis, *Soldier of Fortune*, after the Russian invasion of Afghanistan and the U.S. response to the war:

> They don't like to admit it, but intelligence analysts at the CIA and the Pentagon rely on an adventure magazine published in Boulder, Colorado for some of their best information on Soviet military operations in Afghanistan. Every month the analysts comb through grenade launchers and other Soviet weapons that the magazine's correspondents in Afghanistan have somehow acquired. *Soldier of Fortune* even offers to sell captured Soviet weaponry to the highest bidder, preferably, "U.S. or NATO intelligence agencies." One Pentagon official says that the ease with which *Soldier of Fortune* obtains Soviet arms is a "real sore point" at the CIA.

After the Cold War wound down, the rabble-rousing warrior was continuing to rev up, concocting one scheme or another to keep his trigger finger on the pulse of the head-spinning action that the postwar chaos was creating around the globe.

I MEET THE MASTER OF THE HOUSE OF INTRIGUE

I opened the local paper one morning and read on the front page that the publisher of *Soldier of Fortune* magazine had been shot. Period! No details! Within no time, the international media had gone wild with the news of the "assassination" of the Colonel.

Even the radio talk show king at the time, Paul Harvey, jumped on board with the "rest of the story." He claimed that Sheldon Kelly, a close friend and Reader's Digest reporter who had linked up with *SOF* in El Salvador, and who was allegedly in some nefarious scheme with Brown to smuggle weapons out of the country, had assassinated his co-conspirator and made a run for it. Kelly allegedly was apprehended at the Los Angeles Airport on the pretext of gun smuggling.

I raced over to the "Brown Hotel." I had always made it a point to avoid the notorious Lord of the Den of Who Knows What. But now overcome by a morbid sense of curiosity, I needed to know whether the House of Intrigue had lost its master in some wild jungle or in a combat zone or whether some hit man had really bumped him off.

I knocked, expecting a caretaker or a priest or a bunch of camouflage-veiled mourners. Instead, a very grumpy, unshaven RKB, with his strong aquiline face, his angry piercing blue eyes staring out beneath a baseball cap, cautiously cracked open the door. His thick moustache belied his thinning hair. I hid my shock. He ordered me in. He hobbled back to the massive chair that was his throne, leaning on a sword or a cane, which one I could not tell. He was wearing a short-sleeve khaki safari shirt that exposed his strapping arms, with the top few buttons open to show off his muscular, hairy chest in his macho style, pain or no pain. His safari shorts were hiked up on one side above the bandaged muscled leg of an avid jogger. I was rudely and unabashedly introduced to the first (of what would become many) of his Tourette Syndrome-type outbursts loudly barked out in his deep gravelly voice, a wad of snuff bulging in one cheek. (He bragged he had used some of the finest china in the best restaurants in the world for a spittoon.) His outbursts, to put it mildly, can be mighty shocking even to the most hardened. His seething anger masked the pain in his fair, pale face. He had been shot in the calf with a .22 round and was going to miss his next big adventure.

The "accident," he told me, happened during a moment of one of the "Brown Hotel's" chaotic, drunken fiascos they called a "party." The culprit was Galen Geer, Vietnam vet, who had long joked about being the only mere auto mechanic in Vietnam while all the other vets were Rangers, SEALs, or Special Forces who saved entire villages and fought ferocious firefights on a daily basis. Geer had been mucking around with his Jennings .22 after countless drinks, and while showing the piece off to RKB, accidentally fired. The bullet flew through Geer's hand and penetrated almost all the way through RKB's right calf already scarred from mortar round fragments in Vietnam. The grumpy Colonel found one bright spot in the whacky incident. "The .22 bullet is coated in some kind of wax. Since the bullet went through Galen's hand first, it removed all the wax so when it lodged in my calf, the wound did not have to be debrided. A quick incision with a scalpel removed it, and it dropped into a pan with a loud cling just like one you would hear on Gunsmoke," he said.

"Right," I thought. "You could come up with a better story than this lame one." I found out later that it was true.

PSYCHOLOGICAL PROFILE OF A MERC— A "SOMEDAY I'M GOING TO . . ."

The Colonel was tied in with a global network of professional soldiers and coordinated contacts where I was to study international law, whether it was in Asia, South Africa, London—the land of many mercs—or Paris, the land of many more mercs.

I went on to spend months with the fascinating "dogs of war" of many nationalities, many of which are players in this book. I found the worldly warriors unlike the stereotypes of trigger-happy, unkempt burly brutes that ate raw meat, human or otherwise. I met many soldiers of fortune during those years, including Brits, French, South Africans, Australians and a number of Americans. The least memorable were those wannabes who were legends in their own minds, boasting endlessly of their kills, conquests or trophies, real or imagined. Some who had served from Rhodesia to South Africa, to Lebanon to Oman and beyond spoke matter-of-factly of their adventures. The most fascinating of all verbalized with their wary, piercing eyes, not saying much. They didn't have to— they had fought ruthlessly in vicious battles and survived. Many of their opponents had not.

They were unpredictable, some savory, others unsavory, some complex and some simple, but all so interesting that I determined to write a book about the psychological profile of a mercenary. Another "someday we-are-going-to" brainchild.

A couple of years after the Colonel's shooting incident, in my last year in school, a pompous, narcissitic professor, about whom I fantasized sending some of the Colonel's friends to make sure he had given his final lecture, flunked me after I said something of which he disapproved. The politically motivated Dean of the Law School said he could do nothing because the professor's wife donated hundreds of thousands of dollars to the school. With the hope of shutting me up the fastest way possible because an unfair flunking grade amounted to an unfair expulsion, which could prove to be very uncomfortable for him, he told me he would arrange for me to take another course. He cautioned me to make every effort to score an "A" to average out the bad grade to a "B" or the deal would bomb. In law school "C" is a flunk.

I took the only course available before the end of the next quarter in order to graduate. If I did not earn an "A" to make up for the failing grade, I would probably be joining some Foreign Legion somewhere and would not even be able to defend the ne'er do wells. The course? Trial tactics! Me, who froze in front of any audience? We had to take a mock case from beginning to end, including complaints, responses, motions, depositions, etc. etc. etc. We were required to present both sides, but were to be graded on the final defense of our client. We barely knew what a motion meant.

WHAT JUSTICE?

I get bored easily, and that wouldn't help my efforts to complete grueling exercises in an attempt to earn one of the only A's of my life. Why not make *Soldier of Fortune Magazine's* rogue Colonel as my "client", I thought in one enlightened moment? At the time the Colonel was besieged by legal claims. Apparently a couple of criminals had linked up in an ad in *SOF*, and months later one of them had killed someone. It mattered not that if evil men, however they met that their murderous actions were the responsibility of the evildoers. As soon as the case was filed the mainstream press turned personal "Gun for Hire" ads placed by security guards, personal protection professionals and other independent advertisers into "Hit Man Ads." Then as now, the media attracts a much bigger audience with spectacular half- or untruths, and in this case rather than holding murderous psychos responsible for their actions, the media blamed a publication and its publisher.

Even I, who knew nothing about the practice of law, with what little the Colonel told me about his opponent plaintiffs, was sure he had been sold down the river by a sea of incompetent attorneys. It is no secret that The Flaming Liberal Republic of Boulder is noted for its plethora of pothead, "nose candy" addict and substance-abusing members of the legal profession.

Feeling the crunch, he invited me to observe one trial in Texas that was going forward after months of pleadings and motions being thrown back and forth. For two dramatic weeks while playing hooky from school, I watched in horror as the nightmare unfolded. The case opened to a surreal start.

"What are you trying to do, counselor, make me make a mistake? This morning you give me responses to 51 motions?" the judge told the Colonel's waste-of-time attorneys, one a womanizer more interested in his conquests than the case, even during the trial. Maybe if the judge had a reputation of being partial, which I doubted, it was apparent he had already made the decision and manipulated the trial to reflect it.

I knew that the case was over but the trial proceeded. I desperately tried to convince the Colonel to kidnap the opposing counsel at gunpoint and force him to represent *SOF* and simultaneously bury his defense team alive. I promised that the secret would go with me to the grave.

A slick, well groomed pretty boy in his 30s, with a good old boy's slow Texas twang, the opposing counsel was well aware that the media vultures were all over the case with their cameras. He had hit the big one in terms of fame. He gave an obviously well rehearsed performance that was theatrical, brilliant, and had some of the most convincing presentations I have ever seen, though mostly a pile of lies. The victim's family, by design, was dressed and told to conduct itself in such a pitiable manner that the jury and audience were instantly overwhelmed with sympathy.

Local prosecutors had already convicted the two perps in a criminal trial in which *SOF* had no involvement.

This drama spelled huge trouble for a notorious tough guy defendant with the reputation of publishing the most daring and controversial adventure magazine in history. I doubted that RKB and his army of uniformed former military officials and colossal tough guys charging through the witness stand could ever convince anyone that *SOF* could be innocent of any accusation, no matter how false or outrageous, anywhere, then or ever, especially to a jury of working stiffs who identified with the plaintiff. And to make it even worse, one of *SOF*'s bigheaded witnesses, unprepared, told an irrelevant bold face lie on the stand, which the plaintiff's lawyer exploited to the hilt to impeach his testimony.

SOF lost. After the verdict, we were mobbed outside the courtroom by media vultures scrambling for comments or wanting interviews with the bad boy of journalism.

The case was appealed. And now many media outlets, which had helped create the hysteria, suddenly became terrified that such a meritless case would put a damper on their own freedom of speech and hit them in their pocketbooks when an inevitable slew of cases would be filed against them based on this precedent. So they filed supportive briefs. Personal ads that were likely to attract some pervert or ax murderer had become the vogue in many journals. RKB's skilled appellate attorney won the appeal, which was really a no-brainer for any attorney who was sober. But by then the sensationalist media, no longer threatened, had lost interest. The damage was done.

FREEDOM OF SPEECH COMES WITH A DUMPTRUCK LOAD OF HITCHES

I spent hours of toil and sleepless nights on the case. I picked RKB and the "hotel" guests' brains without telling them why, just feigning interest. I prepped mock witnesses (students), who all eagerly volunteered to participate in the trial of a reputed scoundrel at this private, liberal law school. I chose the jury based on one criterion: rebellious-looking males.

Presenting the "plaintiff's" case was simple: a notorious magazine that shocked the conscience with questionable ads and content had to be shut down.

As the stages of the case progressed, I still picture the Trial Tactics professor—slim, impeccably groomed with a well modulated voice and perfectly timed delivery, enhanced with strategic hand gestures, who well earned his reputation as one of the top trial tactics professors in the region—observing with amusement, fascination and intrigue my bungling. I did not have a read on him, as he was too smooth.

The time came for the closing argument for the defense of my "client." I admitted that some of the magazine's provocative content and ads pressed the boundaries of insanity. I pled the case based on the First Amendment's guarantee of freedom of speech, which in my mind was an obvious, unconditional constitutional right.

Fortunately, not until I taught Constitutional Law did I face the harsh reality that the right of freedom of speech comes with a dump truck load of hitches. Or that political correctness, like an engorged predator blob, had gradually gobbled up what used to be a basic tenet of freedom down to its core; and it was still gnawing.

I can't say that I even liked my "defendant" at first, as I perceived him as rather a loud, foul-mouthed rogue with a "hotel" that had walls overloaded with weird trophies and awards; a showman who loved to shock his audience. His fetish for phony but lifelike-looking skulls placed everywhere—on desks, shelves, t-shirts and posters I still don't get. I can't even tell you whether I believed in his causes at first, but by the time I gave my closing statement, after witnessing the actual trial and reading the appeal I knew he had been given a raw deal.

THE BLOOD SHED IN VIETNAM WAS JUST AS RED

I painted a portrait of a former U.S. Army officer, a man of enormous courage, obsessed by his still raw outrage at the likes of sellouts like John Kerry, Jane Fonda, Walter Cronkite, and other members of the media. Of his fury at the treatment of his team members by the anti-war crowd after their return from Vietnam that had crushed many of the troops who had for a decade risked their lives. He was fighting to vindicate the memory of those who died.

Always lurking in the back of his mind since the war ended so wrongly, won by the military but lost in Washington, was the thought that Vietnam veterans felt sold out by Congress and the Democratic Left. He, like the rejected Vets, resented the fact that they received no recognition for their sacrifices. He worked on the premise that the blood that was shed in Vietnam was just as red as that shed in World Wars I or II or Korea. So he decided to focus on world events as well as provide a voice for Vietnam vets.

The classroom was hushed.

A POSTER BOY FOR TRUE GRIT

Perhaps I was driven by the enormous respect I had for another professor at the law school from whom I took numerous classes, and who despite my not so brilliant performance in his courses was fair and became a friend and invaluable advisor. He was the poster boy for true grit, determination, and hard driving success. He had been seriously injured in Vietnam, yet he completed advanced degrees in tax law after the war ended. I would try to hide my grimace as he would slowly, proudly walk into classrooms through the front door with his arms braced by crutches, often masking the pain in his face. Never complaining, never beaten down, he established one of the most distinguished international tax law programs in the country, and he was the director. He in turn expected hard work and excellence. He often asked about my neighbor, the publisher of *Soldier of Fortune* magazine.

But I realized by the time the class ended that day that a couple of the students never knew their fathers who were killed in Vietnam, and nearly every one of them knew a friend or family member who had been affected by the war. Most of them were not aware of the aftermath that Vietnam vets endured.

My classroom "client," who would never have existed without the real deal and whose story was so gripping that it didn't even have to be embellished, won the case. The jury deliberated for only a few minutes and was unanimous. The entire class voted after the jury. The verdict was unanimous. And obviously that included the professor, who gave me an A. It had nothing to do with legal skills. It had to do with harsh reality.

After I left the neighborhood to go live in Europe for a couple of years to finish my dissertation, the "Brown Hotel" was shut down. The Colonel had his contacts find me when I returned to the States, wondering if I could weigh in on his latest legal tight spot. He looked beat up, worried. He was still having a rough time repairing the damage of those unfortunate days. A few more cases were pending. His insurance had dropped him. The days of lavishness were gone, and along with them most of the hundreds of "friends." He recruited me to help keep his passion alive.

I owed him for unknowingly letting me use him to help me keep my career, and for offering to come bail my sorry butt out of Africa, Russia, the Middle East or other places I was if I got in a jam. A study published while I was living in Brussels had rated the U.S. media on the bottom of the list of truth-in-media in the Western democracies.

We got rid of all the nuisance cases the way the first one should have been dismissed. The public stayed out of it this time, the way it should have earlier but for incompetent fame- and money-grubbing attorneys and sensation-seeking media. RKB did much of the work, doggedly going back and forth with me to the venues of the cases. In LA, I teamed up with one of the greatest attorneys or men I have ever known, Larry Straw. He fought on with us until the end in spite of horrendous pain he was suffering in the last stages of cancer. He died young, shortly after we won the most threatening case, thanks to his brilliant procedural skill. In a bizarre twist of fate, the plaintiff had as bungling of a counsel as *SOF* had in its original disastrous case.

The Colonel and my proudest moment was when we received a public apology from the toad of a City Attorney of the Flaming Liberal People's Republic of Boulder, who had defamed the magazine in the local paper. Or maybe I should say that it was a moment of triumph marred by one of the Colonel's many unrestrained moments to protect an underdog or one less fortunate.

The opponent was a small, wiry 50ish-year-old man who came up no higher than the Colonel's shoulder, and who suffered a gnarled, withered hand and walked with a limp. When he shuffled into the pretrial negotiating room, the chivalrous Colonel, who had sworn vengeance for weeks since he read the lies, had never seen the little, lying toad before. Ignoring the malevolent look in his opponent's eyes, he shot up from his seat, pulled the opponent's chair out to help him sit behind the table and offered to carry his load. Concerned that my worst client ever was going to blow the case, I kicked him in the leg under the table so hard that I was sure that I had killed him by severing an artery or producing a blood clot that would shoot straight to his bleeding heart. I'm not sure whether he came to his senses or whether the piercing pain in his leg dazed him long enough to silence him for me to get the job done.

"Did you ever read the magazine before you allowed that scathing criticism?" I asked the toad.

The weasel of a City Attorney had to admit he had never read *SOF* before he defamed it. His lies were based on old media hype. That is just how it was and still is. Lies and rumors; bigger and better lies; and more unfounded gossip.

A PRESS ROOM WITH A VIEW

I have since been daily watching an unrelenting warrior, a survivor who refuses to give up his passion, who is willing to work tirelessly around the clock to keep his mission alive—that of supporting the troops who have been involved in the War on Terror for over a decade, and the underdog everywhere. Stories of Vietnam vets still run frequently in the magazine.

Don't get me wrong. I am not painting the portrait of a saint—quite the contrary. I often wonder why he is still alive with his smirking cool and his uncanny talent for goading those in his line of fire to blind murderous rages. I am number one on that list, and after a decade of constantly nearly coming to blows, have made absolutely no progress in convincing him that his right of freedom of speech is not absolute.

The side of this business I dread the most is when the normally devil-may-care, boisterous RKB goes silent, and I know he is grieving. I will never get used to it and it will never get easier. It happens far too frequently these days and no doubt it did during those Vietnam War days. It is when some young trooper he knows or former team member or old professional soldier, military colleague, or other great hero who was his friend is killed or dies.

The latest tragic death that clouded his office with an eerie, dark quiet was that of an American hero, SEAL Chief Petty Officer Chris Kyle, 38, who served four combat tours in Iraq, who we spent time with, and who was the cover story of *SOF* in its April, 2012 issue. He was gunned down on a range in Texas while helping a 25-year-old PTSD Iraq War vet. Kyle, like countless other troopers who told us that they joined the military after reading *Soldier of Fortune*, wrote last year when he autographed his book, American Sniper, "*SOF*, thank you for all your great articles. You actually piqued my interest to join the military."

The Colonel is most proud of having served as a catalyst to interest young men in joining the military, whether it be a SEAL like Kyle or some young patriot joining the Army, Marines, Air force or Army to be a truck driver or cook. He takes incredible pleasure in realizing *SOF* indirectly helped send scores of terrorists to Hell.

His dogged determination helps support his unquenchable thirst for global intrigue and adventure, not to mention his unfeigned delight and deep satisfaction when he ruffles Leftist feathers.

RKB is a rebel with a cause—that of battling against tyranny, fighting for the underdog and protecting our First and Second Amendment rights. Here is his incredible journey.

—VS

1

I SCHEME TO BECOME A TOP GUN PILOT, A HARD-CHARGING MARINE, A SPECIAL AGENT OR . . . ?

When I entered college in 1950 when the Cold War was hot, every young buck worth his salt was destined to go into one of the military services either by the luck of the draft or, if one was under the illusion that he could be selective, enlist in the service of his choice. Those going to college had the option of throwing their hat in the ring for a commission via ROTC. I fantasized about flying jets and blasting Commies out of the sky, so I X'ed the dotted line for Air Force ROTC.

When I transferred to the University of Colorado from Michigan State in early 1953 (the Dean of men and I agreed that it was best I leave Michigan State), I was shorted one semester at the whim of the genius academicians. There was no ROTC in summer school, so to get a commission I would have to attend an extra semester. Back in those days, if one did not get a degree in four years he was considered some type of freak and threatened with all sorts of bodily harm by irate parents. Anyone who knew my parents would have no doubt that delaying graduation by even one day would probably assure that I would not live to become the national hero that I knew the world was longing for.

I finally figured out that with my near-sightedness, I was not going to go to flight school, and that if I joined the Air Force I would end up pushing a pencil, a fate worse than death for a restless young lad. So for the remainder of my college, I joined the Marine Corps Reserve to see if the Marines lived up to their macho image.

I MEET A SNAKE OIL SALESMAN

I was also casually shopping the Army and Navy recruiters. An Army recruiter, his name long forgotten, who undoubtedly was a snake oil salesman in past, present and future lives, got his bullshit hooks into me big time. He got my X on the dotted line to become a "Special Agent" in the Counter-Intelligence Corps. Yeah, I know. Time for the tired old ha, ha for those vets who know all about how counter-intelligence is conducted in the Army. Rather than going for two years as a draftee and kissing off my perception that I would have say in what I did, I bought hook, line and sinker the pitch that the Snake Oil Salesman gave me, that if I would sign up for a three-year enlistment I would become a counter-intelligence agent. I fantasized of platinum blonds and Cadillac convertibles. Keep in mind, this was long before James Bond's fast exotic foxes and even faster Aston Martins.

I entered the Army in October 1954, and shipped out to Camp Chaffee, Arkansas before it was upgraded to Fort Chaffee. Although it was the same old stuff that millions of recruits have gone through since the beginning of the army, I took to it like the proverbial duck to water. I lived for range time where I became intimate with the WWII and Korea workhorse M-1 Garand. I got my first formal marksmanship training and I loved it. I spent a lot of time outside . . . running, marching . . . gladly inhaling meals in two minutes, a habit that has long endured, and being thrown in with a bunch of disparate types who had been uprooted from everywhere from ghettos to the Kentucky hills. It was an eye-opening experience for a young punk college boy . . . an experience sorely missed by many of the pill-popping, therapy-seeking, ear-piercing Y generation and other bizarre generations of punks since the discontinuance of the draft.

I FIGHT TO AVOID BECOMING A REMINGTON RAIDER

After eight weeks, I was shipped to what was then the Army Intelligence Center at Fort Holabird, Maryland, where I found myself thrown in with a "casual company" of recently graduated basic trainees, all college graduates waiting for a Special Agent course to begin. After a couple of weeks, forty-some of us arbitrarily were designated to take the "Clerk Analyst" course—hardly special agents. Morale went right into the shitter as all my new classmates and I realized that we had truly been scammed by the Army in a practice that would repeat itself far too often. We had specifically signed up for a James Bond gig but instead we were to end up as nothing more than administrative clerks with a security clearance. Disillusionment heightened throughout the eight-week course.

The courses were torment . . . administrative this and administrative that. According to the rules of the game, if you failed three courses, you appeared before a board, which was pretty much a formality, and you were kicked out of the course. Those ejected would invariably end up as company clerks somewhere. Early on, although we could all type, one learned that you never, I say never, especially back in those days, let your First Sergeant know you could type, or you would sure as hell end up behind a typewriter and become a Remington Raider.

Continuing a tradition I had perfected at the University, I not only failed three, I failed four courses . . . and along with seven other dissidents appeared before a board consisting of a captain, a lieutenant and a couple of senior NCO's. All of the other seven came up with some type of BS excuse as to why they had failed, the most enterprising of which was made by a recruit claiming he was participating in opera rehearsals. I went in, mind you very respectfully, and on being called to account, explained that "with all due respect, I attribute my poor performance to the fact that I had been promised one thing [exerting great restraint in not going off on the Snake Oil Salesman the army had pimped out] and forced into another—that I had purposely passed up getting an Air Force ROTC commission because I didn't want to be a paper pusher." I can only assume this honesty must have shocked the board into allowing me to be the only one of the eight of us that was allowed to complete the course.

That was all well and good, but as far as I was concerned I was still in the shits. Death to paperwork. (Though if I'd paid more attention to "paperwork" while running *SOF*, I'd be a millionaire many times over, but that is another story.)

ON TO THE FORT BENNING SCHOOL OF MASOCHISTS

Though I gutted it through the remainder of the course and graduated, I desperately sought an out, any out. The only option I could find was to apply for Officer's Candidate School. I was sure that nothing could be worse than clerking. I was soon to be rudely awakened from that thought. Two other classmates and I applied, but I was the only one accepted. The only explanation I could come up with was that my fate was decided in the course of the oral interview with the student company commander, a captain. "Private Brown, if you had a recalcitrant NCO, how would you deal with him?" he asked. "Well, sir, I'd take him out behind the barracks and whop on him good," I replied.

I had no doubt that I could pound sense into anyone since I was still playing the part of an amateur boxer, although I was cockier than I was skilled. I'd managed to lose my first fight in the Golden Gloves in Lansing, Michigan when I got slammed with a right cross that dropped me to the canvas in 1:32 of the first round.

Now, you would think that would have sent a message to most normal people. But normal or not I was definitely a stubborn SOB. I went on to be a finalist two years in a row in the intramural fights at CU. I finally got the message after a young Mexican fighter knocked me down four times in a row in the YMCA in Milwaukee. Still, I ended up with a 5-5 record, which is better than a jab in the eye with a sharp stick, but not much.

Back to the Captain, who roared at my response, "Now, Private Brown, you can't do that. Ho, ho, ho. No, you must utilize leadership skills to deal with problems like that. Ho, ho, ho." He ho-ho-hoed for a while and then dismissed me. A few days later, I got accepted for OCS at Ft. Benning, Georgia. Not so fondly referred to by officer candidates as the Ft. Benning School for Boys, it would have more accurately been described as the Ft. Benning School for Masochists.

After completing the Analyst course (no honors there) while waiting for a slot to open up in an OCS class, I spent two months as a file clerk in the Personnel Section where one of my many suspicions about the Army machine was confirmed. A glitch in the Army personnel system resulted in an incredible travesty.

One Pfc. Berkowitz was in charge of assigning personnel to overseas assignments. One would think that the individual who had this responsibility would make an effort to assign a trooper to a country where his language capabilities would be of use. But noooo! Old Pfc. Berkowtz, whether he was simply lazy, hated the army or just didn't give a fig, took the easy way out which was "first come, first served."

If the requisition papers ordered 10 troopers to Germany and they had just graduated from Korean language school, off they went to the land of Frauleins and Wiener Schnitzel. If ten relatively warm bodies were required for Korea, he'd assign the next ten on the list even though they had graduated from German language school. I never did figure out if the Army caught him or if the system was simply screwed up.

Life was good. It was an eight-to-five job with weekend passes, few inspections and little harassment, with the exception of pulling guard duty or being assigned to the pain-in-the-ass kitchen police, not fondly nor very creatively called "KP." Off-duty time took us down to the fleshpots of East Baltimore Street but we came up with damn little flesh, a disenchantment dulled by the free flowing of beer.

I was also working out, sparring in a waterfront boxing club right out of Daymon Runyon, a second-story gym over a smoky pool hall where an ancient pug wracked the balls. Rusty lockers were crammed into the upstairs gym and doors hung askance with more types of exotic fungi than the most optimistic germ hunter could hope for. It boasted one ring . . . dried blood on the canvas . . . peeling fight posters on the walls, and a crew out of central casting, most of whom were knockabout pugs, laborers, stevedores and cab drivers. Just simple amateur club fighters who picked up a couple of hundred bucks a fight without any chance for a shot at the big time. One saw the seamy side of the fight racket . . . the heavyweight who knew he was going to get "home-towned" when he fought in Scranton, or the black middleweight who cried when he told the gym manager he was going to have to go with another manager or he wouldn't get any decent opponents. Of course, punch-drunk fighters were not limited to club fighters.

I had been the co-manager of the Michigan State boxing team in 1950 and '51. Michigan State, "College," not "University" at that time, which produced a National Championship Boxing Team, had some top professional contenders using the college gym facilities in East Lansing. The best of the bunch was the lightweight, Chuck Davies, who had lightning fast hands and feet and enough sense to retire after he got pounded into the canvas in a title fight with Kid Gavilan; Jed Black, a powerfully built middleweight, and Chuck Spesier, light heavyweight contender. Davies didn't have the jerks and mumbles but the rest did, as well as a kid on the college team, 17 years old, who already had 80 amateur fights. So why did I persist? In retrospect, just one of my many bouts of damn foolishness I guess, as well as the fact that I got a visceral kick out of getting in the ring and duking it out with someone.

YOU PATHETIC AMATEURS, I LIVED WITH MY MOTHER FOR 22 YEARS

Next stop was Ft. Benning, which damn near put me into terminal shock. Candidates from other classes were frantically running everywhere they went. I reported in, was assigned a room and class number, and the shit began to roll all downhill on to me. I figured out that 90 percent of the harassment was to see which of the candidates could handle the pressure. The theory being, "If you can't handle the stress at Ft. Benning's School for Boys, you sure as hell can't handle combat." All the modern sophisticated limp dicks stick their noses up at such a concept, but no one has convinced me otherwise.

Why else would all of our supervisors, or "Tactical Officers," like hundreds of thousands throughout generations before and after them, be programmed to see harassment as one of their missions to try and break us, get in our face, cuss us out, scream with an appropriate amount of spittle, and just generally jump in our shit big time for the slightest infraction or, depending on their mood, for no infraction. They made more than one grown man cry.

Frankly, when they got in my face, I simply deadpanned, looked straight ahead at rigid attention, and thought, "You pathetic amateurs, I lived with my Mother for 22 years." Not surprisingly, when they figured out that they were wasting their effort they moved on to some more vulnerable sucker.

Ironically, some of the most experienced candidates—I mean young NCOs with several years of Army experience, who you would think would find the challenge a piece of cake—couldn't handle it and resigned. Apparently, having achieved some status and respect as a junior NCO, they couldn't adapt to being treated like dog shit. I didn't have that problem, as I wasn't all that long out of basic training.

In any event, early on I was seriously thinking about ditching this whole gig and becoming a company clerk after all until I saw the first six weeks' training schedule posted on the orderly room wall. Low and behold! The third and fourth weeks were rifle marksmanship training with shooting gloves… and shooting coats and spotting scopes.

Wow! More bang-bang than I had done in my whole life. I figured I could put up with their West Point-type BS until I got through the marksmanship training. After I completed the fourth week, out of curiosity, I decided to stick around for the hell of it to see if I made the six-week cut. At that time, OCS evaluated all candidates at six, 12 and 18 weeks. Would I make it? Amazingly, I didn't get cut. Well, I thought, let's try for 12. I passed that and then it was gravy. I guess the Army figured that if they invested this much money in the candidates who endured, after 18 weeks they were good to go.

And, by God, I graduated! I'm still not sure how I pulled that off, as 40 percent of our class fell by the wayside. Was I a Distinguished Graduate? Well, depends what you mean by distinguished. Yes, I could boast of two major feats. I had the highest number of demerits in the company (got caught sleeping in ranks on one occasion). And I scored the highest on the machine-gun range, the old but effective Browning 1919-A6 which was fired off a tripod. So what did all that mean? I guess my love of the range pulled me through.

Now, with the gold "butter bar" of a Second Lieutenant, I would no longer be a lousy clerk. So I was sent back to the "Bird," the not necessarily affectionate name for Ft. Holabird, to attend the elusive "Special Agents" school. The course work was the same for both enlisted men and officers and beat the hell out of learning how to fill out forms correctly. I found conducting interrogations a highlight since they fit into my definition of Special Agent. The classroom held about 40 students. Slightly elevated was a room fronted by a one-way mirror that extended the whole width of the classroom. Behind this, the practice interrogations took place. No Abu Ghraib amateur hour crap, but effective.

We also had classes in surveillance which had their amusing moments, especially when the subject purposely walked into the lingerie section of a department store. So how does one follow unobtrusively? We didn't.

MY NAME IS BROWN, SPECIAL AGENT BROWN . . .

As I had made friends in the Holabird personnel section, when I came back from Ft. Benning I had my choice of assignments to any CIC unit anywhere in the world. Beyond awesome! Let's have some adventure! I had my orders cut and was salivating at the thought of going to jump school and being assigned to the 14th Airborne Division's Counter-Intelligence Division unit in Germany.

However, it was not to be, as my father died suddenly, and to fulfill family obligations, I opted for an assignment near home in Milwaukee, Wisconsin, where most of my time was spent conducting background security investigations, one of the cushiest jobs in the Army. The unit I was assigned to only had about 30 personnel and we used to fight over who got to run the odd complaint case, like Johnny Jones getting caught whacking off in a smelly urinal in the city bus station. Although we were always looking for communist agents, not only did we not find any, we didn't even find any communists. Of course, this was Milwaukee, not Berkeley.

We all wore civilian clothes, lived on the economy, e.g. were responsible for our own living quarters, and reported in for work at 0800hrs. If there were no cases, we were free to do whatever moved us, which in my case consisted of spending some time on a 32-foot sailboat at the Milwaukee yacht club. We drove unmarked black Chevy's with shortwave radios, carried .38 Colt Detective Specials concealed, as well as impressive FBI-type credentials. Great for impressing the ladies but didn't result in many affairs of the heart in those days.

I moved in with four civilian bachelors in an old but upscale brick apartment building that had been in the posh area of town back in the '30s. I got tired of hitting the bar scene every night since no one was scoring, and spent most of my evenings riding my 1948 64 Harley with a 74 engine to the gym or the local pistol range. The large apartment, four baths and five bedrooms with a 30-foot living room, served as party central for the neighborhood singles. In those days, most singles lived with their parents or in efficiency apartments. Nearly every weekend we threw a big, loud party, which resulted in our eviction.

Other than that, there was little excitement. I had quickly become bored with paperwork even as a Special Agent, and I opted for an early release to return to graduate school at the University of Colorado. I learned enough to know, though, that the Army was not for me as it became apparent that if one stays in for 20 years, one is bound to have to serve under more than one incompetent dickhead. I wasn't about to put up with that shit since I never have suffered fools gladly, although I have been able to adjust when absolutely necessary.

Back at CU in the fall of 1957, while working on my Master's Degree in Political Science, I joined an Army Reserve Marksmanship unit. I actually got paid to shoot on the pistol team with free ammo. Then there was the occasional active tour of duty to shoot in Army matches or attend marksmanship courses.

Vietnam was calling me, but a lot of twists and turns and calls to revolutions along the road delayed my tour in Indochina.

2

CUBA . . . THE BEGINNING OF THE ROAD (TO PERDITION?)

At Christmastime in 1957 I returned home to Highland, Indiana to visit my recently widowed mother. Bored one night, I decided to drink my way around the north side of Chicago and find some action, whatever form it might take. The cold, windy night was so brutal that few ventured out and there was no action to be found.

I happened across a bar, called the "College of Complexes" which I gathered was a beatnik hangout but no one was hanging. The only interesting aspect of the place was a large room in the rear furnished with about 20 picnic tables and benches. At one end of the room was a podium and microphone. Two or three times a week, some character would speak, discussing various political and social issues with the audience in order to sell a lot of beer. I happened to notice a small wooden container, which held mimeographed programs of upcoming events. I noted that a few days earlier, two individuals had spoken on behalf of Cuban Revolutionaries who were determined to overthrow the then-dictator of Cuba, Fulglencio Batista. By some strange urge, I carefully folded the mimeographed program and placed it in my wallet.

"MACHINE GUNS + CUBAN REVOLUTIONARIES = MONEY FOR BROWN."

The program that by some impulse I placed in my wallet listed the names and addresses of Americans who supported Castro. When I got back to the University of Colorado, one of my buddies, Minor Van Arsdale, had a comment one night as we gulped down a couple of beers after busting some caps. "One of my classmates, who got off on giving the impression that he was connected to the Mafia, claimed he had some submachine guns," he said.

My fanciful mind went into simple overdrive and came up with the equation:"Machine guns + Cuban revolutionaries = money for Brown." It sounded like a lot of bullshit, but what the hell, it might be an interesting story.

I policed up VanArsdale, a pistol club and rodeo teammate, and what seemed appropriate for the occasion, a bottle of cheap Cuban rum. We headed over to the apartment of this would-be thug who bragged about the machine guns. His digs were in a relatively upscale motel on 28th Street a few blocks east of the University. The conversation was banal. Well in our cups after we had slugged down most of the rum, our would-be gunrunner reached under his couch and pulled out a French Mas submachine gun, a Thompson and a Sten gun.

Holy shit!

"Look my friend," I said, "I think we all can make some money. I can get in touch with some Cuban revolutionaries who undoubtedly are in the market for firepower. Let me take the Sten gun back to Chicago and show it to them to prove my credibility." He bought the pitch and I walked out of his apartment with an unregistered fully automatic weapon, which could have bought me some serious time in a Federal slammer had I been caught with it. It wouldn't be the first time I stepped outside the law while supporting causes I believed in.

I waited for spring vacation in 1958 and eagerly headed back to the Windy City with the Sten. In one of my many reckless moments, I walked into the offices of one of the revolutionaries' supporters, who, when he wasn't dallying with the revolution, ran a translating service. On seeing the Sten, he became ecstatic, practically jumping up and down.

"You got cash?" I asked him

"No cash, but I will get it."

"I get the money, you get the gun," I told him.

His promises of obtaining funds never materialized. So I headed back to Boulder with the Sten gun in my trunk. Along the way, I picked up a young hitchhiker by the name of Tony, who had been working in a carnival and gave the impression of being on the lam from someone or something. Tooling along over patches of black ice from a preceding night's storm outside of Burlington, Colorado, I lost control of my red and white '55 Chevy and started sliding sideways up a small hill. In the other lane, coming down the hill, was a ton and a half Chevy pickup. He hit me broadside and, with no seat belts in those days, I was thrown out the door. For a couple of minutes, I verged on panic as I could not see and thought I was blind. I blinked rapidly to get the blood out of my eyes and could finally see.

My next thought was, "Holy shit! If the county sheriff shows up and finds that damn Sten in my car, I will become Brown, the felon rather than Brown the budding revolutionary."

"You talk to the pickup truck driver," I told Tony.

I moseyed around behind my now very sick Chevy, opened the trunk and secured the Sten under the spare tire. Not to worry, as the Sheriff, when he arrived, could have given a hoot about what was in my trunk.

After this episode, I kept the Sten hidden under a bale of hay at the ranch I was living in with other vets. Some of my buddies and I decided to wake up the student body, which was totally apathetic to the dire political situation in Cuba, by launching an anti-Batista, pro-Castro movement. We didn't have a clue who Batista or Castro were, but that was beside the point. At that time, Castro had not shown his true colors and would not until he was well on his way to consolidating power in early 1960. Most of the U.S. media reports, including flattering pieces authored by Herbert Matthews of the New York Times and Andrew St. George in the now-defunct magazine Coronet, hailed Castro as a good-guy type Social Democrat who just wanted to overthrow strongman Batista. I was bamboozled, as were most Americans and Cubans.

I was going to help Castro overthrow the Latin dictator.

I FORM A BOULDER BRANCH OF THE 26TH OF JULY MOVEMENT

Cuba had a violent history, made stormier by the homicidal Batista. In 1933, Batista had launched the Revolt of the Sergeants, a coup that succeeded in overthrowing the Gerardo Machado government. Batista was the Army Chief of Staff and controlled the resource-rich island. He was elected president in 1940 until 1944. He came to the United States for eight years but went back to Cuba and staged another coup that put him in power until 1959. Basically a murderous thug, he was in bed with the Mafia and big business in the United States. As the U.S. tends to do, it supported the dictator who was impoverishing his country and lining U.S. business pockets. The excuse was that he held Communism at bay. U.S. opinion was souring against him when reports confirmed that he was openly torturing and slaughtering his opposition, including protesting students.

In comes the charismatic Fidel Castro, an attorney and the illegitimate son of a wealthy man. He attempted a failed revolution in 1953. In exile, he began building support as an anti-imperialistic savior of the common folks. Castro's July 26 Movement built up momentum and popular support.

By 1956 he convinced a left-wing Spanish loyalist who had fled Franco's victorious fascists, Colonel Alberto Bayo, to train an invasion force in Mexico. The United States, which had been supplying arms to Batista to fight the insurgency, cut off support for the now unpopular despot.

After six months of intensive training under an ex-Spanish Lpyalist officer who had fled Franco at the end of the civil war. Col. Bayo, Castro, his brother Raul, Che Guevara and 80 other revolutionaries landed on the Cuban coast on 6 Dec. 1956. Ambushed by Batista's troops, only 12 escaped to the Sierra Maestra Mountains where they launched their ultimately successful guerilla war. In 1958 Batista fled to the Dominican Republic with planeloads of riches. Castro and his revolutionaries moved in and took power. The rest is history.

A few other rebel classmates and I formed an ad hoc organization and named it after Castro's 26th of July Movement. We publicized an organizational meeting inviting anyone interested. A group of brilliant social misfits, members of the only liberal group on campus, the Young People's Socialist League (YPSL), joined us. Like skilled, power hungry politicians, we preordained who was going to run the outfit with a devious plot.

"We will nominate each other with short, bullshit speeches and then push the nominations through with a quick vote," I said. Castro would have been proud! Of course, so would Lenin and Hitler.

We raised funds for our cause by placing a World War II 20mm Lalhti anti-tank gun out on the university lawn with a ballot box. The sign read,

"Vote with ballots, not bullets." Try exercising that level of free speech today!

One morning, the students and professors flowed onto campus to see the "Viva Castro!" signs we sloshed on the roof of the Chemistry building that was under construction. We picketed Arthur Larson, one of Eisenhower's advisors, who came to the campus for some function protesting the Eisenhower administration's continuing military aid to Batista.

The next step was to go to Cuba and meet Castro, the Man. I had wrangled my way into the offices of a prominent Chicago attorney, Constantine Kangles, a very influential mover in Chicago politics who was serving as Castro's legal consul in the United States. I showed him a letter of introduction from the two limp dick Castro supporters who I had shown the Sten gun to.

"My God," he said, eyes bulging, "if you show this to Castro's people you'll be shot! They're with the wrong group!" This should have been a warning that there was a hell of a lot about revolutionary politics I did not know. However, I was not to be swayed from my mission. I contacted an old Army CIC buddy who I served with in Milwaukee, Pete Jasin, and recruited him. "Pete, old buddy, how about some adventure? Let's go see Castro." I bamboozled the University student paper, the Colorado Daily into issuing press credentials for me by promising them an exclusive scoop. They bought it.

I BECOME A FOREIGN PARTICIPATORY CORRESPONDENT

"Let's do it," Pete replied. I was working for a roofing company pouring gypsum roofs for bowling alleys, super markets, etc., and decided to save up for the trip and head south in August 1958. I met up with Pete in Chicago and we drove to Miami where we contacted the Miami branch of the 26th of July Movement. The lawyer, Kangles, had given us the address and a letter of introduction. The office was located on the fourth floor of a semi-respectable office building in downtown Miami. We met with whomever, telling them, "We want to link up with Castro," as we showed our press credentials and the letter of introduction. We got an initial runaround as the no-name we talked with said we would have to be checked out. That sounded reasonable, though we didn't know why they would have to check out journalists or how they were going to do it.

We left the office and decided to take the stairs instead of the elevators. "Wonder if the FBI is on our trail," we mused as we descended. We'd had some dealings with the "Eye" when we were in the CIC and were not overly impressed. As we got to where we could see the lobby, yup, there were two dudes in coats and ties and straw hats—in the stifling Miami August heat!

Pete and I smiled at each other." Let's walk past them and let them chase us," I whispered. After we bolted, they finally figured out that we were their targets; that we had come down the stairs instead of the elevator.

"Hey. Hey, you two. Wait up," one of the suits yelled. We turned and waited till they huffed and puffed up. They flashed their credentials. "Come to our office." We shrugged. Why not? At the office, they informed us sternly, "Ok boys, we have an agent report that stated Brown was in the process of recruiting a band of college students to invade Cuba."

Ah, a taste of fame. We laughed. No doubt that concept had been bandied about at one or more of our Cuban rum and fun parties with the YPSLs out at the ranch where I was living while in grad school.

The Feds interviewed us separately.

"We know stuff about Castro you don't know," one of them said in a hushed tone. But in typical FBI fashion, refused to get specific.

"You better not go, but if you insist on doing so, you better contact the FBI agent in the American Embassy in Havana who is operating under the cover of the embassy's Legal Consul."

How could we resist such a clandestine invitation to a Revolution? We flew into Havana and went directly to the American Embassy and contacted the FBI guy.

"Any idea where we could get a decent but cheap hotel?" we said. He was taken aback, but recommended one. We said our thanks and promptly left, leaving him somewhat perplexed. We asked a lot of questions of anyone who spoke English and found our way to the anti-Batista underground, which was giving us the necessary underground contacts. We hung around Havana, interviewing a few locals including the Bureau Chief of the Havana AP. After our funds started running out, we decided we'd best head back to Miami to somehow replenish our funds and then return to Cuba. Pete and I were unfamiliar with the Cuban culture and did not understand the "manana syndrome." Being a private revolutionary was becoming quite expensive. We had been told that the overthrow of Batista was not imminent, so we figured we had some time.

BATISTA FALLS WITHOUT ME

On New Year's Day, 1959, Batista and his thugs saw the writing on the wall and fled to the Dominican Republic, at that time ruled by fellow dictator Rafael Trujillo. I decided to head back to Havana and see what was happening, as well as to see if I could come up with a unique subject for my Master's thesis in Political Science at the University of Colorado. I arrived in Havana and wrangled a few free nights at the Havana Hilton, which is all my revolutionary contacts figured my services to the revolution were worth. I moved into a small $25 a week pensione and started hanging out at the Havana bureau of the Associated Press. I had met some of the AP reporters on my previous trip and the bureau was the hotspot for journalists. I picked up a few freelance assignments—$5 here, $10 there—which supplemented my meager budget. I wrangled introductions to the revolutionary community through a number of pro-Castro Cubans I'd worked with in the United States.

After Castro took over, Havana was flooded with real or would-be revolutionaries from a dozen Latin American countries, all of whom fantasized about emulating Castro's success in their native lands. Cuba was the exotic Land of Plots, the stomping ground for Latin Revolutionaries lusting for power, where the hypnotic, hot, rum-sodden air of intrigue intoxicated the masses. Plots were hatched, meetings were held, and proclamations were issued.

Once Castro showed his true colors, which was soon after taking power, I became an active anti-Castro advocate.

A REVOLUTION I MISSED

I was invited to join an invasion of Nicaragua, but passed it up. The poor schmucks who invaded Nicaragua ended up being lucky compared to some other dead revolutionaries. The Nicaraguan fiasco paled compared to another invitation I had to an expedition that was kicked off to overthrow the brutal dictator of the Dominican Republic, General Raphael Trujillo. Trujillo's henchmen surrounded the invasion party and greeted them with a bullet in the back of the head. It didn't take a great deal of insight to foresee that these misguided idealists plotting to invade were doomed to failure from the beginning. So they met their executioners without me.

One of the freelance assignments that I picked up was to interview now "General" Alberto Bayo, a refugee Spanish loyalist who had fled Franco toward the end of the Spanish civil war. Bayo, along with some of his fellow loyalists, had held a press conference where he boldly proclaimed that they were going to invade Spain and overthrow General Franco. That, coupled with a few not very big bomb explosions in Madrid, prompted the AP bureau chief, Paul Sanders, to say, "Brown, go interview this turkey and see what he's been drinking." I did and the story ran worldwide with my byline, and I was flying high. My name was now on the list of international correspondents. The price of such fame turned out to be high later on when the military updated my top-secret security clearance before I went to Nam.

THE MYSTERIOUS MAN BEHIND THE REVOLUTIONARIES

I figured that a story about the fascinating Bayo was worth more ink than the first 750 words printed, so I went back and conducted further interviews. It was time for "the man behind the revolutionaries" to receive some deserved credit for training the two Castro's, Fidel and Raul, as well as Che Guevara and some 80 others, in the rudiments of guerrilla warfare for six months at a secret site 40 miles outside of Mexico City. This was truly a benchmark in the history of wild-eyed revolutions. The members of this core group, in contrast to other revolutionaries who ended up in catastrophic fiascos fueled by rum, fantasies and ignorance, were well prepared.

The prep time didn't do most of Castro's group much good, but had it not been for Bayo's training, the survivors, including the Castro brothers, would be merely a footnote in the history of failed revolutions.

General Bayo was shrouded with mystery. The burly man with grey, wavy hair was the first pilot in the fledgling Spanish Air Force in 1911. He flew combat ops against the Moors in Morocco in the early '20s, fought the last legal sword duel in Spain in 1922, and was an accomplished poet. He was also like a grinding burr under the saddle of the Spanish monarchy with his liberal diatribes. When the Spanish Civil War started in 1936, he threw in his lot with the Loyalists and repeatedly tried to get the government to embrace the concept of guerrilla warfare, to no avail. After losing an eye during a Franco bombing raid, he fled to Central America, where he became involved in a couple of unsuccessful efforts to overthrow the dictators of Nicaragua and the Dominican Republic.

When Fidel approached him for assistance in overthrowing Batista, he blew him off since he was fed up with the incompetence and lack of realism of the previous would-be revolutionaries he'd worked with. Castro kept pestering him and finally Bayo said, "Come back with $20,000 and I will work with you." Bayo didn't expect to see him again, but Castro returned a few weeks later with the money. Bayo leased a large ranch, under the guise of raising cattle, and started his training. Six months later, Castro and his band boarded a decrepit yacht, the Granma, and sailed on to infamy.

BAYO INADVERTENTLY SETS OFF MY PUBLISHING CAREER

Little did Bayo imagine that he was to help shape the bizarre twist my career was about to take. One time when I was interviewing him, he showed me a book on guerrilla warfare that he had authored and used as an instruction manual for training Castro. This book, "150 Questions for a Guerilla," was going to be of great value, I just knew it. I didn't have a clue what it was at the time, but I soon saw the light. My mission became to translate this manual that revealed the techniques—primitive though they may have been—that helped Castro seize power, so it could be available to military buffs and those interested in unconventional and guerrilla warfare. I looked for a publisher. But first I needed a translator.

I fell in with a Cuban exile, Hugo Hartenstein, a Spanish instructor at the University of Colorado. With the slim build of a sprinter, raven black hair and blue eyes, Hugo had graduated from Dartmouth where he set the record for the quarter-mile in track and later ran track in a tour in the Army. Hugo was as violently anti-Castro as I had become and, in his spare time, completed the translation. I couldn't find a publisher, so I convinced an old hunting/shooting buddy and former naval officer who was also working on a graduate degree, Bill Jones, to cough up $800 to publish 1,000 copies of a paperback version of the manual. I authored the introduction.

So we published the first book from our new basement office firm, Panther Publications. It evolved, in 1970, into Paladin Press, which is still operating in Boulder.

I was fortunate that I did not make it up to the Sierra Maestra with the Castros. Even then I knew I would not have been satisfied playing a pencil-pushing war correspondent. I would have picked up a rifle, joined the revolutionaries, and been forever branded as a communist sympathizer, just like those idealists had who joined the International Brigade in the fight against the Fascist Franco.

The trip to Cuba may have been a financial disaster, but I had picked up Bayo's manual on guerilla warfare that was to change my life and launch my career as a publisher. I had met and worked with some of the finest professional journalists the AP had. I had managed to kiss off a couple of opportunities to get my ass shot off with some incompetent revolutionaries, and the girls were pretty, so what the hell.

JOURNALISM CAN KILL

I returned to Boulder where I played hit and miss with my schooling and socked away some money working odd jobs so I could return to Cuba the following year. In Boulder, I knocked out a couple of articles, one of which had a healthy dose of "unintended consequences." One of the articles I had published in Guns magazine dealt with the various types of homemade guns the Cuban revolutionaries used in their fight against Batista. I profiled a certain Regino Camacho who was in charge of building a small arms factory for Castro in Havana. I wrote, "The first openly Communist-controlled arms factory in the hemisphere is to be located in a tightly guarded concrete building outside Havana's machine gun-ringed army headquarters, Ciudad Libertad, formerly Camp Columbia. Called Industrias Militares, it was begun early in 1959 by one Major Regino Camacho . . . a veteran of the Spanish Civil War, the Caribbean Legion, and the Second Front of the Escambray. Camacho is a long-time associate of the famed Col. Alberto Bayo . . ." I had met Camacho through Bayo, gotten a bit of his background, his plans and a few photos. How could I have known that that article would lead to his assassination? Yes, journalism can kill.

Within a year, I heard that a hit team had whacked Camacho in Havana, but didn't pay it much mind. Revolutionaries were always getting whacked in the Caribbean for one reason or another.

It wasn't until the early 1960s that I would, as Paul Harvey would say, get the "rest of the story." My path crossed one or more of the more fascinating soldiers of fortune in Miami as I hung out with the local mercs.

Robert Johnson, in his mid-forties, slim, wavy black hair and a chain smoker, had only recently bailed out from the Dominican Republic shortly after the assassination of its dictator, Generalissimo Trujillo. Somehow, Johnson had signed on with this thug and ended up as his number two in the Dominican Army's intelligence section under the equally thuggish but certainly more dapper General Arturo Espaillat.

Johnson and I bumped into each other occasionally in Miami, and he eventually knocked out a couple of pieces for the magazine I started in 1975, *Soldier of Fortune*. The tales of his intrigue in the Caribbean turned out to be some of the best journalism we ever published. One evening in the early '60s, when we were knocking back a few rum and cokes, he suddenly turned serious, lowered his voice, and said, "You know, Brown, your writing got somebody hit."

Taken aback, I replied, "Huh? What the hell are you talking about?" He swizzle-sticked his drink, grimaced and said, "Your article on the arms factory in Havana caused Trujillo to send a hit team him to assassinate Comacho. They got him."

BROWN IS ON THE GENERALISSIMO'S HIT LIST

"OK, Johnson, let's hear the whole story," I replied as I ordered another round.

Johnson threw back the last of his "Cuba Libre," settled into his chair and began his tale. "I never did like Bayo, though I admit he was a colorful character. His book, '150 Questions for a Guerrilla' which you published was full of bullshit. However, the book has an enduring appeal even though it is written for a 12-year-old and seems childish. But strange things happen to bored or ambitious middle-class youths who read Bayo. He offers them power. He shows them how ridiculously simple it is. And of course, he throws in generous dollops of guerrilla mystique. Kids study Bayo and they're transformed; they feel a sense of power in this world he reveals. It all seems so damn simple. But some of his precepts are not only oversimplified but downright dangerous. Take his famed recipe for cooking up nitroglycerine for example. It's manically simple to produce TNT: boil dynamite and skim off the scum: presto—you've got yourself a powerful explosive. Much more likely: presto—you've got a big BOOM!"

The second round of drinks arrived, I tipped the waitress, and Johnson continued. "Bayo was mucking about stirring up trouble wherever he could. We had to do something about him. I asked my boss, General Arturo Espaillat, also known in trade circles as 'the Razor' or 'the Yellow Cat,' who was Trujillo's intelligence chief, 'How come the Old Man has never tried to eliminate Bayo? We had a perfectly good stable of hired killers sitting around doing nothing. At the time, they were merely between gigs . . . or hits.

"'Of course, we don't do things like that,' said Espaillat, a West Point graduate who was an aristocrat, suave and cosmopolitan. He could be hilariously funny but he was also the most lethal guy I've ever known. He moved through his world like a barracuda through sardines. 'Why don't you ask the Jefe?' 'Not me,' I said. Palace protocol was that suggestions came from the Old Man, not to him.' "

"So what happened then?" I said, numbed by the cheap booze, but aware enough to know that I had entered into a web of deadly intrigue.

"It wasn't long until an opportunity presented itself," Johnson continued. "I came across something about Bayo and Regino Camacho guaranteed to excite the Generalissimo. I'd been skimming through a stack of intelligence reports when an article from Guns magazine, published in the U.S., stared me in the face. The article, written by one Robert K. Brown, mentioned that an arms factory was being built in Havana.

"I was stunned. Not a word had I heard about this from our high-priced Havana spies. Not a word! Here I'm reduced to getting top-priority intelligence out of a magazine. I tucked the clipping in my pocket. No one would ever see it. I'll write my own report. You don't get any points—or bonuses—in this business for intelligence coups you stumble on in public print."

"The Generalissimo got excited, aright. Until now, his San Cristobal arms factory had been the sole source of weapons in the Caribbean area. The factory had been built at enormous expense and operated at a heavy loss—but the Old Man was enormously proud of it. The San Cristobal plant meant that we'd have local access to arms in case of a U.S. embargo—such as one that had just helped destroy Batista's government and was now being applied to the Dominican Republic."

"An arms factory in Castro's Cuba would wipe out any margin of military superiority the Jefe had over the Cubans. The Generalissimo seemed as upset at another item I'd extracted from your article:

" 'Those dogs are going to use our San Cristobal design to produce weapons in the Havana Plant?' the Generalissimo asked.

" 'Si, Jefe, that's the info I'm getting. I understand from our sources, which got a full account from an American arms expert there, that Regino Camacho is using the San Cristobal design—a modified design, that is. It seems that Camacho's prototypes were overheating.'

" 'This is that same Camacho you've mentioned before? The Camacho who is always making revolution?' the Generalissimo barked.

" 'Yes, Jefe. He's Bayo's man,' I said. 'He's also a genius with weapons. Camacho is the kind of technician who can take a rusty smokestack and turn it into a howitzer. He's been with Bayo for years . . .' "

"The generalissimo made a short, fast chopping motion with his chubby right hand across his neck. I was familiar with the gesture. But I wasn't quite sure who he meant. 'Bayo, Jefe?' I asked hopefully.

" 'Comacho. Draw any extra funds needed from the Officina Particular.' I nodded.

" 'Now . . . this other arms expert. Who is he?'

" 'I really don't know, Jefe,' I admitted. 'He's been in our sights for some time. He is said to represent American arms manufacturers. That may be a cover. Brown'—I was referring to you, R.K.—'is an American and has been all over Havana for some months now. He's been seen with Bayo. . .'

"Jefe gave another short hard chopping motion. 'Bayo, Jefe?' I asked hopefully.

" 'Brown.' I must have looked disappointed. The Jefe added: 'Comacho and Brown only. They can have no arms factories without technicians, can they Roberto?'

"The hit team was activated. Most of Trujillo's agents were Cubans who had been on the payroll for years: diplomats, politicians, corrupt cops, gangsters. They were controlled either directly by the Generalissimo or by his intelligence service, the Servicio de Inteligencia Militar (SIM). Most of these agents had been eliminated by Castro's organization within a few months of his takeover.

"However, a second network survived. One with which I was more closely associated. It was made up of a small group of Chinese-Cubans, a couple of expatriate Europeans, a defrocked priest, a Toronto mobster and an elderly Mexican pistolero who had lived in Havana for years. The network was still functional but was starting to disintegrate as pressures increased on Trujillo's regime. But the old man still was able to have Camacho hit outside Liberty City in January 1960. And you, Brown, had fortunately run out of money and returned to Colorado. You left just in time to avoid being the last corpse chalked up by Trujillo's once-feared 'Network of Terror.' "

I grasped my drink with both hands and was in semi-shock, yet fascinated by how close I had come to buying the farm. I mulled over how I felt about being indirectly responsible for the death of an individual that I had written about." I said, "Let's toast Bayo and Camacho for a hell of a story."

Johnson, who for reasons unknown, never reached his potential as an author though Paladin Press, did publish his book, *How to Be a Mercenary*.

THE HUNT FOR REFUGEES WHO NEEDED RESCUING

Back to 1960, when I made my third trip to Cuba in March. Bob Berrellez, the AP's "fireman" for Latin America for many years, and who was involved to an unknown degree in the overthrow of Salvador Allende in Chile in 1972 while working for ITT, graciously put me up in his apartment to save me a buck. Once again, hanging out with the AP staff I realized that the intentions of the Castro regime had drastically changed over the preceding year. The Cuban press and media in general were under the thumb of Castro, who was successfully moving to control all centers of power in the island, be it student, labor or professional organizations. Concurrently, the anti-American tone of the Cuban government spokesman over and above Castro and Che was taking on an ever more vitriolic tone as well as becoming more supportive of the Russians and Communist bloc nations.

The writing was on the wall but the American government didn't figure it out until October of '60 when it finally broke relations with Cuba.

Castro, the most exceptional caudillo in the history of Latin America, had in fact bamboozled me, but he had also duped the whole world including his own Cuban populace. Hundreds of thousands fled when Castro revealed his true colors. But you have to give the old dictator credit. He was able to confuse the opposition, both latent and active, until it was too late. The problem was that those individuals who eventually withdrew their support from Castro defected, or even went to the mountains to conduct guerrilla warfare against him, did not arise in a mass at one time but, often incrementally over a period of a year, consequently diluting their potential impact.

After all this intrigue I had titled my Master's thesis, "The Impact of Revolutionary Politics on the Autonomy of the Cuban Labor Movement." Most of the former Cuban labor leaders I interviewed, who had been supporters of Castro and in many cases active in the anti-Batista underground, told me, "Ah, we knew that Che was a communist. We knew that Raul was a communist. But we were certain that Fidel would take care of the two when the time came." Yeah, well, he took care of them but not in the way the anti-communist labor leaders had predicted.

I kept in contact with some of the 26th of July activists who had supported Castro and then had turned against him, as I had, once it became obvious that he was a Commie in disguise. In the spring of 1962, about a year after the Bay of Pigs fiasco, I headed back down to Miami to link up with the activists and interview Cuban exiles for my thesis as well as to see what a small cadre of would-be soldiers of fortune were up to.

After the Bay of Pigs, Miami was inundated with patriotic, adventurous young male Americans, some with and some without military experience, who wanted to take a crack at Castro, not realizing that for the most part the CIA had all the action locked up. After sleeping on park benches for a couple of weeks, most got the word and headed back to Arkansas, Alabama or wherever. A straggling dozen or so hung around Miami and were involved in nearly every non-CIA plot to overthrow somebody, somewhere in the Caribbean. They were an interesting group of rogues or renegades who simply wouldn't give in to the humdrum of everyday life. Many plans and plots were discussed, and fantasies fueled by cheap rum were concocted, but none came to fruition.

I gave my "go directly to jail" Sten submachine gun to Ed Collins, a former Army NCO, and instructed him to see "that it was put to good use." It was—I suppose. He sold it a few weeks later for $40 for food money. I was successful in locating and interviewing numerous Castro defectors from the Cuban labor movement who provided a wide and varied insight on the machinations Castro used to slowly take control of one of the most powerful non-communist segments of Cuban society.

I monitored the situation in Cuba as time went on, and in the spring of 1964, after I had completed Airborne School at Ft. Benning, I decided to head out again to Miami to see what kind of adventure/trouble the remaining soldiers-of-misfortune were getting into and with whom. I heard of plots and plans but nothing materialized.

There I met Peder Lund, who had bumped into some of the mercs while working as a deckhand on an inter-waterway tugboat.

"I went to pawn a .357 Magnum and was directed to Nellie's, where I met the boys," Peder recalled. Nellie's was a rundown boarding house catering to anyone with $10–15 a week for a cot and two hots a day.

In an interview before he died, Marty Casey, a former Marine who had been on the Soldier of Fortune scene in Miami for the prior three years in an abortive attempt to pull some refugees out of Fidel land, remembered meeting Peder.

"When Peder knocked on the door at Nellie's, Lil Joe, one of the ne'er do wells, answered. Peder was more than welcome since he carried a two-pound tin of coffee and a carton of cigarettes. A Miami Herald reporter, Don Bohning, had given him our address and told him that we were broke and craving cigarettes and coffee. The cigarettes he bought, and the coffee he found when nobody was looking on the tugboat he worked on. Peder told the boys that he was trying to find a Colorado adventurer by the name of Bob Brown. The name meant nothing to me, but the others perked up and started calling out the various handles this Brown was known for. "The Cowboy," "the Texan," "Uncle Bob," etc., including a few Brown would rather forget. Within a half hour, as they sat swapping lies, there was another knock at the door. Again, Lil Joe answered and let out a loud, 'Uncle Bob!' A big smile on his ruggedly handsome face, "Uncle Bob" called out hello and told us he had rented the empty apartment next to ours, and he would be back in a few minutes. He returned, no longer wearing jeans, cowboy boots and shirt. Now in uniform, Captain Robert K. Brown, U.S. Army Reserve, stood in the doorway showing off his newly won paratrooper wings. He would be in town for only eight days, but that was more than ample time for 'Uncle Bob' to stir up enough trouble for a lifetime," Marty said.

150 QUESTIONS FOR A GUERRILLA

Peder had run across a copy of "150 Questions for a Guerrilla" at a newsstand in Boulder, Colorado, and wanted to meet "Uncle Bob," publisher of Panther Publications. "After a few hours swapping dubious tales, 'Uncle Bob' invited all to get some chow," Marty said. "He wanted seafood and the seven of us stuffed ourselves into a '51 Dodge and ended up at the New England Oyster House, by Miami International Airport. As we chowed down the seafood delicacies we rarely had the opportunity to savor, the main topics of conversation were the CIA and Cuban exiles. At that time the exile movement was a joke and the CIA's operations would have been hilarious if it weren't for the tens of millions being wasted, while a few good souls were being captured and executed. Everything was a mess and very few seemed to care except those who were making big money ripping off the taxpayers."

"We got down to serious business when we returned to Lil Joe's. We still had 12 days left on our boat rental and a lot of weapons. We lacked some ammo and money to buy gas and food; 'Uncle Bob' pledged that. When Lil Joe came home from working at a boat builder's, he called a friend, Edy Mor, a Cuban exile activist. Edy was a member of one of the hundreds of small exile groups who trusted neither the U.S. government nor, much less, exiled politicians. A simple plan was hatched. 'Uncle Bob,' Peder and I would take the Toni to the dock in Black Water Sound. The boys would join us there, bringing the weapons and ammo."

Marty continued his tale:

"We got a late start and I soon learned Peder had quite a bit of boat-handling experience. He took the helm and expertly guided Toni next to the tug on which he was employed. There was no one aboard, so we liberated a small coffee pot, coffee, sugar cubes, utensils and canned goods. We were not making very good headway and were still off Soldier Key when the sun started to set. Two hours later we were no farther south than Elliot Key and dog tired. Heading toward shore, we spied a small dock and headed for it. We finished tying up when we heard noises coming from up on the dock. A man's voice coming from behind a flashlight called out, "Do you want to spend the night?" Peder asked if we could tie up and told the man we were headed for Key Largo and were too tired to go on. The man said his name was Bill and invited us to his house for coffee. At the end of the dock was a sandy beach. Thirty meters farther, now slightly illuminated by a moon peeking its nose over the eastern horizon, sat an eerie looking, large two-story wood frame house, complete with gables, one of which was loose and slowly swinging and creaking in the slight breeze.

"The house was Spartan with a small table and chairs, a wood burning stove and a couple buckets of fresh water. We shot the breeze by the light of an oil lamp. Bill was a former medical doctor who had fallen prey to alcohol, or 'the Irish disease' as he called it, and was now recovering and worked for the landowner, Arthur Vining Davis. Mr. Davis would send his alcoholic friends down to the key to dry out. Bill's job was to care for them. The house, built in 1875 of durable Dade county pine, constructed with all dowel work, without a nail, had weathered many a vicious hurricane. But it was haunted by the ghosts of various alcoholics who didn't leave the key alive," Marty said.

"'You can spend the night here,' Bill told us as he walked us into a small room illuminated by the candle he carried. As soon as he left, Peder dove into a small cot, leaving 'Uncle Bob' and me to share a slightly larger bed. Small beams of moonlight filtering through cracks in the gable and the sound of the broken one added to the eeriness. In no time we were asleep," Marty said.

"The following morning, with a belly full of eggs, fried corn beef hash, biscuits and hot coffee, we were on our way. It took almost five hours to get to the cut leading to Black Water Sound. Once into the sound some teenagers in a speed boat came by and started yelling, 'Cuban exiles, Cuban exiles.' We ignored them as we passed the Caribbean Club, once the main set for the Bogart movie, Key Largo. A few minutes later we were tied up at the small dock. I walked to the Caribbean Club and called Lil Joe, who assured me they would arrive at 9 p.m. It was pitch black. Peder stayed on the boat while 'Uncle Bob' and I walked the few meters to the road, more a single-lane path covered in gravel. The path ran down to the water's edge, then hooked back to the highway. 'They're early,' whispered 'Uncle Bob' as we heard a vehicle crackling the gravel. Slowly the car advanced, its headlights extinguished. The car stopped. I was on the passenger side, Bob on the driver's. Bob asked, 'Are you the Cubans?' as he pulled the door open. The overhead light came on to reveal a pockmarked teenager performing dubious acts who dropped the gear into low and sped off showering us with gravel," Marty recalled.

Peder's recollection of the event was not so thrilling:

> The boys' at Nellie's had a scheme to bring some refugees out of Cuba, film the operation, sell the film to a major TV network, and with the proceeds finance an armed raid against Cuba. As I was the only one working, I financed the rental of the Toni. 'The boys' were to bring weapons by road, and a Cuban captain/guide was to rendezvous. We slept on the Toni when we weren't hanging out in Key Largo. There wasn't much else to do except slap mosquitoes or eat refugee beans and rice, or both. RKB said he would accompany me on the boat to Key West, but would not go on the harebrained scheme to rescue refugees. We, of course, encountered foul weather, ran aground on a sandbar, ran out of food but for refugee beans and rice, caught no fish except for one small barracuda (they are virtually all bones and inedible), and waited a frustrating five days for the boys and captain. After numerous payphone calls, we were told the captain had 'to do his laundry' and would not be joining us.

I started feeling more and more antsy about this mission. Not only had the guns not arrived, it just didn't feel right. My gut had kept me from getting whacked twice in Havana by not joining abortive revolutionary expeditions to the Dominican Republic and Nicaragua. I told Peder, who was young, dumb and full of testosterone, "This is bad . . . I don't like it. I'm not going."

Peder finally agreed, worried anyhow about having no Cuban captain.

I left a couple of Army ponchos with Marty, who later used them to jerry rig sails when the boat's putt-putt went kaput, which allowed them to make it back to Miami. Peder enlisted in the Army to circumvent the draft, and went on to get his commission the hard way as I did, at the Ft. Benning School for Boys.

My Cuban adventures had wound down. I was still alive because I had run out of money and patience and, dreadfully disillusioned, headed back to paradise in Colorado. I had unknowingly avoided being a corpse on the wrong end of an assassinaton. It was not the last time that I would be on someone's hit list.

3

THE NON-INVASION OF HAITI

It was a typical, bright sunny afternoon in the Flaming Liberal People's Republic of Boulder in 1966 when the first phone call came in.

"Brown," Little Joe asked, "do you have any mortar rounds?"

"No, Little Joe, I do not. I have better things to do, like making a living," and hung up. Little Joe had been one of a considerable group of American would-be adventurers who had shown up in Miami, hunting rifle barrels stuck out of their car windows, after the Bay-of-Pigs fiasco, hoping to get a piece of the action. A piece of Castro, that is.

Most gave up and returned home after sleeping in parks for awhile. But there were a dozen or so hardcore would-be soldiers of fortune who would be involved, one way or another, in most of the numerous wild-eyed revolutionary plots that germinated in Miami in the 1960's. Miami was the Mecca for anti-Castro Cubans, Castro spies, adventurers, con men, and the occasional sincere individual determined to bring down one Caribbean despot or another.

I had met a number of them when I had headed to Miami in 1962 to continue gathering information for my Masters thesis.

Little Joe, telephone pole thin with a drooping mustache and balding head from Bowling Green, Kentucky, was one of them. He was a "remittance man" whose daddy, a local judge, sent him $50 a week to keep him out of town after Joe got involved in dynamiting competitors' after-hours night clubs. He also had worked his way up to Master Sergeant in the Kentucky National Guard. I paid his telephone call little mind and went about my business . . . in this case, packing and shipping books on guerrilla warfare for my small, barely profitable publishing company.

Thirty minutes later, another phone call . . . another Miami soldier of fortune. This time it was Marty Casey a former Marine, jet black hair and stocky, who fit the stereotype of the hard-drinking Irishman. "Brown, we need some mortars. Can you help?"

"Look," I said. "Do you think I keep that kind of hardware under my bed? What the hell is going on?"

He whispered, "We're going to invade Haiti!"

"Yeah, well, good luck," I growled and hung up. Ten minutes later, a third call, this time from another of the crew, Bill Dempsey, a handsome, curly haired Canadian who had somehow found his way to stirring the revolutionary pot in South Florida.

"We need some machine guns," he said.

I was hooked.

"OK. I don't have any machine guns, but I'm on my way. I'll call regarding my arrival time." I packed my military gear into a duffel bag, grabbed my scoped Model 70 Winchester hunting rifle and headed to the airport. How often do you have an opportunity to invade a country with which the U.S. is at peace—from the U.S.?

In Miami, I was picked up and driven to "Nellie's," the ramshackle boarding house. Some of the aspiring invaders were hanging around cleaning AR-15's. I was quickly read into the plot. . . .

"We load our guns and personnel on the boat and invade Haiti," pretty much summed up the invasion operations order. It wasn't going to be a repeat of the Normandy invasion that was for sure.

And then the waiting started—for the ship that wasn't coming in. Finally, we got the word to move out to a safe house that turned out to be not so safe. Two carloads of us drove from Nellie's across town to a large white two-story house on a corner lot with a "For Sale" sign planted in the front lawn. We pulled into the driveway in that upscale neighborhood—in daylight mind you—and unloaded the guns, which were somewhat concealed in ponchos.

This was not good. With all the shenanigans of the anti-Castro Cubans, this type of unusual activity was bound to draw the attention of nosy neighbors. And the cops. We went inside and found some 40-odd Haitians with rucksacks. Not a stick of furniture in the house. I said, "This is bullshit, stupid. The snooping neighbors are going to call the cops."

Within 15 minutes, a police car pulled up across the street and an officer went inside.

"Oh, shit, this is one time I wish I was wrong," I said. "He's going to come over here. Let me handle it."

And so he did, rapping none to gently on the front door. So I opened it. "The neighbors report there is some suspicious activity going on over here. What's going on?" the cop growled, as he swiveled his head doing a quick estimate of the situation. Now how the hell do you explain 50 males of military age in a house with no furniture?

"Well, officer, we're attending a Boy Scout convention and rented this house to save money." I replied. He was not stupid. He didn't believe it for a minute.

"And what, pray tell, are all those military backpacks?" he smirked. I replied, "Oh, just easier to carry clothes than in a suitcase." And with that, he departed.

"Ok, guys, we're going to get raided. Get the guns back in my car and I'll take them back to Nellie's. While loading up, one of the gringos reconned the area and saw a four-door sedan parked behind a row of popular trees on the south side of the house. Customs was surveiling the house till the cops could take us down. I backed the car over the curb using the trees as concealment, loaded the guns and took off. Within a half-hour the fuzz raided the house but found nothing—except a bunch of hungry Haitians. Well, one WWII hand grenade was overlooked. Little Joe grabbed it and shoved it down his jock strap. The serrations of the pineapple grenade showed though his pants but the law didn't notice. Nothing really illegal there, so the cops left.

But the operation was compromised. And there still was no boat. Meantime the Cuban exiles in the operation started going down to Little Havana to get their fix of Cuban coffee wearing their camouflage uniforms. One of the Cubans' mothers showed up in front of the "safe house," screaming, "Jose, Jose, you can't leave your mama alone!" The novelty of this farce had worn off and I decided to go back to packing books instead of going to jail.

The core group of would-be invaders continued to fuss around with invading Haiti, until most of them got arrested in January 1967, including some of the American soldiers of fortune. Some went to jail, including a Haitian priest, Father Georges, who had been a Minister of Education under "Papa Doc."

I later wrote a scathing critique of the FBI's involvement in the abortive invasion that appeared in National Review in '67. The Feds knew about the plot from the get-go and at any time could have taken Father Georges, one of the Haitian leaders aside and said, "Father, we know you wish to free your country from a brutal, oppressive dictator. But, Father, you cannot launch an armed invasion from the United States. It is against the law. Now, if you continue to pursue this project, we will have no choice but to arrest you."

This undoubtedly would have brought things to a screeching halt, but the Feds like to hang "trophies on their walls, and it is more exciting to play spy-counterspy in Miami than investigate run-of-the-mill miscreants. This would have saved the American taxpayer hundreds of thousands of dollars.

That put an end to that until 1969, when I was "safely" in Vietnam, when the *SOF*'s and a few Haitians tried again. The plan was to land a Super Constellation filled with Haitian exiles and American adventurers at an isolated airstrip and go from there. The Haitians got cold feet and did not show up. But the gringos, out of frustration, decided to go ahead and do something . . . like bombing the Presidential Palace in Port-au-Prince with 55-gallon drums of homemade napalm. Some of the drums actually exploded, starting an impromptu urban renewal program. Haitian anti-aircraft guns shot up the Super Connie; it was forced to land at a U.S. military missile tracking station and everybody was arrested. Enough already!

It wasn't the last run in I would have with the Haitian exile fantasy. In August of 1972 I got a call from a Haitian self-styled exile leader—name long forgotten as is how the heck he got my phone number.

"How about leading an invasion and subsequent guerrilla war against "Baby Doc," Duvalier's fat, Lamborghini-driving son. You have to come to New York and then we will drive to Montreal to meet with the money man," he explained with a thick French accent.

I was working on a yet-unpublished manuscript on CIA covert operations in Florida, titled, "Ripped Cloak, Rusty Dagger," and was bored.

"Why not," I responded, but being a bit wiser in the ways of would-be revolutionaries I added, "You will provide me with a round trip air ticket to La Guardia—not a one way—and pick up all my expenses."

He agreed and in a couple of days I was winging it to the Big Apple. Yeah, I should have held out for a "consultant's" fee, but like I said, I was bored.

I grabbed a cab to what ended up being one of the spookiest hotels I've had the misfortune to stay in. And I've stayed in some classic shitholes over the years. I checked in. It was not rocket science to figure out that they had put me up in this particular roach haven because the night desk clerk was—you guessed it—a Haitian exile! I could swear that the casting director for the first Star Wars movie got all the customers in the bar scene from this hotel. And going, with some trepidation, to my room, I almost got a secondary high from the marijuana smoke in the hallways. Whatever the inhabitants were offering to sell didn't interest me. I didn't need a case of clap no matter how cheap, much less uppers or downers or inners or outers.

The next morning I met the leadership of the group and we chugged seven hours up to Montreal where we met the moneyman—a Canadian oil baron—and the leaders of this particular boondoggle. In short order I found out that the Haitians had promised the Canadian exclusive drilling rights for oil in the poverty-ridden country, in return for funding the operation.

I was chosen to lead the invasion force. I was, with my team, to assassinate"Baby Doc" and the number two and three men in the dictatorship, all at the precise same time while they were in different locations: But there was a catch—none of the Haitians were going with me!

This was insanity at its apex! To try and take out three targets in three separate locations at the same time means they had been smoking too much of their own bad dope. And none of them were going to risk their sorry asses? God protect me from the loons of the world. I decided to extricate myself from this inanity as quickly and gracefully as possible. I thought for a moment as they continued to babble, and came up with an alternative plan.

"Look, guys, think about this. You say that Baby Doc drives to his beach house with some bimbo every Sunday afternoon in his Lamborghini about 2 o'clock, right? I suggest that I charter an upscale yacht, get a couple of my buddies and girl friends, and sail down to Port-au-Prince where we will hit the casinos. We'll play the part of wealthy playboys and meet fat boy."

"After developing rapport with him, on one sunny Sunday afternoon we'll sail up to his beach house, invite him aboard for drinks, neutralize any of his security and put the grab on him. Then we hold him for ransom, since his mother, who adores him and is in France, allegedly has $450 million in Swiss bank accounts.

"Meanwhile, I have a plane to catch. Give me a call when you're ready."

Needless to say I never got that call. But I had been smart enough to get a round-trip ticket.

4

WANDERING THROUGH THE ARMY; ANGLING FOR NAM

A short-lived, turbulent, to say the least, and totally unsatisfactory marriage to a local bottle-bleached Boulder psycho siren left me thoroughly pissed at the world in the summer of 1963. I had been promoted to Captain and was broke, and the only prospect of earning a decent paycheck to cover alimony and child support was going back on active duty to attend an Army school. I popped down to the local Army Reserve center where I looked for and found the longest school I could attend, the Infantry Officers Advanced Course at Ft. Benning, Georgia. Six months of an Army Captain's pay and I could pay my bills. I should have never been sent there, as my branch in the Army was Intelligence, not Infantry.

At Benning, I found myself in a sorry predicament as I was competing with classmates who were both active-duty and Reserve infantry officers who were about six years ahead of me in experience and knowledge. However, I struggled through once again.

I made friends with the student company first sergeant in a plan to get an assignment to Airborne School. I knew it was unlikely, as the regs stated there were to be no airborne school slots for reservists unless you were assigned to a reserve airborne unit, of which there were none in Colorado where I was stuck for graduate school.

"Sarge," I implored, "any strings you can pull to get me in that damn school?" He gave me a bemused look and said, "Well, Captain, we NCO's do have our ways, but it's going to cost you a bottle of Jack Daniels." No problem there. Somehow (another mystery never to be solved) through the old boy NCO network he got me orders, even though I was not assigned to an airborne unit.

THE MYSTERY OF THE BAY OF PIGS OFFICERS

I had a number of interesting classmates. Three or four had just returned from the White Star mission in Laos. And there were about a dozen Cuban Bay of Pigs officers who had been ransomed from a Castro hellhole only a few months before.

We non-Cuban officers raised our eyebrows as to why this might be, since in a normal infantry officer's career, one first went to Basic Infantry Officers Course (BIOC), then served several years in various assignments before attending the Advanced Course. These guys were going directly from BIOC to the Advanced Course and a couple of them were scheduled, immediately upon graduation, to attend the General Staff and Command College at Ft. Leavenworth, Kansas. Normally one would have to have ten years of active duty before such an assignment. Only explanation we could come up with was that either Kennedy planned another Bay of Pigs or he was manipulating the Cubans' hopes for political reasons. Little did we know that Kennedy had cut a deal with Khrushchev not to invade Cuba. The mystery was solved, but not until much later.

A number of these Cubans, virulent anti-communists, went on to distinguish themselves in combat in Vietnam and subsequent assignments in the States and elsewhere. A couple dropped out of the course to work with CIA-sponsored Cuban exile groups that were conducting para-military operations out of Nicaragua against the Cuban mainland. One, Gustavo Villado, a jovial, blue-eyed, sandy-haired tiger, was in on the capture of Che Guevara in Bolivia in 1967. Nestor Pino rose to the rank of full colonel and was Vice President Dan Quayle's military advisor.

Since I was now jump qualified, I was eligible to apply for the Special Forces Officers Course (SFOC), since back in those days, one had to be jump qualified before one could even volunteer for SF.

WHAT THE HELL, LET'S GET A GREEN BERET . . .

The SFOC was my type of action. Our class of about sixty was split up into 12-man "A" Teams, the basic building block of the SF command structure. The team I was on split up almost immediately into two factions. One faction believed in doing everything strictly by the book and the second believed in doing whatever it took to accomplish the mission and screw the regs. Not too hard to figure which group I cast my lot with. The division almost got nasty on a couple of occasions, with serious punch-ups barely avoided.

Fed up with regs, I contributed to one of those conflicts during our graduation field exercise. After running around the woods for a couple of weeks, the "plan" called for the final exercise to consist of the main body of SF officer students to paddle down a river in rubber boats and blow a bridge—simulated of course. Our specific team was to recon the area of operations. We had a two-man team on 24-hour surveillance near the bridge. As darkness set in, our surveillance team radioed in the warning that gun jeeps of the 82nd Airborne Division, who were playing the part of the counter-guerilla forces and who, according to the lesson plan, were scheduled to win, had positioned their gun jeeps along the bank of the river and would ambush our main force (with blanks of course) as they paddled down the river. Gun jeeps vs troops in open rubber boats? It would have been a massacre. Now, the hassle between the two groups in our A-Team got heated.

One faction said, "Look we're not in radio comm with our headquarters. We are unable to alert them to the ambush. We must blow the bridge before the 82nd gets into their final positions."

The by-the-book bozos said, "No, if we do that, we'll screw up the whole exercise. The grand finale firefight is scheduled for 2000 hrs., which is to be followed by the beer blast and barbeque. We've got to follow the lesson plan."

"Screw the lesson plan! You know damn well that when you develop new Intel that is going to impact on the success of the mission that you adjust your plans."

The argument continued until the by-the-book team leader laid down the law, "We were going to do it according to the lesson plan."

As our detachment moved to its destruction, I grabbed a hold of Captain Lopez, another one of the team renegades, and pulled him to the rear of our column.

"Look, Lopez, this is bullshit! Screw the lesson plan. Since you and I are the team demo men and we have the prima cord and fuse lighters, let's steal a boat and blow the bridge ourselves." He replied. "Let's go steal a boat and screw the regs." Stealing boats was our own brilliant improvisation, and of course against the regs.

We moved down to the river and after 50 yards we found a not-too-waterproof rowboat without oars. We picked up a couple of planks, crawled in and cast off. Quietly paddling for half-an-hour, we beached the boat a hundred yards from the bridge, and stealthily conducted a recon right up to the bridge itself. Ah ha! No bad guys on the bridge. They were all smoking and joking waiting for the fireworks to begin in an hour. We could approach the bridge without being observed.

"Lopez," I whispered, "let's move."

We hustled back to the boat, paddled up to the bridge, wired the bridge with our dummy charges and the prima cord, which would not cause any damage but would make a hell of a racket. We pulled the fuse lighters and paddled like mad. Within moments all hell broke loose. The prima cord exploded and the gun jeeps started firing blanks at who knows what. We paddled to the riverbank and rejoined our team. The referees/exercise monitors were running around screaming, "What happened? It's not time yet! The chicken isn't barbequed! Terminate the exercise!"

The instructors were really pissed at us for fouling up their carefully laid plans and wouldn't speak to us during the rest of the course, though one did admit off the record that we had done the right thing.

BROWN DECIDES HE IS NEEDED IN VIETNAM . . .

After completing SFOC in 1965, I was accepted into the SF counter-insurgency course, which had euphemistically been renamed, "Internal Defense and Development." While there, I made inquiries about getting a piece of the action in Vietnam. One of the instructors, a Lt. Colonel, suggested that I investigate signing on with the USAID program for Nam. He gave me the name of a contact in the State Department who I hustled up to see immediately after graduation. I called in the middle of a Friday afternoon and told him who I was and he told me to come on over—on a Friday afternoon no less! I did so and after a brief interview in which I detailed my publishing experience and interest in guerrilla warfare as well as my pirating around with the Miami soldier-of-fortune, Cuban and Haitian exile crowd, he said, "Let me call someone." He dialed and chuckled, "Sam, I've got somebody you need to see. He's a soldier-of-fortune type . . . would fit right in your outfit."

I suppressed a gasp and figured I was screwed. But what the hell? I headed over to his office about 1600hrs, and after a short chat, Sam Simpson, who was director of A.I.D. recruiting, said, "We've got the perfect spot for you as an Assistant Province Advisor. $15,000 a year plus 25% hardship allowance and 12-month language school in Hawaii." As I had some notion of coming back to the States and getting into academia, this sounded like an appropriate stepping stone. It was an opportunity for action, as well as a chance to do some good. "Brown, it's a near done deal. We'll be in touch and bring you back here for further interviews and a physical."

A couple of weeks later, I winged into DC at Uncle Sam's expense, where I was told, "You don't need to see this guy, no need to see that guy. With your Special Forces background and experience working with those crazies in Miami, you'll just be wasting everybody's time as we're going to hire you in any case." I took the test to evaluate my ability to learn the Vietnamese language and only passed because they had dropped the standards the preceding week. The last hurdle was a physical with one of State's physicians. He was in a hurry as it was again Friday afternoon late, and at the end of it, he asked, "How's your hearing?" I replied, "What?" And he said, "Go on and get out of here. You passed and I'm late for my golf game." "O.K. Doctor Death," I muttered to myself and bailed.

A couple of weeks later I called Simpson and asked him how my application was progressing. "Not to worry. We're in the process of completing your security check and then you're on your way." A week later, I got a form letter, something to the effect: "Dear Mr. Brown, We regret to inform you that we have found we have a number of individuals who are better qualified for the position for which you have applied. Thank you for your interest." The establishment had sold me out and I knew it. I knew enough about the intelligence community to figure out that anyone who was out of the ordinary was as about as popular as a tertiary case of syphilis. I wrote a letter to a Senator to look into the matter but got no response. And that was the end of that. I had no doubt I got deep-sixed because of my shenanigans with the Cubans.

MY DECLASSIFIED CIA FILES TELL ALL

When the Army notified me that I was transferred from the Intelligence Branch to Infantry, I had assumed that it was because I had completed the Infantry Officer's Advanced Course. I figured they had put me in the Intelligence Branch then realized their administrative screw-up and decided that I was now more qualified to be an Infantry rather than an Intelligence officer. I didn't find out the real reason until sometime in the '90's when I was contacted by a A.J. Weberman, who was researching a book on the Kennedy assassination and who offered to trade me copies of documents from my declassified CIA files for a lifetime subscription to *SOF*. Such a deal!

What I read in the files knocked off my proverbial socks. When the CIA investigated me to find out to what degree I was involved in Garrison's investigation of the Kennedy assassination, they pulled my Counter-Intelligence Corps records. The records revealed that:

> Subject's military service file was reviewed by a Review Action Board on 17 September 1964 to determine Subject's retention in the administrative field. Removal of Subject's Intelligence MOS was predicated upon Subject's apparent pro-Castro activities prior to 1960 and anti-Castro activities after then. It was noted that most of Subject's overt activities both pro and anti-Castro took place after his release from active duty with the CIC MOS . . . and during a period when he still had a Reserve obligation. Note was made of Subject's trips to Cuba and his authorship of news articles resulting in an official protest by a friendly foreign government as evidence of Subject's poor judgment. (While in Cuba in 1958 Subject wrote an article for the Associated Press concerning the possibility of General Alberto BAYO beginning a revolution against the Franco government in Spain.BAYO was a former officer in the Spanish Republican Air Force, long time communist sympathizer, and supporter of Castro. The article appeared in the 7 April 1959 European edition of the Stars and Stripes and promptly resulted in official protests by the Spanish Government to the Departments of State and Army. In 1963, Subject published a handbook on guerilla warfare allegedly authored by BAYO.)

> Subject attended the Infantry Officers Associate Career Course at Fort Benning, beginning in October 1963 and appeared to his classmates and faculty members as being irrational in his outlook on anything connected with Communism. This change of opinion on Subject's part concerning Castro resulted in his active participation in affairs of Cuban exiles and attempts to raise fund for weapons to be used against Castro. These anti-Castro efforts on Subject's part were believed to demonstrate a lack of discretion incompatible with the standards of the members of the Counter-Intelligence Corps. On 25 September 1964 Subject's Intelligence MOS was revoked and he was declared ineligible for any intelligence assignment.

All true and I have no regrets. Screw the Colonel Blimps.

BACK TO MY OLD FALLBACK, THE ARMY

So what to do? Might as well go the Army route to Vietnam. I knew full well that the Army would also run a background check and undoubtedly find out the same shit that deep-sixed me with USAID. I confirmed this suspicion in Miami hanging with the soldiers of fortune and the Cuban exiles when I ran into a young SF Reserve trooper. He had volunteered for active duty in S.E. Asia, been assigned to the SF 46th Company in Thailand, and after six months was shipped back home when the investigators found out he had been working with some of the non-CIA Cuban exile groups." Yeah, I said, "But you were just being "unconventional" and working against that bearded tinhorn dictator." He shook his head. "It's not right, but that's the way it is. They don't want anybody out of the mainstream."

I had no doubt what the outcome would be when they updated my security clearance. But I also knew it would take the Army machine six months to complete a background check, and my plan was, after getting to Nam and they found out I was one of Peck's bad boys, I would have had at least six months combat time and hopefully see the elephant—more than once—and whack a few bad guys. And then the Army could go get lost. I submitted my application to return to active duty in 1966, and got rejected because I was too old for my rank. A few months later I tried again and was accepted, as Mr. Charles and the NVA were blowing away too many company grade infantry officers, which included captains.

I got orders for Special Forces and reported to Ft. Bragg on 27 December 1967. I was going to stick to my plan of keeping my mouth shut until I saw that they had assigned me to G-2, which was Intelligence. Upon reporting to the then acting Chief of Staff for Intelligence, I decided, rightfully or wrongfully, I had best fess up to some of the more lurid aspects of my career. "Sir, I think you ought know that I was investigated for allegedly being involved in the Kennedy assassination. Also, I've been working on a manuscript which is an exposure of how screwed up the CIA is in their covert and clandestine operations targeted against Castro and yada, yada, yada." After a few minutes of this, squirming in his chair, he said, "Captain, go on leave and we'll pull your background files." I saluted smartly, about-faced and moved out.

When I returned there was a new Assistant Chief of Staff, Intelligence, who brusquely informed me, "Brown, we've pulled your file. You're not going to be in intelligence anymore. Report to Personnel." "Yes, sir," I replied and once again moved out smartly to Personnel where I was brusquely informed, "Captain, you're not going to be in SF anymore." This moving out smartly routine was getting old.

For a couple of weeks, I was a pariah amongst my Green Beret peers as the rumor got around that I had been doing bad things before I came back on active duty.

I PLAY CHICKEN WITH THE TOP BRASS

Then a full Colonel in the Personnel section of the Pentagon called me. I remember it clearly. "Brown, damn it, someone failed to update your security clearance before you received orders to active duty!!" Gotcha, mother! Having been in the CIC, I was well aware that to revoke or downgrade my "Top Secret" clearance, the Army was required "to prove cause." So, I can imagine the Army establishment's quandary. What do they tell me, which they damn well know would go directly to the media and read something like this:"Special Forces Captain Brown, who has volunteered to go to Vietnam, is being cashiered because while he was researching a manuscript on CIA activities in South Florida, he ripped the cover off over 27 CIA covert operations?" No, I don't think so. I would have given my left nut to be a fly on the wall and see how they handled this hot potato.

The mystery deepens. Couple of weeks later, the same Colonel calls me and asks me what I want to do.

"All I want to do is to go to Nam with Special Forces," I replied.

"Not going to happen," he snapped back."You'll do six months stateside like every other reservist coming back on active duty before shipping out. What schools do you want to go to? Language school? Ranger school?"

This blew my mind. The Army personnel office was not in the habit of asking junior officers what they wanted to do, even if they walked on water. I was trudging thru BS up to my knees. Why he made this almost unheard of offer is on my list of many unsolved mysteries.

The good Colonel told me to hustle my ass over to XVIII Corps G-3 and get assigned for the rest of my tour stateside. I met the assistant G-3, a relatively decent Lt. Colonel who gave me a choice. "Captain, you can either be in charge of ROTC training for the summer or you can be the Officer in Charge of the Corps Advanced Marksmanship Unit." Holy Cow, Marley, throw me into the briar patch. My angel/gremlin scored another one for me.

I couldn't have created a more desirable slot if I tried. Generally speaking, shooters are exceptional troops, since they have the self-discipline to perform under stress on the firing line, so it was far less likely that they would cause problems. Also, it was a whale of a lot more rewarding to spend your days on firing ranges than doing some bullshit job that a lot of my NCO's suffered through in their assigned unit. The fact that such duty encompassed numerous trips to attend matches throughout the Southeast frosted the cake. In the six months as OIC no one messed with me. My immediate boss, the assistant G-3, only visited me once, and since we were kicking ass in Army and civilian matches, I got a letter of commendation from the commanding officer of the XIII Airborne Corps, General York.

I organized a sniper training program for both the North Carolina National Guard and sniper teams for the XVIII Airborne Corps, in case such a resource was required to deal with any out-of-control civil disturbances that might occur during the upcoming summer.

TIME TO KICK MR. CHARLES' BUTT . . .

All good things must come to an end, and by now I was anxious to get to

Nam. My arrival there was no different than the descriptions that have been in scores of memoirs . . . getting off the plane and getting hit with a straight left jab of humidity followed by a right cross of debilitating heat. . . . The grenade screens over the raggedy ass bus windows . . . the smells, sights, for me, of a baroque culture . . . military fumes from the vehicles along with the stench of the food, unwashed bodies and open sewers. No big deal. A couple of million-plus troops had done the same thing.

It didn't take long to get processed and transported to my assigned unit, 2/18th Battalion, 3d Brigade, First Division, which was headquartered in a sprawling, dusty base located at Zion, about 20 clicks north of Saigon. Once again I landed on my feet, as the battalion I was assigned to had their Tactical Operations Center (TOC) in a huge brand-spanking-new water purification plant built with something like, as I remember, 60 million dollars funded by USAID to provide potable water to the inhabitants of Saigon. This project was typical of so many do-gooder projects in Nam and elsewhere, where the intent was admirable but the results a flat ass failure. Oh yes, the plant worked just fine, pumping out hundreds of thousands of gallons of water toward Saigon. Problem was the genius who put this project together failed to realize that all the pipes that carried the water into and throughout Saigon were ancient and decrepit, and therefore contaminated. And so was the water by the time it reached the end user.

But our quarters were comparatively luxurious. Tile floors, bunk beds and air conditioning—most of the time. When I first reported in to the Battalion, the old man, or CO, Lt. Colonel Crow, assigned me as the S-4, in charge of logistics. This excited me about as much as a bowl full of hairballs. The quartermaster/supply section was based at Zion. I slept in a bed of sweat till my body adjusted to the heat. I lost 10 lbs., down to 165 because of the heat. I ordered three tailored suits in Saigon, and within weeks after I got home and back to my normal weight, none of them fit. Well, at $35 apiece it was not a major financial disaster.

5

A-TEAM ADVENTURES: WHACKING MR. CHARLES . . . AND ALMOST GETTING WHACKED MYSELF

After about a month, the Battalion CO tagged me to take over as the S-2, staff intelligence officer. Dealing with the enemy, weather and terrain rather than keeping track of beans and bullets was definitely a step upward. Our Battalion was one of several that had been given an area of operations that blocked the major avenues of approach for the NVA into Saigon after Tet.

Unlike most combat battalions, who were hopping around the country chasing the bad guys, we were in a static location. As a result, I had relatively little to do in my new assignment, as the enemy units in our AO stayed the same, as did the terrain. So I had time on my hands. I established contact with the local Defense Intelligence Operation Coordination Center (DIOCC), which was the local office of the Phoenix program. It was headed up by a young Second Lieutenant, John Kelleher who controlled, to some degree, a dozen-plus thugs he had inherited or recruited, most of whom were VC defectors. He was somewhat of a smart ass but quite sharp and aggressive. His mission was to track down and eliminate, in one way or another, the VC province infrastructure. In our province, his success was primarily achieved by his young thugs moving around in the various villages and hamlets till they saw some of their former comrades and put the grab on them. He had his own informant network, and when agent reports predicted a movement of a VC unit which was too large for him to handle, he contacted me. I went to my colonel and requested a company of infantry to ambush the route of the VC element. Sometimes we scored, sometimes we didn't. In any event, we were one of the few straight leg infantry combat battalions that got kills based on agent reports, and I even got a letter of commendation from James Dameron, who was the Phoenix Province Chief for setting up the ambushes.

I started developing my own wire diagram of the province VC infrastructure, and as time passed I developed an insight into how we were slowly gutting the VC organization—whacking a couple in an ambush here, another in a raid there. Our battalion, along with the ARVN units in the province, were getting a few more every month. It was simply a matter of flooding the province with nightly ambushes—like over 1,100 a month—and sooner or later Mr. Charles would stumble into one and get blown away. We could see the results as we soon realized that various VC leaders were wearing two hats—responsible for more than one area of operations. Inexperienced VC were forced to move up the chain of command. We were hurting them and hurting them bad. No macho SpecOps personnel or fancy Intel moves. Just simple, plain old plodding grunt work.

I also enjoyed the intel bit, especially interrogations, as I got to look inside the heads of the enemy.

However, my enthusiasm for such endeavors nearly ended in disaster. On one sunny, bucolic afternoon my driver, blond, curly haired Spec. 4 Randy Goldman, was driving me and a young recently captured POW from the Brigade Intel shop back to my headquarters at the Bn. TOC, me in the back, the prisoner in the front next to Goldman. I was lolligagging around, enjoying the scenery and greenery as we slowed to make a left turn near a small village. As we did so, the VC bolted.

My reaction was so automatic that I have no recollection of whether I had a round in the chamber of my M-16. I do remember, though, that as soon as you could say, "Stop!" I was running after him, rapidly squeezing off individual shots . . . aiming low . . . no spray and pray shit. I saw him tear into a deserted hooch where I picked up a blood trail. I had popped the little shit. He had run out the other side of the hooch. I moved in, did a "spray and pray" inside to discourage any potential problem makers, and tracked the VC out into a pasture where the little shit had the misfortune of running into a patrol of local ARVN soldiers. I had a rather heated argument with them as to who this slicky boy belonged to, and I guess my uncompromising yelling won out that day, as I had no intention of being hung from the yardarm if I did not return with the prisoner.

Obviously the old angel/gremlin was up to his tricks again in this escapade. I had been purposely aiming low—don't ask me to try and evaluate my decision making in this case—and one bullet had gone through the sole of his right foot as he raised it while running. I could say I planned it that way, but that would piss off my angel/gremlin.

BROWN RETURNS TO SPECIAL FORCES

But this was all about to end, as in late '68 dame fortune turned from a fickle whore into a loving mistress. I found out that an old but not by any means close acquaintance, John Paul Vann, was operating out of CORD Headquarters in Bien Hoa, a few clicks up the road from our TOC in the water plant.

Colonel Wendell Fertig, who had been a major leader of the guerrilla opposition to the Japs in the Philippines during World War II, and had continued to serve as a consultant to the DOD or CIA regarding the communist insurgency in the islands for several years, had introduced me to John Paul Vann. I had met Fertig, who lived in Golden, Colorado, a hop, skip and jump from Boulder. My small publishing firm, Panther Publications, was not only publishing a few somewhat baroque books on unconventional warfare, but was retailing a wide range of titles on the subject by other publishers.

After reading his memoirs I called Fertig, told him of my interest in the field, and that I would like to visit. After a couple of meetings he introduced me to John Paul Vann, a former Lt. Colonel in Vietnam, who had resigned his Army commission as a protest over the way the war was being conducted in 1964. In 1963, he went public regarding the true state of the conflict—that the South Vietnamese were getting their asses handed to them by the VC—which went against the Army establishment's line of official bullshit. When I met him, he was working for defense contractor Martin Marietta and he was angling to get back to the action in Nam. Now he was Deputy for Civil Operations and Revolutionary Development for III Corps, and based out of Bien Hoa.

Though we had met only a couple of times, I later contacted John Paul Vann and he invited me to breakfast at his home in Bien Hoa. He picked me up at 0700 at my TOC. After pleasantries, I got right to it. "John, I've got to get out of this leg outfit and back into Special Forces." I explained how I got kicked out of SF and my assumptions as to why it occurred. He sympathized with me and said, "I'll see what I can do." And, bless him, he did. Shortly thereafter, I got a copy of a letter he had sent to Colonel Arron who was commander of the 5th Special Forces Group in Nam. He tooted my horn saying something to the effect that I was one of the Army's leading counter-insurgency experts, etc., etc. This was rather embarrassing, but no way was I going to throw a wrench in the works and disillusion the good Colonel Arron and jeopardize my chances for getting transferred back to Special Forces.

Shortly thereafter, I got a transfer to the 5th Group. Getting an in-country transfer like this was highly unusual, but who was I to complain or contradict John Paul Vann, who eventually held the civilian rank equivalent to a Major General. I saw him only one other time, when I arranged for him to attend a demonstration of exotic small arms at the nearby ARVN Infantry School in South Vietnam in the fall of 1968. Also in attendance were high-ranking ARVN officers, U.S. military personnel and representatives from the CIA. After the demo John Paul Vann spent an hour with us busting caps and left in his helicopter. I never saw him again.

Yet if John Paul Vann had been running that war, and if the dickhead McNamara, his whiz kids and the politicians had played with themselves instead of the lives of our military and our allies, we would have won the war. As it was, John Paul Vann gets most of the credit for playing a decisive role in defeating the North Vietnamese by calling in B-52 strikes on the NVA armored columns during their March 1972 Easter offensive. He was a brilliant tactician and strategist who might have won the war in Nam if he had not died in an ill-timed chopper crash.

I never did find out who the unlucky Infantry Captain was who thought he was going to Special Forces and instead ended up assigned to a leg outfit in the First Division.

My good fortune continued when out of the blue, a TV crew from CBS showed up at our TOC. I noticed a familiar face. It belonged to a cameraman who had been filming the abortive Haitian invasion attempt in 1966. We did the "Hi, howdy," bit and he informed me, "Guess who jetted over here on the same flight?" "Ok, who? Papa Doc?" I responded. "No, Mitch Werbell, III, with all of his goodies. He's bunked up at the Astor Hotel on Tu Do Street."

Werbell was one of the most if not the most flamboyant snake oil salesman I've run across in my nefarious career. Mitch had an unparalleled gift of BS. He claimed his father was a Russian Cavalry Colonel in the Tsarist Army. Who knows? Over time, I learned to take everything he said with a grain of salt. If he said the sun was going to rise in the east in the morning, I would say, "Mitch, I'll wait and see." He often claimed he had been in the OSS in the Burma-China-India theatre during WWII. I was suspicious of this until one weekend when I was visiting his semi-palatial farm and saw him and Lou Conien, a famous CIA operative who played a major role in the Diem assassination and then ran the DEA for several years, reminiscing about the big war as they looked at faded snap shots. Werbell and Conien were similar in the respect that with both of them one could never separate truth from fiction.

Only Werbell wasn't selling snake oil, but something far more deadly—state of the art submachine guns, like the Ingrahm M-10 and M-11 as well as the then state-of-the-art Sionics suppressor or silencer to the U.S. military or at least trying to. I had first crossed paths briefly with Werbell in Miami in '66 when we were both dicking around during the attempt to overthrow Papa Doc Duvalier, I then started running into him when I was the OIC of the XVIII Airborne Corps AMC in the first half of "68 when he was attempting to peddle his wares to the Army stateside at the various Army marksmanship centers, such as Ft. Bragg and Ft. Benning.

As soon as I could bamboozle a jeep from my CO, I headed to Saigon and the Astor hotel. "Got some hot intel I got to pass on to the Intelligence Center in Saigon. Hush, hush you know."

Well, anyhow, I got the jeep and linked up with Werbell, who took me and my driver out to a nearby French restaurant where I was introduced for the first time to French baguettes which were backed up by some sort of mystery meat which was passed off as steak. Plus, real, honest scotch which I hadn't touched in four months.

Werbell, in turn introduced me to Connie Ito who was one of the Colt M-16 reps in Nam and Peyton McGruder, who was, though a civilian, a work unto himself. Peyton, a fine human being, had played a major role in engineering the B-26 bomber that became famous in WWII and was used in a number of unconventional conflicts for the next 20 some years, including the Bay of Pigs and S.E. Asia. Peyton had a villa on the outskirts of Saigon, which he made available to me when I was passing through.

Werbell lent me one of his suppressors for my M-16. During the first firefight I got into the new toy ended up rocketing down a few meters toward the enemy. I hadn't screwed it on tight enough

BROWN GETS HIS A-TEAM . . . IN THE GARBAGE PIT OF III CORPS

I reported into 5th Special Forces Group, headquartered in Nha Trang, where I was assigned to Company A, headquartered in Bien Hoa, who in turn, assigned me to a B-Team located in Hon Quan, near An Loc. When I arrived, Lt. Colonel Michael Lanter, tall, lean, black-haired and pleasant, decided after looking at my personnel file to make me the B-Team S-1 or personnel officer. I suppose that since I had a master's degree he assumed that I was reasonably literate and could handle all the Team's bullshit paperwork.

I bit my tongue for a couple of weeks, and in a letter to John Paul Vann, dated 18 February1969, wrote, "Dear John: My long sought after transfer to Special Forces finally has happened. However, if it is a blessing it certainly is well disguised. I reported to the SFOB in Nha Trang on 24 January. I asked for IV Corps but was told SF was at full strength and therefore I was assigned to Company A, and later to Detachment B-33. I was promised an A-Team in about 4–6 weeks when in Bien Hoa but apparently my CO here has different ideas. If I don't get some type of operational slot in the relatively near future, I should pick up my ball and bat, terminate with SF and ask for a "leg" outfit.

I continued: "It is both disgusting and frustrating to be placed continually in staff positions because of my educational background, writing and publishing experience. Furthermore, the war effort receives damn little benefit from my extensive (and expensive) training in unconventional warfare and counter-insurgency . . . "

Shortly after writing John Paul Vann, I confronted my boss, Colonel Lanter. "Colonel, with all due respect, I came up here to fight, not fill out forms. If I can't get an A-Team and get some action then I might as well de-volunteer from SF and go back to a leg outfit where I at least will get some trigger time." He smiled and said, "We'll, see." Well, we saw all right. Shortly thereafter, he sent me out to A-334, commonly known throughout the B-Team as the "Garbage Pit of III Corps." The previous team had a lot of problems and the team leader and several of the team were relieved and sent to some purgatory somewhere. I took over with a hand-picked crew of some of the most competent SF NCO's around. And God knows I needed them, as our basic mission was to interdict the NVA's LOC, or Lines of Communication, from their supply depots in Cambodia into South Vietnam.

Not only was Tong Le Chon a shithole, it was nonfunctional. There were gaps in the barbed wire that you could parade a marching band through. No trip flares, No claymores implanted. No minefields.

My Team Sergeant, Master Sergeant Jim Lyons, reminisced about his experiences at Tong Le Chon: "Upon my arrival at TLC, I set out to repair the defenses of the camp and the general police of the camp, i.e., putting in new wire barriers and claymores, picking up garbage lying around the inner and outer perimeter. Upon Captain Brown's arrival, he immediately took charge of the situation, developing a crash program to upgrade the camp defensive positions. This included building new fighting positions, repairing existing bunkers, installing additional tons of wire and thousands of claymores and trip flares. At the time of his arrival we had no outer berm per se—except tin and some dirt that was pushed in front of it. We instituted a program whereby all the fighting positions were improved—in some cases cemented, overhead cover was installed, and the entire berm was revamped. The policing of the entire camp was improved at least one hundred percent."

Lyons noted in an interview on 24 April 1999 that, "Detachment A-334 (Tong Le Chon) had been there for a long, long time but it had never been built into a fighting base. It was just wire strung around a bunch of sandbagged bunkers."

So, confronted with this mess, I decided to lie. Now, I had promised myself that there was no way I was going to bullshit anybody when I got to Nam. I'd been around the rodeo arena a few times and knew there was no way that I was going to make the Army a career. So forget kissing up to and lying to some limp-dicked superior officer. But lie I did. The Standard Operating Procedure (SOP) at that time called for half of my battalion of

Civilian Irregular Defense Force (CIDG) to be out on operations at all times. Well, we can't do that when I don't have a camp that I can fight. So in went the phony operations reports, while my CIDG and my team constructed a reasonably impregnable fortress. As Lyons points out, we put in the requisite barriers of barbed wire, mines, claymores, flares, etc.

WHEN BROWN WAS KING AND MINISTER OF . . .

As an A-Team commander I found myself in what was to be, looking back on it, the most challenging, frustrating, yet rewarding period of not only my bizarre Army career but also my life. I was a "King," albeit of a rather small kingdom. I was also the de facto Minister of Defense, Minister of Justice, Minister of the Treasury and Minister of Health, Education and Welfare. I was superintendent of roads and low-income housing—very low income housing. I mediated personal problems such as how to handle the marriage of a Buddhist nurse and a Catholic. I was ultimately responsible for the lives and safety of over 576 mercenaries, Vietnamese, Cambodians and tribesmen along with several hundred dependents.

Every day presented a new set of challenges, with Mr. Charles doing his best to contribute to our uncertainty. I knew when I took over the camp that I should keep a diary, even though it was forbidden. One got around such a restriction if one had a mind to by titling such a work a "Memo for Record" or a "Log." But what with the responsibilities of my position, I simply just did not have the necessary self-discipline to do what I should have done. The only decent record of specifics are parts of letters that I sent to my then close friend, attorney and rodeo buddy, Robert Bruce Miller, who, for whatever reason, kept them.

One, dated 17 February 1969, reads as follows: "Yep, I've finally scored. I've got an A-Team about seven clicks from the Cambodian border. Most of the elephants, tigers and other wild life have left the area or have been eaten and been replaced by a much more dangerous animal whose initials are 'NVA.' I've got one of the most forlorn asshole camps of the world—but I'm almost the 'king' though the official policy is that I and my team are supposed to advise and assist rather than command. I've got 374 motley Cambodians (who are waiting for the right time to desert and get assistance in the overthrow of the present Cambodian government), Montagnards who are ready and willing to slit any Vietnamese throat,

North or South, and some shifty Vietnamese thugs who would stick it to anybody for a Piastre.

"Haven't had a mortar attack in two days. Since we blew the back off the head of a VC mortar section leader three days ago. I didn't, but one of my 15-year-old Montagnard mercenaries did the job. Now the only thing that keeps me awake sometimes is our firing H&I fire with the 4.2's and 81mm mortars."

OTHER THAN THAT, TODAY IS QUIET

On 7 April 1969, I wrote; "A busy day today. Old Charles tried to liven things up by firing a rocket into our camp but his aim was off by about 600 meters. Then, about 2100 hrs, a couple of clumsy NVA, who were trying to penetrate our defensive wire set off a trip flare. All our mercenaries on the south wall opened up with mortars, .30 and .50 caliber machine guns and their M-16's. This is the third ground probe in three days so we're expecting to get hit in the near future. Our concern was heightened after examining the documents on one of the KIA we got during one probe which stated he was a member of a Recon unit of the 7th NVA Division that recently got its ass kicked to our south. We speculate that they may hit us to regain some face."

While on radio watch on 23 April 1969, I wrote: "Interesting job. A typical day was yesterday. At 0500, Charley dropped in 35–40 rounds of 82mm (mortar rounds) on our runway, killing two ARVN Rangers and wounding three as well as destroying the chopper refueling point. At 0700, laid on detail to police up debris so planes could land. At 1000 almost got into fight with three Rangers who got pissed when I wouldn't sell them any beer. Chased them out of the compound. At 1200 one of four Montagnard children set off a claymore wounding one Air Cav trooper. They were thrown in jail for a couple of hours and everyone yuk yuked—except the Cav man who has a hole in his arm—course, he may be yuk, yuking cause he got medivaced to the rear. At 1400 went over with 1st Sgt (Lyons) and chewed out the 4.2 mortar crew cause they weren't working—much yelling and screaming. Made more enemies. Found out that the VC mortar crew that disturbed my sleep got dumped on. An Air Cav unit found their position—bloody bandages, blood trails and a blown up 82mm mortar. Called in air strikes and arty in support of field element yesterday afternoon and eve. This morn, went up in Cav chopper for visual recon. We got called in on a downed chopper shot down by ground fire and burned. Rescue chopper got out one seriously wounded. Back to our base to refuel—landed—Ranger 3/4 truck nearby —backed up to get out of our way—over two Rangers who were sleeping behind truck—one had broken pelvis so had to get medivaced. Other than that, today is quiet."

OLD CHARLIE GOT ME

On 20 May 1969, I wrote: "Old Charlie messed me over on the 15th. We took 27 rounds of 107mm rockets within our perimeter . . . was running back from artillery position and got hit 20 meters away . . . 16 holes in me . . . mostly small . . . face pretty screwed up for a while . . . one fragment went through my right cheek and out my right lip . . ."

25 June 1969: "Got some good action last week. Had a combined operation—100 of my little people and a troop of the 11th Armored Car. Went around shooting up NVA bunker complexes in the Michelin rubber plantations. Sighted five gooks one afternoon and got two on our way back. Charles ambushed us. The Armored Cav. Troop commander, a Captain, in whose APC I was riding took a .50 cal round which blew half of his wrist away. Missed me by less than a foot. The Buddha I wear looks out for me. We shot our way out. Took one U.S. KIA, three WIA and five CIDG WIA. Two nights latter Charles lobbed RPG rounds into our perimeter we had set up with the Cav. Troop. Two of my CIDG were wounded by friendly fire from our perimeter. I had sent them out on ambush but instead of moving several hundred meters away from the perimeter as ordered, they only went out about 50 meters and, playing the part of laggards as they were prone to do when not supervised, sacked out. And being where they weren't supposed to be, got shot up. I was glad to get back to Tong Le Chon, shit hole that it is, where we just get mortared occasionally . . . though I'm a bit more cautious about standing up on top of a bunker and watching the mortar rounds explode. Yea, I'm out of the hospital and have been since about 24 May. Got bored and became so obnoxious the head nurse discharged me five days early."

TROUBLE IN THE CAMP

As time passed, I found myself more and more at odds with my counterpart, a Captain Long, who commanded the resident Vietnamese Special Forces detachment. Hypothetically, I and my A-team were in the camp to advise and assist the Vietnamese. In fact, in my camp and most A-team camps that was not the case. We ran things as we controlled the funding of the camps' operations as well as the salaries for all the CIDG mercenaries. We decided when and where to conduct combat operations, as well as, for the most part, camp policies.

Early on, it became apparent that Captain Long was less than enthusiastic about scheduling our combat patrols in areas where we might run into the enemy. Sergeant Lyons also was not impressed with Captain Long. He remembers, "I had noticed for a month prior to Captain Brown's arrival that Captain Long was a very hard-to-understand, hard-to-get-along-with individual. While he was with you, he was always patting you on the back and telling you what a great job you were doing, and how great it was that you were fighting alongside the Vietnamese. Upon departing from your company, however, Captain Long would revert to his old individualism and would ignore our advice and suggestions. . . . We never could seem to get them (LLDB) to work or conduct aggressive combat operations . . . When an operation was planned which seemed to promise a hairy situation, Captain Long always seemed to have a reason to go to Bien Hoa or An Loc. Captain Long only ran two combat operations in the six months I was in Tong Le Chon, and he was ordered by his superiors to run both of these operations.

"There was also a strange feeling among the detachment members in TLC about Captain Long. It seems that every time he left the camp during the months of May and June, we would receive rockets, mortars, or a probe of our perimeter. My Intel sergeant, Fletcher Blocksum, would make an intelligence assessment as to where our efforts would most likely produce results. Captain Long would always suggest an area least likely to encounter the enemy."

After being in my camp for a couple of weeks, I developed a rapport with the commander of the Cambodian company who were of the Khmer Serei political persuasion, and who after Lon Nol took over the Cambodian government in 1970, were sent along with all the other SF Cambodian companies to bolster the Lon Nol regime. The Cambos were far superior to my other two companies of Vietnamese and Montagnards. The Montagnards were of the sub-tribe, the Stang, and simply were not as aggressive as other Yard tribes like the Bru or the Rhade.

The Cambo company commander, once he felt he could trust me, told me what was really going on in camp, e.g. the corruption. Captain Long had come to see the camp as his own personal money machine. For instance, he had his own PX, through which he sold fresh food to the CIDG and their dependents. We had about 576 troops and another 400 or so dependents that lived within the wire of the camp. Tong Le Chon was somewhat unique in that we were the only one of the 50-some A-Team camps that did not have a village nearby where fresh food and other necessities could be purchased and the troops' dependents could live. Since the road from Hon Quan, where our B-Team was located and which was the nearest village, was unsecured, all supplies and fresh food for the 1,000-plus inhabitants had to be airlifted in. I found out, from my Cambo Captain, that Captain Long was essentially extorting money from the CIDG by charging exorbitant amounts for the necessities of life like $50 for a live chicken—when the average monthly salary was only $50! I put a stop to that shit by not allowing him to bring goods for his PX into camp on U.S. aircraft, and thus gained an undying enmity from Captain Long.

Sergeant Lyons confirmed the treachery: "As far as graft and corruption go, in our camp Captain Brown made an earnest attempt to get to the bottom of the problems. This was probably one of the factors which led to the deterioration of rapport. Captain Long was opposed to Captain Brown's efforts as Captain Long was making several thousand dollars a month through profiteering.

"Captain Long ran a PX at Tong Le Chon. He would bring fresh food, black market cigarettes and whiskey on U.S. planes and would sell it at outrageous prices to the CIDG. I remember one instance when his 'co-op' sold a small cucumber for 80 piasters. A live chicken would cost as much as 1,400 piasters. His younger brother, who was on the CIDG payroll, ran the PX. This character commuted to Bien Hoa almost weekly to get goods. . . . During the six-month period I was there, Captain Long's brother was never out of camp on any type of operations—even local security."

Captain Long also fostered dissent in TLC by showing favoritism to the Vietnamese over the Cambodians or Montagnards. An example of this and how it adversely affected our combat effectiveness, Sergeant Lyons recounts:

> During the month of April, we had a recruiting program going. Captain Long sent his Reconnaissance Platoon Leader to An Loc to recruit individuals for the CIDG. He recruited about 170 people in the course of a week. Long took trained personnel from the two CIDG reconnaissance platoons and put Vietnamese recruits in place of the Cambodians, which caused dissent. (CIDG assigned to the recon platoons received slightly higher pay than regular CIDG personnel.) These people went on operations and aggravated an already dangerous situation. Beyond that the recruits (Vietnamese) were inept, lazy and poorly trained.

DENS OF THIEVES

Speaking of food, at some point in time I became suspicious (I don't remember why) that we were somehow being cheated on the amount of fresh food we were actually receiving from our food supplier, a devious Chinese who had the contract to supply all the A-Teams in the area. I asked the B-Team for a scale to weigh the food. Not surprisingly the response was, "No funds available for unauthorized purchase." So, I went out and bought one on the local economy. The next time the fresh food was flown in on the twin-engine Caribou, I and my ever faithful Team Sergeant, Lyons, were on hand with our scale. We started weighing each category of food. And suspicions were confirmed. Instead of 110 kilos of watercress, we got 100 kilos. The 150 kilo pig, 135 kilos, etc., etc. The son of a bitch Chinese food supplier was overcharging us 10%. I was infuriated. Shortly after the food arrived, by pure chance, Lt. Colonel Robert Campbell, the C Team commander stationed at Bien Hoa, choppered in on an unannounced inspection tour. I blew it. I had planned on sending the scale around to all the other A-Teams in our B-Team area and have them weigh fresh food shipments and then have an irrefutable case. But I was so pissed that I had to blow off steam to the good Colonel. He listened politely, as I recollected, promised nothing and departed. However, within an hour an Air Force major, who was in charge of getting food and supplies to the camp, flew in.

"Look, Captain Brown," he said, "You're mistaken. Maybe your scale is wrong. We weigh every shipment that leaves the airport to see that the manifested weight is correct." "Bullshit," I muttered, "Mr. Hon is screwing us with the U.S. government and your help." He turned red and stomped off to his chopper. Perhaps I was being unfair to him, as he may well have thought he was telling me the truth.

As I was being transferred from my camp, I had an experience that provided an insight about how such errors could occur without the good Major being aware.

From the time I assumed command of A-334 in February, an assistant of Mr. Hon, who had been a former camp interpreter who went by the nickname of "Cassidy," was always trying to get me involved in some sort of illegal activity which would make him big bucks. Early on, I told him, "Cassidy, do not bring us anymore free 10 kilos of meat and 10 kilos of French bread." I did not want my team to be indebted to the Chinese food supplier.

"Not to worry, Dai Uy." The third time it occurred, I told him, "We cannot accept this, Cassidy. Next time you bring that out here, I'm going to feed it to the pigs." Once you get on the take with this kind of trash, you'll pay for it eventually. Then it was, "Dai Uy Brown, you get birth control pills from States, we make big money from bar girls." "NO." Then later, "We go PX, you buy cameras, scotch, we sell on black market." "NO." And so it continued, one scheme after another. And he was always trying to entice me to party in Saigon, all expenses paid. And it was "NO" again.

Then I got my order to report to my next assignment. Cassidy, ever optimistic and not knowing I was being transferred, once again approached me. "Mr. Hon want you to come to Saigon for dinner. Number one Chinese restaurant. He pay all. You be his guest," He was unexpectedly overjoyed when I said, "Tell Mr. Hon that I would be highly honored." Well, old Cassidy about wet his pants. After months of trying, the persistent con man thought he had finally suckered me in.

The dinner was delightful, the scotch acceptable, the company charming. Slicky boy Cassidy and the insidious Mr. Hon were as happy as cats in a bird's nest. This was all well and good but Hon was also hosting three young Air Force enlisted men—with free food, booze and bimbos and presents of gold Buddha's. And it just so happened that these young troopers were in charge of weighing, loading and manifesting the fresh food and supplies flown out to the camps, including TLC. I remember thinking, "My, what a generous chap Mr. Hon was."

It was now clear how the wily Mr. Hon got phony manifests of the food sent to the A-Teams. He compromised the young enlisted men loading the aircraft.

As I finished the meal I shook hands with Cassidy and then Mr. Hon, saying, "It was so good of you to throw me a going away party. Wish me luck as I'm off to my new assignment at SF Headquarters in Nha Trang tomorrow." Doing an about face and striding off, I turned and smiled to see the two crooks start to go into terminal shock. A victory. A small victory, but a victory nonetheless. Heh, heh, heh.

SURVIVING THE PSYCHO B-TEAM COMMANDER

Sometime in April 1969, I led a company of my CIDG on an operation outside of our normal Area of Operations (AO). Shortly after, we broke out of the bush into the Michelin rubber plantation. The plantation's hamlets had long been deserted. The rows of rubber trees had a foreboding look as there was no movement from humans or animals. After having moved out into the rows of trees for 50 or so yards, we ran across the tracks of half a dozen or so VC, a Ho Chi Minh sandal and a pole that was used to carry bunches of bananas. We had obviously spooked a small VC infrastructure unit who had heard us tromping into the plantation.

There was no way that you could move a hundred or so men silently through the bush, and the bad guys bolted. It was getting towards dark and I decided to set a defensive perimeter for the night. Concurrently, I sent out a couple of patrols to check out the area. Within the hour, one of the patrols returned with a young Vietnamese male in his late teens. Since there was no legitimate reason for him to be in the deserted area, we assumed he was a VC and advised our B-Team, who sent a chopper out to pick him up and take him back to B-Team headquarters for interrogation. The next morning they choppered him into our perimeter, as he had agreed to lead us to his base camp a few clicks away.

A couple of Montagnards on each side of him, they prodded him along with their M-16's, hoping against hope that they would have an excuse to blow him away. The Yards hated the VC, the North Vietnamese and the South Vietnamese equally, as the Vietnamese in general considered the tribesmen savages, calling the Yards "Moi," which had the same meaning as "nigger" did in our country. They were oppressed and exploited on a long-time continuing basis. And tragically, they still are today by the communist government.

The young VC lead us into his camp which had obviously just been abandoned, as a couple of cooking fires were blazing; the rice was still warm. Once again, our numbers had announced our arrival, giving what we estimated to be eight to ten bad guys an opportunity to flee. We saw no point in trying to track the VC, and made our way back to Tong Le Chon, where we secured the prisoner behind barbed wire.

The following morning, our B-Team commander, Lt. Colonel George R. Murray and his B-Team counterpart, a Vietnamese by the name of Major Long (no relationship to my camp counterpart), choppered into TLC. I hopped in a jeep and drove down to meet them at the chopper pad. I walked up to Murray and saluted. Murray opened the conversation without pleasantries, growling, "Brown, how many VC have you killed this month?" I knew Murray was a glory hound, determined to make his mark and reputation no matter what it cost or whom it killed. I had already had several run-ins with him from the time he took over command from Lt. Colonel Lanter, who was a decent human being and a competent SF commander.

On one occasion, Murray had approached me, suggesting, "Brown, take a couple of your team and a dozen CIDG, put on VC black pajamas, grab some AK's and go interdict the 5th NVA Division's main supply line." I replied, "I don't think so, and Murray did an about face, grumbled and stalked off. True, I disobeyed a direct order. But there was no way this sorry excuse for an officer was going to bring me up on charges since at the time no American forces were allowed within five clicks of the Cambodian border and U.S. aircraft were not allowed within two clicks. He wanted us to emulate the highly effective SOG operators who ran recon operations into Cambodia and Laos, but without any air cover, extraction assets or artillery support. He was only interested in body counts and didn't give a shit if we were the ones providing the dead bodies.

Another time, I had a company of CIDG who were making a helicopter assault into what our intelligence had reported was likely a hot LZ. The SOP for such an operation called for half the helicopters to disembark their troops who would immediately secure half the perimeter. The remaining troops would land and secure the other half of the perimeter. Then, once again according to SOP, we would immediately high tail it into the jungle to reduce the possibility of being attacked on the Landing Zone. But no! Murray instructs us to remain in position so he can land his chopper and come over and congratulate us for a successful insertion. Everyone thought he was insane. Fortunately, it was not a hot LZ and nobody got killed. No thanks to our fearless leader.

On another occasion, Murray was with one of our sister A-Teams in a firefight, picked up a burning smoke grenade and hurled it on top of a bunker for reasons unknown, and later had the audacity to put himself in for a Purple Heart. The commander of the C Team, LTC Campbell rejected his award and wrote a scathing memo that went out to all SF personnel condemning such gross self-promotion. Campbell even sent Murray a barbeque mitt.

Murray, we found out, had never been in Special Forces and was not Special Forces qualified. He was one of hundreds of officers who had been placed in a position that he was unprepared for but would allow him to get his six months of "command time," which was imperative to have if an officer had any hopes of promotion.

AN INVITATION TO COLD BLOODED MURDER

Now as far as the young VC prisoner we had taken, after I told Murray we hadn't whacked anybody during the month, he raised his bushy black eyebrows and offhandedly mentioned, "Well, Brown, if the prisoner is killed trying to escape tonight, you'll get a body count." Major Long, his Vietnamese counterpart, simply smiled. I was stunned! This was a blatant invitation to commit murder. The prisoner was no threat to the camp. I was at a loss for words. I should have told him that he could go fuck himself. But for reasons unknown I didn't, and have regretted it ever since. Instead, I said, "Look, I've had a fair amount of experience interrogating VC . . . let me see what I can get out of him." Murray and Long stalked off, obviously not satisfied with my response, and they choppered back to the B-Team.

Sergeant Lyons received an almost identical proposition. As he recounts it: "Major Long and Lieutenant Colonel Murray arrived at Tong Le Chon after the POW was captured. I met Lieutenant ColonelMurray at the airstrip. Lieutenant ColonelMurray came up to me in the jeep and I got out. He took me aside and asked, 'How is your body count coming this month?' I told him we hadn't gotten anyone and he said, 'Well, you have one POW out there. If he was to try to get away tonight, and you people were to shoot him, you would get a body count for it.' I immediately thought Lieutenant ColonelMurray was joking, and I said to him, 'Sir, you must be kidding.' He replied, 'No, if the man should try to escape and you were to kill him you would get credit for a body count.' I said, 'Sir, I don't want any part of what you're talking about. If you want anything from me, I will be up at the team house.' And I got in my jeep and left."

The next morning I rousted out the Vietnamese Special Forces intell sergeant, got the prisoner, my intell sergeant, Sfc Fletcher Blocksum, a raw-boned redhead WWII and Korean vet from Texas, and my interpreter and went down into the CONEX which served as our communications center. I conducted the questioning about his family. After a few innocuous queries, I got to the meat of what I was after. This youngster claimed he had been impressed into service by the VC, which was not all that unusual. I was stern in my questioning but not threatening. For a while, that is.

"Nguyen," I asked, "what did you do with the VC unit you were with?" "Oh, Duy Uy, I provide security for my team when they go to village to propagandize, collect taxes and rice." A few more unimportant questions, like what the food was like, etc. Then I casually asked, "Did you ever carry a gun?" "No, no," he shook his head vigorously. "Never carry gun."After more insignificant questions, I let out the clincher. "Well, Nguyen, when you were providing security for your unit, how did you warn of the approach of the Americans or South Vietnamese?" "I fired my carbine in the air three times." Gotcha! "All right, you lying piece of shit," I yelled in his ear as I hovered over him. "I've caught you lying and you better damn well tell the truth or I'll turn you over to the Montagnards." He quivered and I started on him. After an hour, I had elicited intelligence of incredible value, easily worth the elimination of a battalion of VC. Spilling his guts, he gave me a list of the names of the VC in small infrastructure units in the area, the location of mines and booby traps, weapons caches, etc. I was in hog heaven. A big score for the good guys!

Sgt. Lyons documented the episode:

"Captain Brown continued his interrogation of the POW, and the man agreed to go back to the area he had been taken from to point out meeting places and quarters of VC and NVA and to identify VC infrastructure personnel. A couple of days later, however, we were told that the individual had tried to escape and the airport outpost had to shoot him. We were not notified of the incident until the next morning; and when we asked where the body was, they said they had already buried it. Later the Intelligence Sergeant of the VNSF admitted that they had received orders from the VNSF B-Team that the man was to be executed."

The next morning, in choppers, Lt. Colonel Murray with his toad-like counterpart showed up. I barrel-assed down to the chopper pad to gloat over the invaluable intel I had wormed out of the POW. After enthusiastically detailing the info developed from the VC, there was a toe-in-the-sand type of embarrassed silence. Then he looked me in the eye and said, "Do you know the prisoner was killed trying to escape from the camp last night?"Once again, I damn near went into terminal shock. I have no recollection what I said, if anything. Murray and the toad departed and went up to the camp team house to discuss the situation with the rest of the team. I was in a white-hot rage due to the fact that this was nothing less than cold-blooded murder. So, the question was, "Why?"

There were a number of factors that led me to believe that he was killed because he knew too much; that Murray and Long ordered him liquidated because, since he was spilling his guts, he might well implicate the Vietnamese Special Forces collaborating with the VC. I figured the kid was part of a commo-liason unit in the Province. Therefore, he might well have known the nature and scope of the contact between the LLDB in TLC and the B-Team and the Province VC. My theory was based on the fact that when my patrol picked up the kid, he was wearing a clean, short-sleeved khaki shirt and shorts; he had a recent haircut; his exposed body extremities were clean and without sores or scratches; he had clean paper money in his pocket. Now, there was no way that he had been living on a long-term basis in the primitive camp he led us into which had no running water and only rickety lean-to's covered with torn plastic ground clothes.

Sergeant Lyons recollects, "One night we had Captain Long over to the team house drinking. Captain Long got pretty drunk and admitted in front of Sergeant Blocksum and me that he had been told by the B-

Team that this man would be executed. He did not give the names of the individuals who told him this. I made a statement for the record at the time, and it was put on file in the safe in the intelligence folder."

This is another one of the funny instances to show that whenever something happened, Captain Long was not available. He was visiting the B-Team on the night the POW was shot.

Sergeant Lyons continued: "I have been in the Special Forces for approximately sixteen years. I have had a number of team leaders, good and bad, but Captain Brown was the best team leader I ever had, bar none. This individual will listen to anything anyone has to suggest and will evaluate and judge it on its own merits. As to Lieutenant Colonel Murray's remarks on Captain Brown's efficiency report, which Captain Brown showed to me, some of the things stated can be summed up as being true, but it is a one-sided story. Reports were repeatedly made to Lieutenant Colonel Murray concerning the VNSF corruption and lack of aggressiveness. Such reports were consistently ignored. Lieutenant Colonel Murray would suggest that an individual do something which was almost suicidal; Captain Brown repeatedly opposed these hair-brained schemes.

"I can quote three separate examples: During the six months I was at TLC, Lt.Col. Murray repeatedly tried to get us to go to the Fishhook area, where even U.S. troops with gunships would not go. On one occasion, Lieutenant Colonel Murray took me to the Fishhook area and dropped me off with 100 CIDG in an area which was known to be a VC cache and supply area for the entire 5th NVA Division. Murray sent us, with 100 CIDG and one interpreter, into this area to look for a division. Another time he sent me to a firebase with two other Americans and three Vietnamese to look for a battalion. It was supposed to be a reconnaissance mission, yet we had no artillery or air support on call. I interpreted this to be a death mission. If we had been killed in making contact I am sure Lieutenant ColonelMurray would have thought only about the body count he got out of it. On one other occasion, Lieutenant Colonel Murray sent me, with only 120 CIDG, into a known VC-infested area where there had been no American units operating for two weeks because of the activity there. He picked me up by vehicle after that operation and dropped me off in another area, approximately 15 kilometers from our camp, to recon back to the A-Team. I was going through the First Division Tactical Area Of

Responsibility (TAOR). Murray failed to notify anyone of my presence there. I was spotted by a FAC that was flying in the area. By chance he happened to call my A-Team and ask if we had anybody in the area. I happened to be monitoring on the radio and overheard him. The FAC was in the process of calling in 175mm artillery on us from Quan Loy.

"These are only a few of the examples of the mistakes Lieutenant Colonel Murray made while he was in command of B-33," Lyons wrote. "In my personal opinion, which is only the opinion of a Sergeant Major, Lieutenant Colonel Murray is not Special Forces material. He is not a competent individual capable of commanding in such an operation as we had in Vietnam."

Over a couple of beers in 1999, when I asked Lyons why he didn't get along with Murray, he meditated a bit and said:

"Because I think Murray was trying to make a name for himself at everybody else's expense . . . I don't know if you were still there or you had already been medevaced when he sent me and two other individuals out to one firebase west of camp. I don't know where it was but we had to leave at midnight and he gave us a time that we were to arrive on station and then we had to RON there that night. And we didn't go. We went and looked and there was nothing there and we backed off . . . I wasn't remaining there because I thought the guy was crazy," Lyons said.

I asked Lyons, "Why did he want you to do it?"

Lyons replied, "I don't know. I never did know what he wanted me to do. He gave me grid coordinates that were supposedly the location of an enemy base camp and we were supposed to go and verify that. I had said, 'I'll send somebody out' and he said, 'No, I want you to personally go.' I had made him mad about a month before. We had gone on a mission and ran out of water and couldn't find any—they didn't bring us any. I made the decision to walk out back to the B detachment and he was going to have me court martialed for this. He read me my rights and everything.

"Since we didn't have water I decided to come in. He said he had Intel that it was being occupied by the VC. That is when I got sprayed with Agent Orange. They sprayed all over us."

I asked, "Any after effects?"

He chuckled, "Well, prostate cancer and bladder cancer . . . both at the same time. I beat them both though. It's been nearly two years and I'm supposedly cancer free. The VA declared me 100% disabled. I laugh all the way to the bank every month." (Command Sergeant Major Lyons died in 2008.)

I could expect no assistance in dealing with this apparent murder and unraveling the mystery from the B-Team for obvious reasons. It was pointless to go to the USAID Province advisor, who was located in Hon Quan, as I was told he was one of Murray's West Point classmates. After a couple of weeks, I was able to get to Saigon accompanied by my team medic, Robert Bernard, where I looked up my CIA contact, briefed him on the situation and asked for his advice. "Look, Brown, this kind of shit happens all the time over here. In any case, there's nothing I can do about it since we do not have a CIA presence up where you are located. Sorry about that." So, that was where the case rested until I could find some excuse to get up to a higher headquarters to file a formal complaint.

CAPTAIN LONG TRIES TO GET ME WHACKED . . .

A couple of weeks later, on 7 May 1969, I got my trip to higher headquarters, though not in the manner I expected or chose. The monsoon season was beginning and the day opened overcast with a light, persistent drizzle. About 1400hrs, I was in the team house when I got a call on the radio from my counterpart, the omnipresent Dai Uy Long. "Dai Uy, you come down to end of runway . . . see rockets."

We had a battalion of the 1st Division that had been located in a temporary base about 200 yards to the west of TLC, which was moving out by C-130's using our airstrip. Mr. Charles took exception to this and decided incoming and outgoing planes were targets too juicy to pass up. Every day, he was dropping 82mm mortar rounds on and around the airstrip, inflicting one or two casualties. It got so annoying that every time a plane landed or took off, we had to have fast movers overhead to keep the bad guys' heads down. I decided to humor the little shit and hopped in my jeep to go down and see his blasted rockets. Sure enough, in front of the grinning Captain Long and his little band of sycophants, there were two 107mm rockets on crossed bamboo stalks pointing straight down the runway. Then Long said, "Dai Uy, go up to camp, get camera . . . take pictures." "OK, you little shit," I thought, "all in the interest of good counterpart relations."

I wheeled into camp, went into my hooch for my Cannon SLR camera, and then into the team house when the first round landed inside our perimeter. . . . More followed . . . 82mm rounds and 107mm rockets . . . we started taking casualties with the first round . . . while in the team house we were in touch with our CIDG company that had just left a couple of hours earlier on an operation. Sonny Elrod, my commo sergeant, told us they could hear the rounds flying overhead. We looked at the 1:50,000 topographical map and drew an azimuth from our camp to our unit in the field and off the map; we then identified all open areas 100 yards on each side of the azimuth as possible bad guy firing positions out to the maximum range of 82mm mortars which is about 3,200 meters. We had two 105 howitzers, manned by South Vietnamese artillerymen, who were already firing, who knows at what. I will give them credit, however, as they were loading and firing in their gun pits while all of the rest of us kept out of harm's way in our bunkers.

We had the eight-digit coordinates of suspected enemy firing positions, but how to get them to the ARVN artillery? We had no direct commo with them and it wouldn't have mattered anyhow since we had at that particular time no interpreters inside the perimeter, nor did any of my team speak Vietnamese. There was only one way to get the info to the arty. . . . Someone would have to run the info over. Though the ARVN could not speak English, they could read and understand map coordinates, and that was where they were to fire. "Who wants to volunteer to run these coordinates over to the artillery?" I asked. The silence was deafening except for the rounds continuing to fall in the camp perimeter raining death and destruction.

"No volunteers? Well, gentlemen, I'll do it myself." And with that, I burst out the door, rockets and mortar rounds be damned, and set a new record for a 50-yard dash as I legged it over to the ARVN firing pits and gave them the coordinates. They nodded their heads enthusiastically, cranked in the necessary changes to adjust elevation and windage on the coordinates I provided, and started firing away. I waited while they fired a couple of rounds, looked around—for what I don't know—and started dashing back to the team house the way I came. About 25 yards later I suddenly found myself on the ground . . . I was unconscious . . . don't know how long . . . got hit right next to the camp dispensary. . . . I felt for all my limbs . . . they were all there . . . so were my cojones, and I could see. I groped my way along the side of the dispensary and staggered into the charnel house that the dispensary had become ... the dead, the dying, the wounded. ... blood streaming from a number of holes, most noticeably from my face.

Sfc. Robert Bernard, nicknamed "Bac si," or Vietnamese for medic, looked at me, checked me for sucking chest wounds, slapped pressure bandages on the most bloody of the 14 places I had been hit, and told me, "You've got no problem. . . . get out of here." I stepped over a withered mama-san who had half her brains exposed, and sprinted another 20 yards to the team house as the shit still continued to impact. We all figured this was a softening up process for a full-scale ground assault on the camp as soon as it got dark. I turned command of the camp over to my rock-like dependable Team Sergeant, Jim Lyons. Trying to play hero, or as Lyons said, "stupid!" once in the day was enough. Shock took me flat out of the fight.

I FINALLY GET TO HIGHER HEADQUARTERS . . .

The next few hours were a blur . . . in and out of consciousness . . . helped into a medevac chopper. . . . Off-loaded into some sort of forward-based medical facility where they stabilized you so you would, hopefully, live until they got you to a major field hospital. I blurred my way onto the gurney and into surgery about 0200hrs . . . freezing . . . I swear they put ice water in with the intravenous medication . . . woke up about 0700 or 0800hrs . . . looked around and saw two of my team members sitting by my bedside. I had sent them to Bien Hoa to trade the Air Force a bunch of captured AK's for cases of steaks and buckets of ice cream, and they had followed the attack by monitoring the radio traffic between Tong Le Chon and SF headquarters in Nha Trang. There was no ground attack; why we never found out.

My head cleared and I told them, "I want to get out of here, now!" Whether I muttered or screamed, I have no recollection. "You can't do that," Sonny Elrod objected. You just came out of surgery. That's insane." But white-hot rage had returned and I was not to be denied. "Listen, go get me a uniform and boots and help me out of this shroud," I demanded. Reluctantly they took off and returned with an out-of-the-box, brand new set of jungle fatigues and a pair of boots. Obviously, no hospital staff were around and we sneaky-peted out of the hospital. "Take me to Company C

Team Headquarters," I directed them. Next thing I remember I was standing in front of the A-Team commander.

I don't recollect what he said, if anything, just that I was yelling how Captain Long was a VC; that he tried to get my team and me killed. Lt. Col. James Lillard, as I recollect, was calm and listened until I ran out of volume. I knew he knew what had happened. And I must have been a sight coming out of the hospital bed four or five hours after surgery, looking like the Bride of Chucky or a Frankenstein without the plugs in my neck . . . a dozen plus sutures holding together the wounds on my face and mouth. In any event, I stalked out, struggled into the jeep and rode back to the hospital where I had them drop me off at what I thought was the hospital entrance. Wrong again. I didn't know where I was. I didn't have my team members take me back inside because I didn't want them to get in trouble. I was lost. My medication was wearing off and, damn it, I started to cry. That I remember. How I got back to my bed is another mystery, as are any comments about my actions from the hospital staff.

The next day, one of the surgeons told me they were going to ship my sorry ass to Japan to a convalescent hospital. "Wait a minute," I said, "you've got me all patched up. I don't want to go to Japan. I want to go back to my camp." After a "discussion" we compromised and he agreed to send me to the convalescent hospital at Cam Ranh Bay for two weeks. Why they didn't send me there in the first place . . . another mystery. While awaiting transfer, I reflected on the whole sorry incident and puzzled as to why I had failed to insist on seeing the body of the executed VC. And I haven't figured that one out either. Just plain dumb.

BYE-BYE, TONG LE CHON . . .

My usefulness at Tong Le Chon was at an end and it was time to move on. I wrangled an assignment as the 5th Group Political Warfare Officer serving under my former B-Team commander, Lt. Colonel Lanter, where I primarily edited translated enemy documents while awaiting approval of my request for extension of service for another six months in-country with the then-mysterious Special Operations Group. SOG had been conducting, officially denied at the time, cross-border operations into Laos and Cambodia. I figured another six months would put me close to my discharge date and I might as well spend it in Nam where the action was.

Furthermore, in my new position, I looked forward to traveling throughout Vietnam.

While at Group Headquarters, I once again bitched about Lt. Col. Murray, the duplicitous Captain Long and the "disappeared" VC, all of which essentially fell on deaf ears. In retrospect, what with the turmoil churning from the Calley massacre, the last thing my superiors wanted to deal with was another scandal. Within a couple of weeks I got word that my request for extension had been denied. Whether it was because of the withering officer's efficiency report authored by my nemesis, Lt. Col. Murray, or because of my stirring the pot regarding the trouble at Tong Le Chon, or perhaps the fact that Special Forces Headquarters had only then become aware that I had, unbeknownst to them, somehow wiggled my way back into a Special Forces slot, remains a mystery. Or, maybe it was because higher echelons became aware that I still did not have a security clearance.

While with the 1st Division and later with SF, I periodically would drop by the intelligence section and inquire regarding my clearance, only to be told that I had an "Interim Clearance." This security clearance limbo dragged on through the remainder of my active duty service and continued all the way through my subsequent attendance at the Command and General Staff College at Ft. Leavenworth, from which I graduated in 1973. I undoubtedly had set another record, over and above being kicked out of SF twice, for being the only student to attend said school with no security clearance. My orders to Command and General Staff College read: "Security Clearance—None."

BACK TO THE WORLD OF THE GREAT PX . . .

Once again, I lucked out. I was assigned to Ft. Leonard Wood, Missouri as a Basic Training Company Commander. Had I stayed in SF and returned to Ft. Bragg, I would have been simply one of hundreds of Vietnam veteran Special Forces captains. As it was I ended up commanding a company, a position considered by nearly all infantry officers as the best job in the Army. Granted, a basic training company was not a line company, but it was the second best thing. I ramrodded 250 young trainees through their eight-week introduction to the rigors and discipline of the U.S. Army. Seeing them graduate was almost as rewarding as calling in artillery on a concentration of NVA regulars.

Of course, there were a couple of assholes in every cycle of trainees. Two or three problem children took up 99% of the time I spent dealing with personnel problems. Back then discipline was going to hell in the Army, not only in Nam but stateside. I had young punks telling my Drill Instructors to "Go to Hell!" and they couldn't lay a hand on them. Which was a bummer, as sometimes the only way to deal with such miscreants was to lay a right cross to the head bone out behind the barracks. For instance, one little shit, let's call him Private Smith, a thin, slack-jawed whiner, was particularly vocal with the four letter words. Finally, on a sunny Saturday afternoon, good Drill Sergeant Minton, from a small town in Mississippi, had had enough. Minton, who was the Charge of Quarters for the day, had also had a few belts of moonshine. Private Smith walked by the Orderly Room and Sgt. Minton yelled, "Private Smith, go into the latrine and get the mop!" "Sergeant Minton," Smith sniveled, "there's no mop in the latrine." Minton followed up, "Get the mop in the latrine." "But there's no mop in the latrine." Minton growled, "Get in the latrine." Smith did. And so did Sergeant Minton. A few blows to the body and they both exited. Private Smith now had just cause to snivel.

Shortly thereafter, my First Sergeant smiled his way into my office. Now my Field First was a hulk of a big, no-nonsense black who had been a contender in the '48 Olympics in the quarter mile. "Captain Brown, Private Smith wants to see you. He has a complaint." And in came Private Smith, crying like a weenie wimp. "Captain, Sergeant Minton hit me. More than once!" I shot him my most unsympathetic glare, and said, "Well, Private, I guess we'll have to look into it. Dismissed. Get out!"

I knew that we were going to see some shit rolling downhill right towards us shortly. Sure enough, he called his mommy who of course called her Congressman.

I saw this coming and called my First Sergeant and Sergeant Minton into my office and said, "Here's what we're going to do. We're going to flat ass lie. We'll portray him as the trouble-making sniveler he is. We all stick to our stories. He has no noticeable bruises. He must have fallen down."A couple of days later, I was notified that a Congressional investigation for brutality was in the works. But we all held to our stories.

The investigating officer knew we were lying. The battalion commander, Lieutenant Colonel Harold Riggs, knew we were lying. The brigade commander was sure of it. But they couldn't break our stories and the investigation went nowhere. Private Smith was eventually busted out of the Army for being unable to adapt. There was a plus, however. Word got out to the trainees, and we had no discipline problems the rest of the cycle. No more, "Screw you, Sarge." It was nothing but, "Yes, Drill Sergeant" or "No, Drill Sergeant."

Come April 1970, my tour was up and I returned to Boulder, which had become Hippietown, USA.

After such an untidy career, I still puzzle as to how I got promoted to Major and then Lt. Colonel in the Reserve, much less how the Army, in its questionable wisdom, selected me for the Command and General Staff College. But I did not complain.

Though I stayed in the Reserves till my mandatory retirement date in October 1984, nothing much of significance occurred. My days of fun and games with the Army were over. But other challenges were waiting.

6

JUMPING INTO HELL

"Who the hell is it?" I fumed over the phone, reacting to a rather nasty hangover. I had been tossing a few down the night before and was not in a particularly good mood, especially since it was o'dark thirty.

"Brown, it's Hemming, Gerry Hemming. I need you to recruit a team of paramedics and fly down to Peru."

I had known Hemming, tall, half-crazed and creative farfetched storyteller extraordinaire since the early '60s and he was always involved in some kind of weird scheme, mostly involving Cuban exiles, though they seldom reached fruition. My foggy mind started to brighten up a bit. "Hemming, what the hell are you talking about? It's not even light here!" I grouched at him.

"There was an 8.0 earthquake in Peru on 31 May . . . 75,000 dead, 25,000 missing, 200,000 injured."

"So what am I supposed to do about an earthquake," I grouched some more.

Hemming replied, "I'm down here with a team of paramedics and we're going to jump into the Cordillera Blanca Mountains to aid the Indians. The roads into the AO have all been destroyed and the only way to get in is by parachute." I said, "Yeah?" He said, "I need another 12-man team. I want you to recruit, find equipment and get them on a plane

ASAP!" Hemming assured me that all expenses would be paid including, of course, roundtrip airfare, which I insisted was to be provided in advance.

Since I was getting the airfare, I figured I'd at least get a trip to Peru. At the time I felt I could use a jolt of do-gooder excitement since I had been bored since I got back from Nam. I got on the phone and started rounding up a team via the old boy net, and recruited a former SEAL, a couple of Green Beret Nam vets, a couple of Israelis, and as my XO, a highly competent Nam company commander and Special Forces A-Team leader who was my business partner in Paladin Press, Peder Lund.

I flew to LA where the team linked up and I purchased a dozen parachutes and reserves, jump suits, boots, the whole shebang. We were on a plane south in 72 hours. On arriving, we were briefed regarding the damage estimates, the terrain, and the types of medical and support problems they were having. A part of the peak of 22,000-foot Mt. Huanascan had slid down the mountainside into a canyon, hitting two cities, Jungay and Rhanrhica, with a wall of mud and water 30 feet high at an estimated speed of 248 kilometers per hour.

"Lima's hospitals had soon been filled to overflowing," Doctor John Peters, from a small mining town in Colorado, recalled. Doctor John, jovial, handsome, heavy set and jump-qualified, headed up the medicine men that made up the first team lead by Hemming. Sixty nations were actively participating in the relief effort.

We were all billeted in the "Hospital Obrero," the Lima's workers' hospital. A huge, drab building, surrounded by a plethora of funeral parlors, did not encourage one to be treated there, so we couldn't wait to get out in the field.

During a briefing, organizers explained we would be jumping into an unmapped area. Hemming had asked, "If we go in and helicopter operations are found to be impossible, how do we get out?" The answer was not very encouraging. A Peruvian Army general told him, "Only two possible ways," he said. "Climb over the Andes in the middle of winter, or follow the Baranon River down to the Amazon to Iquitos." "How far from our area to Iquitos?" someone asked.

"Seven hundred miles," the general smiled. Seven hundred miles through some of the most primitive and remote areas in the world, down a river infested with piranhas and through jungles inhabited by hostile Indians. I asked some Peruvian commandos who were preparing to launch an operation down the Amazon from our launch-site where they were going, and their commanding officer said, "We are going down the river. There have been reports of the Indians selling human flesh in the market again." And that disabused us of the intriguing idea of floating down the Amazon, especially since we had no small arms.

We then started running into delays in getting jump aircraft. The U.S. refused to let us jump from their C-130's. The Argentines offered us the use of their F-27's, but they lost one on a supply drop in a narrow canyon. All of the crew was killed. We finally looked to use the old C-47s of the Peruvian Air Force, but it wasn't till some days later we found out why they came up with excuses not to drop us. There were no maps of the mountainous area, and no emergency landing strips or areas that could serve as an emergency strip. If one of the engines went out on the WWII transport, whoever was on board was dead. The Peruvian pilots were adamantly against flying their decrepit craft. Finally, we contacted officials at the Moa Bay Mining Company who put pressure on the Air Force to get us planes.

Finally we jumped in two four-man teams along with Doc Peters and George Speakman. The last two pushed their luck as they jumped at 15,000 feet over the desolate up-mountainside town of Silhaus, 3,000 feet below, avoiding steep slopes and jagged rock outcroppings. Peters remembered, "I would go first, with Moore following me on a second run. I would be jumping with a drop bag containing 100 pounds of medical supplies, surgical equipment, some drugs and 5,000 doses of smallpox vaccine." "Butterflies were working overtime in my stomach. I exited the aircraft, got a good canopy and noticed I wasn't going down," he told us. "I felt I set a record as my chute caught a thermal for twelve and a half minutes." The drop bag of medical supplies broke away from Doc and was stolen by some renegade Indians when it landed.

Doc Peters called in a medical and food resupply and for the next five days treated the locals until they could get evacuated by a Brazilian Huey—two at a time! Two choppers had already crashed trying to make it over the high mountain passes.

When we arrived back in Lima, representatives from all walks of life greeted us enthusiastically. We were driven to the Presidential Palace, where President Belasco welcomed us back, thanked us warmly for our efforts and announced we would be decorated both for valor and compassion. That afternoon, the Minister of Health awarded us medals created especially for our teams. Ironically, the American Ambassador, who had done nothing for us, showed up grinning, backslapping and posing with us for pictures. So with that we logged another adventure in our journals.

7

HOW I WAS TO BECOME DEFENSE MINISTER OF A NEW NATION

While attending Command and General Staff College at Ft. Leavenworth during the last three months of 1972 and the first three months of 1973, I became friends with a classmate who was a major in the Cambodian army. With such a contact, I decided after I graduated that it would be an interesting break from the tedium of work at Paladin Press to go to Cambodia as a sniper. I saw an opportunity for a little adventure as well as popping some bad guys. We had a long weekend break over the Easter holidays so I flew down to see my favorite rogue, Mitchell Livingston Werbell, III, who was now a self-styled Lt. General in the Free Afghan Army. How he came by this title I do not know, nor does anyone else. Nor had anyone heard of the Free Afghan Army. However, wearing the appropriate rank, it gave him another badge of importance, at least to those who didn't know him.

You'll recall that I first bumped into Werbell when he was mucking about during the abortive attempt to invade Haiti in 1966, and then ran into him before and during my trip to Nam. He was hanging around the army's Advanced Marksmanship Unit promoting various weapons systems, and since I was the OIC of the XVIII Airborne Corp AMU, we crossed paths many times. Supposedly the purpose of my visit was to get the latest scoop on what would be the most appropriate sniper system to take with me. In fact, I just wanted to get the hell out of the boring environs of central Kansas.

I arrived at the "Farm," a small mansion on 40 acres of Georgia pine, where Werbell conducted outrageously expensive personal security courses, marketed his Ingraham submachine guns and Sionics suppressors, and hosting an eclectic group of ever-changing arms dealers, rogues, veterans of various wars, law enforcement personnel, etc, etc. The usual aura of "excitement" was unusually high this time.

As the weekend wore on, I knew that some nefarious scheme was afoot. The "Farm" reeked of intrigue, guarded glances, whispered exchanges. Though I was never told what the plot was, simply by looking at numerous newspaper clippings scattered about and overhearing fragments of guarded conversations, I deduced that Werbell was heading up some cockamamie scheme to prevent the island of Abaco from becoming part of the Bahamas, which was scheduled to receive independence from Great Britain in the summer of '73. The majority of the inhabitants wanted to remain under the British Crown as the new black administration, led by Prime Minister Pindling, was corrupt, and the Nassau government already had a reputation for sucking out taxes from the outlying islands and giving next to nothing back. The racial mix of Abaco differed from the rest of the Bahamas, which was 90% black and 10% white. With a 55% black, 45% white racial mix and boasting the second largest land area in the Bahamas, Abaco had enormous potential for tourist development with its plentiful supplies of fresh water, sand, sea and sun. During this time period, there was a significant amount of racial unrest in the Caribbean and investors were looking for "secure" areas to develop to take advantage of growing tourism. Abaco could be the island that provided that security.

I decided it would be a worthy goal to cut Werbell out of the project, as I was convinced, for all his bluster, that he would never take any action to achieve independence for Abaco. He had huffed and puffed about bringing veterans of the United Kingdom's "Highlanders" to fill out the ranks of the would-be independence advocates. Concurrently, the House of Lords was trying to preclude Abaco from being separated from the British Crown.

How to do this? Well, first I had to establish contact with the Abaco resistance. I decided on the perhaps foolhardy but most direct way to make contact. I flew to Miami and caught a white-knuckle flight to a dirt strip that proclaimed itself "Abaco International Airport," which had flights to and from Miami. I guess that justified it tagging itself as "International." I checked into a local hotel, grabbed a shower and beer, and toured the capital of Abaco, Marsh Harbor. It didn't take much "touring" as there were only about 1,000 inhabitants.

Following the direct approach method of revolution, I simply walked into the local dispensary and asked the first nurse I saw, "Can you put me in touch with the resistance?" A cute little thing, without makeup and curly brown hair, she smiled, "Why that's easy. The leader is my husband, Harley." And so it started.

After being introduced to Harley I said, "I am planning to conduct a short and promising area assessment and see what can be done—if anything. The islanders have only a few sporting weapons but on the other hand, there were only three Bahamian police on the whole island, armed with obsolescent .303 bolt-action Enfield rifles. No problem there. I think the project is worth further research."

I flew to Nassau to meet the mouthpiece for the Abaco Independence Movement (AIM) Chuck Hall, a chunky, blue-eyed, dark-haired businessman.

"I am planning to recruit a small number of Special Forces Vietnam veterans to help seize the island, repel any foray of Bahamian cops from Nassau, and train a multi-racial militia. If the Bahamian cops struggle ashore, they would be easy pickings for our snipers since they are city cops, not infantrymen. We could pick them off at long range without the survivors being aware that we're involved. The American operators, in the best of SF tradition, would remain unseen in the background but would provide guidance, training and advice to the new provisional government and militia," I told him.

I recruited an old friend, a former Time journalist, Jay Mallin, who had made his bones in the Cuban Sierra Maestra by following Castro's march to victory. Mallin was going to be the PR spokesman, would control all contact with the media, and shield my team's involvement.

But I was broke. In order to get funds to implement our coup, I first contacted an old acquaintance from my Cuba days, a Chicago attorney by the name of Constantine Kangles, who was well connected. By this, I mean

I had seen him walk into Mayor Daley's office right past the receptionist without any introduction. He was the one who was Castro's legal counsel prior to the success of the revolution and had given me a letter of introduction to the Castro supporters in Cuba.

I was politely trying to hit Kangles up for money for my brilliant plot. He arranged a meeting with a former Illinois state insurance commissioner who had been kicked out of office for some kind of skullduggery. We were to meet for lunch in the main restaurant of the prestigious Blackstone hotel. I showed up at the appointed time in my normal cowboy boots, levis, sheepskin jacket and cowboy hat. The maitre'd in black tuxedo looked me over with a haughty demeanor. "You must have a coat and tie."

I, with an equally affected accent, stuck my nose in the air and said, "How unfortunate. I am here to see Mr. X."

He paused a moment and muttered in disdain, "Walk this way sir." There must have been 200 people in coat and tie. He led me to Mr. X. I explained to him what I had in mind and what the potential rewards were as I saw them—in exchange for funding he could have casino rights. He wanted to run the whole deal and control the whole island.

Negotiations ceased and I thanked him for the meal. I went back to Kangles and explained what had happened so he set up another meeting. Keep in mind the time frame—the mafia still played a significant role in running Las Vegas. He set the meeting up with two guys in Caesar's Palace named, believe it or not, Frankie and Johnnie.

I recruited a man whom I will call a man whose name I would rather forget, not much more than five feet with as big a pair of balls as anyone I have ever known, and who constantly lived life on the edge, to go with me to meet the contacts. We approached the information booth.

"We are here to see Frankie and Johnnie."

In come two guys with bouffant hairdos and polyester leisure suits with two heavily made up bimbos in mini-skirts. After a brief introduction they took us up to one of the two or three penthouse suites in Caesar's Palace. In the cheesiest of nouveau riche fashion, the décor was mainly of Italian marble and the bedspreads were mink. There we met some other individuals right out of Cosa Nostra central casting. In the room was a gnome-like accountant with Coca Cola-thick glasses, stooped shoulders and comb-over, and a couple of swarthy, obviously hoodlum types with slicked black hair, pockmarked faces, sunglasses and appropriate bulges under their jackets. Once again we went through our pitch of what it would take to accomplish the operation.

"We are looking for half a mil and your rewards will make the investment worthwhile. You can have all the casino rights in the island." I gave them an offer they could not resist.

Frankie and Johnnie and the accountant and a couple others exited the room for a private conversation, and after fifteen minutes came back in. The meeting terminated with one of the two guys saying, "If we wanted to take over this island, we could send our own 'soldiers' down to do it."

They were gracious enough to offer to put us up for the evening in Caesar's Palace but we were not in the mood and took the next flight out.

Later I ran the plan by an old friend of mine, Lee Jurras, who had achieved no small amount of fame in the gun industry in the '70s by developing a profitable new brand of high-powered pistol ammunition, which became quite popular. He, with a couple of his friends from Indiana, came up with $50,000. I wasn't sure we could pull the operation off for that much but it was a start. At the same point in time our main contact in the Bahamas was Chuck Hall.

"I don't want you to have communication with Warbell," I told him. "That loudmouth has no intention of going through with his boastful promises. He is doing this just for the publicity and his own ego. I am going to be able to pull this off with a dozen Vietnam Special Forces vets I recruited at summer camp and $50,000."

Hall went straight to Warbell and told him what we were up to. Warbell promised him half a mil and 450 mercenaries. Prior to this, we had flown in a load of guns in a friend's two engine Cessna, including a .50-caliber machine gun and a bunch of AR-15s. It was a dirt strip on a little island without an overly long runway. We had set up a plan to meet a reception party from the Abaco underground who came to the island with a boat to pick up the guns and transport them and hide them in a cache. We offloaded the guns and turned them over to the Abaco underground. Just about this time the owner of the island tried to get us to stop, yelling at us, "What are you doing here?" as we taxied by him, waving vigorously. We had not followed a flight plan, as our landing strip was so close to Abaco. We barely lifted off as we outran the length of the runway.

Chuck Hall, who really had no knowledge, much less experience, of any type of military operation, let alone Special Forces operations as far as we were concerned, had blown the project. He was bamboozled by Warbell's BS. To him, 450 mercs and half a million dollars seemed a much more doable project then 12 ex-Special Forces and $50,000. I had taken $10,000 cash on my last trip to Abaco to demonstrate my sincerity. When he wouldn't buy into my plan, I put the money back into my pocket and flew back to the States and gave the ten grand back to Jurris and his friends.

So ended my dreams of becoming the Defense Minister of Abaco, and with it my aspiration of getting a couple hundred acres of prime beach property to develop as I saw fit.

For all I know the guns are still buried in Abaco.

8

HELPING OUT IN THE BUSH WAR

Independent Rhodesia, with its short and violent history, had captured international attention for years. In the early 1960s, Southern Rhodesia had been a self-governing British colony in the Federation of Rhodesia and Nyasaland that also included Zambia. Nyasaland broke off in 1964 and called itself Malawi. In 1965 the Rhodesian government got together with the British government to try to sort out a way to end the war that was smoldering and about to explode. But the 1965 decolonization talks between the United Kingdom and the de facto Rhodesia white government accomplished nothing. The Brits wanted one man, one vote. Ian Smith, the governor of Rhodesia and leader of the Rhodesia Front, would have none of that because, of course, that would mean blacks would get into power. It would devolve into a case of "one man, one vote, once." How right he was! So the white Rhodesians unilaterally implemented the Universal Declaration of Independence (UDI) in 1965.

By the late 1970s, Rhodesia was falling to the insurgent terrorists after a rocky 15-year existence. In 1978, in an effort to put an end to hostilities, an interim agreement was signed in Salisbury. A white vote referendum approved the establishment of an interim government. It consisted of an Executive Council made up of white Ian Smith, and blacks Bishop Muzorewa, Ndabaningi Sithole and Jeremiah Chirau.

The "internal settlement," proposed in a desperate attempt by the Ian

Smith government to put an end to the civil war, resulted in a new constitution being drafted and an election scheduled. The country was renamed Zimbabwe Rhodesia.

Elections were held and the Union African National Council (UANC) won. Josiah Gumede was elected president and Muzorewa prime minister. But the odd men and losers, the two main terrorist leaders, Robert Mugabe and Joshua Nkomo, refused to accept the results of the election and ramped up their bloody terrorist insurgencies. In 1979, Ian Smith and Muzorewa were having Lancaster House talks with Margaret Thatcher.

The Cold War was still hot and Russia and China had essentially taken over the two major terror organizations by providing abundant amounts of training, indoctrination, weapons and other war supplies. The communists had infiltrated the blacks, and there was heavy fighting the entire year before the elections. Anti-Smith guerrillas launched a terror campaign against the white farmers. For the white government and its black citizen allies, it was nothing but anti-terrorist warfare.

From the beginning, Ian Smith's Rhodesia had only a handful of friends, including South Africa and Israel, which recognized it as a sovereign state and helped keep its economy alive. The United States and the United Kingdom banded together, refusing to recognize Ian Smith's Rhodesia and forcing him to recruit foreign volunteers to help his undermanned army defend his country. In spite of the fact that the country once boasted one of the most vibrant economies in Africa and loads of resources, it was landlocked and choked out by the neighboring African states.

The Bush War, or the War of Chimurenga, was the most exotic of the many prolonged and vicious African wars of decolonization that glamorized the 20th century merc. It was a civil war that relied on hired guns, a war of terror for both white and black Rhodesians. The non-conventional, racial war of independence was shattered by betrayals, whether blacks against whites or blacks against blacks or whites against both.

In addition to Vietnam vets, Dogs of War from all over the globe, from Europe to Australia to South America to Canada and Africa, itching for a good old fight against a bunch of savages terrorizing farmers and Bushmen, signed up. All sorts of adventurers, ne'er do wells and fugitives from all over the world headed for the land of hired guns, some intent on fighting the communist-backed terrorists and others just to kick some butt. Rhodesian Army recruiting posters splashed in the pages of *SOF* magazine and on the walls of merc recruiting offices lured those of all ages hankering for a risky adventure. Foreign volunteers, seeing the invites, trotted off to Rhodesia to fight the commies who were supporting the terrorists or just for a good firefight.

The counterinsurgency regiments, the famed all-white Rhodesian Light Infantry and the Rhodesian Special Air Service (SAS), fighting the commies had built up formidable reputations. The daunting Selous Scouts, the covert elite special force regiment of 1,000 that consisted of black and white, with a majority of blacks, were credited with gathering spot-on intelligence for the regular army. They would pose as terrorists and develop intelligence. They would infiltrate the guerrillas; find out where the terrorists were, and radio in their coordinates to the Rhodesian Army. They took out nearly two-thirds of the main terrorists during the Bush War. For a foreign volunteer to join up with them would be a mercenary's reverie.

THE BUSH WAR

Upon returning from Vietnam, I entered into a partnership with Peder Lund, the Vietnam vet you will recall I first met in Florida while soldier-of-fortuning with a group of anti-communist adventurers. I bought out my partner, William Jones, a close friend and hunting buddy who had put up the initial seed money to publish a thousand paperback copies of Panther Publications' first book, "150 Questions for a Guerrilla," by General Alberto Bayo, the trainer of Castro's invasion party in 1956. Jones and I started selling other books on unconventional guerilla warfare as well as publishing a few original titles. But the business sputtered for lack of capital. Lund, who put $10,000 into the new partnership, got 50 percent of the action and I changed my publishing firm, Panther Publications, to Paladin Press. We did not want to be affiliated with the Black Panthers.

After four years, I got itchy feet. I gave Lund a "buy-sell" offer for Paladin and he decided to buy. And I got $15,000. It was time to see more of the world and some adventure . . . of which there was damn little in Boulder, Colorado.

I contacted Mike Acoca, a superb journalist who produced major feature articles for Life magazine from their Miami office. We had crossed paths numerous times as the Miami soldiers of fortune and I tried to flog stories to him about the daring, ambitious, but for the most part foolhardy schemes to mess with the Castro regime. In fact, Acoca hired me as a "stringer" for Life when they were running an intriguing but unsuccessful investigation of Jim Garrison's 1966 investigation of the Kennedy assassination.

"Mike," I said, "I have completely run into a writer's block regarding my manuscript on CIA operations in Miami. How about co-authoring my book?"

Acoca left Life after they closed down the Miami bureau, and had gone on to be a contract stringer for *Newsweek* stationed in Madrid. "Sure, you can come to Madrid and bunk in my apartment while we develop the book," he offered.

All this journalism sounded good to me but there still wasn't much action. "Why not go to the dark continent after Madrid?" I asked myself. There's plenty of action there. Why not, indeed? Choosing a country to visit on my first trip to Africa was a no-brainer. I had been corresponding for some time with a young American, Bruce McNair, who had up and gone to Rhodesia which was now fighting for its life in the vicious, no-holds-barred, communist-supported and inspired guerrilla war with black terrorists.

In one of his letters, McNair described his experiences chasing terrorists on the Rhodesian-Zambian-Mozambique border. He joined the Rhodesian police and offered to play host and show me around if I could get there. Of course, no way I was going into that kind of situation without being armed. I selected a Springfield Armory M1-A, a civilian rendition of the Pentagon's select-fire M-14, with a Leatherwood Adjustable Ranging Scope, a system that had made its bones with the Army sniper teams in Nam. Since I was always looking to pick up a few bucks freelancing gun articles, I took over a .44 caliber Auto-Mag that had just come on the market. No one had tested it in Africa, and an article describing its use on four- or two-legged critters would pick me up a few hundred bucks.

The stay in Madrid proved less productive than I had hoped. Acoca had difficulty in sitting down at a typewriter for any prolonged period of time, at least to work on a book. He had to take the poodle for a walk, buy cigarettes, get the car washed, yada, yada, yada. We did complete one chapter, a fascinating exposé of the CIA's involvement with the mafia. It included Henry Luce of Time-Life, the CIA, and William Pawley, a wealthy Floridian who helped form the Flying Tigers in World War II. We wrote about the mystery of the Cuban exiles who allegedly tried to bring out Russian missile experts who would testify that offensive missiles still remained in Cuba. The team of Cuban exiles who were going to retrieve the Russian defectors were launched from Pawley's yacht, the Flying Tiger, on a wildly turbulent night, and were never seen or heard from again.

Mike was a professional journalist and had good contacts in Madrid. One day, knowing my interest in unconventional warfare, he asked me, "Brown, how would you like to meet Skorzeny?"

I was a bit taken aback and replied, "Do you mean the Otto Skorzeny, the famous Nazi commando? But of course!" Mike set up the meeting in Skorzeny's Madrid office where he was operating under the guise of some phoney-baloney kind of construction company. I had no reason to believe he was an "ex" Nazi. Many strongly believed that he was still playing a key role in the infamous Odessa network that was responsible for smuggling hundreds, if not thousands, of Nazis out of Germany to South America.

Skorzeny was an imposing figure. Six foot plus, with a linebacker build and a jagged dueling scar running across his left temple, he exuded power. The conversation drifted to Vietnam and I told him about the success of our snipers, whacking bad guys at 8–900 yards with accuracized M-14's topped off with Leatherwood ART scopes. He took exception and grunted, "Vell, I had vun sniper on the Eastern front that killed 275 Russians . . . never more than 300 yards!"

It was just an interesting conversation worth a short antidote over a couple of beers with friends but not much more. I regretted not getting a photo with him so I could give the Boulder fruits and nuts something else to snivel over.

COMMIES REVOLT IN PORTUGAL

However, on 24 April 1974, an event would occur which sounded the beginning of the end of white control of southern Africa. A communist revolution in Portugal! It was time to head to Lisbon.

The revolutionaries, bless their rotten communist souls, were quite clever. The leaders of the coup decided for whatever reason that it would be advantageous to get all the foreign journalists out of Lisbon. How to do this? A "freebie" of course! A free all-expense round trip to the guerrilla war in Mozambique. The foreign press corps, such as it was, bit hook, line and sinker, especially since until that time no journalists of any persuasion had been granted visas to that guerrilla-infested country.

All major media were desperate to get reporters on the scene. *Newsweek*'s office in London called Acoca and told him to get his ass to Lisbon ASAP. So within the hour, he and I were ripping through the Spanish countryside in his red, 1967 Matra sports car. So much for finishing my manuscript on the CIA's anti-Castro ops in Florida.

In Lisbon, I quickly became bored with the rabble marching through the streets. No action here. So on to Africa. I returned to Madrid to pick up my guns, which were in bond with Spanish Customs. I had one anxious moment as I was boarding for Johannesburg, when two Spanish cops came racing down to the boarding gate. I just remembered I had not declared that I was carrying my Auto Mag in my carry-on baggage. But fortunately they were after some other miscreant.

I MEET A MERC WHO WOULD CHANGE MY LIFE

I caught an Air Rhodesia flight with all my baggage, guns and ammo from Jan Smuts to Salisbury, Rhodesia. Rhodesian Customs welcomed me, as they were always happy to see foreigners bringing in small arms. There was a dearth of rifles and pistols for Rhodesian civilians because of the embargo implemented by the U.N. for the Rhodesians having the audacity to declare "Unilateral Independence" when it decolonized from the Brits. The Brit government, caught up in a frenzy of guilt for having ruled over the Third World, or more accurately 24th-world Africans, insisted on the Rhodesians holding a "one man, one vote" election. The Rhodesians said "Bugger off" and declared independence, knowing full well what a one-man vote would mean. And of course, when Rhodesia finally caved and held elections, they ended up with one of the most brutal dictators of the 20th and 21st centuries. But that story comes later.

By chance, McNair, whom I had been corresponding with over a couple of years, was just returning from a six-week patrol in the bush. We met and spent several days together, during which we reconned the terrorist-infiltrated northeast front area around Mt. Darwin. Heavily armed of course.

McNair's story of how he ended up hunting terrorists, or "terrs" as the Rhodesians called them, was one of resolve. He had alternated several semesters in college with race car driving in Australia and England. Finally giving up on the books, over the next five years he jacked around as a longshoreman, offshore roughneck, deep-sea diver and professional hunter.

He decided combat would be good to test his mettle, but was rejected by the U.S. Army because of arthritis. Then he heard of Rhodesia's bush war. He was rejected by the Rhodesian Army's Officer Candidate School for being over-age. He flew to Rhodesia at his own expense in hopes of obtaining a waiver on his age, but again was turned down. So he joined the Rhodesian national police, or British South Africa Police, a title the Rhodesians had carried over from their British heritage.

Though McNair had no formal military or police experience, he was only required to complete four weeks of counter-insurgency training because he had experience with small arms. After six months of police duty, McNair requested transfer to the BSAP Support Unit. Somewhat unique in the annals of military history, this elite unit was staffed with 30 to 40 European volunteers and 300 black Rhodesians. Their sole mission was to track down and eliminate terrs.

"I received an immediate approval on my transfer request, as the local Support Unit instructor had seen me operate in the bush," McNair explained. "I also had a reputation of being a damn good shot."

McNair commanded eight Africans as an acting section officer. During the next year, he and his section spent most of their time on six-week patrols in the desolate, wild Zambezi Valley, which counted more rhino, Cape buffalo and elephants than humans.

In the ensuing months, McNair had a steady diet of hot, dusty patrolling, interspersed with short periods of violent action. On 18 September 1973, his Land Rover hit a mine while he was leading a reaction force to come to the aid of a white farmer's compound. Though it demolished the vehicle, McNair escaped with just a slight concussion and a temporary eye injury.

Let me dispel a stereotype no doubt fabricated by those who've never left their offices. The word mercenaries, or "merc" as they are called in Southern Africa, conjures up a picture of a grizzled, devil-may-care trooper who fought in the Congo, Biafra, the Sudan and other African hotspots.

However, the Americans, Australians, Canadians, New Zealanders and Europeans serving the Rhodesian armed forces received the same pay and benefits as a native Rhodesian, and were subject to the same types of rules and regulations utilized by any modern army. Much like the 20,000 Canadians who joined the American forces and served in Vietnam.

Hardened white merc veterans who fought in the Congo in the '60s initially staffed the BSAP Support Unit. At first, the unit's mission was riot control, which then evolved into providing security and ceremonial functions when Rhodesian leaders determined the unit's personnel had quelled riots with excessive force. With the increase of terrorist activity, however, the Support Unit was committed to a full-time anti-terr mission. Normally they spent six-week patrols in the bush followed by one week at BSAP headquarters in Salisbury. While in the bush, they lived out of their 60 lb. packs and supplemented their dried rations by shooting game. No chopper resupply like in Nam.

As is the case with most low-level insurgencies, the terr war in Rhodesia found most of the counter-insurgent forces frustrated by the continued game of hide-and-seek with the enemy. Weeks and months of daily patrols and nightly ambushes often resulted in nothing more than sore feet and a distaste for dried rations.

Obviously, it was not a job for the faint of heart, nor the impatient.

A BSAP superintendent told me, "Most recruits are obtained by word-of-mouth as the U. N. sanctions against Rhodesia precluded establishing recruiting offices or advertising in foreign countries." He further noted, "After we put together a comprehensive file on a volunteer and he is approved, he is invited to Rhodesia. We pay all travel expenses in advance or reimburse the volunteer once he arrives." He went on to say, "If the volunteer fails to pass the Recruit Selection Board, we refer him to the immigration department. If he cannot find employment or desires to return home, the Rhodesian government will repatriate him at government expense."

The BSAP depot, home of the Support Unit, consisted of a large complex, housing some 3,000 personnel including families with a sports field, recreation areas, an auditorium and training facilities.

Training courses varied in length. Regular patrol officer recruits attended a basic course of four and a half months, which was followed by a two-week driving course where one learned to handle both Land Rovers and motorcycles in all types of terrain.

Basic training covered physical exercise, hand-to-hand combat, close-order drill, police procedures, accident investigation, counter-insurgency, first aid, radio procedure, typing and riot control.

BSAP personnel served tours with the Police Anti-terrorist Units (PATU), which consisted of teams of four European officers and one African constable. They received extensive training in small unit operations, patrolling, ambush and counter-ambush tactics before going to the bush. PATU teams remained together during advanced training, which included bush craft, map reading, terrorist procedures and immediate action drills.

Speaking of volunteering for the Rhodesian Army, Major Nick Lamprecht, Recruiting Officer for the Rhodesian Army, told me all volunteers had to pass a two-hour interview conducted by five field grade officers.

SOF *IS BORN IN THE BUSH OF AFRICA*

I had met up with an American, Bruce McNair—a member of the Rhodesian police. Over Lion Lagers one evening, in the upscale Monamatapa bar, one of Campbell's buddies mentioned: "When our contracts are up with the Rhodesians, some of my mates and I are going to sign on with the Sultan of Oman."

At the time, Oman was suffering a low-grade insurgency sparked by Yemeni rebel tribes. The British Army and the Royal Marines had been in Oman off and on to protect the Sultanate from tribal rebellions and invasions. Mercs of different nationalities supplemented a number of British officers "seconded" to the Sultan.

"Mitch, can you get me the address for the Sultan's Defense Minister?" I asked.

"No problem mate," he replied.

When I got back to the states, I sent an inquiry letter with my resume and DD214 to the Defense Minister of Oman and received a reply in a couple of weeks. Along with a contract I received 40 mimeographed pages describing the pay, benefits, the insurgency, culture, climate, etc.

Although in between odd jobs that included private investigator, cement foreman, freelance author, roofing laborer and other unsavory gigs, I didn't fancy running around the desert after some "ragheads." But, just but, I thought, "Maybe this info can be turned into a money maker."

I put together a cheap ad that ran in Shotgun News about four column inches long, which read something like,

"BE A MERCENARY IN THE MIDDLE EAST! All necessary info including pay and benefits. Forty pages. Send five dollars to . . . "

Orders started pouring in from all over the U.S.

Then *Newsweek* published an article, included in its international edition, featuring Vinnell, the first U.S. corporation that had signed a contract with the oil-rich Saudi monarchy to train the Saudi Arabian National Guard. The feature included a sidebar on mercs. Some editor with a sense of humor ran my printed ad as it appeared in Shotgun News for a graphic. When *Newsweek* hit the stands worldwide, the response was overwhelming. I received requests from Greece, Bangladesh, Indonesia, Pakistan, and of course the Anglo countries of the United States, Canada, Australia and Britain. Many of the Americans were Vietnam vets.

SOF was born! Having realized the audience was out there, I decided to take a big leap and go from selling packets of merc info to publishing a magazine. I kicked the concept around with my Nam buddies and finally decided to roll the dice. I started running small classified ads in gun magazines and spreading the word by mouth.

I sold the merc packs for a profit that came to about $5,000.

I also started selling subscriptions. In no time, I reached my goal of 4,400 subscriptions at $8.00 apiece for $35,200, which would allow me to publish four issues of *SOF* during the year. I did not have to send back the uncashed checks stashed in a shoebox that I was committed to return if I didn't meet my goal. All the other adventure magazines, like True and Argosy, that were very profitable and popular in the '40s, '50s and '60s, had gone out of business. So, I speculated, maybe, just maybe there might be a market for a hard-core adventure magazine that supported Vietnam vets. I discussed the concept over a period of months with a number of his Nam buddies.

An article, entitled, "American Mercenaries In Africa!" was the lead article in the first issue of *SOF* back in the summer of 1975, and immediately aroused the disapproval of the powers that be, including our Congresslady from Denver at the time, "Peppermint" Patty Schroeder, the bane of defense spending and general liberal sniveler. She subsequently initiated an

FBI investigation as to whether *SOF* was recruiting "mercenaries" for Rhodesia. No luck, bitch. No laws violated. We were simply publishing information. Now granted, it was true we provided info on how to join the Rhodesian Police and Army. We even provided the Rhodesian Army Recruiting Office address. And in future issues we published a full-page, color copy of a Rhodesian Army recruiting poster, complete with addresses. Once again, just publishing the facts.

Now just because Major Lamprecht told me in 1980 that, of the roughly 450 Americans who served with the Rhodesian armed forces, around 75% joined up because of articles we published in *SOF*, recruiting it is not. Ha, ha, ha on you, madam liberal tightass Congressperson Pat Schroeder and the left wing Denver fraud who formed some ineffective, bloated anti-mercenary committee.

And, of course the left wing loons of the U. N. had to stick their noses in the situation. On 29 March 1976, a little slimy punk, Ricardo Alarcon de Quesdada, the Cuban Ambassador to the U.N., held up a copy of *SOF* while condemning it. Buzz off, Ricardo.

A number of young men who drew their first blood in Rhodesia came back to the States and had a successful career in the U.S. Army. Command Sergeant Major Kelso, who joined the Rhodesian Light Infantry for a tour and retired from the U.S Army as the CSM of the Army Infantry Center at Ft. Benning, Georgia, comes to mind. Kelso said he became aware of the Rhodesian Bush War by reading about it in *SOF*.

Al Venter, a very creative, aggressive dude, based out of Joburg, was our main correspondent, though we had other contributors like the famous pistol guru, Jeff Cooper, and a Nam veteran of SOG who left his right leg in that disastrous conflict, Tom Cunningham. Tom, after he left *SOF*, went to become a successful lawyer and judge in Connecticut.

SOF *HEADS FOR THE BUSH WAR*

In 1976, I packed up my kit, and with John Donovan, a Special Forces acquaintance who was on the *SOF* masthead as our Explosives and Demolition Editor, went back to Africa. By this time, I had figured out a gimmick of how to take a duffle bag full of guns to Rhodesia, circumventing federal regulations limiting the number of guns you could take out of the country. One was required to bring them back upon return, a regulation implemented with hunters in mind. Yes, the guns were designated for hunting, but for two-legged game—and they weren't ostriches.

I had met Lou Lowry, a former kicker for Continental Air Services (CAS), which did covert and not-so-covert work, along with Air America, during the unpleasantness in Southeast Asia. When CAS, a subsidiary of Continental Airlines, closed out its operations, Bob Six, who owned Continental at the time, did his best to find employment in his organization for his air spooks. Lowry ended up in charge of security for Continental's operation in Denver. Whenever I took a load of guns to southern Africa, I would call him: "Hey, Lou . . . "

He interrupted me, "Yeah, yeah, you only call when you're headed to Africa with too many guns."

I replied, "Come on Lou, it's for a worthy cause. I'm not making a nickel on these guns. They go to the white farmers, some of which don't have anything but rocks to throw at the terrs."

"OK," he said. "What's your flight number and date of departure?" I would tell him and he would meet me at the Continental ticket counter and tell the agent, "You don't need to check his baggage and don't charge him for excess baggage." And away went my baggage, guns and ammo, checked all the way through to Joburg and then to Rhodesia. I figured I smuggled enough small arms to outfit a reinforced platoon. Thanks Lou, wherever you are.

9

THE BETRAYAL OF "GENTLEMAN JIM"

Since southern Africa offered some of the most interesting and intriguing opportunities for the professional adventurer, *Soldier of Fortune* decided to send a team of staff members for an on-site inspection. Also, we all had great admiration for the Rhodesians who were thumbing their collective noses at the U.N., the disloyal Brits and most of Africa, as well as a plentiful helping of tawdry, hypocritical third world buffoons, boobs, bums and thugs.

Explosives and Demo Editor John Donovan, Roving Correspondent, another unnamed correspondent (who "roved" over Port au Prince, Haiti in 1969, napalming the presidential Palace from a Super Constellation) and I laid over for a day in Rio de Janeiro. We managed to get stoned by a couple of shoeshine boys. Donovan was rudely dumped off in the slums by a cab driver who didn't like gringos. So much for Rio. Our intrepid crew linked up with *SOF* African correspondent Al J. Venter in Johannesburg, where they agreed it might be more adventuresome to travel by vehicle to Salisbury than by Air Rhodesia. Of course, at that time terrorists had yet to shoot down two of Air Rhodesia's civilian passenger planes and bayonet all the survivors. At the Rhodesian border, customs officials indicated that there had been no ambushes in the area so they decided to proceed north without the benefit of convoy. Anyway, it would be interesting to see if the terrorists' marksmanship was as bad as reported.

We arrived in Salisbury without incident though our adrenalin level spiked whenever we encountered cattle or sheep on the highway, as terrorists often blocked roads with livestock in conjunction with ambushes.

In Salisbury it was business as usual even though terrorist operations had escalated in the border areas. Police were seldom seen and still did not carry sidearms, which indicated to us that the African populace was not as "oppressed" as many of the Western liberals liked us to believe.

We bunked in at the luxurious Monomatapa Hotel, which had been dubbed "The Claymore" by the Rhodesian "troopies" due to its semi-circular construction. A few phone calls and a couple of hours later, we were quaffing Lion Lagers with three members of the Rhodesian Light Infantry in the hotel bar who gave us the scoop on the foreign fighters. For obvious reasons, all foreigners who served with the Rhodesian security forces were given a nom de guerre.

Bob Nicholson, 29, from Fortune, California, spent eight years in the U.S. Army, including four years in Nam. Airborne and Ranger qualified, Nicholson left the Army in 1975 because of its rampant drug problem and lax discipline. Bored with civilian life, he simply packed his bags, flew to Rhodesia and enlisted in June 1975.

Chris Johnson, 26, from Houston, Texas, served two tours with a Marine Recon Battalion followed by a five-year tour with the French Foreign Legion's Second Parachute Regiment. After his Legion discharge, he returned to Houston, where a Houston PD officer told him of the opportunities in Rhodesia. Within days, he was on his way.

The third member of the trio was Andy McLease, 26, from Scotland, who served nine years with the British Parachute Regiment. He opted for Rhodesia after receiving glowing reports from several of his buddies who had already made the move.

"I simply couldn't handle civilian life," McLease recounted, as he sipped on his Lion Lager. "I'm satisfied. There's action and a lot of bloody good people in our unit."

McLease's basic training unit consisted of 28 foreigners and five Rhodesians. The Rhodesian Light Infantry, which consists of three assault companies, one training company and one support company, had thirty to forty percent foreigners, most of whom had come from the U.S. and Commonwealth countries.

We spent the next five days hunting and talking to local farmers and troops. One of the farmers Al Venter introduced us to was Art Cumming, a strapping, cheery fellow whose farmstead was located about 50 kilometers from our safari camp. We were with Cumming and his wife Sandy, the week before in Rhodesia's northwest operational area, codenamed "Operation Ranger," when their farm was raided by terrorists.

What made no sense about the attack is that while it was made in the name of terrorism, few families in Rhodesia enjoyed such excellent relations with the blacks who lived on their farm as the Cummings did. A week after our visit, terrorists attacked the Cumming farm. Chillingly, Arthur Cumming told us on the last morning we were with him: "I've grown up among these people. So did my dad and his dad. They know us as we are, and we know and accept them in the same way. There is trust and understanding, so why would they try to kill me, or my wife or brother or mother?" Why indeed.

A pride of lions that had come across from the Wankie National Park had attacked Cumming's cattle and Arthur was eager to drive them back to the sanctuary. It was our job to kill one or two members of the pride, which had accounted for the loss of at least a dozen head of cattle during the previous week.

Our routine was the same each day of the hunt. Each morning before dawn we would arrive at the Cumming estate atop a small hill overlooking the nearby railway line. There we would pick up the local tracker, a man named Tickey, who had been with the Cumming family for more than 30 years. If only we had known that Tickey was already playing a pivotal role in the events to follow.

Movement about the farm was unrestricted. The only signs of a security presence were armed patrols along the railway line checking each day for landmines, which might have been placed on bridges and culverts during the night. Nothing was found while we were in the area, though the terrorists had blown a span of the Metesi River Bridge a few weeks earlier.

We were on the lion spoor but they were always two or three hours ahead of us. One amusing incident occurred while tracking the lions, but John Donovan would not think so. Venter, ever the prankster and who was always trying to impress J.D. and me with his machismo, grabbed the tail of a six foot King Cobra that was slithering across our path and was intent on retreating into its hole.

Now there is a myth or legend or whatever, that if you grab a snake's tail and whip it over you head, you can break its neck. Venter attempted such folly but didn't have the technique down pat. He did have six feet of now very angry Cobra hissing and spitting. He finally let it fly and it bounced off the chest of Donovan who became as angry as the cobra. The cobra fled to its hole and we all had a good laugh with the exception of J.D. who threatened to do a number of unprintable things to Venter.

Venter, bless his black heart, had a great gift for bullshitting. He arranged for me to go hunting with Gregorio Grasselli, then owner of Central African Safaris. I was to get three days of big game hunting in exchange for a Ruger Mini-14, half a dozen banana magazines and 500 rounds of 5.56 ammo, which I had smuggled out of the U.S. Grasselli had a small but beautiful facility consisting of a lodge and half a dozen roundavals which lodged his client hunters. The first day, Donovan and I had puzzled over the fact that his facility was not fenced and that he exhibited no concern about mines or ambushes on the 30 some clicks of dirt road that lead from the tarmac to his camp.

That night, over sundowners, I asked Grasselli, "Aren't you vulnerable driving on that dirt road all that distance and having no security fencing?"

He blew us off, saying, "We don't have a problem here. I'm not worried." J.D. and I felt uneasy about this and kept our guns next to our beds. But, we reasoned, he was the local and should know what the situation was. The lion hunt was unsuccessful and our party settled for a fair-sized sable and a near record kudu. Days later, the attack which rocked northwest Rhodesia took place: Arthur Cumming's wife was widowed, soon to give birth to a child who would never know its father.

Details of the actual attack were sparse, a tight security blanket being thrown over the area by members of the security forces who engaged in follow-up operations directly after Arthur Cumming had been killed.

A JUDAS IN THE CAMP

Arthur and Sandy were alone on the farm that fateful night. Lawrence, his younger brother, had left earlier in the day for Bulowayo, where their mother, one of the earliest pioneers in the northwest, had been spending a few days.

At about nine in the evening, according to Sandy Cumming, Arthur got up from his easy chair in the lounge to lock the outside doors. Moments later, she recalled with horror, three black men in the uniforms of the Rhodesian Army—complete with camouflage cloth caps—entered the room from the kitchen. Sandy's first words were: "Arthur, what is the Army doing in the house?"

A moment later, Arthur shouted a warning. "Run, Sandy. Run for your life, out of the house." A fusillade of shots rang out in the close confines of the house and Arthur Cumming staggered backward into the lounge. He crumpled in a heap on the concrete floor. That was the last that Sandy saw of the attack, for she had already slipped out through one of the side doors. Moments later, she heard another burst of AK-47 fire. Sandy could hear bullets ricocheting off the concrete and she knew the terrorists had again shot her wounded husband.

It was clear from the start that the terrorist band of three, who apparently had come across from Zambia, were aware that Sandy Cumming had escaped. They also knew that she was almost nine months pregnant and could not go very far.

Crouching in a low clump of bushes at the end of the garden, Sandy could hear one of the men, obviously the leader of the killer band, give an order. One of the terrs immediately began to search for her around the house while the other two set about raiding the farm store, about 30 meters from the homestead. Sandy remained hidden for what she termed "about 10 or 15 minutes, I can't remember exactly how long." All the while, she was desperate to know the fate of Arthur, for no sound came from the house. Meanwhile, the one terrorist searched through the house for her.

Eventually, Sandy could restrain herself no longer. She waited until the searching terrorist had gone around the corner of the house and then quickly scrambled towards the building, slipping into the house once again by the same door she had exited from. Like a phantom in the dark, she made her way to Arthur who lay in a pool of blood where he had fallen. He was not yet dead. Trembling, but with cool calculation, Sandy moved slowly towards the Agri-alert system which had been installed in their home only a few weeks earlier. She knew that she would have instant contact with a distant police station, but she was also aware that if she tripped the alarm switch, the noise would bring the terrorists running.

Sandy carefully moved the switch marked "Talk" over to the "On" position. Lifting the telephone receiver to her ear she whispered a few words. "Can anyone hear me?" she said softly.

The firing had already alerted an Army patrol near the railway station, but they were several kilometers away. They had, however, contacted base and reported the shooting, and thus the command and control center was on the alert.

Yes, they could hear her. What had happened, they asked. In as few words as possible, Sandy recounted the story in a low voice.

"Arthur is dying," she said. "Please send help."

Once again, she slipped to where Arthur was lying. She returned to the Agri-alert to tell them that Arthur's condition was critical. Having spent much of her adult life as a nursing sister in Salisbury, Sandy Cumming knew a serious case when she saw one and she did not mince words.

Several more times, Sandy went to her dying husband and each time she returned to the Agri-alert phone to report his condition. On one occasion, a terrorist banged at one of the doors as he passed and she froze. But he moved on. Eventually the inevitable report came through. "Arthur is dead," she called over the intercom. By then the terrorists had gone, having set fire to the farm store while a military patrol was fast approaching the house.

Ten days after we had been with Gentleman Jim, he was murdered in cold blood.

Unbeknown to Sandy Cumming, the entire drama, as it unfolded, was being followed by the entire farming community of northwest Rhodesia; at least that portion that was linked by Agri-alert to Victoria Falls Police Station. Each one of the sets installed on the farms was in contact with the other, so that when one farmer speaks, every other link can follow the conversation. In this way, if the alarm is sounded on a farm, it goes off simultaneously on every other farm. In all the farms with the Agri-alert system, weapons as well as the system were next to the farmer's bed once the security gates had been shut for the night.

For a radius of more than 100 kilometers, families were horrified by the drama as it unfolded. "Gentleman Jim" Cumming, as young as he was, was already a well-known figure within the community. George Grasselli, our guide who lived about 50 kilometers from the Cumming farm, expressed the helplessness:"There we were, listening to this terrible story and there was absolutely nothing that we could do about it," he said. "Nothing!"

BETRAYAL

Rhodesian security forces were quick to follow up the attack, but first, questions were asked among those Africans working and living on the farm. Shockingly, the tracker, Tickey, who had been with the family for three decades and had helped during our hunt for lion, had led the terrorists to the Cumming home on the night of the attack. Apparently, he had been feeding and hiding the group for a week, in spite of the fact that Tickey had often looked after young Cumming when he was a child.

"He carried him on his back as a little boy and helped to kill him once he had become a man," one of the security officers said during the investigation. Tickey was taken into custody in Victoria Falls. For helping terrorists in a terminal attack, he probably received the death penalty.

Arthur Cumming had mentioned another farmhand, "Boss Boy," when he explained why he believed the homestead would never be attacked. "Boss Boy" was a senior card carrying member of the ZAPU faction of the Rhodesian African National Council (ANC). He had told Arthur that the farm was safe. He was told that everyone knew that he paid his labor well and was kind and good to their families. There was no reason, the African told Arthur, why the insurgents should want to attack the Cumming home. So relying on such authority, Arthur Cumming never had his home enclosed with cyclone fencing. This ANC member was in Wasalso being held in close custody by the Rhodesian police. His role in the murder was not detailed.

When we heard of the Cumming murders, we all reflected on a strange situation that had occurred on the third day of our hunt. About 0530 hours, we were traveling toward the Cumming farm in Grasselli's land mine-proofed Land Rover. Roll bars had been installed along with steel plating in front of the firewall under and behind the front seats. We were crossing the railway near the Metesi bridge as dawn was sneaking over the African bush, when one of our party observed three Africans 150 meters down the track.

"They are armed and in uniform," someone whispered. Grasselli halted the vehicle; we bailed out and began uncasing our Zeiss-scoped .375 H&H magnums.

We had been hoping to get a shot at some terrorists and it looked as if it was time.

Grasselli glassed the suspects as we moved into the prone position. "I can't make out their weapons but they're wearing Rhodesian cammies," he said. We shrugged our shoulders and reluctantly went back to looking for lions.

When we heard that Cumming had seen terrorists, we zeroed in with 20-20 hindsight and determined we should have confronted the suspects—especially since when we had first observed them, they were moving toward the railway and when they saw the Land Rover, they walked the other way.

While we were in Rhodesia the war continued unabated, except that Ian Smith's security forces appeared to have achieved a major breakthrough. On our trip to Salisbury by road the previous October, we passed numerous operational centers along the main southeast highway from Beit Bridge. A month later, when we returned once again by vehicle, the entire operational front had moved further towards the east and the Mozambique border, the back of the insurgent offensive having apparently been broken by cross-border raids into the neighboring Marxist state.

The extent and impact of these raids is not fully known. While some critics maintain that they came too late and were not on a large enough scale, unofficial but reliable Salisbury contacts indicated that the three cross-border operations stymied the full force of the terrorist summer offensive. Government sources in Salisbury speak of "several hundred terrorists killed." Other reliable sources indicated that the true figure was nearer 2,000 terrorists killed, in three separate operations.

The daring, imagination and effectiveness of these raids can be compared with the Israeli raid on Entebbe and the U.S. raid on Son Tay. According to one of our contacts, on August 8th a Rhodesian force of 72 men—both blacks and whites—drove into a terrorist training camp in Frelimo vehicles, dressed in Frelimo uniforms, singing Frelimo songs and armed with AK-47's. Their operational plan had them driving onto the camp's parade ground as the terrs and Frelimo troops were holding reveille about 20 minutes before dawn. When in position, the Rhodesian force opened up, killing approximately 300 terrorists and 30 Frelimo.

Days after the first raid the Mozambique government broke silence with a brief announcement that 618 had been killed. The broadcast alleged that the attack had been made on defenseless refugees at " Nyagomia village, 40 kms inside Mozambique." A British newspaper, under the headline, RHODESIA IS ACCUSED, repeated the Mozambique accusation that "hundreds of women and children" were killed in an attack on a "refugee camp" and quoted the Mozambique government's publication of photographs of "massed graves of women and children refugees."

The British government further stated that it preferred to believe the United Nations' account to that of the Rhodesians'. On August 29th, the Rhodesian government released a fairly full and documented account of the raid, including a captured map of Nyadzonya camp. In addition, captured documents included a "master roll" of more than 2,000 names of camp inmates, listing their real names, their chimurenga ("'war of revolution") names and details of their village of origin, district, educational standard, occupation and marital status.

Words on the map clearly indicated the military nature of the camp: words such as "security section," "security guards," "commander's residence" and places for "Red guards." Other documents showed there were three battalions based at the camp at the time of the raid. On August 5th—three days before the raid—the A Battalion had a register of 1,128 of which 1,070 were on parade. Some were sick and 36 were "missing." Each battalion was broken down into three detachments and with each detachment were a commander, a political commissar, a medical officer, a deputy commander and a person responsible for logistics.

A further document included a list of SKS rifles and rocket launchers—curious equipment for a refugee camp.

As an editorial in the Rhodesian Sunday Mail (Aug. 29) stated, "No one who sees the documentary evidence can question that the Nyadzonya camp . . . was in fact a terrorist camp. To suggest, as has been done outside our borders, that it was a refugee camp has been proved absolute nonsense by the documents. They are packed with references to the military structure of the camp, its battalion formations, their chain of command (including political commissars), lists of revolutionary names, records of weapons and instructions on them, lecture notes with the thoughts of communist chairman Mao Tse-tung, records of punishments inflicted on dissident revolutionaries (including women), and personal testaments of recruits.

"It is all there for the world to see—and to nail the refugee camp lie. Refugees do not have military battalions, terrorist indoctrination, communist commissars and weapons of war.

"Obviously efforts were made in Mozambique to cover up the true nature and purpose of Nyadzonya—sufficient to fool a representative of the United Nations, not that that body would require much convincing of anything anti-Rhodesian.

"There have been suggestions that after the Rhodesian raid, Frelimo took the opportunity to do some eliminating of its own. Likely or not, it is interesting to note that the camp Rhodesia attacked was at Nyadzonya, 50 km inside Mozambique, while the United Nations' representative admitted the settlement he saw was called Margonha and was near the Rhodesian border."

During one raid, a massive arms dump was destroyed in the Tete region of Mozambique involving almost 100 tons of Soviet and Chinese ordnance. The explosion lit up the sky for 50 kilometers, and there were a number of "foreign advisers," including Eastern Europeans, killed in the blast.

One of the results of cross-border raids was that Rhodesian army morale was at a zenith. This was reflected in the activities of those terrorists (estimated to number about 2,000, about a fifth in the northeast), still in the beleaguered country. Terrorists captured by Rhodesian security forces in late November indicated that they were well aware of Rhodesian raids into Mozambique and the effect they were having on supplies and logistics. There was also serious doubt in insurgent circles about the security of their home bases—an essential aspect of insurgency or guerrilla warfare.

For this, and other reasons, bands of terrorists in Rhodesia were running for the border and trying to get back to Mozambique. It was these groups that were decimated the most, simply because they no longer effected caution and became easy targets while on the move.

Further problems faced them once they entered Mozambique, since strict instructions were given by Frelimo authorities not to allow terrorists active in Rhodesia to return to bases behind the lines. In some cases returnees were shot out-of-hand by Frelimo forces for disobeying these orders.

In a desperate bid to prop up the offensive, the Mozambique command—directed by regular army officers from Tanzania, Zambia, Mozambique and Botswana, together with a sprinkling of Cubans, Russians, Chinese, East Germans and North Vietnamese—were sending into Rhodesia half-trained combatants.

It became a challenge for the Rhodesians themselves, with their small population, to neutralize them.

10

RHODESIA: THE LAND OF MERCS AND HIRED GUNS

When I heard about how the terrorist leader Robert Mugabe threatened to steal the elections in Rhodesia in 1980, I was outraged, although not one bit surprised.

I had almost given up on getting to fight some terrs after six visits to Rhodesia from 1974–80, each time itching for a firefight but leaving without having found one. The only excitement I had found was on my first trip, in May 1974, before I launched *SOF*, when I linked up with McNair. We careened about on dirt roads in terr-infested northwest Rhodesia for a few days, but the only excitement was provided by the driving of the merc.

Finally, unexpectedly, in March 1980 I found my firefight when I decided that we had to be in Rhodesia for the elections, which were bound to be bloody. Though I and a few of my staff of editors had made several trips to the Rhodesian war zones, it wasn't until that year that *SOF* had the funds to send a team to cover the upcoming elections, which would determine if the small, besieged country would elect a moderate black–white government or a terrorist dictator.

I figured we needed a sizable presence during the elections since all of our contacts and sources warned that after the elections the whole country would go up in flames. If the inevitable occurred, we knew that no stuffy Rhodesian bureaucrat would be in any position to prevent us from linking up with a unit not choosy about where a few extra guns came from.

Former U.S. Army Major Darrell Winkler, commander of the elite Rhodesian Armored Car Regiment, a rugged, fearless and seasoned Vietnam vet and warrior, had come to Rhodesia a couple years earlier. I had heard about him through the merc underground in the United States and met up with him on previous trips to Rhodesia. His story was typical of those Vietnam vets who came back after the war disillusioned with the U.S. Army, and for a time floundered around, searching for somewhere to fit in.

"I was in New York and I met a Rhodesian," Winkler said. "He asked me if I wanted to go to Africa and fight for Rhodesia. I said, 'not really.' I had spent two and a half years in Vietnam, first with the Long Range Reconnaissance Patrol (LRRPs) until my unit changed to the 75th Rangers. We spent most of the time in the Mekong Delta. I was injured three times.

"But after the war ended and I came back, the Army had changed, so I decided to get out and find some law enforcement job. That is when I ran into the Rhodesian. Anyhow, he gave me a number to call in London. I did out of curiosity. They were looking for officers with mechanized or armor background. I was in an armor unit in Germany, so I fit the bill.

"'Come to Salisbury,' they told me, 'just for a visit. If you go to Toronto there will be a ticket waiting for you.' So I went and they offered me a position as commander in the armored car regiment."

I had met Winkler in '78 in Rhodesia while researching an article on the Rhodesian armor regiment. He made it a point that he was actually a member of the Rhodesian Army and that he was a Foreign Volunteer, not a merc. He and other volunteers from France, Belgium, the UK, Australia, Canada and New Zealand received the identical salary and benefits as the regular Rhodesian soldier.

SOF, *MERCS AND THE RHODESIAN AFRICAN RIFLES REGIMENT*

The first priority when we got to Rhodesia was to link up with Winkler, since we felt he would be in the best position to conceal our presence from the Rhodesian Combined Ops which had prevented me from accompanying any Rhodesian unit on combat ops. This proved to be the case, even though Winkler had been transferred to the Rhodesian African Rifles.

After joining Winkler, we contacted an old Rhodesian friend who just happened to be a quartermaster of a large unit. We traded Johnny Walker

Black and *SOF* t-shirts for Rhodesian cammies and kit. The next morning we were on our way.

Winkler took us in to meet up with O'Brien and Reb, the MAG machine gunner, who we had not met before, in Salisbury on a Monday morning just before the elections. I had brought *SOF*ers Art Director Craig Nunn, Associate Editor N.E. MacDougald, and Tom Wilkenson. We hooked up with Yves Debay, a French Foreign Legion veteran from Belgium and "the Mechanic," the only white Rhodesian. The remaining members of the 14-member outfit were all black troopers of the Rhodesian African Rifles (RAR).

British merc Jerry O'Brien was one of the regiment members who had come to Rhodesia the previous year. Around 5'8", he was muscular, with strong, full features, cautious smoky blue eyes always on guard, and a loud contagious laugh to match his keen sense of humor. After completing his five-and-a-half-year tour in the Legion, serving his time in Corsica and Djibouti, he wanted to kick some butt, see some combat. So he and a Legionnaire friend hatched a plan to go find some action in Rhodesia. Jerry tried to join up with the RLI (the Incredibles), a regiment of professionals including many RAR foreigners, but they rejected him. "All I could figure was that they didn't want former Legionnaires," Jerry said.

Acting on a lead from the local who was driving them around in search of a regiment, the two met up with Winkler and joined his Armored Car Regiment. Later they followed him to the Rhodesian African Rifles.

Meanwhile, back in the States, another American—frustrated crusader Michael Pierce, aka "Reb"—had been hell bent on joining some military and fighting some commies somewhere. He had not had a chance to fight the evil empire as an American soldier. He was sharp, nimble, good looking, and full of piss and vinegar. He looked like a musician, and he was, but he was there on a mission that was hatched after he read an article in *SOF*.

"I was playing and writing music in Hollywood. The Yankee Army had turned me down (according to them, blind in my left eye). I had pulled off some pretty cool stuff in LA and developed delusions of grandeur, deciding I could take some time off and go fight for people whom I thought were worth fighting for. I traded my guitar for a light machine gun," Pierce told me.

After reading an article in *SOF*, titled "The Black Devils of the Rhodesian Armored Car Regiment" in January 1979, Reb imagined that he heard the Black Devils calling him. He wrote to a Rhodesian Army recruiter who told him to get lost because he had no combat experience. Undaunted, Reb sold his belongings and bought a one-way ticket to Rhodesia. Just as Jerry had interpreted the rejection letter he had received from the recruiters in London as a "get your ass down there" invitation, Reb interpreted the negative response his own way, as "come on over."

As soon as Reb landed in Salisbury, he made inquiries about the American commander he had heard about, figuring he could not turn a fellow American down. The merc underground network was very active in the United States. He tracked down Major Winkler.

"I gave Reb five minutes to convince me that I should accept him into my regiment. Whatever the dogged 'I won't take no for an answer' Rebel told me, which I cannot even remember, it worked," Winkler said.

For the next year, the two Brit former Legionnaires and the two Americans, one a seasoned veteran and one a volunteer, fought terrorists together in the ferocious Bush War in Winkler's Armored Car Regiment.

The members of the regiment filled us in, trying to make sense of the impending disaster.

The West, they told us, in all its witless glory, in a pattern of familiar missteps that conjured up memories of the murderous Pol Pot in Cambodia, had sided with Robert Mugabe and his terrorists, never mind their brutal, vicious tactics.

"The terrorists were relaxed in comfortable assembly areas tended by the commonwealth monitoring force, and were fed and supplied by the British and American governments. Thousands more roamed the countryside, intimidating the local populace and laying the groundwork for an overwhelming political victory," Reb said.

"We even did a raid into Mozambique to take out a terrorist base camp. Terrorists were coming in from Mozambique and Zambia. Mugabe's terror campaign was communist-backed. A lot of Cuban fighters were with him," Jerry said.

"The country was about to crash, I was still in the Armored Car Regiment with Winkler." When he got seconded to the RAR demonstration company, he planned to train them to take out Camp Romeo, one of the camps where all the terrorists were going to turn in their weapons. Winkler took me, Reb and the Belgian, Yves Debay, with him. But although we trained to take out the camp, they never did and I still don't know why," Jerry said.

"We weren't told why Winkler was seconded to the RAR, but it was very obvious the government didn't want an American in command of the most powerful regiment in the army at a delicate time politically," Pierce added.

Anyhow, here we were with the British merc, the two Americans and the well-known Belgian war correspondent Debay.

"The war has to end somewhere. That kind of guerrilla warfare could not go on forever, and I heard that Ian Smith could no longer afford to continue the war with the United States and United Kingdom imposing sanctions. All the terrorists from the Mugabe and Nkomo camps were going to come in to rendezvous points and hand in their weapons. The British Army would monitor the elections. What the Rhodesians decided to do if Nkomo won was to deal with him, since he was sensible. If Mugabe, a nutter, won, they were going to storm the government buildings and take out the rendezvous points where the terrorists were hiding their weapons," Jerry said.

Rumor had it that the terror chief Mugabe was going to steal the upcoming elections. We were warned that Mugabe and his savage followers were going to win no matter how much violence and mayhem would occur. The terrorist attacks against the white Rhodesians were escalating as they gained confidence, with the backing of both sides in the Cold War, East and West.

Together, our unconventional group ran into terrorists in what was the Regiment's umpteenth firefight and *SOF*'s first and last firefight in Rhodesia.

We were piled up in two cars and headed to the RAR to patrol with the regiment. A few days passed, and then one day when we were out on patrol we saw smoke from a campfire. Winkler split us up. Reb, O'Brien, Craig Nunn and I went with him. N.E. MacDougal had gone on a patrol with someone else.

The Demo Company had been assigned a task for the anticipated election punch-up. They were to make an assault crossing over a river, and together with Tenth Battalion, Rhodesian Rifles, take out Assembly Point Foxtrot. A last minute re-evaluation of pre-election security priorities prompted a hurried transfer of our company from the Sanyati Tribal Trust Lands (TTL) to the Que Que Silobella area.

Screw the disapproving politically correct, publicity shy senior army officials with cameras and weaponry—we were all geared up for action. That night the major hosted a get together for the officers, senior NCOs and *SOF*ers.

We were showing off our high quality equipment and webbing. The kit and equipment–starved European members of the regiment lusted after the lightweight American assault rifles.

"The Africans viewed them as interesting novelties, preferring the aging but lethal FN FAL," Reb recalled.

We were in one of the Tribal Trust Lands, Silobela, which contained about 70 or so terrs. After about 12 to 14 clicks from the base camp, security was posted around the seven-fives and last-minute instructions were quickly given. Drivers were given pick-up points, time frames were checked, and off we were.

Just before the firefight we awoke as the sun came up. We loaded the seven-fives armored vehicles and rode to the operations area. The machine gunner, Reb, informed us that Winkler had found terrs on more than 70 percent of his operations. This looked real promising.

"When we deployed there the cops told us there would be no terror activity for a number of months. But the major said he smelled gooks (terrs). I tended to believe the major, whose instincts were good," Reb said.

In silence, we neared one of the branches of the Gwelo River, heading southwest. In each village the RAR sergeant questioned the locals about the terrs. They told us where the terrs camped overnight. Winkler decided to split the group of 14. His section would delay and head straight for the terr camp. We were to cut a big arc behind and set up an ambush.

A little over two kilometers from the branch of the Gwelo, the Damba River dip, we were to intercept with the terrs. As soon as we hit the village, we realized that the terrs were already there, judging by the look of fear in the villagers' eyes. They had been intimidated by the terrs the past November. Another five kilometers after crossing the Totololo River, we heard the contact about one klick north of us.

Craig Nunn and O'Brien went right flank, walking through an empty village, and Winkler and Reb and I went forward and the others went to the left.

"It's the terrorists, we have contact with the terrs," I shouted and began shooting. Craig and O'Brien came in from the right. O'Brien fired two rifle grenades. A terr shot a grenade at us that went off right behind us.

Reb sprayed a short burst with his MAG 58, then rifle grenades; AK-47s and the Remington 870 shotgun Craig was carrying burst fire. We ran about 700 meters up to a tree line. Debay wanted to charge into the contact, but we had no radio and the major could not know from which direction we were coming. Friendly fire is not what we came to Rhodesia for.

As Reb recalled, "We got out in the bush looking for trouble and walked and walked (as always). At 1500 hours my own instincts kicked in and I sprayed the bush with my MAG just across a minor stream. Two rifle grenades came flying back at us. I went prone and fired again, watching a tracer ricochet back at me, seeming to come right at me. I knew the physics of it—it couldn't hit me; but for a few seconds I was hypnotized.

"I looked to my left and Brown was standing up firing a Ruger Mini-14 with one hand and snapping pics with the other. In the background I heard the loud bang of a shotgun, which was coming from Craig Nunn's Remington 870, who was with our other team blasting away—not sure what at," Reb recalled.

"I fired another burst and then my MAG jammed. I couldn't clear it, so I reached for my pistol and it was gone. The cheap shit Rhodie holster had torn off my belt when the scrap started. Luckily for me, the bad guys gapped it and ultimately ran into our stop group, where they were taken prisoner. The Rhodesian Army worked close to the bone," Reb said.

"The Rhodies were broke. We ate 1939 British rations, and our weapons, while adequate, had been around. The AK I used for a while still had blood stains on it, which I didn't really mind, in an Apache sort of way. I was annoyed with the mercs' equipment failures. Brown has brass balls. That was real ordnance flying at us that day and you'd have never known it by his reaction," Reb said.

WHAT THE HELL AM I DOING HERE? I'M NOT EVEN GETTING COMBAT PAY

The way I recall it, a few kilometers out from the base we prepped our weapons and started watching the bush. We were told that the Rhodesian armored vehicles we were convoying in were mine-proof except from the larger Soviet tank mines, so we were not to worry about moving through mine fields.

As the first AK rounds cracked overhead, I come to a micro-second conclusion: corn stubble makes lousy cover. I peered through, around and over the stalks. Looking for a target, preferably one of the terrorists who were trying to ventilate me.

Reb, on my right, triggers short bursts on his MAG light machine gun. Where are the bastards? Will they fight? Or will they shoot and run as usual? Blam! Blam! Two terr rifle grenades explode on a line 10 meters to the right of the MAG. Right range, wrong windage. A hell of a way to shuck corn. Major Winkler yells out above the fire, "Cover us. We'll move up on their flank."

Winkler and I are on our feet, green and brown Rhodesian camouflage uniforms patched with sweat . . . Ruger Mini-14s bucking . . . sprinting . . . to where? Nothing but more damned corn stalks . . . might as well hit the dirt here . . . breathing hard . . . providing covering fire as Reb moves his MAG another 30 meters . . . rest of the stick to the right of the MAG also on the money . . . on the double, bent over . . . jerking heads left and right . . . searching . . . firing into ant hills, bushes, trees.

The MAG jams . . . I run over to the gunner . . . can't eliminate the malfunction . . . well, no incoming.

On our feet now, sweeping forward line . . . searching for spoor . . . (movement . . . reflection from an AK 10 to 15 meters apart . . . no incoming fire . . . then, blam! A terr rifle grenade explodes 10 meters directly to my rear.

This time the terr windage was right on but the range was 10 meters off. It's probably just as well they didn't try a third time. I remember thinking, what the hell am I doing here? I'm not even getting combat pay!

We obtained fire superiority and they ran. We radioed to the other patrol and they captured three of them, who dropped their weapons. The three were handed over to the police and the next day they won the elections. Taking out the rendezvous point never happened because the British Army was there.

IT HITS HOME: THE TERRORIST MUGABE HAD STOLEN THE ELECTIONS

That evening, we partied with Demo Company. Reb was checking out my weapons and we were getting well into our cups, which was probably good because it numbed the news that blared over the radio that the thug communist-backed Mugabe had been elected as prime minister.

Winkler issued all the ammunition and grenades his team could carry and they eagerly awaited the order to march on Salisbury. Rumor had it that General Walls, commander of the Rhodesian Army from 1977, had sold out. (Suspicions were especially raised when Mugabe appointed him in 1980 to oversee the transition from white to majority rule. But Mugabe later accused Walls of planning to assassinate him while he commanded the Rhodesian Army.)

As Reb recalled, "On the way to Salisbury we stopped at Que Que South African Police station. The Major, Jerry and I did anti-riot duty in Que Que. We patrolled the streets with evil in our hearts, then planned the great escape." It hit home that Mugabe and the terrs that escaped from the firefight had won. In Salisbury, we heard rumors—plans to burn the city. That is when we heard of a hit list Mugabe's people had of military and civilians; that included all *SOF* members."

We had previously reconned the Rhodesian Art Museum, intending to liberate the more prestigious pieces of art when the city started to burn. The problem was that none of us were art experts. The only name I was familiar with was Picasso's name on some drawings.

According to some, the whites and even many of the blacks were to join up in a massive column and fight their way to Beit Bridge on the South African border, where they would be welcomed by South Africa.

But all the carefully laid plans to take the country back went nowhere. Instead, the Salisbury streets were bloodied as Mugabe supporters swarmed the streets, stoning and beating anyone who had opposed him. A Special Branch guy came and warned the Major that he was on a "war crimes" list because he'd killed a lot of gooks.

We all hung out at O'Brien's apartment for a couple of weeks, figuring that staying in a hotel would be a bit risky considering that we were on Mugabe's hit list. Meantime, Winkler discharged O'Brien and Reb. O'Brien is currently working security in London and spending what he saves in between gigs on his next adventure. Still going strong, he regularly meets up with his former Legionnaire buddies in Corsica at the annual FFL reunion. He and Reb, back in the United States are still in touch and he visits Winkler in the States often.

Nunn, who had been in the Special Forces Reserve, finally fought his first battle in Rhodesia. The fearless Nunn died tragically, way too young, just a few years later in Boulder in what was another daredevil act on his motorcycle. He was still with *SOF* at the time.

I finally found my first and last firefight in Rhodesia. To me, that'll always be its name.

Ian Smith stayed active in Rhodesian, then Zimbabwe, politics and wrote two books about the betrayal of his government. He died at the age of 88 in South Africa in 2007, a broken man. His only son and business partner had died a few years previously. My big regret is that I was not able to visit him in South Africa, as I had planned, before he died. The corrupt, evil and invincible dictator Mugabe has hoarded billions and impoverished his country, which used to be called the "Bread Basket of Africa." His opponents are regularly eliminated while the West looks the other way.

11

CONS, PSYCHICS AND AN ABORTED SEARCH FOR POWs

In early 1981 I received an urgent call at the office from a voice from the past. "Brown, we need your help," the gruff voice bellowed so loudly that even with my half-deaf ears I about dropped the phone.

"We were recruited by Bo Gritz to participate in a POW rescue operation in S.E. Asia which has turned out to be the mother of all cons. I need you to go to New York with me and see a guy who laid down a bundle for the mission and convince him of what was going on with our getting stiffed. He's George Brooks (Chairman of the Board of Directors of the National League of Families of American Prisoners and Missing in Southeast Asia). You know, the guy whose son Nicholas was shot down over Laos in 1970. He gave Gritz over $20,000. Some of it was to pay our expenses. We did not get a dime," the angry voice roared.

It was Jim Monaghan, a hard drinking, blue eyed, hot tempered, curly haired, medium height, muscle bound Irishman. He was a former SF Captain with four tours in Nam and a chest full of decorations. We had crossed paths several times when the restless, half-mad vet who recklessly lived on the edge was trying to suck me into some wild scheme or the other. I was on guard.

Monaghan had been a member of the elite Mike Forces, Special Forces units composed of a small number of specially trained SF personnel that led company-size units of Montagnard tribesmen. The Mike Forces were deployed throughout Vietnam, mainly when A-Team camps were threatened or overrun. The vast bulk of Special Forces personnel and their Montagnard mercenaries only operated around the A-Team camps. Monaghan had become a legend for his fearless actions in the Mike Force Third Company—China Boy 3—and made his bones several times over in his four years in Nam.

Monaghan had touched a raw nerve.

"Slow down, tone it down and fill me in," I told him.

"My buddies and I went to Florida to join a group of Vietnam vets and other former SpecOps guys to join a POW mission, a convoluted mess that Gritz concocted and called Operation Velvet Hammer. Like I said, it never got off the ground," he said. "All expenses were to be paid, plus a lump sum. Or so Gritz told us."

"OK, you have my attention. Go back to the beginning," I told Monaghan.

"It all started in February, when Gritz called Medal of Honor recipient Fred Zabitosky, a friend of Senator Jesse Helms, inviting him to participate in a POW rescue attempt. Gritz asked Zabitosky to recruit other Special Forces Vietnam vets."

I knew the tight community with its active network and was not a bit surprised that in no time over a dozen recruits were on board. Monaghan went on to describe the haphazard fiasco.

"In addition to Zabitosky and Earl Bleacher, a Son Tay Raider, we recruited several other vets who jumped at the chance to participate," he said, rattling off the names of the volunteers, most of whom I knew or knew of.

Fred Zabitosky had come under heavy enemy fire with his reconnaissance patrol team in Nam. He took charge of the defense and counterattack until rescue helicopters arrived. The first rescue helicopter crashed and Zabitosky, although injured, saved its pilot during the battle. Zab was tall, dark and a bit shady looking with a contrived attitude that said, "Don't mess with me because you don't know who you are messing with."

Another member of the dirty dozen or more was Bleacher, a mean SOB, handsome, dark, tall, slim, with a sloping forehead and piercing eyes. He was part of the Son Tay Raid to rescue 70 POWs held in a torturous prison camp 23 miles outside of Hanoi. In November 1970, 56 Green Berets were divided into three groups, each with a different mission. Blueboy was the 14-man assault group assigned to crashland its helicopter in the small prison camp with fighter cover above. The 22-man Greanleaf group would land outside the prison camp to support Blueboy, and blow a hole in the compound wall. The helicopter carrying Blueboy departed from the CIA-operated security base in Thailand at 11:25 on 20 November at 02:18. It successfully crashlanded inside the compound at Son Tay. Greenleaf landed a quarter mile from its intended LZ, and attacked a North Vietnamese barracks. Within 27 minutes on the ground, the Green Berets killed between 100–200 enemy soldiers sleeping in the barracks. Blueboy reported that there were no POWs in the compound. They had been moved the previous July, but the mission was still considered a success because no American lives had been lost while a strong message had been sent to the NVA.

Another guy who came to Florida for the project was Lt. Colonel Mark Berent. He was a decorated pilot with three tours, totaling four years in Vietnam from 1965 to 1973. On one tour, he flew F-4Ds out of Ubon Air Base in Thailand with the Night Owl Squadron as commander of the famous Wolf Forward Air Control (FAC). Berent flew the F-100 jet aircraft on over 250 missions out of Bien Hoa from December '65 to December '66. In one of his following tours, he flew 250+ missions in the F-4 aircraft out of Ubon Royal Thai Air Force Base (RTAFB), from November '68 to November '69. The first seven months he was a flight commander in the Night Owl squadron. The last five months he was the commander of the Wolf FAC unit.

Berent and Monaghan had first hooked up in Saigon in 1966. After the war, Berent recalled, "Monaghan called me to see him in Florida to meet with Bo Gritz about the POW/MIA search and rescue. "I then called Lieutenant Colonel Dick Hébert, and San Sok (Sam), a Cambodian Army Lieutenant who had saved my life several times. He was trapped in the States when Cambodia fell in 1975 and I had taken him in for six months. They agreed to come down to Florida (Sam at my expense)."

"I brought Dick with me down to the Velvet Hammer affair," Berent said.

"We flew down to Florida where the operation was being organized to join over a dozen other former special operators in early March. We were broken down into different sections including intel and planning. We were just hanging around awaiting the promised intelligence. Reporters were to be present to publicize the search for the POWs so Gritz could raise more funds. The flashy Gritz, who did everything with the main focus on himself, even claimed that he had organized a parade down 5th Avenue in New York," Monaghan said.

OF PSYCHICS AND HYPNOTISTS

"To top off the show, Gritz, who used spiritual mind tricks and claimed to be a hypnotist himself, had hired a hypnotist and psychic to give the intelligence brief. She went into a trance in this weird séance and gave a spooky vision of the sight of captive Americans in a cellar," Monaghan said.

"A few days of Gritz's stalling and after several whacko meetings with psychics, we were beginning to get antsy and smelled a con game. Each day, we asked for reimbursement for our expenses, but Gritz kept blowing us off. For the next two days, nothing happened other than the smoke and mirrors.

"Finally the elusive Gritz showed up and asked us if we knew anyone who could provide automatic weapons and transport them to Thailand. We contacted an international arms dealer we knew who promised to get the weapons as soon as he received a down payment. The money never came and there still was no intel. One more psychic session, and fed up with the BS from this big time conniver, we once again asked Gritz to cough up our expense money and give us enough to get back home. No go. If we had hung around much longer, it would not have ended very well for Gritz or for us, so we booked flights back home on our own nickel," Monaghan said.

Berent contacted Fred Smith to see if he could help with the POW search. "Fred, the owner of Federal Express, which he founded it in 1970, was a former Marine and Vietnam vet who had worked for Dick Hébert in an A-4 fighter squadron at Da Nang," Berent said.

"After that fiasco, we decided something needed to be done, so Hebert and Monaghan and I went to Memphis and met with Fred Smith who said he would put everything at our disposal if we could give proof of just one POW being found. While we were in Florida, Ann Mills Griffiths of the National League of Families had said that she had the proof.

"So I called Griffiths and had to really coax her to come to Memphis. I had to pick up the tab on all of this, including Monaghan's, and flew her into Memphis," Berent continued. I'll never forget what happened when she showed up at the conference table where Fred Smith and his number two guy (a Marine buddy whose name I don't recall), Monaghan, Hébert and myself were seated. Ann Mills Griffiths started just drawing circles with her finger on the table and said she could not release the proof. This she told Fred Smith, who had had many personal conversations with President Reagan. And just then we got a phone call from somebody who said that Gritz had released everything to the press. I made a panicked phone call to an Air Force three-star general at McDill AFB who had been getting ready to provide us with maps and told him to back off. It was a disgusting day," Berent said.

Indeed I knew Griffiths, who for years was head of the National League of Families—a player in her own mind who got off on the power she accumulated in that position, using everybody's first name, e.g. "Nice to see you Colin [Powell]."

Perturbed at not seeing a shred of evidence about the presence of Americans at Gritz's target, Nhommarath, Laos, and having been fleeced out of their meager bucks and time, the formidable team told the oft-decorated Lt. Colonel Gritz to perform a long piss up a short rope, bid adieu to his Florida Follies, and decided to cast its lot with me if I was game.

"You became involved after that and helped finance the Center for POW/MIA Accountability (CPMIA) that Monaghan, Hébert, and I set up," Berent remembered.

How Gritz had the cajones to mess over that formidable team escaped me.

The SpecOps community was all too familiar with retired Lt. Colonel James "Bo" Gritz, a tall, ruggedly handsome, charismatic, highly decorated (though often awarded upon his own recommendation) Special Forces veteran. Some respected him for his Vietnam record. I did not. A legend in his own mind, Gritz became notorious in the SpecOps community when he later conducted several highly publicized private missions into Asia to rescue POWs, all to no avail. He paved a rocky if not hostile road for recovery teams to tread in the search for any POWs over the next few years when *SOF* was operating with his twisted missions that cost a lot of hopeful donors and families of POWs big bucks.

I strongly believed we still had some Vietnam POWs imprisoned in some dank unknown prison in Southeast Asia, if alive, or lying in some unmarked grave if not. I had been watching for over a decade while official agencies and the scores of private parties searching for POWs in one mission after another could not get it right. With one unsolicited call, fate sucked *SOF* into a foray to take over where the prissy, lethargic bureaucrats or bungling private operatives had failed. Colonel Mike Peck mirrors my disgust for the political bunglers. He was chief of the POW-MIA Office, a division of the Defense Intelligence Agency (DIA), a position he resigned from because of principle.

"The U.S. was not sending active agents into Laos or anywhere else to locate the missing. It took a civilian using his own resources to do what the government wouldn't. I always felt that we had abandoned a number of our men in Southeast Asia for political expediency, and no one in Washington was willing to admit it. 'Peace with Honor and a Nobel Prize,'" Peck said.

"It was not until later," he continued, "that I discovered that the real mission of the organization was to bury the POW's and the missing, along with the entire issue—quite literally. I was continually shocked and dismayed at what I witnessed, and could not believe the naysaying and obfuscation that was the organization's norm. A number of politicos in Washington were responsible for the fact that not everyone came home, and they were hiding behind phony organizations infiltrated by insiders, the POW-MIA flags, the postage stamps and insincere commemoratives," Peck said.

12

SOF *IS SUCKED INTO THE HUNT*

In April '81, after visiting George Brooks of the League of Families at my own expense (but of course that was the reason Monaghan called me), and convincing him to no longer fund Gritz, the now former Gritz loyalists and I returned to Boulder to hash out some plans for launching our own POW mission.

Once word got around that *SOF* was heavily involved in the Yellow Rain and the POW search, Bill Guthrie, who was with *SOF* wearing many hats from 1981–86, fielded a parade of resistance movement chiefs who came begging.

"The POW search was something that needed to be done and finished at the time, and you and Perot were the only people with money who had the balls for it," Guthrie said.

"Your involvement in Laos drew to the office a parade of people who either represented resistance movements, many of which we'd never heard of, or in some cases more frauds who wanted money for nonexistent campaigns. We were approached by Karen splinter organizations, other Burmese tribes, and Armenian and Kurdish organizations, largely because of the fame of the POW and Yellow Rain searches." Guthrie had to help ward off the stampede while he held down the fort.

GENERAL VANG PAO COMES ON BOARD

After making a whirlwind estimate of the situation, I flew to Washington,

DC with a couple of my guys to brief Rear Admiral Allan G. Paulson, the director of the POW/MIA office of the Inter-Agency Group, and the Deputy Director of Collection Management of the Defense Intelligence Agency (DIA) of the *SOF* teams' research and buy-out plan.

Berent had first been the assistant air attaché, then the air attaché at the American Embassy, Phnom Penh, Cambodia in the '70s. Through some of his contacts, he introduced me to Admiral Paulson.

"I was at the initial meetings with Paulson and I remember him being an absolutely superb guy, and I remember also that he was kind enough to give you a Pentagon china cup so you could spit your chewing tobacco into it," Berent recalled wryly.

Admiral Paulsen gave me the green light to hunt for American POWs in Laos. He never promised U.S. Government support, but he did promise to provide identifying questions to ask the POWs to vet them once we had a list of names.

"I think that you should contact General Vang Pao, the Hmong general who led the CIA-sponsored war against the communists in Laos. Hopefully he can provide a source of reliable intelligence through his anti-communist contacts still deep inside Laos," Paulson suggested.

The General and his Laotian entourage, including bodyguards, were eager to come to Boulder. I had already met the General when I invited him to be a banquet speaker at the 1st *SOF* Convention in Columbia, Missouri a few months earlier in September 1980. His visit to Boulder clinched the *SOF* mission to search for POW/MIAs.

"Gentlemen," the small, dark, round-faced, tough-as-nails General began, as he leaned forward on my black phony leather rocker in my den and stared at me with his steely black eyes. I braced myself. His words were more of a calculated command than a request. "I realize what you really want is information about your missing comrades in Southeast Asia. I can help to provide such aid. But I want the following before my side can give you anything, and what I want will have to be in three phases. First, I want the issue of chemical and biological warfare against my people in Laos by the Vietnamese brought before the United Nations. Second, in exchange, I will have my organization turn over 17 sets of remains of missing Americans to you. Third, you must assist me in arming and equipping a battalion of my men in Laos who, in turn, will form the nucleus of a fighting force which will eventually throw the Vietnamese out of Laos."

He drove a tough if not impossible bargain, but the General was the one to open the door for getting *SOF* firmly established in Southeast Asia. Rather than antagonize him by asking why he had not turned over the remains of the Americans to the U.S., the country that supported his "Secret War" efforts and had given him asylum, I decided to play.

Aha, he had given me a tall order, but at what cost? *SOF* could hardly convince the world that a Laotian Revolution was feasible—or fund the purchase of arms for a battalion to overthrow the commies in Laos and eject the Vietnamese occupiers. But his was the best offer on the table thus far.

"I will agree to your conditions, but I have to have hardcore proof of the POWs," I told the General, my mind swiftly stacking up the cost in terms of time, manpower and funds for the multi-faceted mission.

"I can do that," the wily General said as he handed Zabitosky a letter of introduction to one of his agents in Santa Ana, California.

Zabitosky and Bleacher flew to the west coast to meet with Gen. Vang Pao's agent on 13 April 1981. The General's contact produced a letter to be given to the chief of staff of the Laotian resistance forces covertly headquartered in a Lao refugee camp on the Thai-Laotian border. *SOF* staffer Jim Coyne, rugged, bearded, mocking blue-eyed, a Huey door gunner in Nam and former 12-year National Geographic photographer, joined them in LA. The three flew to Bangkok on 26 April 1981.

INTO THE WILDS OF THE GOLDEN TRIANGLE

For the next two years *SOF* POW/MIA teams journeyed to the mysterious and treacherous environs of the "Golden Triangle" of Thailand, Laos and Burma, and into the wild, foggy hills of communist-occupied Laos. Our Lao sources confirmed sightings of some of the 534 missing Americans, mainly air crewmen who had been shot down over Laos and never seen or heard from again.

The hard core *SOF* team, Zabitosky, Coyne and Tom Reisinger, a former SF medic, all of them seasoned Nam vets and familiar with the smoggy, over-populated city of Bangkok which had been a popular playground for those on R&R during the war, knocked around the old familiar city for days.

Bangkok, like many other Southeast Asian cities, was a melting pot for Chinese, Indians and other nationalities. It very much had a European influence, although Thailand had escaped European colonialism. Thailand had become a neutral playing field with seaside resorts and cosmopolitan shopping districts that catered to worldly tourists and other fat cats. East met West in Bangkok, where hit men, gold, drug and weapons traffickers and other nefarious characters met and plotted. The streets were lined with small ethnic shops and upscale designer boutiques. Fashionable men and women drove or shoved each other through the streets or were driven in rickety carts pedaled by humans in baggy pants and sandals. The smell of roasting coffee and chickens hanging in the marketplaces, rotting, mixed with the scents of exotic spices and freshly cooked hot Thai cuisine floating out from the many restaurants that lined the streets and backed up into alleyways. Thailand was the "Land of Smiles," not counting the periodic palace coups by the military, and the Thais were outwardly quiet and gentle. That reputation is all well and good as long as you'd never dealt with them, and even then learned to watch your back.

Whether in smoky bars on the infamous Pat Pong Street in Bangkok, where for many years clandestine legitimate and illicit rendezvous and plans had been hatched, at the Bangkok Foreign Press Club, or through the "old boy" network, the *SOF* team established contacts. Some of those included U.S. Embassy officials and various indigenous personnel. Others were Americans in the expat community in Thailand up to one shenanigan or another.

Having gotten as much as they could of the POW scoop in Bangkok, the *SOF* team slipped up north toward the Laotian border to meet up with Vang Pao's contacts. They reported to home base after getting a feel for the lay of the land and for the dicey political situation that had changed considerably in the decade since the war had ended.

"Brown, this mission is not going to go far unless we have a launching pad in Laos, right across from the Thai border in the north. From there, we can conduct training of local Lao United Liberation Front (LULF) troops. Recon teams and intelligence agents could infiltrate Laos to search for U.S. POW/MIAs or provide security if a cash-for-POWs plan came through," they told me.

"What about crossing the Thai-Laotian border?" I asked.

Coyne said, "No country likes folks crisscrossing its border without so much as a greeting to immigration control and customs. But there are places in the world where governments can't do much about it. Laos and along the Mekong River are obviously one of those places.

"We've laid contingency plans to make a wild dash back into Thailand from Laos and a quick lawyering-up in case hostile Americans or Thai officials pursue us. Just imagine vastly outnumbered Thai border security forces and their Kuomintang Chinese irregulars trading fire with totally pissed-off Vietnamese and/or Pathet Lao chasing after our "round eye" scalps. Large-scale hostilities heating up between the two Southeast Asian rivals would put the names of *SOF*ers at the top of the American Embassy's bad guy list. Or worse yet, we could end up in some rat infested Thai or Lao slam, or spend a few seconds against a cold concrete wall facing a firing squad." The team, concerned about our shifting Thai and American "allies," sounded the alarm regarding the shaky political landscape.

I gave their fears due thought—for a couple of seconds. After all, the two tall, blue eyed, English-only-speaking Vikings who towered over the natives, TR and Coyne, and the mean and tough-looking, dagger-eyed Zabitosky, conducting all sorts of irregular activities made a very visible target among the smaller even more dark-complexioned locals.

"Continue to march," I said. "Build the bloody camp. I'll finance it myself."

The Thai officials, who played their cards close to their vests, never openly approved of our highly trafficked safe house in Chiang Mai or our trekking across their border with arms and supplies; but they did not stop us either. That is, until five months later when, out of the blue, they ordered us to shut our operation down.

The intervening five months, until we were ordered to shut down the site, were some of the most eventful in the magazine's history. One bizarre event after the other kept our heads spinning. We found ourselves so entrenched in other projects that we kept on operating in Thailand for the next two years. We recruited 125 armed ethnic tribesmen to man the camp we established and called "Liberty City" (FOB '81), the only permanent anti-communist installation in Laos in the early '80s.

Now some good intentions are just that, while others cost a bundle, and this one almost sucked me dry. I doled out at least $250,000 (probably

$680,000 in today's currency) from *SOF* coffers to fund the command center in Laos and other POW/MIA related projects. The various cunning actors whose support I needed demanded that we operate on several fronts before they would cooperate.

Remember, to get General Vang Pao on board, we had to produce a sample of Yellow Rain, a chemical warfare agent allegedly being used against the Hmong. His second condition was to train a local hostage rescue force. We were strong-armed by a former CIA agent in Thailand into helping support a Laotian revolutionary movement in exchange for a hoped-for recovery of American prisoners. But it got better. We planned to take down an opium lab.

I dished out over $72,000 alone just to William Young, the American mastermind of a Laotian Resistance revolution plot, a clever former CIA operative and a man of great intrigue. Little did I know that he was a Lahu tribesman in a white man's body. Skilled in the Thai/Lao way, he used bribes, cut underhanded deals, and, knowing just how to trigger my lust for adventure, kept me hanging on with fantastic plots so he could keep the purse strings open. But as you will soon see, he wasn't the only villain. Thailand and Laos were full of them, both native and Western. I admit that I was completely seduced by the adrenalin-raising adventures and missions impossible. But first let me get to the search for Yellow Rain, the first hoop we had to jump through in order to meet General Vang Pao's bargaining conditions.

13

YELLOW DEATH IN LAOS

At the same time that plans were being laid for Liberty City, in an ongoing saga that lasted half a year, we had gone in search of samples of Yellow Rain.

On 4 May, soon after arriving in Thailand, the *SOF* team went to Laos to visit a refugee camp. Through General Vang Pao's contacts, they were introduced to and interviewed individuals who claimed that they had suffered from Vietnamese attacks of Yellow Rain.

There they hit pay dirt.

"We happened on Soua Lee Vang by chance, while gathering background for a story on the state of the Lao resistance, and asked about refugee reports of the use of gas. "Absolutely! Would you like to talk to a man who has just come out of one of the gassed areas inside Laos?" our contact asked.

"But of course!" Coyne said.

The following story that Soua Lee Vang told *SOF*, if true, would confirm our worst fears.

An old biplane, flying high and slow, approached the village on Ban Paa Ngum mountaintop. Without warning, in one loud, low pass over the village the previous October, a wide trail of yellow mist poured from the wings and whipped into the slipstream, then fell quietly over the village center. Villagers, including Soua Lee Vang, convulsed coughing until they collapsed from severe abdominal cramps and spasms, many dying horribly in their own blood and voided bowels. They bled from their eyes and ears, and profusely from the nose and mouth. Men, women, children and animals died one by one, and the only sounds were of weeping and the brush of wind on the yellow covered leaves.

With the aid of an old Department of Defense escape-and-evasion map of Laos that our source had stashed with his few belongings from "the old days," he began the trek toward Thailand. He meticulously noted the co-ordinates of the attack on Ban Paa Ngum, including date, time, type of aircraft, direction and results: 21 people dead, approximately 500 people critically ill with vomiting and bloody stools, approximately 400 people with skin disease, blisters or spreading infections.

Then, on 2 April 1981, he witnessed another attack, this time on the village of Ban Thong Hak. A MiG-17 appeared suddenly out of the sun to the northwest and dropped its lethal cargo of chemicals on the defenseless Hmong men, women and children: a brownish cloud in which Soua Lee Vang believed 24 people died horribly, and 47 became desperately ill.

With the chemical sample wrapped in plastic and tape, he reached the Ban Vanai Refugee Center in Thailand, six grueling days later.

At least five similar gassings occurred since the previous October in the areas he had been in. Hundreds, even thousands, had died. *Soldier of Fortune* had heard rumors for some time that the Soviets, and their client states, had been routinely and systematically employing chemical, and possibly biological, weapons in Laos, Afghanistan and Cambodia, but had been unable to prove it. The agent or agents used were unknown and elusive, and gassings always occurred deep within hostile, virtually inaccessible areas, far from inquisitive observers. The evidence itself seemed to just disappear. All that remained were the results, the accounts from survivors, and blank abandoned areas on the maps.

"Would you like a sample of the chemical?" Soua Lee Vang's words hit us like a sledgehammer.

"Yes, we damn well would like a sample."

Soua Lee Vang soon returned with the small, well-wrapped parcel he had carried so long and so far.

We held back our enthusiasm lest we end up with mud on our face. We had heard from reliable sources that one major Laotian charlatan, General Phoumi Nosavan, who headed U.S.-backed anti-communist military forces in the '60's, had sold Australian ABC-TV what was purported to be a canister of Yellow Rain for $10,000. It looked like a RPG round painted yellow. When the TV station purchased the canister and it was taken to Australia for evaluation, it was found to be an RPG round painted yellow. No Yellow Rain.

All we needed was to be suckered in with a bogus sample. ABC was painted as a victim, whereas *SOF*, already on top of the media outlaw list, would become a liberal laughing stock.

Within 48 hours, Bleacher flew the sample, concealed in a toothpaste tube, to the United States to have it tested in a private laboratory. We were suspicious that an official government agency might not provide an honest analysis, as some government personnel might object to giving *SOF* credit for the find.

A MAJOR COUP FOR SOF!

The private lab proved to be useless, giving us negative results for the sample. We turned the remaining residue over to Congressman Jim Leach's (R-Iowa) office through a third party, who in turn gave it to the appropriate U.S. laboratory where it was analyzed and found to contain a deadly mycotoxin.

When he was in West Berlin, Secretary of State Alexander Haig declared that for the first time the United States "had definite evidence" of the use of chemical weapons in Laos, Afghanistan and Cambodia, which were manufactured by the Soviet Union, one of which was provided by *Soldier of Fortune* magazine.

In November 1981, *SOF* staffer Jim Coyne went on the talk show circuit and testified before the Senate Foreign Relations Committee regarding the Yellow Rain issue. *SOF* itself exposed the use of chemical and biological warfare in March '82 in an article called Yellow Rain. Dismissing the State Department's confirmation that they had obtained four samples, one from *SOF*, the New York Times criticized the State Department in an article, "Too Quick on Yellow Rain." We figured the NYT was just miffed because their reporters were not part of the story. But the people of Laos were suffering and dying for such lack of concern.

At this time, *Soldier of Fortune* magazine offered a $100,000 reward to the first communist pilot to defect to the West in an aircraft with intact samples of Soviet chemical or biological warfare agents. Unfortunately, there were no takers.

We were certain that the use of chemical and biological agents by the Soviet Union and its satellites was an integral part of their strategy and tactics. They would, without hesitation, poison Cambodian refugee-camp water wells inside Thailand, or spray lethal chemicals on Laotian villages, or gas an Afghan town. Fortunately, for reasons unknown, this did not happen.

14

POWs ON OUR MIND

All the while we were on the hunt for Yellow Rain, we were on the lookout for POW's.

The anything goes Bangkok bars, where anyone could buy almost anything, were the favorite hangouts and the most likely places to find expats. A seedy bar did not let us down this time either, when we met the contact who was to open doors for us. Zabitosky, on the prowl for local bimbos, was in a smoky bar in Bangkok one night when an American Indian, Rob ("Mingo," aka "Crazy Horse") Applegate, a former Air Force sergeant who had spent much of the previous year in northeast Thailand, a few kilometers from the Thai border, approached him.

"I hear you are searching for POWs," said Mingo, tall, swarthy and who, with sharp Indian features, never did mince words. This gung-ho, if off-center loner and self-styled soldier-for-hire later smashed a flower vase against Zabitosky's skull during one of what was to become too many brawls between *SOF* members at our Chiang Rai safehouse, or penthouse, in Bangkok.

As Coyne put it, "The Indian Mingo was a crazy mother. At one point he knocked Zabitosky into the fireplace when he came down from Liberty City and wanted to know where all the food and gear they were promised was. Zabitosky was, well, feeling no pain at the time and was with a young waitress he had brought home. Apparently his answers did not satisfy Crazy Horse. I just remember thinking, 'Holy Cow, this is one tough SOB. He just punched a Congressional Medal of Honor recipient into the flaming hot fireplace!'"

"A U.S. embassy official in Thailand gave me information that live POW sightings have been made both in Bangkok and up north in Chiang Rai," Mingo claimed in that smoky bar. "The U.S. government won't pay for the information. But my Lao contacts will love to give you the information if you are willing to help them."

"Help" and "love" in Thai, or Vietnamese for that matter, as we had learned during the war in Nam, translates into "Pay dollars, Sucker."

So that is how we recruited "Mountain Man" Mingo Applegate and his cohorts, Messrs. Buni and Tor, who provided intros to the two alleged eyewitnesses to the target, the Muong Sai POW camp supposedly containing American POW's.

A few days later, Zabitosky, Mingo and Coyne flew to Chiang Rai in northeastern Thailand to meet up with Mingo's resistance contacts. After checking into the Wiang Inn Hotel, the *SOF*ers were introduced to a Mr. "T," who represented himself as the Chief of Staff of the Lao United Liberation Front (LULF), and a Mr. "B," his deputy. "T" headed up the medical section of a refugee camp and "B" was employed as an instructor in a secondary school in Chiang Rai.

"T" claimed that there was overwhelming evidence of a POW/MIA presence. Coincidentally, two recently released prisoners of a communist re-education camp at Muong Sai, Laos, had returned to Thailand where, through the grapevine, they related stories of seeing Caucasian prisoners during their respective confinements.

The team interviewed the two informants on the spot: a Hmong we referred to as "LP," and a Lao, "TS." Their separate accounts were amazingly similar in regard to the information concerning the camp layout.

The Lao claimed that while being taken to a building for interrogation, he saw two roundeyes, both in their late 30s, being escorted to another building within the compound. The Hmong sightings involved two Americans working on an aircraft on the adjoining airstrip. Neither, however, was able to give any clues as to the identities of the Caucasians.

DATE OF INTERVIEW:

16 June 1981; Name: "LP"—a Hmong; Age: 32

"I was taken to Muong Sai on 30 March 1981 where I stayed for 21 days until about the 24th of April. I had been charged with murder of a village headman and was arrested with two others. I am headman of the Hmong resistance and was born in the village of Sang Num Om in Laos.

"Pathet Lao troops accompanied me to Muong Sai. We were awakened at 0600 hours each morning and then cleaned our room. There were about 20 others with me.

"On or about 9 April, I saw two Americans. The first was tall with a beard and less than 50 years of age. He wore dark pants and shirt but had no shoes or hat. The second man was shorter and heavier with no beard. Again, he wore dark pants and shirt and had no shoes or hat.

"Both men were guarded by two Pathet Lao soldiers armed with AK-47s. I was about 10 feet away from the Americans as they walked by on their way out of the camp.

"I was told by friends that more than 20 Americans are held prisoners at Muong Sai along with at least one Thai prisoner.

"The camp where Americans are kept may be called Nado or Nadoo which is known to be a large jail for criminals and high-ranking enemy officers."

DATE OF INTERVIEW:

16 June 1981; Name: "TS"—a Lao; Age: 37

"I was a prisoner in Muong Sai until six months ago. During 1972–73, I worked in Laos under General Vang Pao at his headquarters at Long Tieng. The Pathet Lao felt I needed to be re-educated so they sent me to the prison for five years from 1975 until January 1, 1981. My job was to cut wood. I was released because I had finished the re-indoctrination program.

"On December 26, 1980, I saw two Americans sitting in a truck with about seven Laotian soldiers also in the truck. They were on the way to the airfield where the Americans worked on planes.

"One of the Americans was blond, less than 40 years old, had no beard and wore dark yellow clothes, the shirt having long sleeves. The other man had dark hair and a beard. I could not tell his age."

After several hours spent debriefing each informant, we decided that there was at least some hope that their accounts were accurate, even if the stories contained circumstantial information at best.

We realized that with our limited resources, mounting a raid based on these intriguing but unconfirmed reports would be stupid. It would be foolhardy for us to storm into the camp unless we could be certain that we could affect the safe release and return of all POWs in the compound.

Then, while we were debating back and forth the probability of success of the mission, Mingo, sensing our hesitation, trotted out another Laotian, "Ko Long," an engineer who was supposedly tight with the Pathet Lao governor at, of course, Muong Sai.

Mingo's sidekicks, Tor and Buni, swore this guy was legit. They said Ko could arrange a mass jailbreak should I decide to pay and play along. Ko's buddy, the governor, see, would get his Pathet Lao buddies to ice the NVA guards, then grab the American prisoners, pile 'em into trucks, drive at breakneck, bone-wracking speed to the banks of the Mekong to an agreed upon meeting point, then send them across one at a time as I simultaneously launched bags full of $20,000 U.S. greenbacks for each vetted POW.

Movie plots don't get that wild.

A summary of his interrogation follows:

DATE OF INTERVIEW:

17 June 1981; Name: "Ko"—a Lao; Age: 43; Occupation: Engineer

"I have known the governor of the province in which the POW camp is located for five years and last spoke to him 10 days ago for about 30 minutes. I feel quite certain that for $200,000 U.S., my friend will consider using the Pathet Lao military under his command to rescue by force the 10 to 14 American POWs at Muong Sai. There are approximately 100 Vietnamese at the camp but they will be killed when the camp is attacked. They will use commandeered trucks to drive the 140 kilometers to Pak Bang that will take about two to three hours. When we arrive, it will be necessary to be met at the Thai-Lao border by a representative of yours who would exchange the money for the Americans. Naturally, all involved must be guaranteed political asylum in the United States."

We gave "Ko" instructions to report on the Vietnamese unit designations and strengths at Muong Sai, along with trying to obtain the governor's files on any American hostages or at least their names. "Ko" stated he would depart for Laos on 22 June and return with the information on 4 or 5 July.

If "Ko" was not speaking with a forked tongue, all we had to do was concentrate on working out the details for the exchange, i.e., money to pay for POWs. First, though, we needed the names of the POWs, and once we had the names, we could contact Admiral Paulson who had promised to provide questions that only aircrew members would know the answers to. Paulson was putting his ass on the line as he was going to provide us with highly classified info. Besides, we did not have security clearances. We sure as hell weren't going to pay $200,000 for dirt-bag deserters or dope-heads posing as U.S. POWs.

I again rolled the dice, even though Buni & friend were not exactly batting a thousand: We were still without confirmation from Muong Sai, and receipt of the "Yellow Rain" artillery round and grenade we had heard about was "delayed." However, we figured, all bases should be covered. Thus, with the first $500 installment of *SOF* dough, Ko Long, codenamed "Brave One," set out through the wilds of Laos to follow up on the buy-out possibilities.

I was thrilled with the preliminary findings of the interviews. I decided it was time to go to Thailand myself to scope out the territory and try to figure out what was fact and what was rumor. I arranged for further and more in-depth interviews with our sources in Chiang Rai.

Once there, after two days of discussions, I decided that *SOF*'s financial backing would be thrown behind "T's" organization if it could assist in our POW/MIA mission. We got wind that the leadership of the LULF, who were expecting us to arm them for the revolution after they led us to the POWs, was getting restless because we had not provided them with any funds for the operational base inside Laos.

They threatened to attack the POW camp on their own, hoping to free two or three of the POWs that they then planned to ransom to the U.S. They said they would use the money to fund further operations against the communists.

They made it clear that it was do-or-die time for the mission—either I fund a LULF base inside Laos, or they would launch a half-assed attack on the camp which would, even if successful, jeopardize the POWs. But there were a lot of "ifs." If in fact the POWs were there. If we had a base, it would provide a facility to train a Lao resistance unit which we would use to provide us with security when the money/POW exchange was made at the border — if it was made.

Two hundred thousand dollars in U.S. greenbacks in my hot little hands in the wild ass jungle of the Thai-Lao border meant that I was going to need a company or two of friendly guns. After all, here one could purchase a "hit man" for $10, and a raw gut-wrenching bottle of bad Mekong whiskey thrown in to boot.

Granted, we could purchase automatic weapons on the black market, but trying to purchase and carry a large quantity of M-l6s or AK-47s would undoubtedly irk Thai officialdom, who would in return give us free room and board in the local gray bar hotel.

Reason kicked in. We decided that we would limit our support of the LULF camp to assistance in the design and construction of Liberty City, and the purchase of uniforms, building supplies, tools, boots, webbed gear and food—but no weapons or ammunition.

ROUND-EYE SPIES

Back in Bangkok, before finding a location for the camp and beginning construction of Liberty City, Zabitosky, Jim Coyne and Tom Reisinger, whom I had stationed there full time, had been on hold for several weeks at the zero-star Nana Hotel in Bangkok awaiting back-channel clearances to get our armed reconnaissance off square one.

"The Nana was a palace compared to the hotel that General "Heinie" Aderholt got us," Jim Morris, another *SOF* Special Forces vet who took three AK rounds in Nam, who also joined the team before going to Lebanon, said. "Heinie" had a Thai friend who owned a run-down dump that catered to Pakistanis. Every time you walked into the lobby, it was like walking into a Paki armpit that hadn't seen a bar of soap in a couple of weeks. We were interested in saving money, but this was too much.

That meant that TR, Coyne and Zab were hanging around with a lot of dead time in Bangkok, which triggered a lot of rumors of undercover CIA agents and high hopes of making some quick bucks by the indigenous irregulars signing up for Liberty City. The hype about the CIA round eyes went viral as the weeks and months rolled by.

My protest, "Really guys, we're not CIA!" went nowhere with the gung-ho Doubting Thomas locals. They did not buy the story that some lone crusader, or maniac, would cough up the dough to launch such a costly mission without the support or anointment of Uncle Sam.

The expenses were piling up, and raising $200,000 for the POW exchange would be quite a feat. I needed to try to recruit potential contributors. We heard a lot of flag waving and emotional ranting from several donors who offered to kick in big bucks, but such offers were just hype. The one that still gives me heartburn was from future presidential candidate H. Ross Perot.

George Petire, a former SOG operator in Nam, worked for Perot. He arranged for a meeting between us and the billionaire, or so he thought. Two *SOF*ers and I, at *SOF* expense, hopped a flight to Dallas believing that Perot would be eager to see us after he had given some song and dance about wanting to bring the POWs back home.

Once we arrived, rather than being welcomed into Perot's den, we were ushered off to his Number Two who blew us off, muttering that without "concrete evidence" Mr. Perot would not be endorsing any checks. I should have taken a lesson from the ruthless businessman who had no doubt been fleeced in previous POW efforts, but at the time, I was highly irked because the blowhard bastard had not told me about the "concrete evidence" requirement before I wasted our time and my money.

By 7 July the Thai officials finally approved the construction of Liberty City. Once our ticket to action, "Mr. Dieng," a Thai Border Security operative and our liaison to host country intelligence, showed up, we set about tackling the logistical nightmare of feeding, clothing, equipping and training upwards of the first 90 "enlistees" who had drifted into the campsite. More and more were trickling in every week. Why the Thais "authorized" our operation still falls into the category of unsolved mysteries. We all had our theories, but Coyne's rang as the most likely.

"I believe the Thais were content to allow Liberty City to operate as long as they knew about it and trusted what we were doing. It was in Laos, not Thailand, and beyond the Kuomintang (KMT) picket, so the Thais had nothing to lose from an intel collection standpoint. The Thais' request to close down Liberty City coincided with the on-the-cover *SOF* revelation of it's existence—then it was no longer plausible to deny knowledge of Liberty City and may have spurred the Thais to have us shut it down," Coyne said.

The team could not operate from Bangkok, hundreds of klicks and damn near a 12-hour drive away from the Laotian border in northern Thailand. So we decided that we would set up a safe house in Chaing Rai, just south of the Laotian border where we had interviewed our informants.

Zabitosky, who was running the show, said, "Since we need a secure training camp, I want Reisinger and Mingo to go with me into Laos just over the Thai border and select a site. Coyne, you go back to Bangkok and complete any stories Robert K. Brown wants done, hang loose and be our contact man. We'll set up a safe house here in Chiang Rai and coordinate things in this area using runners to go back and forth between here and our training base in Laos."

With roving correspondent Coyne down in Bangkok, updating and putting the final touches on articles for the magazine, and me shuttling between the continental U.S. (CONUS), South America, Thailand and the Republic of South Africa (dabbling in big game hunting), Zab and TR held down the fort.

The locals watched closely the flurry of activity around the Chiang Rai safe house. No wonder—we found after leasing the place that it had previously been used as a safe house by the Drug Enforcement Administration (DEA)!

Rumors began to fly that Zabitosky and TR were actually DEA agents arranging a bust on a well-known local narcotics kingpin.

As if TR and Zabitosky did not have enough problems, their numero uno problem became a nasty newly received rumor via our Lao intel net, specifically "T," that a Thai narcotics kingpin had selected two specific heads, Zab and TR's to roll: Those attached to the farangs (foreigners) residing in the mansion on Utrakit Road whom he fingered as being new sheriffs in town.

When the boys voiced concern about their impending death, I told them, "Hell, you guys should be paying me! A lotta people would shell out thousands to be where you are right now! Catch ya in a few days. Out."

After "T" reported rumors that the two round eyes were on the drug-syndicate hit list, they put out the word to the locals that drug busts were not in their job descriptions. "T" was successful in his efforts to dispel the rumors, and the hit contract was lifted. A week later a messenger delivered word of their reprieve via messenger to the front door with an apology.

In Chiang Rai, the boys decided that playing cloak and dagger would only serve to attract even more gratuitous attention from already-suspicious neighbors. To add to the intrigue, the two often left for several-day periods to supervise construction of our base in the clouds, Liberty City. During their time spent in town, over meals or while browsing through shops, they let slip their cover: merely journalists interested in churning out magazine pieces on off-the-beaten-path tourist getaways.

LIBERTY CITY

The team refocused on our primary mission at the moment: infiltrating into Laos to the desolate village of Muong Sai, some 160 kilometers distant from our FOB '81, or "Liberty City," where our agents had placed four Americans only several months before.

After an all-night stay at the safe house, Zabitosky, Mingo and TR, along with eleven LULF troops, began the brutal trek into Laos, splashing through rice paddies, up gently rising slopes and then up the rain-slicked rocky trails for the last nine miles into Laos. Most of the walking was up 60-degree inclines with only slight respites from the agonizing climb.

With Mingo remaining behind to oversee things after they chose the site, Zabitosky and TR flew back to Bangkok to meet me and brief me on our A-Team site location. All was agreed upon, and Zabitosky and TR left to supervise construction of Liberty City. Due to possible security problems involving the Thais, Zabitosky recommended that the site's location be moved several kilometers farther into Laos from the original choice. Some of our troops had reconned the area, and its higher ground coupled with its panoramic view of the Mekong River made it a strategic site.

The "old boy" network in Bangkok and up-country also helped us procure the material just as it had helped us with the troops. We were given the OK to hump the supplies into Laos. Our go-to guy, a Mr. Dieng, who was no doubt with Thai intelligence, had secured road clearances enabling free access to and from our Liberty City training site for transport of non-lethal materiel.

TR called then-*SOF* Managing Editor Jim Graves, who wired $18k in greenbacks to a Bangkok bank within 72 hours. It was the first of what was to be far too many more wire transfers.

The team set about purchasing construction supplies for the camp, clearing ground, digging trenches and building bunkers. Zabitosky and

TR shuttled back and forth to Chiang Rai while Mingo remained on-site at Liberty City to supervise construction.

Anticipating a worst-case scenario such as an air strike, the team threw bunkers together as fast as possible and explored a nearby cave complex. FOB 81 was a virtual A-camp minus the claymores and concertina, inside communist Laos. Far from being a symbolic gesture toward publicizing the POW/MIA issue or ink-generating Hollywood-style hype for *Soldier of Fortune*, the outpost, constructed under the on-site supervision of former U.S. Army Special Forces personnel, was a bona fide launch site for a planned armed foray to the Muong Sai prison camp.

I VISIT SOF'S "A" CAMP

Once it was done, time came for me to check out the camp that I had paid for. Tom Reisinger and I were going up to the base in Laos to meet up with Coyne, Zabitosky and troops of the LULF working with us at the base.

We stopped in the mud clearing near a small village of 30 huts on stilts, greeted by curious locals trying to get a peek at the two farangs and two Laotian guides who had come to their village just as the other two farangs had done the week before, armed only with cameras and tape recorders. As the villagers watched and chatted quietly at a distance, our Lao host showed up to join us and we headed toward Laos, some seven kilometers away across the rice fields, and up into the mountains.

The LULF supplied the Lao guides who picked us up in the village at various times. The LULF was established in May 1981, in response to deteriorating economic, social and political conditions within Laos. It hoped to resist further occupation of Laos by Vietnam, and establish a free, independent Laotian state in northwestern Laos. The number of people in the LULF was difficult to estimate—total armed strength was allegedly about 4,000. And I emphasize the word "alleged."

Individual units, although widely dispersed over northwest Laos, were under one command, and came from the hill tribes most common to the region: Hmong, Lao Tung, Lahu, Yao, Liu and Lao. Many of the cadres were veterans of the clandestine war waged by the United States in Laos against the North Vietnamese in the 1950s and 1960s. The ranks were routinely trained, armed and equipped by the People's Republic of China at Szemao in Yunan Province.

General Vang Pao and his contacts gave us the names and introductions to Laotian resistance representatives in Thailand who arranged for the guided trip over the border to a LULF camp. After a hasty briefing outside the village, the LULF guide led us toward the hills.

The villagers stared at us as we headed into their villages armed with cameras and recorders. For the villagers, *SOF* was a ray of hope.

Although TR had made the trek before, he was in a world of hurt as much as I was. Yuppie-style jogging along the Boulder creek and trails as we did daily in Colorado had us thinking that we were totally buff. Did we ever fool ourselves.

All the jogging and macho working out in the office gym had hardly come close to preparing us for this straight-up mountain trek. We were hurting big time as we sucked in oxygen. Only Mingo, the wiry Indian in good enough shape for trekking across the globe, and several years our junior, was keeping pace with our 110-pound escorts. Mingo got great pleasure out of showing up out-of-shape, ex-Special Forces veterans. More than once we yelled for the guide, who was walking point, to slow down, but all we got was a ration of shit about not being in shape. I could only reply, "You've been here playing games for a year asshole; we've only just arrived."

Meantime we would sigh with relief at the sight of a Hmong village coming into view. The naked kids, animals and curious villagers watched with amusement as we dragged ass into the village headman's house for a welcome break. The syrupy sweet tea so common in Asia revived my sagging energy. After an hour's break, we would head off again.

Hours seemed like days, until finally we arrived at a Thai outpost, a "Shangri-La" set upon a mountaintop we had sighted through a surreal field of clouds. Our prearranged hosts greeted us warmly, and after more sweet tea we departed on the last leg of our forced march.

Curious villagers on their way to the Thai rice fields scattered quietly out of our path as our small group passed. Jim Coyne, who had paved the way for my visit, had warned me about the grueling nine-hour trip, but his warnings, which I dismissed, were coming back to haunt me as I hiked straight up in the back-busting trek which was worse than the killer technical climb I made up Mount Rainier in 1966.

Our wiry little Hmong guides, with legs like coiled steel springs, literally jogged up the steep trails, carrying all our gear without difficulty as we grunted and panted behind them, trying to keep up. We crossed the last deep stream and kept climbing. After another hour of straight-up climbing, we stopped for a 15-minute break and looked up at the increasingly rugged hills. By the third hour we had to stop every 25 meters so that we would not keel over.

To our right, two klicks off the trail, was a CPT (Communist Party Thailand) redoubt, under daily pressure from the Thai Air Force and Border Patrol Police, but we were told that it was not a problem. The CPT wanted to join with the Lao resistance to fight the Vietnamese!

KMT (Kuomintang) soldiers, stationed in strategic locations, glared at us suspiciously. When the Chinese communists drove Chiang Kai-shek out of China in 1949, portions of his army retreated southwestward into Laos, Thailand and Burma. The KMT forces were used by the Thais in some places as border pickets. They provided border security where it would be impractical, or impossible, to garrison regular Thai troops. In return, the KMT was provided limited support, resupply and medical evacuation capabilities.

The KMT guards looked us up and down but never threatened us. Anxious to see any form of life in this Godforsaken country, they offered us cloudy home-made, sweet spiced-ginger whiskey from a gallon jug. We rudely grabbed the welcome brew. The local proverb, "The more Mekong whiskey you drink, the more languages you speak," made a lot of sense just then.

Crossing the Laotian "border fence," a single strand of rusty barbed wire, into the eerie, wild, lawless hills was a creepy, anti-climactic nonevent. The whiskey had worn off and my head was pounding. My legs were numb from endless miles of slipping and falling down in the mud after a downpour; grasping for a tree branch then grasping for the next so as not to go sliding backwards down the steep slopes.

TR and our wiry legged guides were only alive because I needed both of them. Besides, I did not have the energy to waste TR with his annoying chant, "Time flies when you are having fun." Its funny how such statements can stick in your mind for years. I eased the pain by fantasizing about filling out the pink slips for those sitting back at the office who called the treks into Laos "boy scout hikes."

But we had to make it another klick in the dusk to get to the camp at the mountain elevation of 5,000 feet.

Coyne had given the LULF heads up that I was making the journey to meet the anxious freedom fighters who would not give up until they had their independent Laos. Word had spread fast, and several tribal leaders and chiefs were waiting for me when I arrived. They were standing at attention beneath the *Soldier of Fortune* "Death to Tyrants" banner flapping there in the hills of Laos.

"I swear, with your appearance, the sun came out for the first time in weeks," Coyne said.

The LULF troops raised their flag, the ancient symbol of Laos: three white elephants co-mingled on a field of red. The tribesmen were convinced we were representing the U.S. government and nothing we could say would disabuse them of this belief.

From dawn until nightfall, we had been humping straight up the mountains in the constant mist and fog, but we were far too achy and tired to sleep. As one man who had been to Laos many times before told us, "If you sleep in Laos, you should always be half awake."

Our superman hosts, who probably never slept, awakened us in the "guest suite" as soon as we dozed off in feverish sleep, bringing us tea before the foggy sunup with smiles in response to our groans and moans. These men made that trek constantly without a whimper, some of them daily, down and up for needed supplies or to relay information. Finally with daybreak, I could see the camp I had funded and the lay of the land. The "cooks" offered us the traditional stomach-ripping bowl of boiled rice covered with hot red peppers for breakfast.

I could see the camp more clearly in the daylight. It was built of bamboo and thatch and it sat on high ground above the Mekong River. Zigzag trenches linked defensive bunkers built to ring the compound in case the communist Pathet Lao decided to foreclose on our lease.

It reminded the group of us, all Nam vets, of some of the Special Forces "A" camps in Nam. The four or five hootchs (small thatched huts) in the main area were all dug into the ground with dirt banked up against the sides. Log bunkers were placed with good fields of fire and heavily fortified with dirt and rock.

An estimated 20 people lived within the main area, while other LULF troops scattered in nearby sites in the mountains. The troops had a miscellany of weapons: M-2 carbines, a few M-16s, the rest AK-47s or Chinese Model 56s, but all of them were well-oiled and maintained. Ammunition and magazines were in short supply. Many men had only one or two magazines full of ammunition with an additional few rounds loose in their pockets.

The Vietnamese had a nearby garrison of approximately 200 men, 12 klicks away, but they kept to themselves. When the team first got to the camp, they were told how the easternmost LULF outpost had surprised a six-man Vietnamese recon team a quarter klick away the previous week. But the Vietnamese, once they realized they'd been spotted, faded away into the tall grass because the villagers had been spreading the rumor that there were four battalions at the camp. It's funny how rumors would fly through those hills devoid of cyber space and electronics. When the LULF troops went to investigate further, they found skid marks all the way down the hill where the Vietnamese had tried to break their rapid retreat with their heels.

The LULF troops spoke virtually no English, and the interpreter they provided didn't speak much better. The tough little warriors did not have much military training, but they had a common enemy, the Vietnamese who occupied their homeland, and they wanted blood. What held them back was the shortage of enough weapons and ammo to make their fight a success. They mainly engaged when surprised by the bad guys on the trails or in the villages where they went to resupply themselves.

Occasionally, a runner would charge in with news that a 20-man Pathet Lao patrol was going from village-to-village about two klicks below the camp asking questions about the farangs. The camp would immediately go on alert. Earlier, one courier ran into the camp from the lowest outpost that was closest to the patrol: six of the Pathet Lao had pistols, four had binoculars, one a rocket-propelled grenade launcher (RPG-2), and the rest AKs.

The first training we provided our people consisted of basic hand and arm signals, and a straight-from-the-textbook version of a squad-size immediate-action breaking contact drill.

Some of the men had been to China for training, but the training didn't amount to much, although the Chinese had provided equipment and uniforms, including brand new Type-56s (AKs) and a basic load of stick grenades. Each small squad was also issued an RPG-2 and as many rockets as they could carry. Uniforms and webbed gear were basic Chinese-issue green with leg wrappings that looked no different than the uniforms of the Pathet Lao or Vietnamese in Laos, who wore the same soft, short-billed cap as the Chinese, but with a shiny black brim and trim.

DIA JOINS THE SEARCH—HALF-ASSED

The U.S. Defense Intelligence Agency had been collecting various reports of American POWs allegedly sighted throughout Vietnam and Laos. A report of the Senate Select Committee on POW-MIA Affairs, issued several months after Admiral Paulson gave me the go-ahead and our mission was in full force in Southeast Asia, summed up some of *SOF*'s activities:

"On 30 July, 1981, Admiral Paulson requested the appropriate DIA element to research the Lao resistance forces to help answer the question . . . as to whether it may be more profitable (strictly in terms of accounting for U.S. MIAs) for the U.S. to deal with the Lao resistance forces or attempt to continue to secure a full accounting from the Lao People's Democratic Republic (LPDR)."

The assessment was also to consider the possibility of penetration by Lao or Vietnamese hostile intelligence services or even allied resistance groups such as those under former South Vietnamese Army Colonel Vo Dai Ton. DIA favored two major resistance groups: the Hmong in northern Laos and the Lao People's United National Liberation Front headed by Phoumi Nosovan.

The Agency Report went on to say: "League employees and the Joint Casualty Resolution Center (JCRC) were not the only persons searching for POW/MIA information from Laos and Thailand. Early in August 1981, staff members of *Soldier of Fortune* magazine contacted the Joint Casualty Resolution Center (JCRC) coincidental with *SOF*'s own effort to establish Camp Liberty, a base for Chinese-trained Hmong resistance forces in northern Laos. During this period, *SOF* had contacts from time-to-time with the various private Americans operating in Thailand and collecting POW/MIA information. *SOF* also learned quickly that a major POW/MIA information peddler, Phoumi Nosovan, operated from the area of Nakhon Phanom, Thailand, and that he was notoriously unreliable and someone to avoid."

We were happy to be of service to the U.S. Defense Intelligence Agency, and flattered that they found *SOF*'s findings useful. But I still think they might have ponied up some funding of their own for the project rather than having it come from my own pocket.

KMT WANTS TO GET ON BOARD

Meanwhile, back in Thailand during the weeks that followed, various Lao tribal leaders, many of whom had been at odds before, held one conference after the other. Zabitosky eventually cemented together a tight coalition of tribes including the Hmong, Lao, LaoTseung and Yao.

As our band of tattered musketeers continued to beef up defenses and living quarters up at Liberty City, disturbing word arrived that several hundred Yao tribesmen from farther north wanted to hook up with us for a share of rice and beans and a crack at the North Vietnamese.

Then came news of a force of some 340 Kuomintang, which was offering back-up support for our thrust into Laos. The KMT commander was chomping at the bit to engage with the Vietnamese just across the Mekong. He promised that his guys would back us, guns ablazing, should we stumble into deep shit and need to beat feet toward the nearest friendlies.

TR, a Special Forces medic in Nam, had figured that a late-night medical house call to aid one of the KMT commander's ailing NCOs needed to be rewarded. So payback was the promise of hundreds of armed allies just in case our activities would trigger a very large war!

I was, at the time of this most gracious but potentially costly-to-*SOF* offer, jetting back to the U.S. from a Chilean cesspool called Tierra del Fuego. TR knew he better squelch the offers of troops that would surely trigger an all-out war. All of this, undoubtedly on Uncle Bob's nickel, meant that within 96 hours I'd be filling out their pink slips.

They did some fast-talking and by the time I touched down at Don Muong International Airport three days later, the offer had been graciously refused.

All this time we had heard not a word from the engineer "Ko" to whom you will recall I had given $500 for his efforts to arrange for the local governor to spring POWs, until the conniving little bastard finally slithered back in late August mouthing just four words: "Governor say not interested." *SOF* was out another $500, a drop in the bucket in the whole scheme of things, but at the time this spoiled drop made a real splash. Had we been conned from the beginning? No doubt.

Because we had tens of thousands of dollars invested in Liberty City, we decided to research the feasibility of having the LULF conduct recon patrols of likely POW sites inside Laos.

Since it looked like we were there for the long run, we all got sick of no-star hotels with big cockroaches. The *SOF* team located a five-bedroom penthouse apartment on Soi 4S, Sukhumvit Road, Bangkok, that they set up for orchestrating the operations up north and over the border. This led to parties with the locals and dignitaries who were delighted to be invited to the *SOF* digs which soon became notorious for lavish bashes.

ENTER THE MISSIONARY'S SON

A few weeks into the construction of Liberty City, a renowned, highly decorated chopper pilot for the DEA, Robert Moberg, who had served several tours in Nam and as a special adviser in Laos, introduced us to William Young. Moberg had been awarded the Distinguished Flying Cross and half a dozen other medals. He was ruggedly handsome, the quintessential tough guy, with thick features and piercing eyes through large glasses who had gone native and made his home in Asia, mainly Thailand in between trips to CONUS, China and the Sudan. Over drinks, Moberg had promised to steal us a chopper if we needed one to extract POW's. He bragged about Young's extensive background in and around "The Golden Triangle." Young's family had been missionaries and he wove tales of hazardous horseback sojourns for God through hell-raising Kuomintang Chinese bastions.

1949 Burma, where Young was born, was as deadly as 1880 Tombstone. Moberg boasted of Young's contacts with local hill tribes and raved about his expertise, which would be very valuable to our mission. Zabitosky was reassured that Young's polygraph exam as well as his CIA agent background checked out positive.

We set up a meeting with Young in Chang Rai. Since we'd never laid eyes on him, we didn't know whether to expect a hell and brimstone nerd with thick horn-rimmed glasses or a swashbuckling plant sent our way from "Spook Central." TR fretted, "Young could be a burnout who'd bang the table as he embellished war stories or bitch about how the world had screwed him around."

The tall, handsome, by now portly American in his 50's, who stood out in stark contrast to the locals, looked more like a professor than a renowned anti-communist fighter. He climbed out of his late-model pick-up truck accompanied by his local much-too-young girlfriend, "Lek." The *SOF*ers inhaled a fair amount of cocktails while the former hard drinking Young, who was on the wagon, abstained.

As the night wore on and our defenses with it, he started looking more and more like a perfect match for *SOF*. A master storyteller, he told us of a run-in he'd had with his CIA superior, a well-known backstabber ever eager to bolster his career. Young, flying high as a kite in 1967 during the Vietnam War, paid the SOB a visit and thoroughly kicked his ass. His CIA gig was over. "You'll never work in this town again," he was told. Needless to say, he sounded like our type of guy.

He went freelance after leaving the agency, picking up investigative assignments whenever he scored gigs, which was often, since he built up a smashingly respectable reputation. His low key and very polite manner sucked us all in, except for Zabitosky, who thought that anyone who didn't take a drink or light up a cigarette had two strikes against them.

We plotted into the wee hours how to photo recon Muong Sai. With our already wild imaginations enhanced by the booze, we concocted guidelines for future recruitment and training of our Liberty City contingent. Our initial major worry was that the possibility of initiating armed hostilities between Thailand and Laos, which would no doubt drag Vietnam into the fray, was real. It was *SOF's* "Super Bowl," as TR said, and I wanted a tight, disciplined unit without a bunch of Rambos getting creative and slipping across the Mekong to settle personal scores.

I would make a site recon to Muong Sai, Laos with 30 of our Liberty City troops, TR, Zabitosky, Coyne and Mingo. Some of the team members had repeatedly slogged their way up the eerie, cloud-caped mountains of northern Laos, passing through KMT Chinese strongholds amid late-night thunderstorms—locales where white faces just weren't seen.

If we could confirm American POWs in Muong Sai, we assumed, some heavy cash and favors could be called in to finance a snatch op.

Young was especially intrigued by the pan-tribal coalition Zabitosky had organized, claiming that it would score points for some quid pro quo as the mission progressed.

The multi-lingual Young, who spoke four dialects (Meo, Lu, Lao and Lahu) like a native (which he was), would act as our interpreter for the Laotian tribesmen. He upped the ante by offering to serve as intermediary between *SOF* and the powers that be, both Thai and American, down in Bangkok.Little did I know at the time that that his machinations were slowly tightening the noose around my neck. The U.S. Embassy knew good and well that I was in the country and up to some hanky panky in Chiang Rai and parts north. While the Embassy officials had assured us that all was "no sweat," they had been non-committal regarding our planned recon.

I was so impressed with Young, I ordered him put on the *SOF* payroll. He would be the linchpin to cement the diverse (and oft-times warring) elements of our newly formed Lao "confederation" and dispatch them quickly down the road to Muong Sai.

Zabitosky, via some secretive sources which we never did identify, had formulated the theory that Muong Sai prison might hold a missing Air America crew downed by hostile fire on 27 Dec '71, for which the CIA had offered 2kg of gold per man. Whether Roy Townley, George Ritter, Edward Weissenback and non-Air America pilot Clarence Driver, or four other U.S.-types, were held there remained uncertain. What was crystal clear was the fact that the team faced 30 very rugged days in, and at least 30 out . . . and God knew what in between.

CHINESE "CHECKERS" AND SHAN NASTIES

Days later, Young dropped some disturbing news on us: some at the People's Republic of China Embassy, he said, were salivating over our growing in-place armed force up at Liberty City, and were dancing around the idea of joining hands to do a major number on the mutually despised Vietnamese. Confirmation being impossible, we dismissed it as but the first of Young's over-dramatizations and he never brought it up again.

Young continued (he said) to grease the skids with our Embassy. The officials there were cordial enough but we had to remember that Bo Gritz and his coterie, back in March, had made international news for their stupid and incompetent over-the-border incursion into Laos on a POW rescue attempt of their own.

(When Gritz ran for President on the Populist Party ticket, and conservatives asked why I would not support him, I responded: "Anyone who takes eight people armed with only three semi-automatic Uzis and one .38 caliber revolver into a hostile situation, in this case communist Laos, is not playing with a full deck." No one could argue with this and that quickly ended any argument.)

During the hellstorm that followed, veiled warnings were tossed our way: "If you guys try anything, keep it low-profile. And watch your asses. Because if you get grabbed inside Laos there won't be anyone coming to get you. The American Vice-Consul from Chiang Mai dropped by and gave us the same big-brotherly warnings from on high. Suspiciously, his visit came only days after my in-depth Washington D.C. briefing to Admiral Alan Paulson, mentioned above, after which we were green-lighted to continue with our search for MIAs. Keeping Young on board was seemingly a necessity.

THE CIA AND U.S. EMBASSY: WARNINGS OR MANIPULATIONS?

We'd assumed since entering Thailand that the CIA had been tracking our movements. Since the Gritz missions of misfortune, Embassy-types were a trifle testy over independents roaming at will over Thai turf with the potential of inflicting diplomatic black-eyes or setting off nasty bloodlettings with neighboring dictatorships.

Untrained in diplomatic signal-watching, we were slow to pick up on gentle hints. Young clued us in. He'd heard, invented (or had been spoon-fed) a vicious little rumor that the Shan National Army from over in Burma was planning to off several Americans, and that any round eyes who were venturing north out of Bangkok were apt to get themselves whacked.

Was our Embassy saying, "We have empathy for your objectives, but don't get careless"? Or in other words: "You're on your own boys. We never knew you."

Lt. Colonel Denny Lane, at that time the Army Assistant Military Attaché in Thailand, summed up the official position, maybe:

"I didn't know that you had built a camp inside Laos, let alone why the Thais went along with the project. Apropos the U.S. Government and *SOF*, all that I remember was getting a message saying something to the effect that I was to assist Robert K. Brown and *SOF* but not to get involved. I think that Dick Childress, who was then at the National Security Council, had something to do with that. Also, if I remember correctly, when Bo

Gritz came out with his gaggle, we were told that Dick Childress drove him to the airport. Ergo we never really knew if Gritz had at least tacit backing from the NSC."

With that he reconfirmed why Zabitosky and TR sensed mixed signals at the time. Had the Vice-Consul's visit been to warn us off from bringing a POW back, or to simply alert us to a genuine danger posed by anti-American elements?

Several of our contacts advised us that there were numb nuts in the State Department, Pentagon, CIA and DIA who didn't relish seeing any MIA Americans staggering out of the Laotian bush. Whether diplomatic maneuvering was a higher priority than locating live Americans, we hadn't the foggiest. I suppose they were miffed that former Vietnam vets were attempting to pull off what American intelligence agencies and the American military should have carried out years before.

We became aware that certain elements of State and the intel agencies wanted us to pack our tent, leave Thailand and jet on home. Others we came to know covertly supported our efforts. Still we were always wondering who for sure was on which team.

The chief of the U.S. Office for POW/MIA Affairs in Hanoi for over a decade, Bill Bell, whom I met at the time, confirmed my suspicions. With four tours in Nam, he was a highly decorated Airborne-Ranger. In spite of the fact that he had endured enormous tragedy when he lost his wife and daughter in the first Babylift flight from Vietnam at the end of the war, which crashed, he returned to serve DOD in Thailand.

As Bell put it, "The Ambassador and senior staff appeared to be more concerned that your activities as private citizens might add to the number of missing Americans already listed, rather than effective efforts that might reduce the list. Almost all of the staff on the lower end of the diplomatic totem pole seemed to be supportive of your private efforts and they generally regarded the POW/MIA issue as being one of traditional mom and apple pie variety. I think it would be fair to say that regarding your private recovery efforts, most American expatriates, in both official and unofficial status, were in the bleachers rooting for what they perceived to be 'the good guys.'

"Of course," Bell continued, "there were a few diplomats in the Political Section who were proverbial 'nervous nellies.' These guys were primarily concerned that your activities, especially the cross-border forays from Thailand into Laos involving 'resistance forces,' might result in an even stronger level of animosity than the extant degree of mistrust between Thailand and the paranoid Lao Peoples Democratic Republic.

"Certain American officials stationed at remote camps throughout Thailand were also monitoring your efforts. Sometimes in a place like Thailand there are so many unilateral and bilateral operations being conducted that it is difficult to determine which are private, which are official and which are simply tourism. After all, that is the name of the spy game—use a cover op to hide an even more highly classified op. I recall that in my office we also submitted periodic reports on anyone we became aware of that intruded into our Area of Operations."

So, *SOF* was being watched, monitored, followed and, in all likelihood, infiltrated. But the question remained: who was for and who was against us?

WE LAY PLANS TO GO TO MUONG SAI

I was never sure which team Young was on, other than his own. He seemed to say and do the right things. But we assumed that very few in actuality leave Agency employ or association. We fervently hoped he was one of the good guys, not a career suit who'd kiss off any confirmed POWs to garner points with higher-up puppet masters. At the time we needed him in the fold. If he were somebody's inside man, we'd have to chance it.

Zabitosky repeatedly said that the Agency was highly interested in the Muong Sai area and had conceivably blinked its green lights to Young, allowing us to proceed with our missions.

China was still doing a bit of low-key, saber-rattling in regard to launching their Lao-led insurrection. It was imperative that we get to Muong Sai, obtain confirmation photos of Americans, and put into operation our project to snatch these guys. If we failed, they'd be relocated—or dead. We had seen that the People's Republic was continuing in its attempt to create difficulties for the Vietnamese, especially in Laos, where we did confirm that Col. Bounleuth (who we found was worthless) and a cadre of Laotian troops not under his command then cooling their heels up in Liberty City, had indeed received formal military training near Kunming, China.

To hell with the warning that the PRC was expanding its sphere of influence; it was the thought of any Americans up there twisting in the wind that bothered us.

But meanwhile we were on hold, stuck in the "no sweat" world of Young, whose "Just hang in a bit longer, Bob" routine was wearing thin. But he was hardly the only barracuda circling the good ship *SOF*.

In the meantime our armed troops at Liberty City, many of whom had trekked down from China, were antsy to get on with the recon to Muong Sai. Young dragged on the waiting game, citing diplomatic difficulties in getting his official OK for us to launch the incursion.

With Coyne and I heading back to the U.S. to take care of other business, Zabitosky and TR settled in for the wait; two weeks stretching to nearly three months. Buni and Tor, and then Young, coughed up all sorts of excuses: monsoons, sick relatives, non-cooperative Thai border guards, and on and on.

I returned to Boulder, trying to line up some heavy-bread business-types to whom I was pitching this latest buyout proposal. There was a good deal of interest—but no forthcoming cash.

With Mingo's, Buni's, Tor's and Young's credibility sinking, only their two Muong Sai eyewitnesses could save them from being sacked and thrown off the gravy train. Young, I suppose in desperation, latched onto my support for the "ever-growing"—but thus far invisible, to us at least—Laotian resistance movement, which had now allegedly targeted Sayaboury Province as the kick-off place for their grand offensive.

Young continued to shift focus from the POW effort, saying that now was a bad time to perform our recon, since our Thai hosts were getting cold feet. But while we just waited, why not thrill the Supreme Command and move up the Resistance to front-burner priority?

SHUTDOWN

In October, we heard rumors of a large number of Vietnamese troops moving into locations across the Mekong from Liberty City, which now contained more than 200 LULF freedom fighters.

In November 1981, high-ranking Thai officials pressured us to close the camp. We had no choice but to follow their directives as our only source of supply was across the Thai border.

Questions I had then and now will never be answered. Were "T" and

"B" conning us with POW reports simply to fund their dream of returning to Laos? Were POWs in Muong Sai? Did "Ko" actually know the Pathet Lao governor? And, again, what was the Thai motive in letting us establish Liberty City in the first place?

We put austerity measures into quick effect: Our Chiang Rai safe house was closed and Young was placed in overall command of *SOF*'s operations. Zabitosky was understandably miffed at being replaced. But I thought, at the time, Young possessed the contacts and expertise to permanently weld the tribal coalition into a formidable military force, and keep his ear to the ground for any intelligence on POW intel.

Young assured us that all would again turn butterside-up with the Thais. He insisted on giving our boys up at Liberty City the bad news personally . . . with cash bonuses for their efforts. In light of what we found out about Young later, I question whether any "cash bonuses" were paid to the troops.

The *SOF* team reluctantly folded their tents and headed for the Don Muong Airport to board a JAL 747 to Tokyo's Narita airport. "My thoughts raced back through the previous four months," TR said. "We thought we'd made headway but it had cost more than $125,000 to do it. I should know; I picked up the money. In relative terms, though, we hadn't seen nuttin' yet."

Four time zones away in Chiang Mai, Young was laying out his mother of all schemes: *SOF*'s solo financial takeover of the mysterious Laotian Resistance Movement!

15

DETOURING INTO A LAOTIAN REVOLUTION

I am sure you are wondering how I got bamboozled into wanting to support a Lao revolutionary force and how I allowed my head to spin with a whole roulette wheel of con artists who had been on the take. Right after I got back from Nam, in June 1975, after the communist defeat of South Vietnam and Cambodia, communist-sponsored riots ripped through the center of Vientiane, capital of Laos. U.S. dependents and the USAID (United States Agency for International Development) staff were evacuated.

USAID had provided cover and support for clandestine military operations in which the U.S. had supported since 1961. General Vang Pao, commander of the U.S.-backed army of Hmong tribesmen, who had convinced us of this mission in the *SOF* office in Boulder, a few members of the Laotian royal family were the go-betweens. On 23 August 1975, the commies proclaimed Vientiane a "liberated" city. Kaysone Phoumvihane was named prime minister of the new Lao People's Democratic Republic (LPDR). Kaysone for years had been one of the leaders of Doan 959 (Group 959, the Laotian political infrastructure, which had a forward base in Sam Neua Province, Laos, but was headquartered four kilometers outside Hanoi).

He had his time in the sun, but darkness had descended on the people of Laos. Six years after the fall, when we were in Laos, it was the communist governments of Southeast Asia, particularly those in Laos and Cambodia, that faced growing problems of insurgency. Anti-communist resistance had increased and become more powerful and effective. Although factionalized by regional and ethnic differences, the anti-communist resistance in Laos had the broad-based support of all Lao peoples. The Vietnamese were considered as occupiers, not "friends of the revolution." If a spare tire was stolen in Laos, the people blamed the Vietnamese for it, most often with justification, always with hate. The economy of Laos was a shambles, largely because of the high cost of garrisoning the Vietnamese occupation army. (The Vietnamese did not supply essential foodstuffs to their troops in the field; they were "provided for" by their "hosts.") The baggage of monumental bureaucratic and economic mismanagement, which seems to follow closely behind every communist government, was about to destroy Laos. Defections among lower-ranking Pathet Lao troops were commonplace. Rumors floated that many high-ranking members of the government were looking for ways out, or were under virtual house arrest by their Vietnamese "friends." People were becoming refugees for economic reasons.

PLANS TO TAKE OUT A HEROIN LAB

Bill Young kept TR and me abreast of alleged goings-on within the resistance via convincing cables, phone calls and elaborate MOPSUMS (Monthly Operational Summaries). Wishful thinking ruled, so there was a chance, however slim, that Young now was flying straight. I could not abandon the POWs, so I bit the bullet and continued forwarding monthly pay and expense checks (covering everything from new tires for Bill's pick-up, down to the last bowl of rice and copy of Time).

SOF's other financial obligations were formidable, but Young's fledgling proposal of supporting the Resistance "on a very limited scale" to the tune of only $10,500 monthly (plus, of course, his salary and expenses). For the average 30-day period, I was laying out about $13,500 minimum.

From financing a POW hunt to backing construction of Liberty City and supporting more than 130 armed troops, to this new nest of snakes—the Lao Resistance Movement!

I sensed we were being shafted big time, but I opted to saddle us up for another Southeast Asian go-round. It's hard to pull out of quicksand.

Young was very clever about coming up with some project or ploy to keep his hook in me if I became restless. For instance, on one occasion, he suggested we cross over the border into Burma with some of his Wa tribesman buddies, take out a bunch of druggies running a heroin lab, blow up the lab and turn the dope over to the DEA.

"Of course," he continued in a conspiratorial voice, "We will need to buy half a dozen M-16s on the black market at $600 each."

I gave him $3,000 to get the guns. We never saw the opium lab or the guns. Young should have been writing comic books, and I should have had my head examined. But it did sound like a great way to spend a sunny Sunday afternoon.

But I vetoed Young's next "viable" backburner project percolating in the wings—the backing of a no-lie, sure-thing Wa tribal insurrection over in Burma. "My resources are limited," I told him, "so I trust you'll understand that I can finance only one fucking revolution at a time!"

Wanting to pursue to the nth degree all potential routes to information on living American POWs, I decided we would head to Bangkok for only a short period.

I had, indeed given our loyal Liberty City troops their "discharges," placed Mingo on waivers and had him shipped out of country. I also gave Buni and Tor unceremonious heave-hos before expanding Young's dual role as *SOF* liaison and gentleman schemer.

ZABITOSKY RETURNS

Unbeknownst to us, Fred Zabitosky, no longer on the *SOF* payroll due to downsizing and my being warned that he was on the take, as were most of the players by that time, had returned to Thailand, still in a snit over being replaced by Young, but more than eager to get things to a rolling boil up at what was left of Liberty City. He believed that Young and the Thais had orchestrated its demise.

Zabitosky was still hanging around with Tor, scrounging for hard MIA intel. This time he was being funded by PROJECT FREEDOM, another activist POW/MIA outfit I liked, and to which I from time to time contributed. *SOF* had its show to run and Zabitosky had his, both of us with Muong Sai still very much on our minds.

So again, Zabitosky trekked up to Liberty City, where, surprisingly, 20 to 30 troops were still hanging about. Talk of POW rescues and Lao insurrections was still thick in the air. However, Zab's stay in Thailand was short-lived. After several weeks, Project Freedom opted to stand down his activities due to extreme financial pressures back in CONUS. Out of luck and ready cash, Zabitosky was forced to head home.

Before his departure, TR ran into Zabitosky at the Nana Hotel, where he sprang some new info on us: The previous summer, after I'd departed, Zabitosky arranged/convinced the CIA to send over an interrogator, a "Dave Klaxton," and a polygraph technician who did some studies on the hand-drawn maps produced by our two Lao. According to SR-71 aerial shots of Muong Sai, our witnesses' diagrams were only one building off. If the CIA had already gotten hold of photos of Muong Sai, there had to be something hot up there—and our Laotian eyewitnesses had to have been there.

In addition, the previous winter, while leafing through some files at a member of Project Freedom's New Mexico home, he discovered a 1969 CIA document pertaining to a Pathet Lao prisoner of war camp—at Muong Sai, Laos!

Why Zabitosky didn't drop this on us before, we were not sure. We could only surmise that it was because he was bitter about being replaced as *SOF*'s in-country Project Director.

Zabitosky said that the Agency couldn't get near Muong Sai during the Vietnam War; that it was completely controlled by the Red Chinese and that they had poured people into that vicinity. It was and still might be loaded with high tech communications and radar gear, and maybe some anti-aircraft systems.

The road north of Muong Sai leads into Yunnan Province, PRC, and was constructed completely by the Chinese. For some strange reason, it was put off-limits to American bombers during the war.

There had been one aircraft that went down right at Muong Sai, and the pilot had been a Taiwanese civilian, Chi-Yuen. His name appears on the Alpha Roster where he was listed as Category I (i.e. missing). What Zabitosky could not confirm—but strongly suspected—was that the crash sites within our 1981 area of operations were where aircraft with civilian crews only were downed (i.e. Air America planes).

Was there a possibility that we were secretly being utilized by the Agency to go after some of their missing personnel—something they hadn't been able to do? Klaxton never insinuated that we'd been wasting our efforts in focusing on Muong Sai.

There were six civilian MIAs in the area from three different aircraft, with one being listed as KIABNR (Killed In Action Body Not Recovered). With other crash sites so close to Pak Beng it would make sense to take all prisoners north up the highway to Muong Sai.

The two missing Americans closest to Muong Sai were James Ackley and Clarence Driver, who went down in a C-123-K near Pak Beng on 7 March '73. At a second site another C-123-K crashed; its missing being Roy F. Townley (his daughter, Janet, was part of the Gritz operation) and George L. Ritter. Presumed dead was Edward J. Weissenback. They went down in Sayaboury Province on 27 December '71.

Two Americans were spotted working on Vietnamese or Russian light aircraft that flew into Muong Sai. Whether they were housed at the prisoner compound, or at a holding area three to five kilometers away at a cave complex called Na Do, was undetermined.

Zabitosky said, "I waited for a report that one of those Americans was black (Driver was an African-American) but neither came up with that. Since I'd seen a recent photo purporting to be Roy Townley in a hospital bed, gut feeling told me that the two Americans were Townley and Ritter. See why the Company was so interested in Muong Sai? They were their boys."

But what then of the "4" or "10" or " 18" or "22" other POWs that we heard about in the beginning, which motivated us to push on? We may never know, since Dave Klaxton, if that was his real name, zippered his mouth, secured his wallet in-pocket, and kept his massive ego firmly engaged.

The CIA did not shell out a single dollar to Zabitosky or to our witnesses to even defray personal travel expenses to Chiang Mai, where interrogation sessions were conducted at the Prince Hotel and polygraph exams at the Railway Hotel—all of which Zabitosky was not allowed to attend, Congressional Medal of Honor recipient or not.

Zabitosky, one irate and disenchanted CMH recipient, left Bangkok just days after.

A "BOUN" TO YOUNG'S EFFORTS: I BECOME A MAJOR GENERAL

Young, meanwhile, was polishing up his icing-atop-the-cake scam. One

"Colonel" Bounleuth Saycocie, Young's designated "future savior of Laos," had just returned from China with an alleged bevy of troops aching to utilize their recent training. He laughed off any comparison to Zabitosky's former rabble at Liberty City, crowing that Colonel Bounleuth's guerrillas (yet to be seen) were the only officially ordained and feasible unit to take Sayaboury Province.

Changing Laotian politics was not my main objective. I wanted to liberate some POWs and generating articles for *SOF* (in that order). Sucked in again, I decided to play another round with Young, on the off-chance that supporting Bounleuth would finally pay off. Bounleuth graciously made me an honorary Major General in the LULF. Being the modest soul that I am, I accepted the honor but suggested that the title Colonel would do.

Long time friend, retired Air Force Brigadier General C. "Heinie" Aderholt, paid a visit to Bangkok on a furniture-buying expedition, and again threw in with us for a few days. Heinie, who came just to my shoulders but had a very commanding presence, had an impressive military record. Skeptical of Young, he contacted some in the know, who warned me to be wary. Heinie had been CO of MACTHAI at Nakon Phanom, Thailand. He spent 7 years in S.E. Asia, where he flew 240 combat missions and was one of the founding members of the Air Commandos. He was an expert in unconventional warfare and had received the prestigious Air Commandos' Bull Simons Award.

Young had given us a professional looking "position paper" that looked so credible that it could have been written by the NSC to substantiate his belief that an insurgency was not only imminent but would succeed.

The plan laid out in the paper was that *SOF* was to cough up the seed money for an eventual takeover of Sayaboury Province, Laos, by Young and Bounlueth's LULF. *SOF* would then be positioned to run further forays into remote AOs where American POWs might be held. The paper presented a brilliant spin of optimism. "How can a Lao insurgency have any chance of success? Vietnam has 50 million people with one of the most powerful and experienced armies in the world, with massive support from the Soviets. It would certainly seem that encouraging an insurgency in a small country of 3,500,000 people that is poor and undeveloped and which lost a war against the Vietnamese only seven years ago will only cause more suffering and death. But the Lao insurgency is an established fact that is ongoing and will not cease until it is successful." Translation: "Jump in boys, and don't forget your credit cards."

General Aderholt warned us that Young's whole concept was based on a false assumption. There never was any established Lao insurgency. The Lao did not fight during that war, even with unlimited United States assistance. The mountain Hmong did most of the fighting, but they had not, since 1975, been a factor in any significant resistance because there were no stay-behinds or caches of weapons or resupply. Aderholt's bottom line assessment: "This paper is a well-conceived and concealed plan to get financing."

In other words, I had been conned. But the game wasn't over yet.

Promising that Bounleuth's "army" was just about to conquer Sayaboury Province, Young again had us playing his waiting game while, as always, coming up with one excuse or another to prevent us from actually seeing any of the LULF units and cautioning us against meeting directly any of the key Thai or Laotian players. Bob Moberg was still vouching for Young, as were others, so we checked our attitudes at the door and allowed Bill to deal his hand.

He stuck to his game plan, bringing to Bangkok from Chiang Mai an intel operative named "Sam," and then began chairing lengthy, nightly roundtable meets with the esteemed "Colonel" Bounleuth.

The revolt in Laos was put on "indefinite hold" and, when I questioned him, he said, "No, it's not possible to visit the areas and involved players. That might upset the Thais, you know."

That did it.

As I tend to do before giving anyone their marching papers, I agonized repeatedly about canning Young, while wading through a mountain of bullshit paperwork that Young & Co. had produced. Whatever the guy was, he was an efficient typist whose volumes of imaginative monthly summaries (MOPSUMS), were pouring forth with regularity. But never with tangible proof or second party confirmation.

Though his operation was stalled, Young and his boys' salaries and expenses mounted until I decided, during a late-afternoon parley with TR in the summer of 1982, that Young and cronies would be jettisoned forthwith. And *SOF*'s pricey entanglements in POW and Lao Resistance projects would be re-evaluated.

TR recalled my agony in reviewing the straw that broke the camel's back:

> Brown: Okay, T.R., what've we given Young?
> Reisinger: To date, $72,000 and change.
> Brown (gulps): Okay, what's he given us?
> Reisinger: Close to zip. You brought him aboard to gather MIA Intel. Then . . .
> Brown (blood pressure rises): When I talked of shutting things down he latched onto that bullshit revolt in Laos. My money's accomplished nothing!
> Reisinger: No, Bob, it has.
> Brown (eyebrow arches): Yeah? Enlighten me.
> Reisinger: Just found out from Young himself. Ya know that safe-house you were payin' $275 a month for?
> Brown (eyebrow arches higher along than his blood pressure): Yeah, yeah, up-country somewhere.
> Reisinger (pause): It's his family home . . . the one in Chiang Mai.
> Brown (goes absolutely ballistic): I've been paying that rat bastard's mortgage?

The narcissist Young was outraged that I would be attacking his self-righteous reputation, but I had a final card to play.

Jim Coyne had become friendly with a retired Thai military officer and gently broached the subject of our renowned LULF "Colonel" and was assured a background check would be run. I decided to host a dinner party at my favorite upscale eatery, the "Twin Vikings." Where it got its name, I'll never know because there was nothing "Viking" about it. It was just my favorite because it was the only restaurant in the entire world where the maître'd not only remembered my name but the vintage wine I guzzled. I intended to put an end to this charade. It was arranged that Coyne's contact would unexpectedly show up at the dinner.

The lot of us, including Bob Moberg, listened while Young prattled on about Bounleuth's potential of becoming virtual emperor of Laos, when Coyne's Thai contact showed up. I became livid, blood pressure spiking.

Drinks and dinner were a tad strained but I had Young in a vice. Young and Bounleuth avoided our looks, scarfing down their entrees with feigned gusto.

Our Thai guest confirmed that Bounleuth was an out-and-out fraud. No question.

I remained remarkably self-controlled as I ordered the death knell to the projects and with great relief and some sadness, booked a flight home. TR stayed on for another few months, tying up assorted loose ends including the closing of our Bangkok headquarters.

In August 1982, *SOF*'s Bangkok penthouse closed.

A few years later, Coyne told us of a dinner he had in Bangkok with an American ex-pat very familiar with Young. He recounted the Young affair.

"A real shame," sighed the retired operator. "What he promotes always has its grain of truth but this is expanded upon until, I think, he really starts to believe his own tales; that his projects will succeed if sufficiently nurtured and financed. The man is many things . . . he's just not like us. He's just not an American."

He was right. Young was born in a mission station in Burma when his father was evangelizing the natives, and interestingly enough, was on the CIA payroll while the agency exploited his insider information. Bill Young's grandfather had also served as a missionary to the tribal people. The Lahu tribesmen became Young's people, and the hills where he wandered as a child became his home. Rumor had it that he had married an American beauty and moved to America at one point but could not adjust to the culture and went back in a short time to his tribesmen and his fetish for young girls.

He reportedly commanded a whole army of Lahu warriors during the Vietnam War to fight the communists for the CIA. In 2011, he was found shot to death in his home in Chiang Mai at the age of 76, in a very unnerving scenario that symbolized his conflicted life—a gun in one hand and a crucifix in the other. The tortured soul had eaten his gun, putting an end to whatever misery or shadowy demons that had driven the brilliant, one-time alcoholic CIA agent and womanizing preacher's son over the brink.

Hundreds of tribesmen showed up to mourn their adopted son.

Rest in peace wherever you might have gone, old boy; you gave me one of the wildest rides of my life.

A FINAL WORD FROM THE DIA

I left the mission frustrated. *SOF* continued to investigate and then publish articles on the POW situation for the next decade. In 1990 I met up with Colonel Mike Peck, chief of the POW-MIA Office, a division of the Defense Intelligence Agency, who was as frustrated as I was.

Peck, who had two tours in Nam, characterized by General Henry "The Gunslinger" Emerson as the "best combat officer I have had serve under me," recounted, "I had been a reader of *SOF* from its very beginning, and had followed with great interest the articles that chronicled Brown's efforts to find and rescue American prisoners of war that had not been released after the end of the Vietnam conflict. What truly impressed me, other than the amount of time and effort he personally expended in this search, was the fact that he financed the entire endeavor, which was not cheap, out of his own resources. In addition, he was not afraid to risk life, limb and jail to trek into a lawless and primitive environment to set up a base of operations, recruit his own force, and develop his own intelligence.

"I had been hired to run the office because my predecessor had lost a great deal of credibility with many of the families of the prisoners and the missing, who were clamoring for a real investigation and an honest effort at finding them, while he was feeding them canned platitudes. I was in training to be the Inspector General (IG) of DIA, but I suspect I was given the job as POW-MIA Chief because I was Infantry, had a bunch of combat medals, and looked nice in my uniform, which it was assumed would give me a certain standing with the families. The other heads of the POW-MIA Office had been Military Intelligence types, most of whom had not seen any real combat—unlike all of the prisoners and missing.

"Although new to the office, I was immediately impressed with Robert K. Brown, who knew a great deal more about the issue than I did. I still had an open mind at that point, although throughout my tenure with DIA I had heard nothing but unfavorable things about the Office and 'its mindset to debunk.'

"Bob Brown and I discussed how he had spent his own money attempting to discover the truth while the government was wasting billions of dollars on extraneous projects all over the globe, of dubious value to the American people. We generally agreed that a number of politicos in Washington were responsible for the fact that not everyone came home, and they were hiding behind the phony organizations infiltrated by insiders, the POW-MIA flags, the postage stamps, and insincere commemoratives. What a crock! It was especially disheartening that the Office insiders had nothing but disparaging comments to make about Bob and his selfless efforts, which told me a great deal early in the game, and, of course, since everything was a great secret, there was no chance of passing along any intelligence that might have been helpful to his contacts that were still active in SE Asia. Though new to the job, I was already feeling the pressure to be a good boy and read my carefully prepared scripts. After meeting and talking with Bob Brown, I felt a little like Diogenes sans lantern—I finally found an honest man.

"After I left that dreadful place in disgust, Bob and I continued to work together on the POW-MIA issue. I felt I was successful in prompting a Senate Select Committee to convene (in 1992) in order to investigate the POW-MIA miasma. Quite sadly, its efforts were generally subverted by its chairman, (Senator John Kerry) as well as by a sellout senator (John McCain) who had been a prisoner himself, but who acted like a lawyer for the North Vietnamese. The entire Asian POW-MIA story is a sad one, and, as was stated at the time, the only way to get our prisoners back would be to give the VC what had been promised to them in the 'Peace with Honor' deal, which Congress refused to do, or start the Vietnam War up again, which wasn't going to happen. The Vietnamese eventually got everything they asked for in an interesting twist of events, but it is a 'dead' issue now. 'We'll never forget!' Right."

POSTSCRIPT

While researching *SOF*'s Southeast Asian POW-MIA project for this book, I by chance ran across a fascinating article on the subject that reminded me that our POW investigations and research did not end with *SOF*'s withdrawal of personnel and funds from Thailand and Laos. Quite the contrary. *SOF* continued to research and publish articles on the issue on an irregular basis up to 1997. No doubt more than a couple of dozen top articles combined. *SOF* exposed the phonies, the frauds, and the charlatans while the self-serving government bureaucrats and politicians twiddled their thumbs.

One of the most thought provoking pieces of original research on the subject came from close a friend who wishes to remain anonymous so I'll call him "Cicero."

I met him a couple of decades ago in a short-lived, but spirited bang-bang in a rather dismal part of the world. His credentials, experience and investigative skills as well as his patriotism were beyond question. He exposed how the Russians took some 20-plus selected American aircrew POW's from the North Vietnamese army to Russia where they were brutally interrogated with drugs, overdosed and their bodies cremated. What follows are summaries of the intel he obtained and from whom. Even now, he will not reveal the real identities for fear of reprisal in case some may still be living.

1. A retired Russian officer, "General Pavlovich" provided much of "Cicero's" scoop.

   "In the 20 years I'd been researching this subject, I'd interviewed a dozen similar sources . . . but none had ever been able or willing to provide detailed, firsthand information . . . several Soviet and Warsaw Pact sources had presented compelling evidence that either the KGB and/or the GRU had taken American prisoners from North Vietnamese control . . . for interrogation and eventual execution in the USSR." In his 36 years of military service, he compiled a notebook of stark statistics: incidents of American pilots being airlifted to Moscow for brutal, drug-induced interrogations, then they were overdosed and cremated. Keep in mind the USG had records on around 200 air crew who were known to have survived their shootdowns, but never appeared in the NVA prison system. As an example of the type of info amongst several others, the Russkies were seeking, "Pavlovich" detailed info regarding the U.S. Airforce Low Altitude Bombing System which was a low-level, high-airspeed approach to releasing a battlefield atomic weapon, which he claimed was obtained from a U.S. POW.
2. In May 1989, Soviet Air Force Captain Alexander Zuyev defected to the West in a sophisticated MiG-29. Zuyev, who was a guest at a *SOF* convention, confirmed essentially what "Pavlovich" reported about the atomic weapon delivery. Zuyev died in a small plane accident.
3. "Bill Jones," a former Pentagon official was familiar with the intelligence take of Task Force Russia (TFR), the Defense Department's part of a

> Joint Commission, formed with the Russians to investigate Soviet abductions of American POW's during the Korean and Vietnam Wars. Jones confirmed, saying, "To the best of my knowledge and experience . . . everything that officer ("Pavlovich") told you was true . . . unfortunately, TFR was getting close when everything just dried up in 1993." From the fall of the Soviet empire in '91 to the abortive coup in '93, the files were open. After '93, the Russian files were snapped shut and TFR, courtesy of President Clinton, was folded into another bureaucracy.

When you think about it, why wouldn't the Russians want to interrogate U.S. aircrews on their latest techniques, tactics and equipment? Through the initial efforts of TFR in accessing KGB and GRU files, it was proven that American aircrews were transported, during the Korean War, to Russia. And if the Russkies did it during the Korean War, why would they not do it again during the Vietnam War?

16

SOF *BLASTS THE BALLOON WITH THE ROYAL THAI AIR FORCE*

"We are going to jump the balloon!" Jim Morris and Jim Coyne greeted me as I landed in Bangkok. They must have been bored from all the waiting around to find POWs, joining the Lao Insurgency, or believing promises of raiding an opium lab.

Apparently, Coyne, bored to tears, had been chomping at the bit to jump, and the devilish Morris thought he had finally found a scheme that would make me squirm or at least get me to sponsor a jump. We were all staying in the palatial, seventh floor *SOF* penthouse that overlooked the Chokchai Steak House in loud, smoggy downtown Bangkok.

Morris, who had orchestrated this plan, said he had first become aware of the balloon on the Mitrapab jump at Hat-Vai when a couple of guys from Major Mark Smith's U.S. Special Forces Advisory Team (Korea) showed up wearing a pair of unusual wings.

"They're Thai balloon jumper's wings," Smith told Morris, foot propped on the tailgate of a Royal Thai Air Force C-123.

"It's a system they adopted from the British. The Belgians have one too. They use it like the 280-foot towers at Benning, only it's better and cheaper. They have a barrage balloon on a thousand-foot cable. They winch it down; six jumpers climb in the gondola and hook up. They run it back up to 800 feet and go out on individual tap-outs."

"There's no wind blast. You just float out of the gondola. It takes a 6,000 count to open, which scares the shit out of you, and by the time you open you're at 500 feet, which leaves you with about three seconds to get your reserve deployed if something goes wrong. I've got more than 350 jumps and this was the worst!" said Mark Smith, holder of the Distinguished Service Cross, Silver Star and many other decorations.

"If it bothered Smith that much, it had to have a pucker factor of about 9.6," Morris said.

Coyne and Morris had decided that I had to jump the balloon. Far be it from me to not take a dare, especially one that only maniacs would accept. Besides, if the Crown Prince did it, Robert K Brown would.

When I arrived in Bangkok, Morris, the mastermind of this insanity, called Colonel Rut Komolvanich, G-3 of the Royal Thai Army Special Warfare Center. Colonel Rut was known for catering to the Special Forces old-boy network. He put us on the manifest for the following Wednesday.

I pre-empted that jump for legitimate reasons although they thought I was weaseling out. At the time we were all tied up in hours and days of long-range strategy sessions with spooks, phonies and crooks."We will jump as the last thing before we close out," I said. "We have come too far and worked too hard to take a chance of missing some combat patrol for our Lao Insurgency because of an injury like a broken leg.

We used up two months holding secret meetings in hot, stuffy hotel rooms. We learned a lot, most of which we could not print in the magazine without getting people killed.

Finally, "I'M READY TO JUMP THE BALLOON," Coyne bellowed.

Morris called Colonel Rut.

"Sure," he told him. "Come tomorrow. In the morning we jump the balloon and in the afternoon you can jump C-130 if you want."

Morris signed us up.

The next morning we rented an air-conditioned taxi for the day to drive Coyne, TR, Morris and Kat, his photographer wife and me, all squeezed in the small cab to Lop Buri and back. Coyne, professional photographer, took his video tape recorder so we could show the jump at the convention.

Captain Kitti Patummas, who had just returned from the States where he had attended the Ranger and Special Forces officers' courses, met us

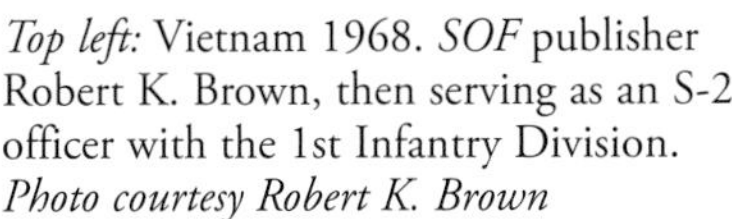

Top left: Vietnam 1968. *SOF* publisher Robert K. Brown, then serving as an S-2 officer with the 1st Infantry Division. *Photo courtesy Robert K. Brown*

Top right: John Paul Vann, examining a MAC SMG as Mitch WerBell looks on. *Photo courtesy Robert K. Brown*

Right: John Paul Vann observing a Special Forces soldier firing an M16 with Sionics suppressor. *Photo courtesy Robert K. Brown*

Captain Brown, Team Leader of A-334, Tong Le Chon, South Vietnam, 5 klicks from the Cambodian border, takes a break with his pet monkey at his camp sometime in 1969. Brown found his long sought position the most challenging but most rewarding time of his life. And special thanks goes to Special Forces Lt. Col. Michael Lanter, who assigned him to that position. *SOF archives*

Photo of RKB at the height of his military career while a Special Forces Team Leader taken in Saigon.

"Special Forces Master Sergeant James Lyons, my Team Sergeant, just back from an operation. In the background, at the rear of the CH-47, is my Intell Sergeant, Sergeant First Class Fletcher Blocksum. Lyons, an exceptional soldier, held my hand through my tour at A-334; took over command when I got hit by mortar fragments. I was blessed with an incredibly outstanding team of NCO's and junior officers. What an exhilarating experience!" *RKB*

Above: Sergeant First Class Robert Bernard, RKB's team medic, with two Montagnards, prior to leaving on an operation from Team A-334, Tong Le Chon, South Vietnam. Bernard patched RKB when he got hit with mortar fragments. *RKB*

Below: RKB on Rhodesian safari in 1976. On left, safari outfitter Grigorio Grasselli, who paid off the terrorists who murdered a Rhodesian farmer on whose land RKB and Donovan were hunting. On right is RKB with his recently deceased Kudu. *SOF archives*

Above: Rhodesian Army personnel and *SOF*'ers pose for a photo during ops before the elections in March 1980 that resulted in terrorist Robert Mugabe being elected. *Top row from left to right:* First three troopers unknown, RKB, with .45 and Ruger Mini-14 he smuggled to Rhodesia, former French Foreign Legionaire Jerry O'Brien, Craig Nunn. *Bottom row from left to right:* Unknown trooper, "Reb" Pierce with MAG machine gun, Major Daryl Winkler, also with Ruger Mini-14 RKB smuggled to Rhodesia, and former Legionaire Yves DeBay who was recently KIA as a correspondent in Syria. *SOF archives*

Left: John Donovan, a Major in the U.S. Special Forces Reserve, on safari with RKB hunting two and four legged game in Rhodesia in 1976. RKB and Donovan could have taken out terrorists that killed a Rhodesian farmer but were thwarted by safari operator Grasselli who was paying off the terrorists. *SOF archives*

Below: Poster that ran in *SOF* that got RKB investigated by the FBI for allegedly violating the Neutrality Act. No law was violated as RKB, ". . . was simply making information available." *SOF* was responsible for the majority of the 450 Americans serving in the Rhodesian military who enlisted. *SOF archives*

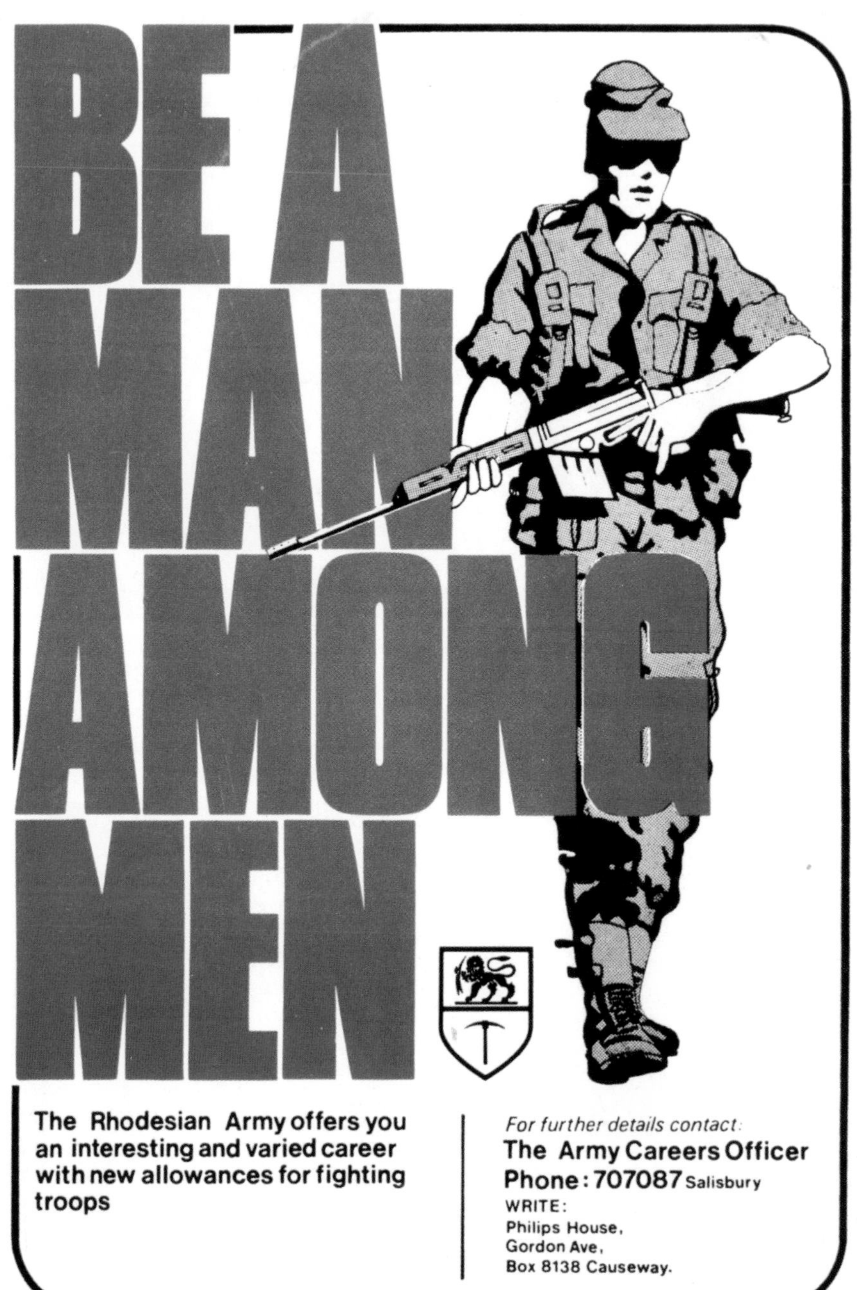

Above: On the hunt in South Africa, 1992, Donovan, on left, and RKB on right link up with agruably the most successful merc in the 20th century, in the middle, Frenchman Bob Denard, who essentially ruled the Comoros Islands for 11 years. *SOF archives*

Below: John Donovan, wearing the first latex Frankenstein mask seen in Rhodesia, in March 1980, terrorized the local help; did not wear it in hotel lobby, concerned he might get shot. *SOF archives*

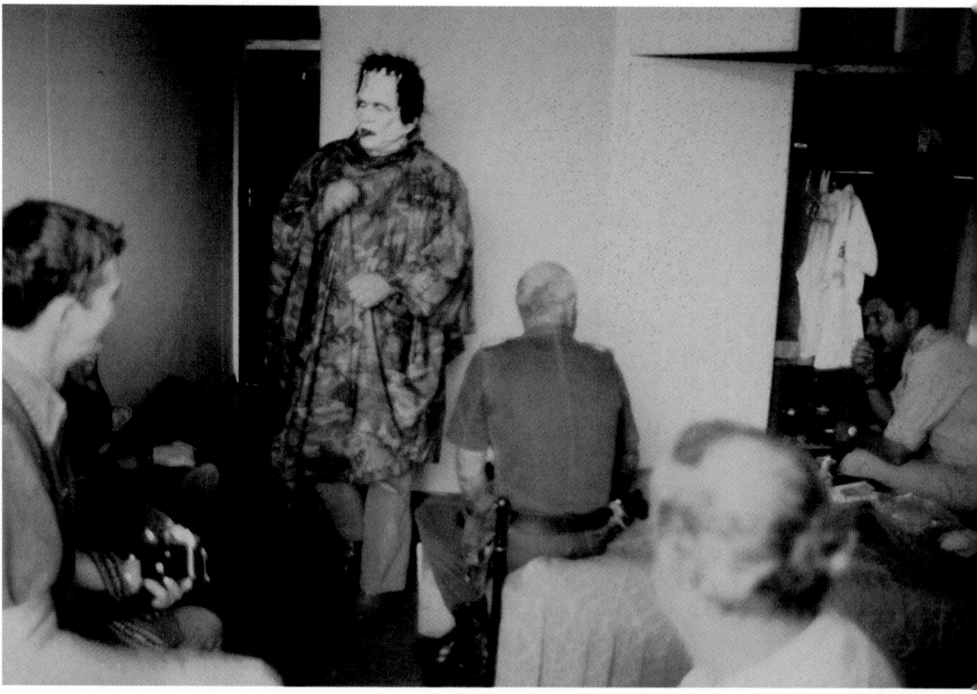

Right: Robert K. Brown is congratulated by Col. Rut Komolvanich, Royal Thai Army Special Forces G-3, after receiving wings. *SOF archives*

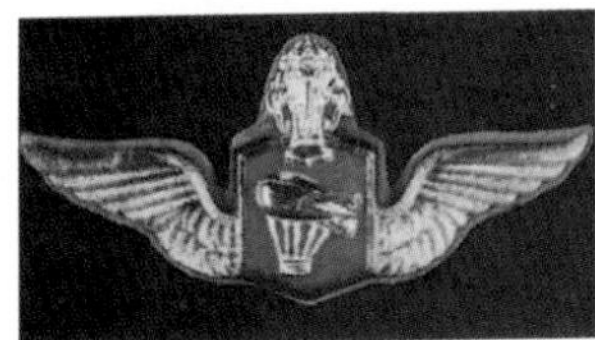

Above: Thai balloon wings awarded to *SOF*ers. *SOF* crew were 13th through 16th foreigners to have jumped the balloon. *SOF archives*

Below: RKB, Green Beret Nam vet and *SOF* reporter Jim Morris, *SOF* staffer and former Nam Green Beret medic Tom Reisinger, prepare for the spookiest jumps of their careers—from a Thai balloon. *SOF archives*

Morris, severely wounded in Nam, reported for *SOF* from many of the world's hotspots; author of the classic military action books . . . "War Story," "Fighting Men," and "The Devil's Secret Name." *Jim Morris archives*

Transporting goods in an open truck across Sarajevo gives new meaning to the term "mean streets." Former Brit Army Leyland truck, still in U.N. white, provided little more than psychological cover for *SOF*'s team of intrepid smugglers. *SOF archives*

Don't shoot at GOFRS fire/rescue workers when they're saving lives, or you may find yourself in a firefight of a different stripe with honcho John Jordan. Jordan and his legendary M1A provide up close and personal protection for rescue workers who have enough to contend with without snipers. *SOF archives*

SOF Publisher Bob Brown (right) helps GOFRS personnel in Sarajevo try on donated Scott Air-Paks, smuggled in for firefighters by *SOF*/RRI team. *Courtesy Phil Gonzalez*

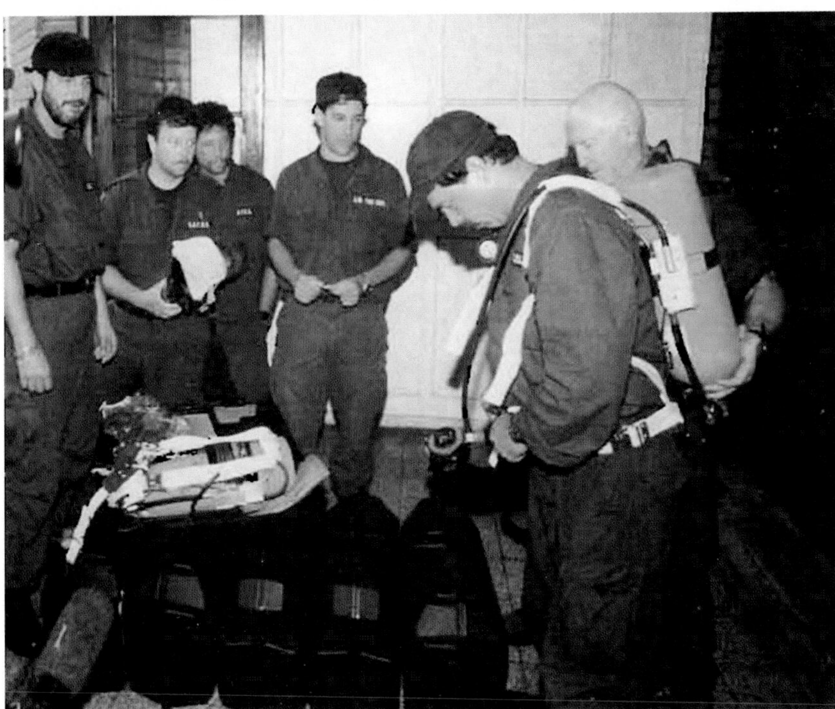

Left: At a guerrilla jungle base in Surinam, *SOF* Assistant Special Projects Director, Derry Gallagher, left, RKB, and Robert MacKenzie pose with a homemade bomb they plan on dropping on a Surnamese patrol boat from a hijacked aircraft. Bomb did not explode. *SOF archives*

Center: RKB poses with guerrilla "bomber." RKB brought in a three-man team of Rhodesian SAS veterans to conduct an assessment of what it would take to overthrow the Surinamese dictatorship. Could be done but *SOF* plotters could not raise the necessary $500,000. *SOF archives*

Below: RKB yuks it up with some French Foreign Legionnaires stationed in French Guiana, along with Derry Gallagher. Legionnaires offered to desert if we could guarantee combat. *SOF archives*

WANTED

**SOVIET Mi-24 "Hind D" ATTACK HELICOPTER
INTACT AND FUNCTIONAL**

— Reward —

$100,000 U.S.

Offered by SOLDIER OF FORTUNE Magazine

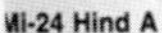

Mi-24 Hind A

Hind D

SIT REP

Soviet-supplied Mi-24 "Hind" attack helicopters are currently being flown by Sandinista pilots and aircrews against Nicaraguan Freedom Fighters. We consider that unwarranted and downright threatening to the struggle for freedom in this hemisphere.

Someone's got to do something before these deadly aircraft are used to extend communist tyranny beyond Nicaraguan borders. That's why we're offering ONE HUNDRED THOUSAND DOLLARS to the first pilot or aircrewman who delivers an Mi-24 into sanctuary in any of the neutral countries bordering Nicaragua.

Reward money will be paid in specified increments to either pilot-aircraft commander or an entire aircrew once the Mi-24 has been surrendered and recovered.

"We are making this offer as a gesture of support for the gallant Nicaraguans who recognize and resist the tyranny of the Sandinista regime. Delivery of a Soviet-supplied Hind helicopter from the hands of the oppressors will be a symbol of solidarity to all the freedom-loving people of Central America."

—Robert K. Brown
Pubisher, SOF

Copies of this poster are available at $3.00 each from SOF, P.O. Box 693, Boulder, CO 80303

ARCH 85 SOLDIER OF FORTUNE 101

SOF offered $100,000 reward to first Sandanista air crew to defect with their MI-24. Lt. Colonel Ollie North offered to come up with an additional $900,000. *SOF archives*

Above: On top of a Mafia-owned Havana hotel in the spring of 1959, from left to right: Commandante William Morgan, one of few American soldiers-of-fortune to fight with Fidel, holds Sterling submachine gun; next is one of his aides holding a Thompson; RKB, who did not fight with but supported the anti-Batista movement, much to his chagrin holds a Thompson, and American Jack Nordeen, whose polio disability did not hold him back, holds a Sten subgun. Morgan was executed for alleged counter-revolutionary activities by firing squad on 11 March 1961. *SOF archives*

Below: Ricardo Alarcon de Quesdada, Cuban Ambassador to the United Nations, condemns *Soldier of Fortune* before the U.N. Security Council, March 29, 1976. Alarcon, along with Somalia, Poland, India and the United Republic of Cameroon, complained about South African "aggression" in Angola. Of course, no mention was made of Cuban or Soviet intervention. *SOF archives*

Above: RKB, on far right, went wheel-to-wheel during the "*Soldier of Fortune*/ Parts Pro Championship," in Atlanta, 28 February 2000. RKB, who took second in his heat because smart ass Jim Fotis blew his engine trying to pass him. RKB insisted all drivers would receive trophies as he was determined to win one. *SOF archives*

Below: Bill Jones, right, played a significant role in RKB's publishing career, as he lent him $800 in 1963 to publish his first book, "150 Questions for a Guerilla" by General Alberto Bayo. Bayo, a Spanish communist, trained Castro's initial invasion force prior to landing in Cuba in December 1956. Left of Jones is Paul Fanshaw and RKB. *Photo courtesy Marty Kufus*

Above: SOF reporter Jim Coyne, left, and RKB hold a press conference detailing their investigation of the use of "yellow rain" by the communists in Laos at the National Press Club in Washington, D.C. *SOF archives*

Below: In March of 1980, Vietnam vet Galen Geer penetrated into Afghanistan longer and farther than any reporter to that time. He brought out the first Russian AK-74 ammunition which was turned over to US intelligence. *SOF archives*

Above: From left to right: Rhodesian Army foreign volunteers Brit Jerry O'Brien, American "Reb" Pierce, *SOF*'er Tom Wilkenson, Major Daryl Winkler, American and former OIC of the Rhodesian Armored Regiment, RKB and *SOF* Art Director Craig Nunn between ops somewhere in Rhodesia. *SOF archives*

Below: At the Queen's Birthday Party, Bangkok, Thailand, 1982. From left to right: Intrepid *SOF* reporter and Nam door gunner, Jim Coyne; RKB, General Pichitir Kullavanijaya, and Tony Paul, Regional Correspondent for the *Readers Digest*. A friend of *SOF*, the good General arranged the invitations. *SOF archives*

Left: RKB in Rhodesia rides with ranch security personnel in the late '70's. *SOF archives*

Below: SOF'ers at ARCE Bn., Salvador, after returning from op in Gulf of Fonseca, Sept. 1984. Standing, left-to-right: Karl Kline, Paul Fanshaw, Robert MacKenzie, Harry Claflin, Carlos Cucualon, Larry Morton. Kneeling, left-to-right: unknown photographer, RKB and John Donovan. *Photo courtesy Carlos Cucualon*

there. He led us into the balloon hanger, where it hovered menacingly against the wall.

A young Thai sergeant gave us gondola training. He taught us the difference between the exit of a balloon and an aircraft. You just step out of the balloon, not jump like from an aircraft. If you jump up and out you could get wound up in a wire.

A two-and-a-half ton truck with an enormous winch on the back towed out the British-made balloon while we were doing some refresher PLFs (parachute landing falls).

The most startling thing about riding in a balloon occurred the moment the gondola swung free and the ground dropped away. Then it was so quiet and the breeze so pleasant one believed he could be on an imaginary cloud. Our jumpmaster, or "dispatcher," in the British jump system, decorated with Thai, U.S. and British jump wings, assured us that they had never had a malfunction. He sensed our anxiety

"How often do you jump balloon?" Morris asked him.

"Almost every day," he boasted, which I guess was a boast well earned. "It's my balloon."

It was my turn.

I saw my life flashing before my eyes. "If the Crown Prince can do it, I can," I chanted. "If the Crown Prince can do it, I can." I let out a great Hail Mary when I went over the edge. It's just a battle cry, I told the boys.

Then it was Morris' turn. He described blow-by-blow his jump. "I wheeled into the door and assumed a standard door position. The DZ was way down there, stationary, almost like a sand table," Morris said.

"Ready!" said the dispatcher.

Morris came to attention, grasped his reserve at the sides and took one step forward, as he said, "like a tin soldier."

"It wasn't like skydiving," he wrote in an *SOF* article. "Where you don't feel weightless until you get away from the aircraft. There was a feeling of instant buoyancy, like the Moonwalk or the Big Slide, only longer and better. My legs just sort of floated up until I was sitting in midair in the shape of an 'L.' Then I felt the first little tug at my back, my trash streamed out and ever so slowly billowed and inflated.

"I reached for the right toggle, as I checked my canopy. The plan was to hold against the wind, saving a long walk to the turn-in point. For a while I seemed to be dropping straight down on one of the two trees on the DZ, but I drifted away without correction. Then the ground got close and I locked my eyes on the horizon and got my feet and knees together. For most jumpers the moment of truth is the exit; for fat boys it is the parachute landing falls."

Like a great proud peacock, Morris strutted to collapse the chute but two little boys beat him to it.

Meanwhile, in the air, Coyne was in a panic, trying to find his toggles. He swore he was jumping a blank T-10. He got in a stiff position and crashed in for a right front PLF, moving at about ten knots, hitting his left heel and twisting his ankle. "Mekong Jim," as Morris called him, was done.

A little over an hour later, Morris, Reisinger and I sat on the tailgate of an airborne C-130 staring out at a sea of eager young faces of a class of junior cadets at the military academy preparing for their fifth jump. The balloon had been installed in September 1981, and had jumped 5,000 jumpers by the time we took the challenge. The first two of the five qualifying jumps for the cadets had to be from the balloon. The military ran the country and paratroopers ran the military, so paratroopers they trained. Up to 100 small, lightweight Thais would shove into a C-130, sitting on the floor in the up position.

Morris made a good assessment of the balloon: "It does one of the basic things that parachute training is good for. It teaches the soldier to perform simple mechanical tasks while scared shitless, which is pretty much what soldiering is about."

I was first on the left. Morris was the first man in the right door, with T.R. right behind him. I prepared myself for my "Hail, Marys," a ritual I do mechanically every time I jump.

The light went green. The third man was going out the left door. Morris disappeared.

"Out and open I grabbed and pulled, turning to make a surprising discovery. The cadets were in T-10s. They had no directional capability, other than a slip. As I held into the wind, the entire stick from the left door drifted directly toward me, a ragged, solid line of olive-green parachutes. I wondered what the kid below thought when he saw the imprint of my size 12s sprinting across his canopy," he remembered.

Morris and I landed fine, but T.R., tall slim and looking totally fit, landed flat on his ass and messed up his spine. He had a football-sized bruise on his hip and wanted to disappear. Morris chalked our fitness compared to the others up to the daily jogs that he and I took in Boulder.

"Well, we finally did something," I said with big-time pride as I walked off the DZ.

But I swore that I would never do it again, and I never did there, though I went on to earn jump wings from Israel, Guatemala, El Salvador, Taiwan and Peru. Not very impressive when compared to Donavan who earned jump wings from 28 different countries.

17

SAY GOODBYE, COMRADE JAWS: SOF *BREAKS BREAD WITH THE KGB*

The wire-service reporter next to *SOF*'s man-in-Bangkok, Jim Coyne at the bar of the Foreign Correspondents Club of Thailand, nodded toward the crowded bar and whispered, "The KGB's here."

"You mean TASS?" Coyne referred to the Soviet "news" agency synonymous with spying. "No, the KGB." His eyes darted around as he spoke. "Him—the big smiling guy with the beer."

Coyne toasted the Russian who was looking in his direction. The burly man, probably in his late 30s, toasted back, with a smile on his lips but not in his mind.

I sat nearby with a crowd of journalists. I was serving as a panelist with a group that was going to discuss the issue of "checkbook journalism."

Television networks and others with megabuck budgets to spend, as far as I figured, come from the "money talks, bullshit walks" school of journalism. The end result is often very far from the truth and can be very damaging. They had no clue of the importance of our POW mission or the use of chemical and biological weapons by Vietnam or the Soviet Union, subjects they were reporting on.

I had been looking forward to this verbal combat for several weeks, and many journalists had shown up. That is probably why the big Russian was there. *SOF* was making quite the impression in Bangkok. We had rented a penthouse suite and I had two of my staffers investigating full time for months.

Alan Dawson, another panel participant, and author of the book 55 Days: The Fall of Vietnam, other panelists and I verbally blew away some clueless participant who was a former State Department spokesman.

At the bar, the big Russian and Coyne had hooked up, both chugging their beers and looking like the best of friends."Anatoly Korolev, Soviet Embassy," the Russian introduced himself to Coyne.

"Jim Coyne," Coyne said. "*Soldier of Fortune* magazine; no doubt you've heard of us."

"Of course. I've read your magazine, but it's very difficult to get," the Russian told Coyne. "What brings you to Bangkok?" he asked.

"Chemical and biological warfare violations by Vietnam and the Soviet Union," Coyne said with a smile.

"Oh, that," he said in perfect English, and shrugged. "We're not doing any of that stuff."

"I wouldn't expect you to confide in me if you were," Coyne said.

Anatoly said, "We should have lunch sometime," then wrote his name, telephone number and address on a cocktail napkin. He was staying just a few blocks away from the *SOF* apartment. Coyne, intrigued, gave him his name and number.

We were scheduled to leave for Pakistan the next day. But Coyne told the Russian, "We're going to Aranyaprathet," naming the Thai-Kampuchean border town 200 kilometers east of Bangkok. 'I'll call when I get back."

"Fine," the Soviet said, preparing to leave.

"What exactly do you do at the Soviet Embassy, Anatoly?" Coyne asked him. "I'm chief of the Political Section," he answered with a smile.

The panel discussion was over and I won another small, humble victory over the forces of darkness and legions of evil.

I asked Coyne who his new friend was after the stranger left.

"Chief of the Political Section at the Soviet Embassy," he said.

"No shit? KGB!" I was impressed. "What did he want?" "He wants to have lunch next week," Coyne said.

"Fuck a bunch of Russians," I said, not in the mood to meet up with the Chief of the Political Section or any other Russian.

Coyne and I headed to Pakistan the next morning, and were in the filthy hellhole Karachi by noon. After a week of participating in a couple of skirmishes in Afghanistan and nearly suffering sunstroke along Pakistan's rugged Northwest Frontier Province, we returned to Bangkok.

We headed for the Grand Prix bar, a favorite watering hole for journalists in Bangkok's notorious Pat Pong District. Rick Menard, an American Nam vet, had owned Grand Prix for more than 16 years. The last thing on our mind was the big Russian.

"Anatoly's been asking about you," Menard told Coyne, who nearly choked on his drink.

"What does he want?" Coyne said.

"I don't know," said Menard.

"Bob," Coyne said, "the KGB guy's been asking for me."

"Tell him that we were in Afghanistan," I told him, as impressed as I was the first time Coyne told me about the KGB guy.

Robert Moberg walked into the crowded bar. "Mo" had flown anything the U.S. government would give him for more than nine years, based out of the American Embassy in Bangkok. He wore a U.S. Special Forces Decade lapel pin on his western-cut jacket.

Coyne described Mo in *SOF*: "He looked like 'McCloud,' only nastier. He spoke with the low whisky drawl known only to southerners and army aviators. "I am," he often said humbly. "A legend among my peers."

"Moberg had commanded the 281st Aviation Company in Vietnam during 1966 and 1967. Twenty-five helicopters known as radio call signs: 'Intruders' for the slicks, and 'Wolfpack' for the gunship platoon. They were always in the shit. I first heard of him in 1966, when the gunship I was gunner on was dispatched south along with one other ship to assist the 5th Special Forces in Nha Trang. Two 'Shark' gunships from the 174th Aviation Company. We flew some of the hairiest missions of the war during the day, and were often parked in Nha Trang by nightfall."

Mo at the time was working for United Oil and Gas Services in Singapore and was well connected. He was as impressed with the fact that the KGB wanted to meet up with us as I was.

The next morning Anatoly phoned Coyne at our penthouse. "Jim, this is Anatoly, remember? I've been trying to reach you. Where have you been?"

Coyne told him that we had been in Afghanistan, and when Anatoly reminded him that he had said we were going to Aranyaprathet, Coyne, one of the funniest editors I had ever hired, gave some bullshit response.

"Something came up. Apparently the Soviet Union invaded Afghanistan a few years ago. Maybe you remember reading something about it in the papers."

"Brown get up!" Coyne yelled at me to wake up in the other room, "The KGB guy Anatoly wants to meet us."

"I'm not talking to any Russians." I said. Coyne would have none of it.

"I'm not going alone," he said. "I told him we were in Afghanistan. Let 's go meet him and see what he's up to."

" OK," I said, "but I'm not shaking the hand of any KGB puke."

"Even if you told him everything, he'd never believe you," said Coyne.

We headed for the Narai Coffeehouse, a decaying hotel and guesthouse. None of the waitresses spoke English. We chose a 2:00 meeting time when there would be little traffic so we could monitor who was coming and going. And in best spook tradition we arrived an hour early to see if any other KGB bad guys arrived before Anatoly. I sat in a rear booth, facing the door. "I'm not sitting next to him."

Anatoly walked through the door alone, on time. He hesitated while his eyes adjusted to the dark interior of the coffee shop. He spotted us and walked toward our booth. We stood up and Coyne shook his hand. He seemed surprised at my presence.

"This is Robert Brown, publisher of *Soldier of Fortune*," Coyne said. "Bob, this is Anatoly Korolev from the Soviet Embassy." Anatoly extended his hand, and after a brief hesitation, I shook it. What the hell.

"So," Anatoly began, "I understand you've been in Afghanistan. Where were you? What did you see?"

"We were in the countryside with the guerrillas," Coyne replied. "We watched a T-62 get hit. A couple of mortar attacks. A couple of doomed outposts of the Kremlin. We were invited there to help the government put down the insurrection."

The Russian shrugged, then laughed at the outrageousness of what Coyne had told him.

"Afghanistan is not my area of specialty," he said.

"How long have you been in Bangkok, Anatoly?" I asked.

"Oh, for a few years now," he said. "Before that in other areas of Asia."

"It must be difficult to go back to Moscow after Bangkok," Coyne said, no doubt basing his statement on all of the rumors of the stiff, austere Soviet Union in comparison with the party town that never slept and where anything goes.

"Not at all," he laughed. "I just get on an airplane. You should come to the Soviet Union. See for yourself."

"I don't think I would be welcome there," Coyne said. *SOF* made no secret of its rabid anti-Soviet stand.

"Why did you want to meet with us, Anatoly?" I was tired of the bullshit and wanted to get this meeting over with.

"Well, I was . . . curious. I wanted to see what *Soldier of Fortune* was really like. I'm here for the same reasons you're here, you know." He relaxed and leaned back confidently in the booth and ordered a beer.

A 30ish small, wiry Thai man with sunglasses sat down in the booth behind Anatoly, facing us. Hardly anybody else was in the restaurant so Coyne and I assumed the Thai was Anatoly's tail.

We ordered lunch on the Soviet Union. I ordered my normal white wine with a cup of ice and found the most expensive seafood entry on the menu, as did Coyne.

Coyne livened up the party. "What are you going to do when someone, somewhere comes up with one of your chemical and biological rockets, and says 'Here it is'?" he asked. "What about the flagrant CBW attacks by the Vietnamese in Laos and Kampuchea, assisted by the Soviet Union?"

Anatoly didn't flinch. "Oh. Jim, really," he said. "We could never do anything like that. The consequences would be too—how shall I put it—expensive for us. We stand to lose too much. This material you mentioned, it is extremely dangerous. We cannot allow it to be given to anyone: especially not the Vietnamese. Why should we? No one will produce such a rocket, or evidence, because there is none."

He was good. He spoke with a straight face and even some passion as he was lying through his teeth.

"Well, Anatoly," Coyne said. " It's only a matter of time. "

"What do you mean?" he asked.

"Communism is dead," Coyne said. "Finished. Communism is dead, Anatoly," the ballsy Coyne said. "Russia itself is a contradiction of the 'workers' paradise.' If Marxism were paradise, workers wouldn't be in the streets of Warsaw. If it were paradise why would anyone want to leave?"

He didn't let up. "Your 'client states,' such as Poland. Cuba, Angola, Nicaragua, Laos and Vietnam, are literally on the edge of bankruptcy. The false economic and ideological principles upon which your nation is based might best serve as models of mismanagement."

Still cool, Anatoly lit a cigarette.

Coyne still did not let up. "The anachronisms of Marx no longer appeal to the unaligned peoples of the Third World. They are now well aware of the internal and external conditions imposed by the acceptance of the 'Gospel According to Moscow.' They need only take a look at the condition of your 'clients.' The ideal of 'sovietism' is a fraud. It's all over. I hope Brezhnev has a sense of humor."

Anatoly was still unruffled. The Thai spook behind Anatoly laughed to himself and played with his ice-cream sundae.

"Jim, you needn't take this all so personally," Anatoly said. "I wouldn't want to have you arrested for anti-Soviet acts."

"We're in Thailand, Anatoly, remember? Not Kabul or Moscow," Coyne goaded him on.

"We've just come from Afghanistan, Anatoly," I joined in. "You're in deep shit. Excuse me." I wandered off in search of the men's room.

"Changing tapes?" Anatoly asked Coyne.

I had had enough of this bull. I thanked him for the lunch when I came back. We parted, went out to the loud streets of Bangkok, flagged down a taxi and Coyne ordered the cabbie to make a U-turn and get us the hell out of there. He cornered the cab on two wheels, heading back to the apartment.

"Did I ever tell you about the time I 'helped' some Bulgarian diplomat 'defect' from his consulate in Chicago?" I asked Coyne. He raised his eyebrows indicating he wanted to hear more.

"Some bozo undersecretary of the Bulgarian consulate in Chicago writes me a letter, on their stationery, requesting all these technical weapons manuals, right? Well, I wrote back and thanked him for his letter. 'But,' I said, 'I cannot assist you in the ways you've mentioned. If you are serious about defecting to the United States, however, I suggest you contact so-and-so at the State Department for further information, etc. etc.' He's now probably picking potatoes in a windy field in Poland somewhere."

We arrived at the apartment.

I invited Coyne to go to the American Embassy with me. "No, thanks," he said and got out of the cab. "I've had enough spooks for one day."

I came back from the embassy, changed into my jogging gear preparing for my daily run, and found Coyne in the hotel pool.

"I was at the Embassy, right? Somebody made a crack about Anatoly Korolev, as an aside. I said, 'Who's this Anatoly Korolev?' They didn't want to tell me. Finally, one guy warned me never to go near him. He wouldn't tell me who Korolev was, only that he was 'brilliant. The Kiss of Death. Maybe one of the few men authorized to use the big sleep as a bargaining chip.' He told me I was probably already being watched, only I'd never know it. It was perfect. I ran out into the streets. The thought of Anatoly watching me had made me very happy. I was in a Cold War movie. Only it was real."

Coyne later asked a friend whether he knew the Russian diplomat.

"You mean 'Jaws,'" the friend told Coyne. "Sure, everyone knows what he's up to, but nobody's said so in print. He's very good at what he does, you know; that's why we call him Jaws." Coyne then asked what would happen once the article was published. "Two things," the friend said. "One, Jaws will probably be reassigned; the KGB is humorless, you know. And, two, what happens to you will be another story."

Korolov left Bangkok three days after the issue of *SOF* blowing his cover appeared on the newsstands. I never heard from or about him again.

Coyne is currently working in Bangkok, three decades later.

18

AFGHANISTAN, ROUND ONE: TRUMPING THE CIA

At Christmastime in 1979 the Soviet Union invaded Afghanistan, inadvertently biting off more than they could chew, just like other superpowers before them and since. The ensuing jihad, or holy war, was a confusing mixture of history and present Afghan problems. The war's general purpose, both the tribal and political factions in Peshwar, Pakistan agreed, was to rid Afghanistan of Russians. Each group seemed to be going in a different direction, however, and Western observers were left confused and frustrated. To understand the complex war fought against the Soviet Union, the Mujahideen who fought it, and why all help from soldiers of fortune, even if offered for free, was steadfastly refused, one must go back more than 2,300 years in Afghan history.

In Afghanistan the basis for fighting is centuries old. Most Afghan dealings with other cultures, particularly since their acceptance of Islam in the 10th century, have centered on war. These wars have included everything from family feuds to repelling various invaders. When there was no "real war" to be found, these fierce people took just as much pleasure in fighting each other. Even without a holy war against the Russians, the Afghans would be happy to fight them because it is good sport.

Because Afghans have spent generations fighting in holy wars, local brush wars and national wars, each family, each generation, has its own history of glory. The jihad, for many of the Afghan men, was a chance to expand that glory. By appealing to their religious devotion, their sense of injustice over the destruction of Korans, mosques, the murder of women and children and the bombing of villages, the groups in Peshawar had a bottomless well of manpower. Their only real shortage was weapons.

There was no death for the Afghan fighters in battle. Because they became Mujahideen, or holy warriors, they already had their Islamic last rites and believed themselves to be dead. When they do die in battle they are accepted into heaven by Muhammad, they live forever and their graves become shrines.

Mului Lalai Up Din, military commander of the largest faction of the Hezbi-Islami of Afghanistan (one of the half-dozen groups operating with political offices in Peshawar, Pakistan) pointed out that for every Mujahideen killed by the Russians, "ten more will rise in his place." This might sound like spiritual blustering to Westerners until one witnesses the fever pitch of Mujahideen leaving Pakistan's tribal areas for Afghanistan and listens to the tales of glory surrounding Mujahideen who have fallen in battle. New recruits, when they hear these stories, leave the refugee camps around Peshawar to join the fight.

The seeds of this jihad were first sown two decades before the war when many of the Mujahideen political leaders began to denounce the communists then active in Afghanistan.

Shortly after the coup that led to the first communist regime, these political and spiritual leaders were able to whip up an anti-communist fever among the people, leading to the first phase of the Russo-Afghan war. Though composed of disparate tribes, the Mujahideen had a common bond in their desire to establish an Islamic state.

BRINGING OUT A RUSSIAN AK-74 FOR THE CIA

In late October 1979, I was having dinner in a Chinese restaurant with a successful but low profile international arms dealer after attending a day at the Association of the U. S Army annual meeting in Washington D.C. While shoveling in some tasty Moo Goo Gai Pan, not surprisingly, talk turned to the subject of small arms.

"You know, Brown," the slightly built, blue-eyed, blond, mysterious arms dealer smiled and spoke in a hushed tone, "Rumors in U.S. Army technical intelligence circles have it that the Russians have developed a new assault rifle to replace the AK-47, along with a new cartridge. Rumor also has it that the Russkies will be, naturally, issuing it to their elite units."

I pondered this for a moment and said, "Hmm, well, if it's better than the AK-47, that will be something."

He went on to say, "I'll pay $10,000 for one of them. But I'm more curious about the round itself. Rumor Control theorizes that the ammo could include a new flechette, an armor-piercing round, a hollow point and a tracer round. Do you think *SOF* could get some of the ammo and/or one of the rifles?"

No Western intelligence agency—including the CIA—had been able to procure the weapon, designated the AK-74, or the round, even though the weapon had been issued to elite Russian units four years previously.

"Sounds like a project for *SOF*," I joked. "But even if we found one, how could we get it out of Pakistan and into the U.S.?" The arms dealer, who is now retired, had prepared himself for the question, "You get one and I'll send a man to Pakistan who will bring it out and into the U.S." He didn't elaborate. I knew enough about the international arms trade to know that international arms dealers, at least the successful ones, developed their own little local underground networks in third world countries that knew which government officials to bribe or pay off.

On 24 December of that year, the Russians invaded Afghanistan. Various news media reported that Russian airborne units were involved in the fighting. I thought about my conversation with the arms dealer, which at that moment seemed like one of those coincidences that proved to be much more than chance. I figured, "If Russian paratroopers are involved, they are probably equipped with this new assault rifle. And no matter how good they are and how bad the Afghans are, sooner or later they are going to lose some of these weapons to their opponents."

Bob Poos, a type-A personality, small, wiry, veteran foreign correspondent, with sky blue piercing eyes that saw through everything and everyone and who had worked for the AP for fourteen years, was my Managing Editor at the time. Poos had done a tour as a combat correspondent in Vietnam and was known as one of the few reporters who was actually out in the field as opposed to most who got their news in some bar in Saigon. After that he was bureau chief in Tokyo for a year and his next step up the promotion ladder was as bureau chief in New Dehli. His gut told him that he had best fly to India and check it out before he accepted the position, which he did on his own nickel. He flew to India, spent one day, was disgusted by the filth and backwardness, and flew back the next day refusing the assignment. That was the end of his AP career. Poos, hard-driving and full of piss and vinegar, who had first made his bones as a Marine who had walked out of the Chosin Reservoir during the Korean "Police Action," was always looking for a good story laced with adventure; a scoop. I had just cooked one up for him.

Poos was goose hunting with Galen Geer, a recently discharged Army vet, who had a tour in Nam and Korea under his belt and who had written a couple of articles for *SOF*.

Poos got in touch with Geer: "Are you interested in going to Afghanistan?" Geer, who jokingly takes great pride in claiming he was the only automotive mechanic in Vietnam, whereas everyone else was with the SEALs, LRRPs, Special Forces, SOG, Marine Recon, saving villages singlehandedly, was taken somewhat aback.

"Huh?" he replied, "Yeah," Poos continued. "A dual-mission—assess how the war is going and bring out an AK-74 and whatever else is lying about that looks interesting. And it would be cool if you could do it before the CIA does."

"Yeah, why not. I've never been to Afghanistan—another war to cover. Builds my resume," Geer, so typical of the Vietnam Vets that could not fit into the normal humdrum routine, jumped at the chance.

As I mentioned earlier, I figured that since Russian paratroopers were in action during the overthrow of the Afghan government in December 1979, some of the never before seen AK-74's would have been lost in combat to the Afghans. The arms dealer refused to advance front money to purchase the new rifle, so once again it was *SOF* on its own.

THE MYSTERY BULLET OF AFGHANISTAN

Galen Geer's April 1980 mission was *SOF*'s first surreptitious jaunt into Afghanistan. His trip paved the way for us to go back.

He set out on an 11-day cross-country trek to track down and bring out the Soviets' mysterious new AK-74 rifle round. He developed an insightful characterization of the Afghans and met with a lot of freedom fighters, some of whom the U.S. later faced as formidable Taliban enemies after 9-11. Afghanistan at the time was probably the same as it was a thousand years ago and will probably not change much in the next thousand years.

"For 10 days I trudged through the blazing sun," sad Geer, "my eyes sunburned so badly that they dried up and the crusted film had to be peeled away like a layer of shed skin. I had followed the trail of the mystery bullet of Afghanistan—the ComBloc 5.45x39mm round for the AK-74 assault rifle. I had stumbled across two deserts and climbed two mountain ranges. I had run the gauntlet of Soviet MiGs and helicopter gunships. From one Mujahideen stronghold to the next, I had wandered through Paktia Province trying to find that damned bullet. Now I had it. All I had to do was get it to the United States—half a world away."

His biggest concern was the KGB. If Ivan got wind of his mission, he would be nailed. So he decided it was too dangerous to stop and best to pull a 36-hour marathon walk.

"As I rounded the bend in the canyon, the smell of dead camels, killed by Soviet aircraft earlier that day and already stinking in the desert sun, assaulted my sense. Pulling our shirts up over our noses, my Mujahideen companions and I walked past, reminding me once again of war's trail of death and decay," Galen said.

The Mujahideen are skilled fighting men, acclimated to the nomadic life in the unforgiving mountainous terrain. They somehow manage to hydrate from one carefully hidden water hole to the next, or to a village that could provide grub.

"We learned the same survival techniques, but with a lot of guidance from our toughened guides. After a few hours of steady, uphill trudging, we would find a small mountain teahouse where we took a break and drank their re-hydration concoction of choice: super sweetened tea, sometimes with naan—a dry wheat bread. The teahouses, like rest stops along our highways, have served countless caravans plodding through the deserts and mountains for centuries," Galen recalled.

"A full day's march begins before dawn. As soon as the morning's prayers are over, the Afghans drink a few cups of tea, tear off a few hunks of bread, then gather together their weapons and what little equipment might be carried on camels or donkeys. Then they move out.

"The Mujahideen took small, slow, methodical steps in an unchanging rhythm to conserve energy and moisture in the blazing sun. Unless we learned to match our steps to theirs we would either lag behind or lose them. Through rain or snow, mountains or hills or on flatland, they wore leather sandals, baggy pants cinched up with a rope, a loose-fitting shirt and turban, and carried a blanket over their shoulder that served as a bedroll at night and camouflage during the day when Soviet choppers passed overhead. Each man carried his own weapon—anything from a World War II Russian pistol to a captured AK-74. The most ammunition carried by a single man was 50 rounds. Most had from 20 to 30 rounds at any one time. Their range of weapons included shotguns, ancient Chinese machine guns and British Enfields. A standard weapon was the Afghan dagger, a wicked-looking blade with camel-bone handle that is curled at the end.

"These same men who cherish the small things in life and demand little by way of physical luxury, ferociously and mercilessly executed all Russians they captured, then chopped up their bodies with hatchets and knives. In their simple, unassuming way, the Mujahideen held the Russian bear at bay," Galen observed.

GALEN GETS HIS ROUNDS

After Geer spent 11 days in Afghanistan, going for longer and farther than any Western reporter could boast at that time, he called *SOF* with an update: "Yes I've got the ammo but the gun is going to cost $25,000–$5,000 to buy three AK-47s to use to trade for the weapon . . . and $10,000 for the guy to bring it out." *SOF* wasn't about to front the money as we didn't know this Afghan from Adam. We made a frantic call to the arms dealer who at that time was in Santiago, Chile. The wily bastard agreed only to front $2,500 and another $7,500 when the weapon was delivered. Since we sure as hell weren't going to come up with the additional funds, we decided to keep in touch with the contact in Pakistan, who would attempt to get the weapon out of Afghanistan. If he did, then we would decide what course of action to follow.

By this time, we had developed a full-blown case of *SOF* paranoia. We'd been having a lot of international phone and cable traffic, which was by no means secure. What if the CIA found out that *SOF* could do what they could not? Humiliated, would they confiscate the ammo at

U.S. Customs? We would have photos but no hard evidence.

Solution? Have Geer smuggle the ammo to Seoul, Korea, to await further instructions. Poos would link up with Geer, take some of the ammo and stand by to see if Geer got through U.S. Customs. It is illegal to bring ammunition into the U.S. even if you declare it, so it'd be confiscated. So they give you a receipt, big deal! The likelihood of getting it back was between zero and nil.

Either customs was waiting for Geer or he fit a "stop" profile. His luggage was thoroughly searched and 23 rounds were confiscated and a receipt was given. Incidentally, we never did find out what customs did with those rounds, though we speculate they had no idea what they had, and therefore made no attempt to forward them to the CIA or the Pentagon. No doubt they were thrown into some "confiscated items" dust bin where they may well remain today. Poos returned a couple of days later and received the same treatment. But somehow he managed to get two of the rounds past customs.

Along with the ammo, Geer and a former British paratrooper, whom he had hooked up with in Peshawar, brought out an NBC filter from the latest-model Russian BMP-2 armored personnel carrier. Western intelligence had also not seen this before. They turned the filter over to the American Consul in Peshawar who in turn forwarded it to the Foreign Science and Technology Center (FSTC), a secret agency of the army. This item did not get the public attention that the ammo did but was of value as it was suspected that it might contain residue from some type of Russian gas.

The same day Geer arrived in the States, he and I flew to the east coast carrying the two precious rounds of ammunition and turned it over to the FSTC. The mission of this agency was to produce technical intelligence concerning the ground forces weapons and equipment of enemies and potential enemies of the United States. Bill Askins, at the time Director of Publications for the NRA, provided contact with the FSTC. Askins, a Vietnam vet, had flown choppers for the Marine Corps and had worked for the CIA for a number of years.

Galen was in my office when I called the FSTC. I told the voice on the other end of the line that Geer had the ammo and some other stuff. The voice replied, "Don't you know that is against the law?" I retorted, "What the devil are you going to do . . . put him in jail?"

There was a silence and then he said, "No."

The FSTC representatives met us at the airport and immediately began their "smoke and mirrors" game. They put us in a small plane and flew us somewhere. Then they put us in a Mercedes and drove us around in circles, obviously not wanting us to know where we were going. They were playing spook to the hilt. We were not overly impressed with this amateurish game.

Finally, they took us to a motel. I walked over to the window, pulled back the curtains, looked out and saw a sign with the name of the motel and the city. So much for our not knowing where these knuckleheads had brought us. For the next couple of days they brought in spooks and a bunch of other assholes and pumped us for all the information we could give them. Fed up with their bullshit, I packed up to leave but they wanted to screw around some more.

They were trying to pump some more information but we had no more to give them. They were trying to determine if the Soviet forces were fighting the way they thought they were. They were dying of curiosity. At one point there were four people in the room during debriefing. They bought in maps and photographs of aircraft, vehicles and various weapons. They had a couple of maps of Afghanistan they had taped together. We spent hours going over the route Galen and his guides had walked, trying to get it all pieced together. I would say they covered between 150 and 200 miles. And I was starting to get cabin fever.

I'd had it. "I'll fix those assholes." On the third morning, when they came into the motel, I was sitting in a chair, stark naked, smoking a cigarette (even though I didn't smoke I figured it would add to the intrigue), waiting for them. After about half an hour in which Galen and I were trying to stifle our laughter, getting great pleasure out of watching them squirm and stare at the walls and ceiling while I sat there buck naked, they picked up their maps and said, "Well, I guess we've got all we can use for now." I stood up, still stark naked and said, "Well, when can we leave?" We were gone before noon. However, that was not the end of it.

Later in the summer, I called Geer and told him to come to Boulder; that I had some CIA guys that I wanted to talk to him. He showed up, but the bean-counting spooks were "financial experts." They weren't interested in operations. All they wanted to know about was the currency that was being used in Afghanistan because they were getting ready to dump, I guess, some counterfeit money in the country. We went to our after-hours office, the Hungry Farmer, for lunch. During the very long conversation one of the two identified himself with some sort of law enforcement credentials.

They told us that the Russians were pretty pissed off about Geer's visit and they advised Geer to stay in the U.S. and not go anywhere. They wanted to know what coinage was used, gold or silver, Pakistani rupees, etc. They asked quite a few questions, then left and I never heard from them again.

The NRA arranged for the bullet to be tested on the Aberdeen proving grounds. They paid Geer's expenses and put him up in a hotel across from their headquarters. Galen was dealing with Bill Askins, the former CIA agent, and they built a barrel to test the ammo. Where they got the specs to build the barrel we never found out, but they published the story.

I RETURN TO FSTC AND RECEIVE INSTRUCTIONS

I returned to the Foreign Science and Technology Center later that summer, before leading a team of *SOF* advisors to Pakistan in September of 1980, to discuss what specific items of Russian equipment the FSTC might be seeking. I met with Rodney Van Ausdall, who was in charge of the equipment procurement. He penciled out a list of items and what the Army would pay for each. A container of nerve gas would be worth $250,000; $125,000 for a container of incapacitating gas; $65,000 for an AGS-17 grenade launcher and so on.

"Also, we want another 10,000 rounds of the AK-74 ammo. We'll pay $1.00 per round," Van Ausdall said. I took the list with me, but in London I got concerned that if the list was found in my possession, it could cause me serious problems. I mailed it back to my *SOF* office, but it never arrived. Whether it was intercepted by some government agency or went astray because of a postal mess up, I do not know.

Running around Pakistan with a suitcase full of greenbacks also did not seem wise and I didn't have tens of thousands in any case. So I asked Van Ausdall, "Look, will you pay me in cash or gold for each item as I turn it in? That way, I can pay for a desired item with funds from a previous sale."

Van Ausdall, paused and replied, "We can do that, but make sure you check in with the Defense Attache's Office [DAO] in the American Embassy to let them know you have arrived."

"Furthermore," he continued, "under no circumstances have any dealings with the State Department, as those weenies tried to take credit for obtaining the NBC filter that Geer brought out of Afghanistan." "I have no problem with that," I responded. Or, that's what I thought at the time.

19

SOF *GOES TO PAKISTAN . . .*

In 1980, the Russo-Afghan war was getting hot. So I selected a team to accompany me on an *SOF* mission both to aid the Afghans and obtain whatever Russian armament we could locate.

Big John Donovan, with his shaved head, ham-like hands with knuckles heavily calloused from breaking bricks and board, was to be our demo man. Five foot nine and all muscle but with a brain, Big John was an explosives expert who had his own demolition company in Danvers, Illinois. I had first met him in 1973 at a Special Forces Reserve summer training camp at Ft. Chaffee, Arkansas. Donavan was the type that you would want with you if you wanted to get mouthy in a biker bar with no windows.

Dr. John Peters, an adventurer in his own right, who I had met while leading a 10-man team of paramedics after the devastating Peruvian earthquake in 1970, was hefty, grey-haired and the most unflappable of the team, as well as being an extremely competent general practitioner.

Peter Kokalis, *SOF*'s small arms editor, was slim, balding with a mustache and a mercurial temperament, but with a fine sense of humor. We didn't consider him crazy although he had watched the "Wild Bunch" 247 times and could quote all of the dialog by heart.

Mike Pate, Army vet, was also a weapons and ordnance expert.

We landed at the international airport in Kirachi, and "What are we doing here?" we all said almost simultaneously. As we packed our luggage into a beat-up taxi we were inundated by swarms of hustlers with hands out and their BO up. We chugged in two separate cabs to the Midnight Hotel where Geer had stayed earlier in the year because it was cheap. And I mean cheap! Pothole size fissures in the raggedy ass carpet foreshadowed unknown types of insects walking through the filth in our rooms. A blind man with no taste must have done the interior decorating.

We had become paranoid and decided we would check in as two separate groups and pretend to be strangers. Our paranoia level began to spike when Donovan got pulled into the Pakistani immigration office and was intensively questioned as to what he was up to. With his big frame and bad biker look, they had a hard time buying his "journalistic" cover. He had an "Omega News Service" press card, which came hot off the presses shortly before we left, but they blew it off. (We all had the same cards in our individual names. Good thing the same customs agent didn't interrogate us all, or our "not knowing each other" ploy would have put the authorities on high alert or put us on a plane right back to where we came from.) They didn't believe Donovan was a journalist any more than they would believe that I was Mother Teresa.

We straggled into the grimy, rundown hotel, dodging the potholes in the worn carpet. As we walked up to registration, I looked back at Donovan as if I had never met him before and exclaimed, "Hey, you look like an American!"

He played along, and replied in his gruff voice, "Well, by golly, I'm just a farmer from Danvers, Illinois."

I don't know how this played with the hotel staff, but I doubted if they gave a shit. We caused a minor ruckus when we insisted they open up the "dining room" so we could load up on soft drinks.

"Open the dining room or we'll break the doors down," Big John said after the staff ignored our requests. No wonder they hesitated. As we walked in to the food hall, a good portion of the hotel staff scurried off the dining room tables they had been sleeping on.

Our first battle was against a new variety of mutant cockroaches, as big as small rats, that fought us for our beds, and the air conditioners that failed to condition because of two-inch gaps between the window frames.

The next day we moved to the Holiday Inn, which had everything the Midnight Hotel did not have, although it boasted even bigger cockroaches.

I taxied over to the U.S. Embassy and the DAO's office where I met a young Army Lt. Colonel. Unfortunately, I do not remember his name as I would like to have been able to make him asshole-famous.

"The FSTC told me to check in with you," I told him.

"I'll have to contact the DIA first," he said. And so the 40-second interview ended.

"Whatever," I shrugged, and headed back to the Holiday Inn.

The next day the same Lieutenant Colonel Nincompoop showed up to officially tell me, in an authoritatively staccato voice, "We will not pay you in cash, and any payment we do make will be made in the United States. Furthermore, I have been instructed to tell you that you should not go into Afghanistan, as neither the American ambassador in Afghanistan nor the one in Pakistan will help you."

I then asked him, "What's the security like on the road between Islamabad and Peshawar?"

"The road is secure. There are no checkpoints, no roadblocks, no problems." I flew to Peshawar where the *SOF* team was training Afghans and looking for items on FSTC's "want" list in their spare time. As I mentioned, Van Ausdall had offered to pay a dollar a round for 10,000 rounds of ammo. Days turned into weeks and we were finding zip.

Then two days before our tour in masochism was up our luck changed. We split up. Pate and Donovan hired a taxi and drove for the third time up to the "there are no rules and even less law" town of Darra, which was under tribal control and where you could buy any type of weapon short of a nuclear device, as well as hashish and French pastries. Doc and I headed up to a refugee camp that was off limits. We were going on the presumption that if it was "off limits" it must have something that would interest us.

Unfortunately, the Pakistani military didn't see it that way, nor did the province governor who graciously gave us an impromptu tour of the local jail. Doc and I decided they were right; that there probably wasn't anything of interest there.

So we headed back to our ½-star hotel, the Peshawar Intercontinental, where every day you could find something new on the menu that you would never order again. John Donovan, who had been instructing the Mujahideen how to fuse and emplace anti-tank mines, and Mike Pate, our other ordnance expert, once again roamed the gun stores in Darra looking for a large quantity of AR-74 ammo. They finally were able to buy 5,000 rounds at 70 cents a round. An outrageous price, but it was a seller's market.

Donovan also made his bones, or shall we say additional bones, when while instructing the Mujahideen in the use of mines and explosives, he had an exchange with one of their commanders: "Ah, Sahib Donovan. We have problem with anti-tank mines. We put in front of tank. Tank goes over. No Boom. Bad. Bad!" Donovan raised his eyebrows and said, "Show me precisely what you do."

When the Mujahideen showed him, Donovan, rolling his eyes back in his head, said, "Well, you need to put the fuses in the anti-tank mines or they no go boom!" How many Russian tanks were subsequently destroyed because of *SOF* will never be known.

Donovan and Pate smuggled the ammo from Dara past half-a-dozen Pakistani Army checkpoints between Darra and our hotel risking serious jail time and then took off for the States. When Doc Peters and I returned to the hotel, we found the 5,000 rounds stuffed in two backpacks lying on our beds.

The two of us were scheduled to leave shortly, so instead of driving the three-and-a-half hours to Islamabad, we decided to unload our contraband on the U.S. Consulate in Peshawar, even though our orders had been to have no contact with the State Department. I kicked this around with Doc Peters and said, "Let's dump it at the consulate. FSTC told us not to have anything to do with State, but I mean, we're all supposed to be on the same team, right?" He chuckled and agreed.

I called the consulate where, again posing as journalists, we had been given the standard dog and pony show briefing upon our arrival in Peshawar and told the consul, a Mr. Archard: "We have some items we think you would be interested in. Can we drop them off tonight?"

"No problem," he replied.

But there was a problem. Now it was "James Bond" time as while the ammo may have been worth $5,000 to the U.S. government, it would be worth five to ten in a medieval Paki jail to us if we were caught with it. Like in a bad spy movie, we switched taxis several times, constantly checking our tail.

My anxiety roller-coasted as the driver with the only two English phrases he knew, "No problem" and "I understand," took us past what seemed to be every military post and police station he could find on our way to the consulate. (I later found out that in Pakistan, where English is the second language, that in fact "No problem" and "I understand," translated to "There is a problem but I do not understand.")

After finally turning the rounds over to the head of the consulate, Mr. Archard, I breathed a sigh of relief and we returned to our hotel. We figured it was a case of "Mission Accomplished." Or so we thought.

At 0730 hours the next morning, the phone rang:

"Mr. Brown?"

"Yes."

"This is Mr. Archard. I am calling from the consulate. My superior in Islamabad has informed me that we cannot accept the goods you delivered last night. You will have to come back and pick them up."

I was shocked; shocked, I say, and then started to morph into a state of white-hot rage. How could these State Department wusses totally disregard material that had a direct bearing on our national defense? Had they gotten their sniveling noses out of joint over the hassle they had with who got credit for the NBC filter that Geer had brought out of Afghanistan? I was sorely tempted to tell the gutless State Department puke to take the 5,000 rounds of ammo and insert them into the body orifice of his choosing. But if I did that, I'd be kissing off the $3,500 that *SOF* had paid for the ammo and would deny the U.S. Army the opportunity to use it for further testing.

"Ah, what the hell," I told Doc, "let's throw the dice. We will hire a taxi and take it to Islamabad and the American embassy. That Lieutenant Colonel said the Peshawar-Islamabad road was clear." Doc slid into one of his enigmatic smiles, chuckling, "Why not? We haven't had a hell of a lot of adventure so far."

I hired some local guy with a run-down, clunky, dirt-stained black Mercedes and headed south after throwing the ammo-laden back packs in his trunk. My anxiety level started creeping up again as our driver had to stop to get some type of dismal food; then had to fill up his gas tank (at our expense, of course); then had to stop and pick up a soft drink (which we paid for) and then had to stop and check his oil.

To add more acid to my rumbling stomach, I remembered that Geer had told me that all Pakistani taxi drivers were police informants. So what would I do if I saw this bad-breathed dude in his soiled, droopy drawers mosey over to a pay phone and start babbling? And to whom might he be talking? How would I tell? Should I cold-cock him on a gut feeling or go quietly to jail? Well, fortunately for him and me I did not have to make that decision as he made no phone call.

After all his ass scratching and dicking around we were finally on the road to Islamabad. A beautiful sunny day was made even better by the fact that we were soon to leave the land of no booze, droopy drawers, gut-wrenching food and customs that I had little tolerance for then and now. I relaxed in the cracked leather seats until I saw another checkpoint. Leaning forward, I said, "Driver, what's that up ahead there about 200 meters?"

"Ah, sahib, no problem, is only army roadblock checking for guns and drugs going to Islamabad." I came out of my seat like a shot. Guns and drugs to Islamabad my ass! It's Brown and Peters to a cold, dark dungeon in a Pakistani slammer.

Of course, our faithful driver might have been a lot less faithful if he knew what he was transporting in the trunk of his wretched Mercedes. I muttered, "Doc, we're sure as hell going down."

Doc, who I had never seen ruffled, didn't break character. He just smiled and said, "RK, relax. We either make it or we don't. Heck with these Bozos."

"Yeah, well," I grumbled, "If I find that son-of-a-bitch, soft-bellied Lt. Colonel Nincompoop who told us there are no roadblocks to the embassy, there's going to be blood on the Persian carpets—his.

Over the next three and a half hours, there were five more checkpoints like the first one.

"Abdul, what is . . . " I'd start to ask, only to hear,

"Oh no problem, is only checking for . . . "

I was now in a continual state of white-hot rage. I determined that I was not going to torture Lieutenant ColonelNincompoop. I was going to fire all 5,000 rounds of 5.45 up his greasy ass in one big glorious burst.

What turned out to be the last roadblock came into view.

"And THIS one Abdul?" I asked, smoke slowly curling from my ears.

"Ah, checking driver's license and car papers. I have neither. No problem." Perhaps if we were lucky we could rat out the driver and get him sent to jail with us where I could pound his scrawny ass twice a day.

Strangely, we weren't stopped at any of the checkpoints. Why? I don't know. Maybe the guards just thought that gringos in a Mercedes, even if it was built in 1907, shouldn't be screwed with. At any rate, to add insult to injury, old Abdul got lost in Islamabad, giving us an unwanted, impromptu tour of the city.

Finally, we made it to the embassy. Fortunately for all concerned, Lieutenant Colonel Nincompoop was not there so the expensive, delicately vegetable-dyed Persian rugs would not have to be cleaned of blood stains and I would not end up in jail.

Colonel Harold Mauger, Defense and Air Attaché, greeted us, calmed me down, counted the ammo, gave me a receipt and promised to forward a letter of appreciation. Old Doc Peters, ever the cool one, just looked on and smiled. He hadn't blurted a single expletive the entire trip. A cooler dude than he, I know not. Whether he medicated himself into a stupor I will never know.

We delivered the ammo. *SOF* was paid $5,000 in the States for a gross profit of $1,500. As you might imagine, the $1,500 didn't go very far in covering the expenses of the team's trip. Was it worth it? You bet!

ANOTHER SUCCESSFUL AFGHAN TREASURE HUNT

Staffer Jim Coyne came up with an *SOF* scoop in 1981 with the discovery of Soviet "butterfly mines." These small, unobtrusive, antipersonnel mines that looked like toys had maimed countless Afghan children as well as rebels. Indiscriminately air-dropped by Russian helicopters, such mines littered the countryside, preventing night movement and blocking supply routes.

Coyne was with a patrol of 14 Afghan National Liberation Front guerrillas. They had been walking toward an ambush area in bright daylight, through a broad, barren valley—observed by every Russian FAC and LRRP team within 40 miles.

"After steadily stepping up and over rocks for five miles, my legs had turned to jelly," Coyne said. "We were going over an immense ridge. There was a road on top, which a Russian mechanized infantry unit had been using for three days. 'Watch your feet,' my guide said, as we continued to move up. We would stop at the faintest whisper of a foreign sound. In my mind I heard that ever-present rotor chop of helicopters that had permeated the air in Vietnam. It seemed odd that there were none here now. It made me uneasy.

"We had reached the crest of the ridge, and something of a road, when we stopped again. The man beside me said, 'You're in luck,' and pointed off the road. Everywhere fragments of green plastic were strewn about."

Russian choppers had dropped thousands of the small antipersonnel mines along the crest. In daylight they were not too hard to spot. At night they were deadly. Filled with an as-yet-unspecified liquid explosive, and armed with a cock spring impact trigger, they took their toll along the border of Pakistan and Afghanistan. The Russians were ruthless. In a place like Afghanistan, where medical treatment was virtually non-existent, blowing somebody's foot off was better than killing them—it required at least two or three people to carry a casualty and, within a week, the wounded would probably die from gangrene anyway.

Coyne brought one of these mines back with him to the United States to undergo analysis.

Looking back, it is evident that today there are few, if any other publications that have been able to match *SOF*'s record of intelligence firsts. Having outfoxed the KGB and several times scooped the CIA, *SOF* has consistently beat other defense journals on both sides of the Atlantic in obtaining additional Russian military equipment. However, in all fairness, other defense publications did not task their reporters to actually go and look, find, retrieve and deliver this "go-to-jail" equipment to the U.S. government.

Some of the additional technical intelligence coups *SOF* notched up over the subsequent years included the first two 30mm grenade rounds for the Russian automatic grenade launcher, dubbed the AGS-17, and the launch tube for the Russian counterpart of our LAW. An *SOF* team member smuggled them into the United States. Smuggling small arms ammo was one thing, but 30mm grenade rounds were of a different caliber and probably meant a much stiffer jail sentence. When he delivered these to me in my hotel in Washington, D.C., I said, "You're crazy! Jail time! Jail time! How did you get these through customs?"

Jack, an affable former college football player, who I had met when he was a Special Forces medic in Vietnam and who had been on more than one adventure with me, grinned, "Hell, there just was a long line so I got bullshitting with the customs guy about football and he just waved me through." The gods were generous once again.

I immediately called my international arms dealer contact. "Tom, I've got some more goodies fresh in from Afghanistan. Anybody want to see them?" He replied, "I'll make a couple of phone calls." A couple of hours later Tom showed up with two suits from the Defense Intelligence Agency. I showed them the goods. I don't know what they were thinking or maybe they weren't thinking, but they couldn't do anything about the ordnance, so arms dealer "Tom" called a Dutch dealer he was friendly with who happened to be in town and who bought the lot for $3,000. The U.S. government had to wait six months for the Dutch to forward a report on the ordnance because of those monkeys which must have been embarrasing.

Western intelligence was as curious about this automatic grenade launcher as they were about the AK-74 assault rifle. An *SOF* team helped them learn more. After a year of negotiations and the crossing of many palms with greenbacks, Jim Coyne and our small arms editor, Peter Kokalis, got ahold of an AGS-17 in the outlaw town of Darra in Pakistan's Northern Frontier District. Kokalis test-fired it, disassembled it and came up with an evaluation of the weapon on video, which was given to the U.S. government and was eventually offered for sale through *SOF* for $39.95 a copy. That came only after a complete report had been clandestinely passed off to the defense attaché at the U.S. Embassy in Islamabad. Also emerging from the exercise was the first report together with photos of Russia's RPG-18, a direct copy of the U.S. Army's light anti-tank weapon, or LAW. According to *SOF*'s Soviet specialist, David Isby, then on the masthead, the RPG-18 had been built by Russian scientists who had, as usual, resorted to reverse engineering to steal our state-of-the-art military equipment.

20

SOLDIER OF FORTUNE *JIHAD:* *WE ATTACK A RUSSIAN FORT*

"The most exhilarating experience in the world is to be fired at with no effect."—Winston Churchill during the Boer War

"The most exhilarating experience in the world is to be fired at with no effect; and to fire back."—RKB, Afghanistan 1982

"Incoming," I muttered to Coyne and a bunch of non-English speaking Afghans who were preparing to drop another round into their obsolete British-made 3-inch mortar. "I saw a flash in the fort."

Nobody paid any attention. Coyne continued to swivel his video camera from the Russian fort under attack to the Afghan mortar crew and back. The Afghans simply milled around with their Boy Scout Jamboree attitude while fusing mortar rounds and observing the Russian fort.

I shook my head and hunkered down next to a large rock to keep at least one side of my body protected. A few seconds later, the whine of an incoming Russian round reminded me that I didn't appreciate that sound now any more than I had in Vietnam; nor the results.

Crump! It hit 70 meters away. The Russians had their mortars registered on our ridgeline. Nobody seemed perturbed except me. The Afghans pointed at the plume of smoke where the round hit and laughed, adjusted their mortar and continued to mill. Coyne, a *SOF* roaming reporter, continued to swivel. It was certainly a different way to fight a war.

A few days earlier, Coyne and I, bored in Bangkok, had flown up to Pakistan to look for new items of Russian military equipment we could sell to the U.S. government. There we linked up with Hashmatullah (Hashmat) Mojadedi, the 36-year-old brother of Sibghatullah Mojadedi, a principal leader of the Islamic Unity of Afghanistan Mujahideen. Coyne had gone into Afghanistan with Hashmat in December 1980 and had brought out the first Russian PFM-1 anti-personnel mine seen in the West.

We hadn't planned on a tour of the combat zone when we arrived in Pakistan this trip. But then Hashmat said: "I'm going to Afghanistan on a resupply mission and to make an estimate of the situation. It will be only a few days. Do you want to come?"

Coyne and I looked at one another, pondering. Hashmat, noting our indecision, smiled and added, "We have a Russian fort surrounded and under siege. We are attacking every day."

Coyne and I continued to look at each other. "Attack a Russian fort? Hell, yes." Coyne, who had 12 years' experience as a TV cameraman before joining *SOF*, brought a video camera with him. Perhaps we could get some combat footage. Back at the Khyber International Hotel in Peshawar we started our pre-mission planning during dinner.

I was concerned about being arrested by Pakistani authorities as we tried to cross the border. Coyne had been arrested twice during his previous trips and it does screw up one's schedule. Hashmat, I felt, was being a bit cavalier in his dismissal of my insistence that we should dismount when we approached Pakistani border checkpoints and infiltrate around them on foot.

"No, no, just buy some Afghan clothes and, Brown, you dye your moustache and hair black. You'll look like a Pathan," he replied, naming the famous warrior tribe near the Khyber Pass, completely disregarding my paste-white skin and blue eyes.

The moustache would be no problem, but the hair, what hair? I finally settled on dyeing just the hair around the temples since my turban would cover the rest of my thinning pate. There was nothing either one of us could do about the blue eyes.

After a day's delay due to vehicular problems, at 0600 hours we jumped in the back of a Jeep pickup, the bed of which was covered by a canvas. Clad in our new clothes, we snuggled up to the back of the cab and four Freedom Fighters crowded in after us with their Chinese Type-56 AK-47s.

For the next eight hours, we bounced over some of the awful goat-track roads and through five checkpoints. Coyne and I feigned sleep, pulling our turbans down over our faces when the Pakistani guards casually inspected the interior of the truck.

With the last heart-stopping checkpoint behind us, we cut from the main road onto a track. For another hour the truck lurched through featureless dark wilderness. No road was perceptible in the headlights. We stopped. Glittering against the silent black of night, stars clustered to form a domed ceiling above us, horizon-to-horizon. We were 1,000 meters from Afghanistan.

A large Bedford truck was parked to our right, a black silhouette in the night. A faintly lit, one-room mud hut was barely visible. We were greeted by shadowy figures in hushed, respectful tones. As Hashmat and the others settled in for a long night of discussion, Coyne and I laid out our bedding. We slept on reed cots, covered with warm, bright Afghan quilts protecting against the chilly night air of the border.

The sunlight woke me at 0530 hours. Twenty or more Mujahideen were already off-loading the Bedford, decorated with elaborate designs and paintings. The truck sat heavily on its springs, weighted with arms and munitions.

Coyne and I watched sleepily as the truck was unloaded. Ammunition, weapons and supplies destined for other Mujahideen guerrillas on the offensive inside Afghanistan were moved with deliberate slowness, hand-to-hand, from the truck to the ground. The driver watched and waited nervously, anxious to leave. The pile of munitions grew.

We found that the weapons consisted of ten recently manufactured Enfield rifles purchased in Darra. The care package also included a 7.62mm SGMB Goryunov light machine gun, still covered with cosmoline in its packing crate, with 1,000 Chinese-manufactured incendiary/tracer rounds; cases of antitank mines with fuses; four or five dozen three-inch mortar rounds, circa 1957; 20 cases of .303 British ammo; and the pièce de résistance, two cases of linked incendiary ammo for aircraft. The label on the latter stated that it was manufactured in 1942 and was "not to be fired through synchronized machine guns after 1944"! I never figured out where that came from.

With this, they were taking on the Russian Army? More shocking revelations were awaiting us. We left the next day at 0900 hours with Hashmat and 14 of his security troops, armed with Enfields and Chinese Type-56 AKs. A camel had been loaded with a portion of the supplies and dispatched the preceding day.

The hours passed as walking turned into trudging—up ravines and dry river beds covered with square billiard balls. By the end of our tour, we were convinced that when God, in all his ultimate wisdom, created the earth, he had taken all his surplus square 2x2-, 3x3-, and 4x4-inch rocks and scattered them liberally over Afghanistan.

I kept expecting Mi-24 helicopter gunships to come roaring out of the sea-blue sky bringing death and destruction to *SOF* and friends. The Afghans seemed unconcerned—talking, bunched up and, once again, milling around. Either they knew something we didn't or they simply didn't care.

Inside Afghanistan, at about 1630 hours, we met a lookout who escorted us to our forward attack position—a ridge that had a single three-inch British Mark 5 mortar positioned in defilade about 30 meters short of the crest. One hundred meters to the right of the mortar, a Soviet DShK Degtyarev Model 38/46 12.7mm HMG poked its ugly snout toward the Russian fort.

"What the hell kind of a war are they fighting?" I muttered to myself. I could barely see the outline of the fort through my field glasses! It must have been 3,500 meters away. I was particularly confused since an intervening ridgeline was 1,500 meters closer. I later found out that they had fired from this ridge the night before, but had moved back one ridge because of the VIPs (us) who were going to be observing the attack. I shook my head, puzzled about the Afghan military mind or what I perceived to be the lack thereof.

"Allah Akbar!" shouted the 30 Afghans as the mortar crew plunked a round down the tube. WHAM! The first round arced toward Ivan. The mortar crew raced to the ridge, then hunkered down to wait for the round to hit.

We waited and waited and waited.

Boroki, the leader and mortarman, mumbled to himself. I suspected bad ammo. Even though no aiming stakes were in evidence, they couldn't be that far off. Another round—nothing. Then another and, again, nothing. The mortar crew was disgusted; they stared at the useless ammo and cursed among themselves.

At the first mortar round from our group, another group of Afghans had opened fire on the Russians with the DShK 12.7mm. We heard its rhythmic "doom-doom" from the other side of the fort.

We had been told before the attack that the Russians would return fire with the DShK 12.7mm HMG first. In the gathering darkness the muzzle flash from the DShK was distinct. Unlike the mortar, the "Dashika" was a direct-fire weapon and not much could be done to hide the flash. The Russians followed up with a few mortar rounds of their own.

I shook my head. The attack had lasted an hour with no results. But happily, still no Mi-24s appeared in the sky even though we were no more than 30 minutes by chopper from the Soviet airbase at Khost.

As dusk fell—and there were still no Mi-24s—we moved down to a safe-house located in the bottom of a narrow ravine four or five klicks from our firing position. The safe-house, which didn't seem very safe to me, was simply a framework of branches covered by dried reeds. Inside, a fire pit dug into the ground fiercely burned the cardboard mortar round containers and provided the means to cook freshly slaughtered lamb. As the light from the flames cast shadows on the walls of this primitive dwelling, we imagined ourselves tripping back through time—to any time period during the last 2,500 years. The shadowed, gaunt, craggy faces of the turbaned Afghans could have been part of the forces that resisted Alexander the Great's invading army in 327 B.C., or the conquering Mongol armies of Genghis Khan in the 12th century, or Tamerlane in the 14th century, or the British incursions of the 19th. Only the wristwatches and burning mortar round containers indicated that we were in the 20th century.

Hashmat asked us, as honored guests, to sleep inside. However, looking at the terrain as I caught up on my note taking, using the base plate of the three-inch mortar as a backrest, I figured that if the Mi-24s took a run through this valley, they would observe the base plate that was propped up against the hootch's doorway and waste it. Coyne and I opted to sleep in the open, 50 meters from the hootch, giving us a bit of a chance if Ivan decided to snoop the following morning. The only disturbance during the night came from a scraggly Afghan rooster tethered about three feet from my head. He obviously had his sense of time upset by jet lag, mistaking 0300 hours for dawn instead of 0530 hours. His crowing disturbed what was, at best, an unsettled sleep. I was satisfied that the rooster was suitably chastised a few hours later—we ate him for lunch.

We broke camp and moved out toward our next attack position about 1400 hours the following day. As we moved across the 400-yard-wide valley floor in a gaggle, I continually searched for cover and concealment. In vain, it turned out, since there wasn't any. Apparently, the Afghans simply didn't worry about enemy choppers.

Granted, they had observation posts on prominent terrain features and ridgelines. However, their early warning system, which consisted of them yelling "Helicopters are coming," down the line, was not reassuring. Even though Coyne pointed out, "You can see a chopper much farther away than you can hear it," I still was not impressed. The Afghans had more confidence in their early warning system than I did.

After a five-hour walk that covered at least 20 klicks, we arrived at our new attack position. The Mujahideen had borrowed an additional three-inch mortar from another group because they were dissatisfied with the previous one. Once again, the mortar position was located about 20 yards from the crest of the ridge on the reverse slope. At 1815 hours, once again to cheers of "Allah Akbar!" the Afghans started mortaring the fort. I dropped a round down the mortar tube as I still had a thing about the Russian support of the NVA during the Nam war.

Much better luck was ours that night. The gunner, Boraki, bracketed the target with three rounds.

INCOMING FIRE

Incoming—once again. It was becoming interesting.

Another enthusiastic "Allah Akbar!" was followed by a bright flash and we got a secondary. Soon another bright flash erupted from the main gun of a Soviet tank! The round landed about 100 meters from our mortar position, but only 10 meters from the heavy machine-gun position. Fortunately, a rock embankment protected the gunner, who did not interrupt his firing. The Soviets once again replied in kind.

After 30 minutes we broke contact. We had run out of mortar ammunition even though we had fired only 11 rounds—the whole week's allocation!

The following morning, the Mujahideen received an intelligence report that one of our rounds had landed on a Soviet mortar pit, killing the gunner and setting off a secondary. Not bad results for a lousy 11 rounds.

During the night, which we spent in another dry riverbed, and the following day, I pieced together a reasonable, or at least understandable, estimate of the situation. The Afghan resistance forces had the small Russian fort under siege and had surrounded it for 41 days. The concept of operations was simple and had been used since the beginning of recorded military history—starve them out.

The Afghan resistance expected that when the Afghan puppet troops ran low on ammo and food, they would slit the throats of their Russian advisers and surrender. Two other Russian outposts in the same area had already suffered that fate in preceding months.

The nightly standoff attacks' primary purposes were to maintain pressure on the fort personnel and prod the Soviets into returning fire, thus continuing to deplete Russian ammo reserves. Since the Soviets had their guns registered on our ridgelines but still fired only a few rounds of countermortar fire, I gave the Afghans' assumption a fair amount of credibility.

The Afghans believed that no resupply by land was possible since all main approach avenues to the fort were under Afghan observation and their blocking forces would attack any relief columns. The Soviets would not risk using a chopper to resupply. However, it seemed to me that if the Russians wanted to relieve the fort they could, if they committed sufficient air assets. I thought that a couple of Mi-24 gunships could easily provide sufficient firepower to suppress any Afghan fire.

On the other hand, perhaps the Soviets felt it was not worth the effort. It was hard for us who had served in the U.S. military to believe that the Soviets could so callously write off their advisers. But in light of the fact that several reports had circulated of Russians destroying damaged Mi-24s with crews trapped inside to preclude military secrets from being compromised, perhaps not.

Ultimately the Mujahideen were unable to storm the fort because a 200-meter minefield surrounded it. They had insufficient artillery and no Bangalore torpedoes with which to breach the minefield. Nor were funds available to purchase enough sheep to attempt to run livestock through the mines, a technique of questionable effectiveness.

Their starvation plan was not sophisticated, but it appeared to be working, and one has to make do with what is available, which obviously was not a hell of a lot. However, I certainly did not envy the trapped Russian advisers.

At about 0900 hours, it was plinking time. A bunch of Afghan "good old country boys" showed off their marksmanship skills, which were not very impressive. A meeting followed, which in turn was closed with the inevitable prayer, and then we traversed the "square billiard balls" again to return to the Mujahideen FOB. However, the return trip was not without adventure. We had to cover approximately 30 klicks and the trip led through a minefield. An Mi-24 had sown PFM-1 antipersonnel mines along the border, a few hundred-meters deep, intersecting the trail. It wasn't difficult to spot the little brown foot poppers as the Mujahideen got a big kick out of pointing them out and picking them up to be photographed. I got a big kick out of not touching the damn things, instead following carefully the tracks of the Mujahideen and even then keeping my eyes peeled.

Then it happened! We heard an explosion in the vicinity of the point man, about 40 meters ahead and around the bend. We moved up quickly and found the man on the ground with a hole in his right thigh.

You can explode a PFM-1 by throwing a rock at it. You can also explode it by stamping on it, hitting it with a hammer or butting it with your head. The Mujahideen liked to blow them in situ by throwing rocks at them. In this case, the rock was blown back into the "pitcher's" right thigh. The injured Mujahideen was kidded by his compatriots, patched up and packed out on a horse.

We trekked back to the FOB and returned the next day to Peshawar. We decided that it wasn't a bad week's work. We had illegally crossed into Afghanistan; traveled over 60 klicks; personally participated in two attacks on a Russian fort; survived a few rounds of incoming from Russian 12.7mm heavy machine guns, AK-47s and a 82mm mortar; successfully negotiated a Russian minefield; and cemented a close relationship with some of the toughest fighting men in the world. We had whetted our appetites for adventure and expressed our support for the Freedom Fighters' cause.

As we left, we promised, "We shall return, Ivan."

SOLDIER OF FORTUNE *JIHAD*

In 1988, I invited former Rhodesian Scout Deputy Commander Mike Williams, former French Foreign legionnaire Paul Fanshaw, and Hunter Penn, a 101st Airborne Vietnam vet and rodeo roper, to go to Afghanistan with me. The plan was to go blow up a Russian fort and shoot down a MiG or Hind Mi-24 gunship with a Stinger.

Williams, a tough as mails, medium-height, suave, smooth-talking, broad-shouldered, wavy-haired ladies' man, later said, "I have done a lot of stupid things, including volunteering for Special Forces, commanding a battalion of North Korean and Chinese deserters in the mountains of North Korea, serving as deputy commander of Grey's Scouts in Rhodesia, marrying three American women and lending my daughter a thousand dollars. But . . . the first prize in dumb was letting Robert K. Brown talk me into paying my own way to Afghanistan to 'assist' the Russian withdrawal."

We were to ship all equipment through a third party in Peshawar, Pakistan, over to our Area of Operations, where we would retrieve it and sneak across the Pakistani border to join the ranks of the Mujahideen fighting the Russians.

Our little band of adventurers linked up at Dulles Airport in D.C., where we boarded a British Airways flight to London. Hunter, who had been in Afghanistan just a while earlier, told us that communication between him and his Afghan friends was virtually non-existent—he didn't speak Pushto, and they didn't speak much English.

We, who spoke only English and some French, were soon to find out what a serious problem that could be. We flew to London, and after dicking around old Blighty for a day, we boarded a second British Airways flight, this one bound for Islamabad with an intermediate refueling stop near Dubai.

We soon found out that Pakistani security measures were draconian. Troops armed with MP-5 submachine guns surrounded the aircraft and gun jeeps cruised the outer perimeter of the airfield. The country was on high alert. Khomeini Revolutionary Guard suiciders had infiltrated the country with orders to kill any American, or any Westerner for that matter, they could find.

General Zia, Pakistan's president, had issued a warning to the Ayatollah that Pakistani security forces would eliminate on the spot any Revolutionary Guards found in Pakistan.

The Pakistani troops, particularly members of airborne units, were impressively professional. Signs were everywhere identifying various military installations, and their types of uniforms and saluting evidenced the influence of previous British Army training.

The ride from the airport to the Holiday Inn had us longing for the notorious, madmen New York cab drivers. The driver did everything but look at the road, spending half the time twisting his head over his shoulder to tell us about his cousin in New York and the remaining half-racing other cabs to traffic lights.

After lunch, Williams and I paid a visit to the U.S. Embassy, where we spoke with several officials who clued us in to trouble-spots within the country. The streets of Islamabad were like something out of the Arabian Nights. When in Rome, do as the Romans do, I decided, so I informed the team that we would wear Mujahideen-type clothing. We rounded up their wide-waisted trousers held up by a cloth cord at the waist and a shin-length shirt and turban. We had no clue at the time that we would end up wearing the drab outfits for ten days straight without a bath.

We had negotiated with the commander of the particular Mujahideen group we were to join that we were to go to Quetta, Pakistan (today a headquarters for the Taliban), where we would link up with our group and cross over into Afghanistan.

General Ramatullah Safi, a boisterous, hulking, high-ranking officer with the Mujahideen, who had a very loud and authoritative presence, met us on our arrival in Islamabad and helped us get settled. In perfect English with a British accent he explained, in detail, the situation in-country regarding Soviet forces and the tactical dispositions of the Mujahideen. When we were ready to leave for Quetta, he drove us to the airport to assist in our departure.

As was customary, we dragged along some Al Mar knives to "souvenir" to our hosts. Pakistani security went ballistic. We had to show our passports, open all luggage, swear we weren't agents of the KGB, and bow three times toward Mecca before they'd let us on the plane.

We chilled out when the guards wrote our passport numbers in ink on the heels of their palms. Although it might be a long time down the road, they would have to wash their hands eventually, or the numbers would all be smudged by their heavy sweat.

Finally, we were off to Quetta, in a rickety airplane that soon was filled with thick clouds of body odor and hot air since the air conditioning was on its way out. It finally fired up when we go to cruising altitude. The captain's voice shattered the thick air. "This is captain speaking. We shall arrive at Quetta at 1530 hours, Inshallah [God willing]."

"Inshallah," my ass.

Quetta was a teeming border town that served as a conduit into Afghanistan through which Mujahideen and reporters traveled back and forth. An Iranian consulate in Quetta allegedly provided a base for a unit of the Ayatollah's Revolutionary Guards, whose mission it was to kidnap, or kill, any Americans found in the city. However, thanks to a contact in Washington, we had a list of the license plates of the Guards' autos.

After circling Quetta's airport for what seemed like forever, we touched down. We were met by a large contingent of blue-uniformed security guards marching out to the hardstand. They covered sectors of fire with MP-5s. A jeep with a pedestal-mounted MG-42 slowly circled the inner perimeter. This was our introduction to some of the toughest security measures we had ever encountered. It made the Israelis seem like gentle lambs. We were body searched and, rather than take our shoes off as we have to do in the United States these days, we were forced to put each foot on top of a small bench so that the security guard could check the soles and heels of our footwear for a fake compartment.

The local Mujahideen commander, Mohammed Tahir Khan, who was short, wiry and in his late 30s, met us. Fluent in English, he had been educated at a military academy in India, a reminder that Pakistan had been ruled by the British Empire. Khan was a mover and shaker, having lobbied "Free Afghan" supporters in Europe and the United States. He had moved his family to California.

We loaded into two Toyotas and headed to the local Mujahideen local command post in Quetta's ancient bazaar. It was a typical souk, like in Turkey or other Middle Eastern countries. Shops carrying various products were jammed side by side, and slabs of raw beef and chickens hanging by their heads gave the air a stench of death while providing sustenance to clouds of flies. The mobs scurried back and forth, dodging donkey carts, bicycles, motor scooters and rickety trucks. Cars weaved through the crowds.

The locals were staring at the gringos. We saw the first of many large, red hammer-and-sickle signs screaming: "U.S. OUT AFGHANISTAN." Pakistani Communist Party flags hung everywhere, which unsettled us.

We turned off the main road and entered a narrow side street that had trash strewn everywhere. It was swarming with flies and hungry, mangy dogs searching for food. Tahir stopped the truck and motioned to some turbaned Mujahideen mulling around. They opened a large, iron gate leading to a courtyard in front of a two-story house. The guards, armed with well-kept Kalashnikovs, carried our bags as we walked across the courtyard and into the house. Tahir told us to sit on the carpeted floor in a large room that served as a conference center. Tea was served. Tahir sipped his tea as he spoke in Pashto to one of the many Mujahideen who'd just arrived.

"It is better you go with me now," he told us after a few minutes.

First we had to slip into our new costumes for this gig. We were soon to find that the baggy outfits and turbans served as perfect camouflage in the environment. One of the Mujahideen showed us how to wrap a turban around our heads and secure the baggy-waisted Afghan trousers with a cloth cord attached to a plastic hook which threaded through a loop sewn around the waistband.

Dressed in our new garb, transformed into apparent locals, we were ready to roll. Tahir said, "We will have to pass through Pakistani checkpoints, so cover your faces and look at the floor when I tell you."

Pakistani guards at checkpoints had the option of throwing you in a filthy jail or accepting a bribe to let you pass. Tahir, the designated driver, put Fanshaw, Penn and the Mujahideen guards, carrying AKs, in the rear of the enclosed Toyota pickup; Williams and I rode in the front with Tahir.

We swerved through the chaos of pedestrians, bicyclists, donkeys and cars, passing through successively smaller villages onto roads that were traveled by a series of large Bedford trucks like those used by the Rhodesian Army.

Tahir stopped in front of a small shop and signaled the "pull the bottom half of our turbans across our faces" warning. He got out of the truck and walked inside the dimly lit shop. The lanky Fanshaw and Penn, all cramped up after being jammed in among the Mujahideen the whole time, had no chance to ease the cramps in their calves. They'd ridden that way from Quetta and began grumbling about getting out to stretch lest they get blood clots.

We tried to sneak peeks at the surroundings and passers-by through our turban-covered faces. We coyly looked at them from the corners of our eyes, while looking down at the floor.

Tahir returned, offering us a handful of small oranges and a large melon.

"Can Fanshaw and Penn get out and stretch their legs?" I asked Tahir, worried that the loose cannon Fanshaw might just dart out and start running.

"Not good. There is problem, many spies here for Russians," Tahir said, as he walked to the rear of the truck and handed the remainder of the fruit to Fanshaw, Penn and the Mujahideen, who grabbed it and started chewing away, spitting seeds into the dirt.

We drove over the dusty, narrow, rocky roads that for hours allowed only one car to pass at a time. In the distance we could see that shadows of much higher ridges were faintly visible in the weak, silver moonlight. We spotted two figures toting AKs, standing by a side road that branched off to the right. They recognized Tahir as he slowed to pull alongside them and waved us on.

"Our people. They guard this road." He shifted gears and accelerated. "Important no Pakistanis come this way."

We drove over the mountainous trails that were carved right on the edge of the cliffs for another nerve-wracking two hours. After what seemed like forever, we stopped at a wooden crossbar marking the entrance to a camp containing tents and mud houses. Large stacks of ammo crates were dimly visible. Two Mujahideen sentries raised the barrier and we drove through, turned right, and stopped in front of a small building.

"Please get out . . . come in!" Tahir motioned to the Mujahideen standing near the truck to bring our bags and follow him. Inside, he stopped and removed his shoes before entering. We did the same, placing our boots in a row near the doorway.

By now jittery, the always-on-alert Williams felt edgy, figuring out how he would grab his shoes and run for the nearest hole in case of a Chinese fire drill. Once again, we sat on the carpet with pillows behind us in the dimly lit room next to Tahir, who spoke in a near whisper with three bearded Mujahideen squatting just inside the doorway.

We sunk into the plush pillows, seeing the large group of shadowy young male strangers and old bearded men with their AKs and ammo hung around their shoulders, as we fought the urge to fade. They stared, barely paying attention to what Tahir and the three commanders were saying.

A Mujahideen boy carrying a tray of tea, bread, cakes and fruit made his way through the curious crowd. We inhaled the sugar-loaded brew and gorged ourselves to the last crumb.

Tahir told me, "You will sleep here tonight and tomorrow we will go see our people. Your beds are ready."

We followed one of the guards outside to get our boots and gear and followed him around the side of the building on a trail that led up a steep hill. I never wanted to see another hill again. They had laid out four thick blankets on pallets side by side against the mud walls of a small hut.

Finally, we thought we could crash until morning.

"ALLAH AKBARRR!" A loud chant woke us at two blasted thirty from an exhausted sleep. Now I am half deaf, but the singing and laughter of the Muslim guards roared in my ear. It was Ramadan, the Muslim holy month, when the Muslims fasted all day and stayed up eating and carousing most of the night.

WHERE'S THE RUSSIAN FORT?

We were woken up again at sun-up and choked down the sugar-thick tea, which would probably give us all diabetes by the time we got out of there, plus half-baked naan that was supposed to pass for bread and the usual small cakes and oranges. I picked up the naan, brushed away a few dozen flies and invited the rest of the gang to eat up, saying, "You know, people pay thousands of dollars for a chance to experience something like this."

Then, "What's that smell?" I asked, looking around.

Williams pointed to a sagging, dilapidated wooden shack covered with gunny-sacks just behind our breakfast feast. "The smell is coming from the latrine. That's also where the squadron of flies is coming from that crawled in your mouth with that last bite of bread," smart ass Williams said.

Shortly afterward, a runner, panting as he ran up the hill called to us, "Commander say you come."

"What about our gear? Do we take it?" Hunter asked, pointing to his camera bag. The Mujahideen shrugged and shook his head.

"Maybe we're going in today," Williams told me as I had just begun to enjoy a mouthful of Skoal to dull the thought of the dreadful dining room.

I spit at three fat beetles busily attempting to roll a goat turd down the hill.

"I don't give a shit! I just want to shoot down a MiG with a Stinger," I said, already wanting to get this endless adventure over with.

Tahir was waiting outside the CP, standing near the Toyota. He nodded and said, "Good morning. We will look at Russian fort today. Soon we will attack it." He pointed at a tall, skinny Mujahideen wearing a Fu Manchu mustache with a dull, dazed hashish look standing near the truck. "Your driver, Mahmoud."

"Salaam a Leikum," the ever smooth-talking Williams said, shaking his hand.

"Wah a Leikum al Salaam," the driver answered and smirked, rolling bloodshot whites.

Williams and I got in front while Fanshaw, Hunter and a gaggle of AK-bearing Mujahideen crawled into the back. Finally, off to the fort we went. Mahmoud fired up the Toyota and popped the clutch, and we shot toward the barrier in second gear.

"ALLAH AKBARRR!" he roared as he shot off full blast onto the rocky road.

"Thinks he's Sterling Moss, doesn't he?" I observed.

Mahmoud had the transistor radio blasting some Middle Eastern chants. "AHHHH . . . ALLAHHH . . . AKBARRR . . . OHHH ALLLAHHHH," Mahmoud roared along at the top of his voice. We barely missed the donkeys with the old men dragging behind along the winding road.

Williams kept mumbling about some Arabic curses in a travel book he had read, "something to the effect that the supreme insult alluded to the fact that the cursee's mother was the product of a sexual liaison between a donkey and a syphilitic camel," a curse he figured the old man had placed on our chauffeur.

Whether Mahmoud was one helluva driver or whether hashish enhanced his expertise we didn't want to know. No doubt the latter, but by some miracle he kept us alive on the winding, cliff-hanging road.

"We walk," one of the Mujahideen in one of the vehicles in the convoy said as we approached a narrow trail that led toward a deep canyon filled with Mujahideen who were highly amused at our misery.

A small mud hut and an ammunition dump with hundreds of 82mm mortar and 107mm rocket rounds were hidden in the canyon. The "command center" communicated with the help of several professionally placed antennae, allowing effective communication.

We were invited in and served some more sickeningly sweet tea with the local Mullahs, who offered prayers for our safety. The big moment had finally come. After getting the introductions over with, we climbed back up the hill to take turns firing a Soviet 14.5mm KPV heavy machine gun at a Russian fort near the village of Lara. The fort was garrisoned with approximately 200 Afghan troops and several Soviet advisers.

Next morning, after the same old sickly tea, cakes and oranges, we rode off with Tahir to inspect the troops who were slated to attack the Russian fort. We passed bombed-out villages where huts showed the effects of Mi-24 Hind strafing and rocketing attacks against their defenseless inhabitants.

"Keep a lookout for MiGs. This area is under air reconnaissance by the Russians," Tahir said as we bounced along the exposed trail over a dried up creek bed.

MUJAHIDEEN, ADVANCE PARTY FOR GENGHIS KAHN?

After about four hours, we braked to a halt. Standing in the middle of the road were four of the meanest looking Mujahideen we had yet seen. Bearded, dirty, yet carrying spotless AKs, they spoke with Tahir and studied us, taking in our Afghan outfits and turbans. Hunter, whose previous three months with the Mujahideen in the mountains near Kabul gave him plenty of insight into the Afghan hierarchy said, "They're local commanders in this area."

The system of district and regional commanders within the ranks of the Mujahideen made it lethal for Soviet troops to attempt infiltration of any Mujahideen area. From the intelligence networks that existed throughout Afghanistan, the Mujahideen knew in short order about any new stray dog in a village, let alone an attempted infiltration by a Russian Spetsnaz unit.

Tahir shook hands with the Mujahideen, nodded goodbye, and we jolted along toward the assault force's assembly area. After a while, the road deteriorated into a goat trail leading off into a canyon. Sentries stopped us before we'd gone 100 meters. Then, recognizing Tahir, they waved us on.

Tahir pointed to a huge pile of 107mm rocket rounds lying on the trail, "We will fire 1,000 of those when we attack the fort tomorrow." Stacked on a ledge above the rounds were 12 Soviet mines and a large number of 75mm recoilless rounds. Boxes of ammo for the AKs and RPD machine guns were stacked next to RPG-7 rounds covering a wide area along the roadside.

"Come with me; you will see the commander and Mujahideen." I fell in step with Tahir while Fanshaw, Hunter and Williams followed, taking pictures of the troop activities.

We moved from a cave, deep in the side of the canyon wall where the command shack was located, to the top of a nearby ridge, where we checked out the Russian fort with our Steiner binoculars. It was stifling hot and dusty. No wonder they wore the white turbans and gowns. They kept their brains from frying, since even the turbans got blazing hot.

The Mujahideen were loading stacks of ammo onto carts pulled by Massey-Ferguson tractors at the bottom of the hill. I asked Tahir what the plan was.

"Two more days until we attack." All the mines, 107mm rockets, 82mm mortar rounds and ammo for the AKs and RPDs had to be loaded back on the carts pulled by the tractors and transported to the attack assembly area. This was their idea of mechanized infantry.

"Tomorrow we will look at a captured Russian fort!" Tahir announced as he cranked the Toyota's engine. He waited while our team and half a dozen Mujahideen guards crowded into the cargo compartment.

"STOP!" Williams yelled. Tahir hit the brakes.

107mm rounds were lying a foot ahead of the tire, their noses aligned with the centerline of the Toyota's wheel. To their left and two feet away were about 25 more, scattered in a close group. Tahir reversed the truck, managing to clear the rounds with Williams' guidance.

"What's going on?" I asked, glancing at the pile of ammunition. "Hell, the fuses probably weren't in."

"They are in," Tahir said

Williams asked Tahir, "Do you have accidents with the Mujahideen when they handle ammunition?" He shrugged, "Many."

I couldn't afford to have one accident.

The Mujahideen had fasted all day and were tired and thirsty, and so were we. The water we drank out of a small mountain stream was a lifesaver. We crossed the shallow creek separating the camp from a Pakistani village at dusk. Tahir had the usual Mujahideen commanders waiting for him and they conducted the normal day's briefing while we ate.

The attack was scheduled within 48 hours, Inshallah. All ammunition would be stockpiled at a new reserve site, ready for use in a preparatory barrage against the Soviet fort.

"My plan is to use 400 Mujahideen in the assault with 500 in reserve," Tahir said. "That way we will hold down the casualties."

"The assault force will be split into two groups, one to encircle the fort from the east, the other from the west. I will leave a path open from the fort to the Afghans inside who want to surrender and join us."

"How are you going to establish contact with the Afghans and the Soviets in the fort?" I asked

"After the barrage, which will start at 0300 and last until 0600, I will send in one of my people to talk with the Russian commander." Tahir stretched and yawned wearily. This made no sense to me but nothing about this whole thing made any sense. "Tomorrow we must leave early. I want to look at the captured fort." He shook hands and wished us a good night's sleep.

After the same old breakfast of tea, cakes and oranges, we mounted up and set out for the captured fort. Tahir drove for four hours over the same dry creek bed as before, keeping a weather eye out for MiGs or Mi-24s. We finally arrived at a small village surrounded by mulberry trees.

The terrain had flattened out from hills and canyons to a wide desert floor. A hot, gusty wind blew dust devils across the road and sand particles into our eyes. We pulled the loose ends of our turbans across our faces, to shield noses and lips from the sand blasts. My idea of wearing local garb was a stroke of genius, but about the only one.

Tahir spoke with several armed Mujahideen at the village, then we continued on, driving toward the yellow-brown mud walls of a fort some two kilometers to the east. We stopped a few hundred meters before its entrance. Tahir leaned out of the Toyota and pointed to the side of the road. "Mines," he warned.

No lie, genius! On either side of the road, aligned in successive rows, were anti-personnel mines laid in an area approximately 20 meters wide, in front of a single strand of barbed wire. The Soviet POMZ-2 stake mines consisted of a wooden stake with a serrated iron body containing six rows of fragmentation segments with a TNT charge of 75 grams. Deployed around the POMZ-2s were plastic PMN antipersonnel mines buried beneath the surface. A rubber top and a metal band held the covers in place. The PMNs had a TNT charge of 240 grams and were pressure activated. They were lethal because they were undetectable by standard magnetic mine detectors.

The fort, which covered some three-quarters of a square mile in total area, looked as if it had been transplanted from Beau Geste's North Africa; all that was missing was the Tricolor flying from a flagstaff in the center of the parade ground. However, instead of legionnaires with kepis-blancs, there were only discarded pieces of communist Afghan uniforms—caps, jackets, socks—and assorted notebooks scattered throughout the grounds.

At the extreme southeastern corner of the perimeter were the hulks of two Soviet T-62 MBTs, their turrets blown off and hulls scorched. Dug in near a trench-line was an MT-LB, a multi-purpose tracked vehicle the turret of which, with a 7.62mm PKT machine gun, had also been destroyed. Fifty meters farther along the trench line sat a BTR-152 VI Armored Personnel Carrier with its sides and front heavily pockmarked from Mujahideen AK rounds.

Tahir, our team and several Mujahideen checked the vehicles out. Tahir warned, "Don't walk too far from the center of the fort." He pointed toward the edge of the perimeter. "There are many mines scattered . . . not marked." Water, as always, had become a problem. The large mechanical pump that furnished well water for the garrison had been destroyed before the Soviets and their Afghan lackeys had abandoned the place.

We all gathered at the Toyotas, shaking hands and preparing to leave. A number of the villagers had been designated as a guard force to occupy the fort temporarily, although the possibility of the Russians attempting to retake the position seemed remote, given the proposed withdrawal plan signed by the U.S.S.R. in Geneva, which was soon to go into effect.

DEADLY POTION

Williams bellyached loudly about dying of thirst and we all echoed him. "No problem," Tahir replied. "Good water in village. We will stop there."

At the roadside, 100 meters from the village, was a large pond some 50 meters wide and 70 meters long. Its pale green waters were spotted with leaves and occasionally dotted by clusters of ripe berries that were swept by occasional gusts from a grove of tall mulberry trees on one side.

We had run out of our supply of iodine tablets, but in spite of the appearance of the water, thirst drove us to recklessness. Desperation drove us. Fanshaw knelt by the pond's edge and filled our canteens.

On the return trip to the CP, Tahir stopped frequently at mountain-fed streams, and everyone drank their belly full. In one deep pool, the Mujahideen in the back of the truck engaged in a little Afghan fishing—bursts of AK fire caused spurts of water to geyser several feet in the air and hurl tiny fish along the rocks lining the shore.

The fasting of Ramadan had left the Mujahideen and Tahir totally whipped. He complained of weakness as he pulled the Toyota to a stop in front of his hut. During tea after dusk, he mentioned that we had a choice during the coming attack on the Russian fort of either going with the assault group or remaining with the supporting weapons. We had the impression that he would be directing the attack from the support weapons' position, high on the military crest of a mountain overlooking the objective. We soon found out otherwise.

Before we had a chance to make a decision, he had started another round of talks with newly arrived commanders who would lead the Mujahideen during the attack, and we were left to ourselves. In our honor, Tahir had ordered a small feast. In addition to the usual sickening sweet tea, cakes and oranges, we got tomatoes, greens, bread and pieces of chicken, a real Afghan feast.

"We must sleep. Tomorrow we will leave very early!" Tahir said, fighting to stay awake. We were barely able to muster up the energy to finish the meal and start back up the long trail to the hilltop and our bedrolls.

At "rooster reveille" at daybreak, things were hopping in Tahir's quarters. People were racing back and forth between the Toyotas and the CP buildings, and one of the Mujahideen ran up the hill in our direction. Fanshaw, the eternal organizer, started gathering up our gear. "We'd better get ready. It looks like we're going to move out!" The runner stopped a few feet below us and motioned: "Come now . . . we go!"

The road gradually shrank to a trail leading down an increasingly steep canyon. Rocks, shale, basketball-sized boulders and mud puddles from a small stream blocked the way. Ahead of us, a long column of armed Mujahideen walked on either side of the trail, AKs, RPGs, and RPDs slung. Several hundred meters ahead, three Mujahideen drivers were carefully easing Massey-Ferguson tractors, ammunition carts in tow, over the obstacles. Our Toyota stopped and Mohammed, a former Afghan Army colonel, tapped on the side of the door.

"We walk now."

He led us up a billy goat trail winding toward a cave high on the rock face. Standing aside at the entrance, he waited until one by one we ducked under a low stone overhang and entered the dim cavern. Inside were several older Mujahideen sitting on blankets with their backs against the damp rock walls. The air was filled with a strong odor of hash and a fog of blue smoke.

Mohammed stuck his head inside and spoke to one of the younger Mujahideen sitting near the entrance. "Chai," he ordered. The boy went outside and returned with the usual tray, this time only with the syrupy sweet green tea. The boiled tea was providing most of our liquid intake since the Afghans had no purified water, but Hunter and I had been hit with Montezuma's revenge and were wiped out. Nauseated, cursing this mad adventure, we grabbed our cameras and left the foul-smelling cave. Williams and Fanshaw soon followed behind. Columns of Mujahideen tractors pulling carts loaded with ammunition were passing below.

"Let's go," Mohammed said. Our Toyota had disappeared, and in its place was one of the four-wheeled ammo carts hitched to a Massey-Ferguson. Instead of 107mm rocket rounds, the cart was crammed with Mujahideen who grinned and nodded as we climbed aboard. A 12-year-old boy who had hopped on offered to carry my AK. Mohammad put an instant stop to that, telling me to stay glued to my weapon. Musa warned us about some of the Mujahideen tagging along: "These are bad people . . . some bandits. Be careful." As Williams said, "Some of the Muj looked like members of the Golden Horde who'd formed an advance party for Genghis Khan."

A very bumpy hour later, the cart jolted to a halt and we got out. We pulled out our cameras and started shooting photos of the attack force. Musa, who had a TV camera, began filming the operations, asking Hunter to give a running commentary on the march.

The sun had set and we were soon stumbling through the darkness. We hopped into the tractors and other vehicles with the rest of the "attack force" and hit the flat road. Suddenly, honking horns, lots of yells of "Allah Akhbar" and the sound of sirens shattered the night air. The Afghan Army garrison troops must have been completely stoned on hash because the Mujahideen, with no concern for noise discipline, had alerted the commies in the fort that we were coming to destroy them. Musa's warning may have panned out.

"Do you believe this shit?" I roared, expecting an imminent attack on our battalion of idiots. But we hit the road again, passing by another village, where more Mujahideen joined our entourage.

After another uneventful 15 or 20 minutes, we stopped in front of a clump of trees. The Mujahideen jumped out and formed into a group. I made sure my team was still together. Musa and Mohammed joined us, directing us to follow a column of Mujahideen moving out in the darkness. We stumbled over each other along the road as we followed our guides. Williams fell into a ditch and Musa helped him back up.

Bodies piled into the mosque and by the time our heads hit the pillows, the snoring rumbled. Williams, by now in an advanced neurotic stage, squirmed around on the hard floor, trying not to strangle himself overnight with the neck straps on his chest webbing, and pulled the canvas rig over his head.

"No, no," Musa, on alert, told Williams. "Leave magazines on. Don't let anyone have the Kalashnikov. Put the sling around the leg and not let anyone take Kalashnikov. Many bad people—Khomeini people—take guns from you," warning about some in the group. Why the hell were we marching with some of the enemy? A better question was why were we involved in this insanity?

Three of the Mujahideen slipped out of the mosque, toting their RPG launchers. Next morning we drank the sick chai and chomped on fly-infested bread with a group of Mujahideen inside the mosque while others were eating outside.

NOBODY SAID ANYTHING ABOUT TANKS

A rocket blast shocked us into tossing our tea and running out to see what was going on. Another blast exploded on the far side of the fort some two klicks to the southeast of our position, creating a large cloud of smoke. I reached for my Skoal. "What happened to the 1,000 107mm rounds that were supposed to hit the fort between 0300 and 0600?" I asked.

"Inshallah," answered Hunter, wiping sweat from his face. The sick sweet tea had made us even thirstier and there was no water to be found.

"Where's the water point?" Williams shouted at a Mujahideen trotting past us. He ignored us and headed toward several scrawny trees 100 meters behind the mosque, where other Mujahideen were squatting around what looked like an oasis in the desert.

"That looks like a pond." Hunter started walking toward the group, followed by Fanshaw carrying our canteen.

We caught up with them and walked around a wall to find a good-sized sinkhole, better called a shit hole, covered with a greenish scum. Standing at the far edge were two sheep and a donkey, their feet soaking in the muddy mix. Near them were several sheep turds floating gently near the green scum.

Fanshaw filled the canteen, shaking his head in disbelief, and we started back to the mosque. It was 1000 hours and the weather was scorching and stagnant. The flies had invaded the mosque and covered the food like a black vibrating blanket.

Several Mujahideen were standing on the shoulders of others under four mulberry trees full of ripe fruit next to the mosque. They were beating the tree with sticks and the ground below was covered with the unappetizing red fruit. Along with the flies and the Mujahideen, who were used to their pathetically slow-moving pace of life, we watched our watches slowly tick until it was time to sleep again. No action, nothing.

The next morning Williams, by now nearly hallucinating, ready to forget about the commies and just kill me, asked Musa when the attack was supposed to start. Further, where the hell were the 1,000 rounds of 107mm rockets that were supposed to have plastered the fort? Also, where were the 340 other members of the attack force? Not to mention the reserve of 500 other Mujahideen.

"No problem," came the answer. "The attack force waiting for word from fort."

"What word from the fort?"

"A Mujahideen agent is inside the fort," Musa smiled. "He is speaking with Russian commander. When the commander says hands up, we get four tanks."

Nobody had said anything about tanks.

"They have four Russian T-62 tanks in the fort," Musa wrinkled his brow. The T-62 tank has a U-5TS(2A20) 115mm smooth-bore gun with a bore evacuator. Maximum rate of fire is four rounds per minute, and it can fire HE-FRAG, (FS and OF-IS), HEAT-FS (BK-4 and BK-4M), and APFSDS (BM-6) ammo. A 7.62mm PKT machine gun is fired co-axially. Like other Soviet tanks, it can lay its own screen of white smoke by spraying diesel on hot exhaust manifolds; the smoke exits from exhaust ports on the left side. At 3,000 yards firing APFSDS rounds, first-hit probability is 100 percent.

Musa shrugged.

Williams perked up, hoping that the Soviet commander would indeed "hands up," anticipating the effect of four 115mm tank guns working over the Mujahideen attack formation as it crossed a line of departure in the open area around the fort.

Williams asked Musa, "What tactics do you use when you attack the fort?"

"No problem. First lie down on ground." He demonstrated. "Then stand up." He jumped to his feet with his AK at port arms and hesitated.

"OK, then what?"

"Then stand up straight." He squared his shoulders, brought the AK to an assault position from the hip, and yell 'Allah Akhbar,' then run forward."

It was no surprise that the Mujahideen's infantry assault tactics were bizarre. "Musa, how close will you get to fort before you stand up and yell, 'Allah Akhbar'?" Williams asked. This insanity was about as whacky as Pickett's charging up Cemetery Ridge at the battle of Gettysburg.

"No problem. Maybe 1,000 meters. No problem," Musa said. Insanity!

Later that afternoon, three of us decided to eat our fly-infested bread and oranges in the shade of some trees rather than in the mosque. Before we'd finished our oranges, the rockets whizzed. We rushed off to find Hunter. Musa and two Mujahideen just outside the mosque entrance bantered in Pashto and burst into laughter.

"What is the joke?" I asked.

Apparently on our first night here, the Mujahideen with the RPGs had gone to the village and captured the deputy Russian commander and two Afghan soldiers, all drunk and asleep from hashish.

The flies were so thick inside our new mosque hotel by now that we decided to camp outside. Musa nixed that idea, pointing to a group of Mujahideen standing around a 14.5mm KPV heavy machine gun.

"Those are bad. Better you stay inside."

Again that night, we faced the usual Mujahideen feast of sick sweet chai, bread, oranges and flies. By now, Montezuma's revenge had struck everyone. We were dehydrated and becoming delusional.

The number of Mujahideen was thinning down. The number of rocket rounds fired at the fort increased, but nowhere close to the point where it could be called a barrage. Mortar rounds came from the fort once in a while but nothing of importance.

A FOX HOLE

On the morning of the third day, Williams and Fanshaw scooped out a hole in the event the fort batteries decided to give the mosque and the surrounding huts a pasting from mortars, artillery or, worst scenario, the T-62 MBTs. On the way back, Fanshaw turned and walked toward the 14.5 and a truck that was partially hidden by an adobe wall. While he was looking at the vehicle, a young Mujahideen, maybe in his early 20s, dressed in clean cammies, stopped Williams and in perfect English asked, "Are you a Muslim?"

"No."

"Are you an American?"

"Yes."

"What are you doing here?"

Williams ignored him and found us checking out the fort through Steiner binoculars, watching the exchange of fire between the Soviets and the Mujahideen 107mm rocket batteries emplaced some 100 meters to the southeast of the mosque compound. Musa ran up from the rear of the adjoining buildings and called to us, "You come now."

"Come where?" Williams asked.

"You no come? Why you are doing this to me?" The more agitated he got, the worse his English became.

"Bullshit. We want to know where the hell you are going and how far it is before we're leaving here." Fanshaw shook his finger at Musa, who turned to me for guidance.

"OK, we go," I decided. Hunter and I dragged behind Musa

"They're gonna get their ass blown away going with that idiot," Williams remarked as he just watched us walk off.

BOOMMM! Twenty-two hundred yards, Williams estimated the range from the rocket batteries to the point of impact. CRUMMP, CRUMMP. Fanshaw started running toward the truck, unslinging his AK. All the Mujahideen around the 14.5 began running away from the gun to look at an open field some 800 meters away. By now Williams and Fanshaw had spotted through their binoculars several Mujahideen advancing across the field from our left to the right.

CRUMMP. A 120mm mortar round from the fort landed behind one of the running Mujahideen, temporarily masking him with grey smoke. As the smoke cleared, there was no sign of the Afghan; then within seconds he was up and trotting again. To his left were two other Mujahideen, advancing across the thick grass. CRUMMP. Another round hit to their front, throwing chunks of earth, stones and grass stalks high in the air, covering them with smoke and cordite fumes.

"Paul, if those Afghans in the fort traverse those tubes to the left, we're going to be in a world of hurt. That truck behind the wall is sitting over a grease pit that's deep enough for us both. The wall might go, but the truck will cover us except for a direct hit. Then we're screwed anyway," Williams warned.

The two started toward the truck when Mohammed, standing near the 14.5, waved at them to follow him immediately.

"Hell, no!" Fanshaw shook his head at Mohammed. "If he's going to go back to the mosque, we'll get our ass blown off if they start hitting the buildings."

"No, no. Please come with me. I must speak with you. There is much danger for you here." Mohammed started toward the mosque.

"Come on, let's give him a few minutes. We can come back here." Williams fell in behind the old man, Fanshaw following.

There were no Mujahideen to be seen in the mosque.

"Alright, what's the problem?" Fanshaw asked.

"You must leave quickly. There is a vehicle at the back of the building." The Afghan's face was drawn and his eyes bloodshot. Fanshaw was staring at Mohammed as if the old man was off his rocker.

"You know Mujahideen who ask you if you are Muslims?"

"Yeah, what about 'em?"

"They are Khomeini people from village." He paused and wiped his nose with the back of one gnarled hand. "Many times they meet and take money from KGB in fort. They say when we attack, they will shoot Americans."

"I think it's time we got the hell out of here," Fanshaw said. "I believe the old man."

Mohammad told the two to stay in the mosque until he found a vehicle.

"We've got to tell Brown and Hunter," Fanshaw said as he picked up his AK and followed the Afghan out of the mosque and into the courtyard. Musa, Hunter and I were rounding the comer, with Fanshaw and Williams heading toward us. Several Mujahideen were watching the 122mm mortar rounds from the fort explode in the distance.

Williams was spouting out some gibberish in Spanish about whether we should tell Musa about what Mohammed had said. Musa, insulted, stomped off after Mohammed. Fanshaw and Williams told me what old Mohammed had said.

"I don't believe any of this bullshit," Hunter snorted and wiped his face with the sleeve of his Afghan blouse. "The old man is crazy. There aren't any Khomeini people here, and even if there were there's no way the Muj are going to let them hurt us. That would be the worst possible thing they could allow."

As I reflected on the crazy story Fanshaw asked me, "Where'd Musa take you guys?"

"We walked about a hundred meters over to the 107s. I got a chance to fire a couple of rockets at the fort. Musa took some pictures," I said.

"To hell with the pictures. What are your feelings about leaving?" Williams put pressure on.

"I think we should get the hell out of here," I said. "We haven't got communication with a swinging dick here who's got any authority. We're all sick from drinking pond scum shitwater. There hasn't been shit in the way of an attack on the fort, and sooner or later the Russians in that sonofabitch are going to call Kabul and all shit's going to hit the fan."

We went looking for Mohammed.

"I'll go find him." Fanshaw headed for the area behind the building where Mohammed was last seen. We were getting our gear together when Musa ran in.

"There is no danger. No Khomeini men. Tahir come. Russians go hands up maybe." He was as wound up as before.

"Screw it, Musa, we go," I said.

Hunter made a face and looked at Musa. "Musa, they think some people in the village will try and kill us during attack."

"No, not possible. Mujahideen won't let it happen."

Mohammed suddenly walked in, looked around at the group and sat down near Musa, who said some harsh Pashto words to the old man and stormed out. Mohammed smiled and shook his head. "Musa is boy," he said. "He not understand."

"Is all our gear ready?" I asked Fanshaw. "We're set to get out of here?"

"I will go now to the vehicle. You wait at the wall outside." Mohammed shook hands with us and scurried out the door. We gathered outside at the adobe wall that faced the Russian fort. It shielded us from any of the Russian Afghan garrison that might be scoping the mosque and the surrounding buildings. Williams was focusing his binoculars on the fort, watching for Mujahideen 107mm hits, when we heard a sudden CRACK.

"What the hell's that?" I looked around with nerves dancing from the heat, the cuisine, the chants and lunacy.

ORANGE FLAMES FLARED

An orange-red flame flared from the direction of the highest point on the 1,500-meter ridgeline, followed by another CRACK.

"Holy shit!" Fanshaw yelled.

The flame came from a 115mm gun attached to the turret of a T-62, which was sitting in full view atop the ridgeline and firing at the Mujahideen rocket batteries in the valley. Apparently the commander, who did not bother to go into hull defilade position, which would afford some protection against the 107s, was not worried about the Mujahideen rockets. Suddenly, a ball of fire throwing orange showers of flame erupted near the T-62. One of the Mujahideen rounds had landed short but on line with the Soviet tank. It was only a matter of time before the gunner decided to traverse the turret in our direction.

BLAM. A second orange fireball hit dead center against the T-62's hull, enveloping the tank in flames that kept burning long after impact, sending a column of greasy, black smoke high in the air, obscuring any view of the turret and hatch.

I muttered, "There's Mohammed. Maybe he's got our vehicle squared away." The old man was trotting toward us, casting glances toward the burning tank.

"The vehicle will be ready soon. We will go back into the mosque to wait."

"Horseshit. Another 'no problem' scenario. Let's find out what the hell's going on." Fanshaw turned and stuck his face close to Mohammed's. "Where's the vehicle?"

"The vehicle is back there. Behind the building."

"Paul, take a recce and see what's going on with our ride," I said. The ex-legionnaire left at a run, long legs moving like pistons, Mohammed walking swiftly behind him. "Bob, the Toyota's there, but it's locked and there's no driver anywhere around. What do you want to do?" Fanshaw came back panting.

"Let's go." I headed for the vehicle, ordering the rest to follow, with the old man Mohammed bringing up the rear. When we reached the Toyota, Williams crawled up into the cargo compartment and squatted down with his back toward the wall of a darkened building only a few feet away. Fanshaw took up a position between the truck and the building, giving him a field of fire covering both flanks. Hunter and I stood at the rear of the vehicle, waiting for Mohammed to close up. Musa and several Mujahideen walked quickly around the side of the building and headed for the truck.

There was a series of dull click-clacks as rounds were chambered. Williams and I locked and loaded, my fire selector was set to AUTO.

Musa and the Mujahideen, hearing us chamber rounds in our AKs, skidded to a halt. He raised both hands chest high, turned palms outward and protested, "Bob, Mike . . . no shoot Mujahideen." I pointed my AK at Musa's chest. "I no shoot if Mujahideen no shoot." Musa walked away from me and toward Williams.

"Mike, Mujahideen no shoot you." Williams moved his fire selector from SINGLE to AUTO and pointed the AK at Musa's middle.

"Musa, we go. Now!"

For the next two hours, the Mujahideen ran back and forth between us and the mosque. The driver wasn't available, then they couldn't find the commander. Musa and the Mullah, yelling something about Allah, assured us that we were safe.

Finally, Farouk, the assault party's commander, showed up and the three started shouting at each other. Some Mujahideen appeared with a radio that they set up several feet away from the truck. Farouk knelt down near it and started to transmit. After at least 15 minutes of communication in Pashto, Musa ran over and told me, "Bob, commander say we go now."

Suddenly a driver appeared, and we climbed in the Toyota, followed by some other armed Mujahideen. Farouk ordered Mohammed and Musa into the second Toyota, then joined us in the front passenger seat.

LOST

It was pitch black, but the drivers had no problem following the snaking, rocky road. We were all prepared for a Russian ambush. We approached the village where our Khomeini-supporting assassins were holed up. The villagers had shot a series of flares in some sort of fireworks display and they arched into the black sky.

We drove on for four hours uphill on a sandy road. We arrived at no-man's-land nestled away in a canyon. The Mujahideen jumped out and started climbing in single file. We had no choice but to follow.

The Mujahideen were pressing their luck, laughing as we chugged up the rocky path and across a muddy patch where a mountain stream flowed. We said nothing, numbly putting one foot after the other. Our boots were full of mud, inside and out. Williams threw himself down by the stream. scooping up water in his cupped hands.

The tall Mujahideen grabbed him. "Op ney! Lop ney. No water. No rest." We were in danger from the Russians, and the Mujahideen were in danger from the near delusional, fatigued and murderous armed gringos.

Williams, over the edge, blurted out of the blue "BAHH BAHH!" Our guards, highly amused, started babbling even louder. I suggested that the Mujahideen carry Williams' webbing and ammo.

"Fuck you," he said. Then when he spotted another stream of water, he threw his gear at the Mujahideen.

"Salaam a Leikum. Allah Akhbar. Take this rucker," he said. The laughing Mujahideen grabbed him by each arm and dragged him along. Suddenly, we heard the sound of a Massey-Ferguson that had stopped 50 meters ahead of us. We climbed into the tractor cart, hanging on for dear life, trying to keep our balance on the oily floor as the driver charged ahead to the commo bunker. We reached the top of the hill, climbed out of the cart and walked the last 500 meters. We passed out as soon as we hit the carpet.

In the morning, we were served our usual feast of sick sweet tea and cakes. We hadn't finished when Musa ordered us to go to the vehicle that had just arrived. This time our limo was the tractor and cart that had brought us in there. Three Mujahideen in the cart were fingering their AKs. Mohammed helped us carry our gear to the transport and shook hands, smiling as we climbed up the cart's sides. He stood and watched us until the driver turned the curve. We rattled up some hills and slid down some muddy trails. Rounding one of the hills, the driver came to a fork in the road. When the road branched off, we took the right fork and plunged into a bog hole.

Fanshaw jumped down to the muddy bog side and looked carefully at the tractor's right front tire. The Mujahideen tried to rock the Massey free nonstop for a good hour, only to dig the cart deeper into the mud. Fanshaw, lean and muscular, stripped to the waist, grabbed a shovel from the cart and started digging up the mud in front of the wheel, but that only made things worse.

"Let's walk," he said, and we headed out for the next command post. It was only ten kilometers away. The Mujahideen told us the route to the Command Post was over an easy trail. Paul's map showed a 1,000-meter increase in elevation as we marched up. We reached a valley that ran some 25 klicks to a high range of mountains. Musa led the pack. Fanshaw stopped, looked at a topographical map he carried, took out a compass and shot a bearing to the highest of the peaks across the valley. Halfway up the hillside Musa spotted a small boy. "Wait here. I will go talk to the boy," he said.

"Ask him how far to the CP," I said as I rested my back against a rock.

"Bob, he's lost," Fanshaw said. "We should be going north, not east. Look at this.

I glanced at the route Fanshaw pointed out. "Son of a bitch, you're right," I said, preparing to kill Musa.

Musa came back from talking to the boy and said, "He is a nomad. He says we go that way." He pointed to a road that curved down northeastward, toward the valley floor.

"Bullshit, Musa. That'll take all day, and we'll be stuck on that road all night and tomorrow. Don't forget we're low on water and I've only got one canteen for the five of us." Fanshaw tapped the canteen attached to his belt.

"No problem. We can go that way," Musa pointed again to the winding road. I clenched my fist at the Mujahideen. "No, Musa. We go Fanshaw's way."

Musa shrugged and turned away, sucking on a blade of grass. Fanshaw took out his map and compass once again, checked the bearing to the peak and started off cross-country in determined strides. We figured we had originally gone in completely the wrong direction and were now 20 kilometers away.

Musa joined Paul at the head of the column, marching along without a care in the world, carrying the only AK in the group. We stumbled across scrub brush and rocks and into deep ravines and back up, having to grab branches to keep us from sliding down.

"Listen," I said. It was the sound of jet engines. Musa shielded his eyes with his right hand, looking in the direction of the sounds. Hunter was the first to see them. He pointed and yelled. "MiGs! They're dropping heat flares to stop the Stingers!"

The jets were not visible, but the heat flares were easy to pick up—silvery-white smoke columns against the light blue of the Afghan sky. A few seconds passed, then a loud BOOM shook the earth. They were bombing the village. Hunter turned toward the distant peak marking the CP's location and began to jog down the slope, shouting, "Come on! If those bastards catch us out here in the open we've had it!"

We ran after him running across flat terrain, slowing to a quick walk through heavy bush, and jogging along crumbling banks of dry gullies. We heard no more bombing, only the noise of jet engines. We scrambled up a small rise and ahead of us was a crude hut built of earth and grass, with two shepherd nomads sitting on the ground watching their sheep. At our approach, one of them got up to greet us. Musa shook his hand. "These nomads are sometimes spies for Russians. Don't speak."

We sat down and rested while Musa walked back. The old, wrinkled one motioned to his companion to go to the hut. He came back a while later, toting a large tin pitcher. He offered Musa and his friend a drink. They refused it and pointed towards us. He knelt in front of us and offered the jug to Fanshaw, who took a couple of swallows, then passed it to Hunter who did the same. Then it was my turn after which I handed it off to Williams. We chugged the no doubt bacteria-laden water down. Fanshaw filled our canteen, and we nervously started off again, watching our backs. We had one AK, no food, minimal water for five men and the barest of communication.

We stumbled along down another deep ravine. I kept asking how much farther we had to go before we would reach the CP. No response. "Do you understand," I roared at Musa. "Yes," he nodded several times. Williams called, "Robert, can't you see he doesn't understand a damn thing you're saying?"

"Sure he does. Right Musa?"

Musa nodded his head. "Yes. Yes. No problem."

I smirked at the nervous Williams.

"OK, Brown," he replied, "ask him if he's an astronaut."

I did, and we waited for the response. "Musa, are you an astronaut?"

"Yes."

"Ask him if he's a brain surgeon," Williams said.

"Musa, are you a brain surgeon?"

Again the happy smile, a nod of the head and a happy "Yes."

We picked up speed as the sun began to set. Fanshaw, having replaced Musa as the guide, yelled, "Come on! You've got to hurry. If we're caught out here at night with no water, no food and one AK, we could be in a world of shit."

Musa nodded. "Yes," he remarked.

We ran into another nomad with a small boy and a herd of sheep. Musa stopped them and, after a brief conversation in Pashto, the shepherd pointed straight ahead in the direction we were traveling.

"OK, not far," Musa said, breaking into a trot.

We saw a familiar-looking hill facing a river and the small grove of mulberry trees that marked the CP area. Fanshaw urged, "You've got to hurry! We can't go into the camp after dark; the sentries will shoot us."

"Five minute break," Williams begged.

"To Hell with the break. COME ON! If we were in the Legion, I'd tie a rope around you and drag your ass!" Fanshaw roared. He started trotting ahead, glancing over his shoulder to make sure I was still moving. Musa was well ahead of us, starting down a steep incline, when a shout sounded from atop a barren hill to our immediate right. Hunter stopped short and froze, his head turned toward the summit. A Mujahideen was pointing an AK at Hunter. The click-clack of a chambering round came faintly over Musa's answer.

Musa and the sentry shouted at each other for a while. Hunter was still frozen in place. Fanshaw was kneeling and I wanted to spit my Skoal at the Mujahideen. Musa motioned us up the trail leading to the sentry. "No problem, everything fine. We go."

Fanshaw led the way behind Musa, with Hunter bringing up the rear. Our ensuing feast of chai, oranges and cakes was as good as a big hunk of prime rib and baked potato and a couple bottles of wine this time. Fanshaw cursed Musa under his breath and Williams scratched the fleas attacking his tired ass. Tahir was nowhere to be seen, so Musa was sent down the hill to the CP building to find him.

He came back a few minutes later, smiling. "A vehicle will take us back to Quetta in the morning. INSHALLAH."

Fanshaw walked up to Musa and put his face six inches from the Afghan's. "Musa. We all go to Quetta tomorrow morning! No! INSHALLAH! We go!"

"OK, yes. No problem."

At daybreak, we packed our remaining gear and finished our continental breakfast of chai, bread and cake-flies. Musa, who had slept at the CP, came to the bottom of the hill and yelled to us, pointing to a Toyota parked nearby. By the time we reached the bottom there were several Mujahideen gathered around the truck. Ramadan had not yet ended and the driver was kneeling on his prayer rug a short distance away. His back toward us, his head toward Mecca, he was deeply involved in prayer and oblivious to everyone. Finally, the driver finished his chanting and walked around the Toyota, opened the door and crawled in behind the wheel. He glanced up at some sacred flowers he had in the car and shouted, "Allah Akhbar!"

I got in next to the driver, Williams next to me. The driver cranked the engine and turned on the radio, and off we were to Quetta. The trip was long and dusty, but Quetta sounded like an oasis in the desert.

Tahir sent us a note explaining the reason he wasn't able to visit us at the fort. Shortly after we had crossed the frontier into Afghanistan he was informed that by 15 May 1988 all his arms, ammunition and supplies would have to be out of Pakistani territory and inside Afghanistan, or they would be impounded. Presumably this was the Pakistani reaction to the massive explosion of an enormous ammo dump near Islamabad just weeks before, which was suspected to have been the handiwork of the Soviet KGB.

We made it out, swearing never to go back to that dreadful country. Until next year, that was . . .

21

SOF *NEVER MISSES A WAR:* *MISSION TO LEBANON*

For years Lebanon, the once vibrant cultural paradise, the "Switzerland of the Middle East," with its exotic cedars, picturesque hills and valleys and breathtaking Mediterranean coastlines, had been ravaged by a vicious civil war.

Ruthless Sunni Palestine Liberation Organization (PLO) invasions and occupation; fundamentalist Iran flexing its muscle with its Shia Party of God (Hezbollah) counterparts in Lebanon; Syrian interference, bombardments and occupation; and multiple Israeli invasions and a 17-year occupation of southern Lebanon combined to all but ruin the once-exemplary Middle eastern nation.

For years and through at least six wars, from 1975 to 1990, the battles were fought on a dizzying number of fronts and shifting alliances. The PLO fought the Israeli Defense Forces (IDF) and its allied Lebanese Phalange Christian Army as well as Hezbollah. The South Lebanon Army (SLA), which included both Christians and Muslims in turn, in bed with Israel, was fighting Syria and Hezbollah as well as the PLO.

In 1982, I was all tied up with the POW operation in Southeast Asia, so I sent Larry Dring to Lebanon three times for months at a time to work with Major Haddad of the Christain Phalange. Dring taught the Phalange troop anti-tank warfare, small unit tactics, and advanced demolition. Larry was the perfect fit for training the Phalange. Medicaly retired from his numerous wounds in Nam, he was an icon in Special Forces. During four tours in Nam, most of it in the Central Highlands, he started as an enlisted man and came out as a Captain winning two Silver Stars, four Bronze Stars and Five Purple Hearts. One of his friends said, "Gotta love a guy whose idea of Psychological Operations to bury an enemy along a trail with one arm sticking out of the ground holding up a leaflet that says 'Surrender of Die'."

While he was there Dring found small arms innovations and weaponry that were not in the U.S. technical manuals, such as Russian hand grenades that had zero-to-eight seconds before detonating. The West was unaware that Russia had zero second delays before exploding. Those who relied on the common wisdom that grenades had several seconds before detonating could indeed have a very unpleasant experience. At first, he took it to the intelligence officer of the Marine Amphibious Force then stationed near the airport in Beirut. The First Lieutenant had no concept of what he had and sent it to explosive ordnance disposal to be destroyed. Dring brought back a duffle bag full of weapons that were not in the Army technical manuals on Soviet weapons. He strolled casually through customs with his duffle bag and brought it into the *SOF* office.

On another *SOF* training mission in 1982, when the Marines were in Beirut, Dring, along with Dale Dye, active Marine at the time and later *SOF* editor, met up. The Marines were forbidden to return fire targeting the SLA without express permission from the U.S. embassy. The story came out that someone was shooting back at the bad guys in the hills who were firing mortars or rockets at the Marines. Before long 4.2" mortar rounds would start falling on the enemy and they would shut down. Dring and Dye were the culprit "phantom mortar team."

Dumping a dozen or so in any corner he could find on my always clutered desk, he chuckles, "Look what I brought ya. Never seen before in the West. Live Russian Grenade Fuses," he grinned.

"Holy shit,Larry, you brought me jail time," I roared.

Once I had calmed down, I called the Denver based FBI agent, Russ Hashman, who, I speculated had been directed to monitor what SOF was up to ever since we got investigated for allegedly violating the Neutrality Act.

"Russ," I said, pretending calm. "Suppose, just suppose one of my reporters came back from Lebanon with some active explosive devices that the U.S. Army would be interested in. Would you come up and take them off my hands. Now this is just a hypothetical," I said.

He chuckled, saying that he just might and I replied, "Please get up here ASAP."

He arrived in short order and took the jail time off my hands.

"Dring, no more crazy shit like that," I ordered him. "I am going to round up the editorial staff and we are going to the nearest bar.

Larry passed away from his war wounds in 1983. Rest in Peace, brother.

22

GRENADA—ONE WE WON!

The United States Invaded Grenada in 1983.

"Pack up, we are going to war," I told my then Managing Editor Jim Graves. We packed up and got on the first plane and went to find the war. Or so we thought.

"Where's the war?" we demanded as we charged through the streets of Grenada's capital, St. Georges. Smiling Grenadians answered in their sing-song English, "The Cubans have gone to the hills. Welcome to Grenada." By Sunday, 30 October, 1983, the liberation of Grenada was almost complete. It was no invasion, it was simply a liberation. At least that's the way the Grenadians saw it when former Ranger, Rod Hafemeister, Graves and I arrived on the island.

At Point Salines Airport, we observed an 82nd Airborne artillery battery on the northeast end of the runway, some troops on the perimeter, some foot and vehicle patrols along the road, and numerous vehicle checkpoints, some abandoned. We didn't see any invaders, a single body or any blown-up cars and trucks. Although rumor had it that significant numbers of Cubans were retreating into the hills to conduct guerrilla operations, we saw only three captured Cuban prisoners in two days. There were Cuban antiaircraft guns and several shot-up BTR-60s, but it was obvious that any real resistance had long since crumbled.

We had arrived at the island with the first load of about 160 press people, five days after D-Day. We were enraged that we had missed the war and even more so when the smiling Grenadians asked, "Are Americans going to stay? We want them to. It's a good thing you didn't wait a few more days." No lie!

There was almost no sign of fighting in St. Georges, the Grenada capital from a press holding area at the airport in Barbados. The objectives of the 1st and 2nd Battalions, 75th Rangers, were south of town and the Marines from the 24th Marine Amphibious Unit (MAU) operated on the other side of the island, north of St. Georges.

With the exception of forts Frederick and Rupert, which had taken a pounding from carrier-launched A-7s and C-130 Spectre gunships, the only signs of damage around St. Georges were caused by scavengers and looters.

The Marines, who had moved into St. Georges the previous day (it had not yet been assaulted and was theoretically still in hostile hands), were as puzzled about their reception on the island as we were. The press who arrived with us on Sunday were just as bewildered. One young Marine approached Miami Herald reporter Don Bohning (one of seven newsmen who had slipped onto the island by boat on Tuesday, 25 October, the day of the invasion) and asked: "Can you tell us what's going on? Is the Grenadian Army with us or against us?"

The 1,200-man People's Revolutionary Army (PRA) had started laying down their weapons on the day of the invasion, stripping off their uniforms and putting on civilian clothes to join the crowd welcoming the 6,000 American liberators shortly after dawn. The sky over Point Salines was filled with C-l30s and parachuting Rangers. The ocean turned gray with the fleet's U.S. Navy warships.

Cuban "construction workers," some actual laborers and some from a military engineering unit, put up stiffer-than expected resistance around Point Salines. Some PRA elements did fight back on the first and second days at Point Salines, Frequente and Fort Frederick. However, most of the PRA, like the overwhelming majority of the population, had little love for its own commanders and none whatsoever for the Cubans.

At the time of the invasion Grenada was, in theory, under the control of General Hudson Austin and his 16-man Revolutionary Military Council. However, in fact, power was shared by Austin and Deputy Prime Minister Bernard Coard, and coordinated with the Central Committee of the

New Jewel Movement (NJM). Austin and Coard, dedicated pro-Cuban Marxists, engineered the house arrest and subsequent execution of Prime Minister Maurice Bishop on 19 October, which triggered the U.S.-led assault on 25 October.

Directing the NJM from behind the scenes were Soviet Ambassador Gennadiy I. Sachenev, a four-star general and expert in covert actions with ties to the KGB, and Cuban Ambassador Julian Enrique Tores Riza, a senior intelligence officer of the Dirección General de Inteligencia (DGI), Cuba's KGB surrogate.

After American forces had seized their initial objectives, they moved out into the hills to hunt down fleeing Cubans and PRA soldiers. To the GIs' surprise, they encountered not hostile fire, but a picnic, with Grenadians offering gifts of cold soft drinks, melons, cheers and information about the hiding places of Cubans and NJM leaders. Information from locals led USMC Captain David Karcher, on Saturday, 29 October, to a house near St. Georges where Coard, his Jamaican-born wife Phyllis (also a prime leader of the anti-Bishop forces on the Central Committee) and some other NJM leaders were hiding. Coard initially indicated he would not surrender, but changed his mind when the Marines targeted antitank weapons on the house. Captain Karcher reported that Coard came out muttering, "I'm not responsible. I'm not responsible."

While Coard waited in the Marine compound at Queen's Park to be heli-lifted to the USS Guam, a hostile crowd of Grenadians gathered to mock him, chanting, "C is for Coard, Cuba and Communism!"

Austin was captured in a similar fashion the next afternoon. Locals tipped off the 82nd Airborne that he was hiding in a house at Westerhall on the east side of the island.

A quick trip was made to Fort Rupert by *SOF* managing editor Jim Graves, Washington Times reporter Jay Mallin and Lionel "Choo Choo" Pinn, an Osage Indian who was a veteran of WWI, Korea and SOG operations in Vietnam. They revealed that no one was guarding the NJM Central Committee headquarters, the Deputy Minister of Defense's office or the equipment stores at Fort Rupert. Pinn was going to help us crack the Prime Minster's safe, but as the door was sprung, the money was burnt. We searched all three locations. We found a collection of new Soviet helmets, canteens, mess kits, packs, AK-47 bayonets, military manuals and the NJM flag that had flown over the fort, which we auctioned off at the 1983 *SOF* convention in Vegas. Proceeds went to *SOF*'s Refugee Relief International charity. We picked through the papers scattered around the office of Lieutenant Colonel Ewart Layne, Grenada's deputy minister of defense. We also located documents in Fort Frederick and Butler House, the prime minister's office.

We discovered documents and other physical evidence that had been overlooked by whatever intelligence entity got to them before we did:

1) Cuba and the USSR were turning Grenada into a strategic military base;
2) As in Nicaragua, more weapons than Grenada could ever use had been shipped to the island;
3) Bishop was killed because of a power grab by Coard and because he was not as pro-Cuban as other Central Committee members thought he should have been;
4) The NJM was losing control of the country because of its excessive pro-Cuban and pro-communist attitude; and
5) Some well-known Americans had highly questionable dealings with the NJM.

Highlights from the documents we recovered included the following:

- A USSR-Grenada treaty and three shipping manifests show that the Soviets were pouring in more arms than was reasonable for Grenada's 1,200-man PRA. Based on the shipping manifests and examination of the arms recovered in the five major warehouses at Frequente, it appears that Russia and North Korea had shipped in enough arms to equip a division. All shipments from the Soviets and their satellites were via Cuba. Interestingly, even though there were vast quantities of military supplies in stock, the documents recorded frequent incidents of Grenadian junior officers complaining of lack of equipment for their men. It is entirely possible that Grenada served as a warehouse for arms intended for use elsewhere. (Other East Caribbean nations, including Dominica, Jamaica, St. Lucia and St. Vincent feared they might be used to aid leftist guerrillas on their islands.)

- A counter-intelligence report indicated that President Reagan's assertion that the American students at St. Georges Medical School were endangered was well grounded. The report described one school employee's husband, who was being "monitored" as "suspicious," and five students who were considered "dangerous and posing as medical students, but really working for the U.S. government."
- A number of documents revealed that Grenada had sent military students to Russia, Cuba and Vietnam. A note in one document indicated that the students in Cuba "will undergo courses for a one-year period studying up to the level of Division and possibly Army." Why Grenada would need division and army commanders is interesting in its implications. Another document revealed Grenada had plans to send 40 comrades to Vietnam for training and that Russia would pick up the transportation costs.
- A series of reports on the combat readiness of the militia in August and September reveals why the PRA folded up so quickly when U.S. troops arrived. The 5,000-man Grenadian militia was intended as the backup to the 1,200-man army. According to the reports, turnout for drill averaged 15 percent, and transportation problems, faulty weapons and a lack of leadership turned most of the drills into political discussions or football games.
- *SOF* found one document outlining a proposed training program between Nicaragua and Grenada. The NJM was offering to train 15 Sandinistas in Grenada in basic English with a concentration on military terminology and the military phonetic alphabet.
- One letter addressed to the General of the Cuban Army, Raul Castro (Fidel's brother), from Maurice Bishop indicated that the Soviet Union's traditional equipment and resupply weaknesses continued. Bishop asked for Castro's help because the USSR had sent a complete shipment of uniforms and other gear; however, "a vast quantity of boots are much too small in size." Secondly, Bishop needed help securing spare parts and tires since 23 of Grenada's 27 trucks and eight of ten jeeps were inoperable.
- One of the most interesting documents we found was a report from a double agent named "Mark" who was attempting to infil-

> trate a counter-revolutionary group of Grenadians on Barbados. In it, "Mark" and a counterintelligence officer surmised that the Grenadian exile counter-revolutionary group on Barbados was working on behalf of the CIA, which was trying to determine the size and strength of the PRA and the militia. However, the kicker was the comment that the Barbados-based counterrevolutionaries had learned "that the PRG [People's Revolutionary Government of Grenada] was paying someone at the Harvard University Radio Station."

I won't bore you with the other mass of documents we found. As soon as I returned to Boulder, I called Dick Duncan who at that time was the Assistant Managing Editor for Time Magazine. I described what we had discovered. He was excited and flew out a photographer and reporter to evaluate the documents the next day. They perused through the whole pile.

When a November 1983 issue of Time hit the stands, it carried an article titled "A Treasure Trove of Documents: Captured Papers Provide Insights into a Reclining Regime." It read:

"Additional documents were shown to Time by *Soldier of Fortune*, a Boulder, Colorado monthly magazine that specializes in military weapons and tactics; it said the papers had been overlooked by U.S. forces. The documents indicate that Grenada also had military agreements with Vietnam, Nicaragua and at least one Soviet bloc country. A top secret paper dated 18 May 1982, records a shipment of ammunition and explosives from Czechoslovakia via Cuba. One document, signed last November by Nicaragua's Vice Minister of Defense, provides for the establishment of a course in Grenada to teach English-language military terminology to members of the Nicaraguan Army."

We didn't find a war, but we did find highly valuable intelligence. Either the CIA or Army Intelligence had done a shitty job of retrieving critical documents.

23

A GAME OF "DOMINOS" IN EL SALVADOR

U.S. and *SOF* participation in the El Salvador guerrilla war was riding on the wave of fear that a "domino" effect would come into play if El Salvador, sandwiched between Guatemala and Honduras, fell to a communist guerrilla movement. Nicaragua had fallen to the leftist Sandinistas, who in turn supported the FMLN in El Salvador. Alarms were being sounded that El Salvador would go next. Honduras was seeing communist guerrilla intrusions and there was an insurgent movement in Guatemala. Mexico was wobbly and could easily fall if bordered by left-wing governments. Then, of course, the Soviet Union would be at our back door.

The 12-year civil war in El Salvador was a culmination of five decades of violence riddled with coups and revolutions and government-backed death squads that wreaked terror against their opponents.

In 1931, Gen. Maximiliano Hernández Martínez became ruler after a successful coup. The government's oppression of citizens during his 13-year rule was highlighted by the massacre of peasants (La Matanza) who joined a resistance led by Communist Party chief Farabundo Martí. 30,000 were killed during the civil war between Marti's band and Martinez's military government.

Oligarchic military dictatorships continued to rule in the coffee-rich country until 1979, when a Revolutionary Government Junta (JRG) of military officials and civilian political figures overthrew the military dictator General Humberto Romero, head of the conservative Party of National Conciliation.

The U.S. administration of President Carter backed José Napoleón Duarte Fuentes, the exiled conservative political leader of the Christian Democratic Party. Duarte returned in 1980 to El Salvador to head the military regime, which by then was facing a full-blown leftist insurgency. The United States authorized the largest economic aid package ever granted to a Latin country. Throughout the war, the U.S. poured nearly $5 billion of economic aid into the country and over $1 billion in military aid. The Salvadoran Air Force was the number one recipient.

Catholic Archbishop Romero had become the most outspoken opponent of the government, which continued to deploy "death squads" to assassinate political opponents. Thousands were executed. He urged the soldiers in the strongly Catholic country to defy the orders of the political elite and he objected to U.S. military aid to the corrupt government. Catholic leaders in Latin America have traditionally wielded enormous influence.

In 1980, a brutal bloodbath of a civil war erupted in the tiny, densely populated Republic of El Salvador. One hundred thousand lost their lives in the maelstrom before a truce was called. The war was triggered when Major Roberto D'Aubuisson, head of the Junta's military intelligence, ordered Archbishop Romero's assassination. Over 50,000 angry, grieving country folk attended the funeral of the beloved martyr. The highly charged funeral procession erupted when a bomb exploded, followed by a fierce firefight between anti-government demonstrators and military forces in San Salvador's Plaza of the Cathedral. Forty were killed, many of them crushed against a security fence as they fled the mayhem.

Four U.S. nuns working in El Salvador, accused of treason by the government because of alleged leftist leanings, were savagely raped and murdered the same year by government-supported thugs. The Carter Administration, torn between supporting a savage military regime that snuffed out its opponents and the fear of the spread of communism, suspended military aid to the junta.

Five separate leftist guerrilla groups united, forming the Farabundo Martí National Liberation Front (FMLN). The Marxist insurgents, convinced that they had popular support and that a mass insurrection would follow, launched an offensive against the government on 10 January, 1981, just before President Reagan took office.

Although the armed forces trounced the poorly armed and trained rebels, the FMLN's offensive alarmed the Carter administration. The fear of the fall of Central American countries to communism overcame the revulsion at the way the military government in El Salvador tried to suppress popular opposition. Within a week's time, the U.S. resumed aid to the military junta to the tune of $10 million.

In spite of its initial defeat, the FMLN received international recognition and retained military strongholds in Chalatenango and other rural areas, where its forces settled in for the long-drawn-out civil war. Before the end of the year, France and Mexico recognized the front as a political player.

The staunchly anti-communist Reagan administration issued a special report, "Communist Interference in El Salvador," during its first few weeks in office. The statement warned that the Soviet Union and Cuba were supporting and equipping the FMLN in El Salvador, just as they had the Sandinistas in neighboring Nicaragua. Central America had become another violent proxy battleground of the Cold War.

Airpower Journal summed up the balance of forces:

"El Salvador had a small armed force of approximately 10,000 military personnel and 7,000 paramilitary police in 1980 when the war began. The army, the largest part of the armed forces, had approximately 9,000 soldiers organized into four small infantry brigades, an artillery battalion, and a light armor battalion. The level of training was low . . . there was no training or preparation for fighting a counterinsurgency campaign. In short, it was an army that was not prepared for war.

"The leftist conglomerate of rebel factions fielded a force of 10,000 guerrillas, headed by the FMLN, and most were well equipped with assault rifles, machine guns and explosives. The guerrillas were inflicting heavy casualties on the Salvadoran Army and even on the more proficient Air Force, which numbered 1,000. The tide began to turn in 1984, thanks to U.S. involvement and support from the Reagan administration. By then the FMLN controlled large areas of El Salvador along the Nicaragua border and throughout the provinces."

In 1982 a hundred guerrillas overran an airbase, destroying a large portion of the Salvadoran Air Force, which was small and dilapidated to begin with. The U.S. made good the losses. But in 1983 FMLN forces overran the rural town of Berlin, destroying several companies of government troops and capturing all their weapons. Later that year the guerrillas captured other government outposts and ambushed a 2,000-man brigade, inflicting heavy casualties. On New Year's Eve in 1984 they temporarily overran the 4th Brigade's headquarters in an especially humiliating setback for government forces.

U.S. Military Group, meantime, trained and advised the Salvadoran Army while scores of airforce trainees were schooled in Panama and the United States to attempt to give the government an edge in air power.

SOF *IN EL SALVADOR*

In 1981, two *SOF*ers, Bob Burton, a famous bounty hunter, and Bob Poos, my Executive Editor, who had been down doing the journalist bit in El Salvador covering the insurgency, charged into the office.

"Jefe, we met up with these two Special Forces senior NCOs advising the Salvador military, Tony Paniagua and Bill Frisbee. In a bar one night they whispered, 'Think there is any way that *SOF* could offer any expertise?' We are really low on manpower," the wired duo said.

The communists were invading our southern neighborhood! I ordered a bunch of my guys to convene at a local bar, the Hungry Farmer, where many *SOF* meetings were held, for a skull session. As the night went on, with heightened booze-induced creativity, we decided that the communist threat in Central America was such a pressing threat to the United States that our other project—supporting the Karens in their six-decade battle against the Burmese dictatorship—should be put on the back burner.

It was again time to kick into high gear for some hardcore *SOF* "participatory" journalism. We would create the story, gin up a lot of action and then write about it for the glistening pages of our bad boy magazine. Thus began our dozens of treks down to El Salvador over the next eight years.

SOF *ARRIVES IN COUNTRY*

General Bustillo, a colonel when we first met him, was the Commander-in-Chief of both the Salvadoran Airborne battalion and the Air Force (the Airborne unit was under control of the Air Force, in contrast to the practice of the U.S. and other Western nations) throughout the entire war, from

1979 to 1989. He was an acclaimed officer and pilot who wielded lots of political clout. The General was a strong supporter of *SOF* efforts as he realized the value of the Vietnam and Africa combat experience of the *SOF* advisors. He even sent his private car driven by Special Forces SFC Tony Paniagua to pick *SOF*ers up at the airport.

Prior to the *SOF* team leaving for the land of ripening coffee beans and flying bullets, we had off-the-record meetings with high ranking officials in the Pentagon regarding our planned efforts in El Salvador. No records were kept.

One of the players was Nestor Sanchez, the Deputy Assistant Secretary of Defense for Latin American Affairs who had a sterling career in the U.S. Army after being ransomed from a Cuban prison who, during his three-decade career with the CIA, participated in the coup against the left-wing government of Jacabo Arbenz in Guatemala and was involved in an attempt to assassinate Castro. Also included in the meetings were Ed Luttwak, a brainy Pentagon consultant, and Colonel Manny Grenado, a Bay of Pigs veteran. They condoned our Central American operation but could not offer any official sanction or assistance. However, Luttwak did say, "Brown, if you have any difficulties call me." I said, "Sure, Ed," having no idea I would be taking him up on his offer in a very few days.

In El Salvador, shortly after we got settled in our quarters, we heard from our Special Forces buddies that they had attended a meeting with the number two man of the U.S. Mil Group and the Salvadoran Minister of Defense.

Paniagua told us, "That leg from the Mil Group was trying to convince the Minister of Defense to declare you all persona non grata!"

This was not good. We had to act immediately. That night, I was on the phone to Luttwak. "Ed," I said, "I've got a problem." "Well, what is it?" "Very simple," I responded, "I think we have a case of 'territorial imperative' and the Mil Group wants to give us the bums rush." Without hesitation, Luttwak said emphatically, "Well, I will take care of it," and hung up.

I was skeptical but had no choice but to wait the situation out. I didn't have long to wait. The next day, my team and I were over at the Estado Mayor getting our press and I.D. cards, when the CO of the Mil Group, Colonel Joe Stringham, flagged me down.

"Brown, Brown, I've got to talk to you," he yelled as he scurried over. Not knowing what was coming down, I responded in a low, neutral tone, "Colonel, how can I help you?" He huffed and puffed saying, "Look, I'm not going to have you guys declared persona non grata. Please get Nestor Sanchez off my back!" I smugly smiled and said, "Well, Colonel, I'll see what I can do." What satisfaction it gave me to stick my thumb in his bureaucratic eye.

According to one of our military contacts, "When a Colonel gets the word directly from an Assistant Secretary of Defense, he damn well better pay attention or he will end up in charge of Quartermaster Sales in the Aleutians." We had no more problems with Stringham or any of the MilGroup from that time on. I won't say it was a case of "Yes sir, no sir, three bags full sir," but damn near.

We were all issued Salvadoran I.D.s or "Get out of jail free cards," as well as press credentials which allowed us to carry personal weapons on and off military bases and even arrest civilians on the street though we never did. We had our own arms room, supply room, and ate at the officer's mess at Illapongo airbase. Imagine a bunch of foreigners, no matter what their importance or rank might be, allowed the same privileges and considerations on any U.S. military base. It would never happen.

WE GO ON COUNTER-GUERRILLA OPS

One of our many missions involved accompanying Lieutenant Colonel Jorge Adalberto Cruz, the officer in charge of guerrilla-threatened Morazon Province, and elements of the Morazan and Airborne Battalions that were in the field to observe counter-guerrilla operations. Cruz, who was 5'7" with curly black hair and raven black eyes, was one of the hottest officers in the Salvadoran Army and had received Army military training in Chile. He was among the first graduates of the controversial United States College of the Americas, a military-training school in the Panama Canal Zone that stressed low-intensity, low-level counter-guerrilla warfare tactics which was hated by the left-wing. He also later became one of the hottest faces for *SOF* readers when he and I posed in-country, decked out in full combat gear, well-armed for a sellout poster that had "Communism Stops Here" slapped below our in-your-face photos.

He was up to speed with, and engaged in most of, the techniques necessary to defeat guerrillas to the extent that his scarce resources allowed. He kept his troops and his officers out of the cuartel and in the bush where the bad guys were. He patrolled aggressively, moving quickly and at night. He took prisoners and supported civic-action projects. The morale of those of his troops observed by *SOF* appeared to be good.

On our mission with Colonel Cruz, the *SOF* team included Sheldon Kelly, a hard-charging Irishman journalist with a quick lip and a fast pen, who I was convinced worked for the Agency. We caught a 45-minute hop on a Salvadoran Air Force C-47 that must have made its bones dropping Allied paratroopers over "A Bridge Too Far" during WWII. We were hopping from San Salvador, El Salvador's capital city, to San Franciso Gotera, capital of embattled Morazan Department.

We had more than one anxious moment with pucker factors of 8 out of 10 during the white knuckle flight. When we couldn't get the wheels down on the landing, I was sure I was going to get a belly landing to add to my "why-am-I-doing-this shit" list. Miraculously, we finally rolled to a stop near a 10x10 concrete terminal topped up with a dirty rag standing in for a windsock. This was not uptown, or even downtown.

We happily disembarked after our bumpy, will-we-get-there, flight, and noted two wounded young troopers suffering in silence, lying on their backs on the floor of a truck. Both had bandages on their chests. *SOF* medics Padgett and Gonzalez jumped to the occasion and as any worth-his-salt combat medic would do, rolled them over and found what they expected—bullet exit holes in their backs that meant sucking chest wounds. They quickly applied airtight compresses both front and back. If both entrance and exit holes had not been covered, the two victims would have bought the farm before they could be flown to the hospital in San Salvador. I fought my impatience after the emergency was over. "Colonel, are we going to see some action?"

He grinned and said, "Si, si, just wait." That night we joined a company-sized patrol looking for a 1,200-man guerrilla column that was transporting a shipment of small arms and ammo from Nicaragua through western Morazan at that time. Cruz briefed us, his excitement contagious.

"My intelligence indicates they plan on attacking Gotera and other points on the road between Gotera and San Miguel. Our objective is to fix the guerrilla column in place by engaging them in a firefight they can't break away from. Then my two other columns will smash them from the flanks."

Cruz, later that night, told us, "The guerrilla column is composed of communist units from La Union, San Vicente, San Miguel and Usulutan Departments, as well as local units from Morazon."

We dozed with half open eyes on alert during that night filled with the sounds of discharges from spooked troops, some friendly artillery fire and blinking lights from the guerrillas, but there was no contact.

Kelly described the long sleepless night. "The only place for us to stay was a bunker outside the wire. We laid there wondering if we were going to get hit. Every time I thought we were all asleep, someone would say, 'Hear that?' 'Hear what?' Then we'd ready up for an attack, then, finally get back to the cots. It was like this all night. I doubt if any of us slept much." For unknown reasons, the guerrillas slipped away.

SOF *MAKES IMPACT IN EL SALVADOR*

From 1982 on, *SOF* had teams down in El Salvador nearly year round. For instance, on one of our early trips, *SOF* provided several thousand dollars of parachute-related supplies, equipment and spare parts, which allowed John Early, a Special Forces Nam vet and Captain in the Rhodesian Airborne, to square away the Airborne riggers' loft. He provided training for riggers and taught a bloc instruction on rigging equipment for dropping by air. By the time of our departure, 480 complete parachute rigs were ready to go.

Jack Thompson, a husky, 6'2" former Marine Vietnam vet with thinning blonde hair and blue eyes, was one of the world's most competent small arms/sniper instructors, with kills on several continents. He had also been a Selous Scout Sergeant Major in Rhodesia. He conducted a series of three-day classes for FAS door-gunners. He taught basic sniper techniques for the FAS Airbase Defense Battalion and advanced sniper training for the Atlacatl Battlion. The door-gunner training resulted in significant improvement in engaging targets. His previous sniper class had killed 17 guerrillas between April and August.

Weapons guru Peter Kokalis, known as "Mr. Machine Gun," who was down there 30 times, completely overhauled the weapons inventory of the Atlacatl Battalion. He and Early conducted a three-day ambush and counter-ambush training program for selected junior officers and NCOs of the unit.

Gonzalez and Padgett, our medics who saved the lives of the two troopers at Gotera, conducted Medcaps that treated several hundred civilians, and held classes on field-health and sanitation for Salvadoran troops and civilians. They also trained FAS helicopter door-gunners in basic life-saving procedures and held classes for enlisted medics of the Atlacatl Battalion and the FAS.

At the time Congress, worried about another Vietnam, had authorized only 55 advisors at one time in El Salvador. As one *SOF*er, straight shooting, no bullshit Harry Claflin, who I sent down in 1984 and who stayed in El Salvador for most of the duration of the decade-long war, said during the thick of the chaos: "There was nothing the paltry group of 55 U.S. military trainers in El Salvador could do about it but bitch and get on with the task despite the frustrations of having their hands tied by political considerations. Making waves might swamp the leaky boat in which the soldiers float through their assignment in Central America." When Harry and *SOF* parted ways, he worked for the El Salvador government until the war was over and "it wasn't fun anymore."

The bottom line was that with the 55 advisor limit that the U.S. had imposed, boots-on-the-ground training and maintenance were sadly neglected, and that's where the private sector (us) provided back-up.

SOF *MAKES A SPLASH WITH THE GOE TEAMS*

I first met Harry at an *SOF* convention in Las Vegas in 1984. I asked him, "Harry, you game to go to El Salvador to fight the commies?"

"I would like nothing more than to finish the job that never got done in Vietnam," he responded bitterly, remembering how we were sold out in Nam by the limp dicks in Washington.

Harry was a Marine Recon vet. He was tall, lean, scraggy, and just plain mean. He served two tours in Vietnam as a member of the 1st Force Reconnaissance Company. After leaving the Marines, he worked overseas as a private contractor for four years as a weapons consultant for the Agency for International Development (AID). He then hired on with the U.S. State Department as a security consultant, providing security protection for government VIPs traveling abroad. At that time, Harry owned and operated Starlight Training Center in Liberal, Missouri, which offered courses in outdoor survival, ranger-type operations and parachute ops. His expertise was a perfect match with El Salvador's ill-equipped Air Force and Army who needed all the help they could get.

"The paratroopers were El Salvador's primary special operations, quick reaction force, and a natural attraction for *SOF* trainers, most of whom have similar military backgrounds," Harry discovered.

Harry was in El Salvador for two weeks the first time and stayed for a few months the second time when, in November and December, he returned to Ilopango air base as an *SOF*-sponsored advisor. After he got back the second time, I called him.

"You want to go back? How long can you stay?" No sense being subtle.

"How much?" Harry asked, just as delicately.

"$1,000 a month" I told him.

"Hell," Harry recalled. "It didn't take much to live in El Salvador and I decided to give it a try. I had been all over the world, in Vietnam, in India and other parts of Asia, in Europe, and it was time to try something new."

El Salvador might consider using civilians with extensive military backgrounds to work as advisors without political restrictions, I decided, disgusted with Congress' spineless restrictions on sending U.S. trainers to fight the communist insurgency in our backyard. *SOF* volunteer training teams had already completed several missions to help El Salvador's Army and Air Force, from 1982 to 1984. That training included marksmanship, sniping, patrolling, small unit tactics, ambushes, demolitions, booby-traps, long-range land navigation, communications, insertion and extraction techniques and a host of other skills necessary for combat operations in the mountainous, volcanic countryside.

I heard through the old boy's network that the 4th Brigade Commander, Col. Sigifredo Ochoa, would like to have some assistance from *SOF* to organize and train a small, elite special operations unit. Harry was assigned as the 4th Brigade's Spec Ops advisor in 1984, and was hired by El Salvador's military a couple years later.

"Everything was in a shambles when I got down there," Harry said. "I had to help them with the military's defunct communication equipment, then get their shabby uniforms cleaned up. From the time I went back, that's what I did: commo, clean uniforms, then equipment then jumping once a week."

LITTLE PARADISE, A LATIN DIEN BIEN PHU

"It was now 1985 and I was sent up to El Parisio [the Paradise]. Believe me it was anything but paradise, it was a little Latin Dien Bien Phu. It had been overrun three weeks before I got up there," Harry said.

"A young SF captain, Ed Phillips, who had no idea why we were there, was in charge. I was with Rene Cárdenas, who was a retired SF medic living in El Salvador. *SOF* paid Cárdenas to be a translator. We went up and told Phillips what we were doing. He said we would have to get permission; he didn't want to have anything to do with this.

"Col. Ochoa was commander of the 4th Brigade. Phillips called him and I laid down the plan—we were to train a unit as a direct action team, which means you train them to go out and find guerrillas and shoot them. He then calls Col. Steele, commander of the MilGroup who said 'Yes, Claflin has the blessing of MilGroup, and give him all assistance.' I was good to go, and that started my relationship with the OPACs."

"My first assignment after I got back to El Salvador for the second time in 1984 started out real promising. Col. Ochoa, a seasoned officer, had studied with Israeli advisers in El Salvador, and later gone to Israel for training in the mid-1970s and later studied for over a year in the United States. He asked me to train teams of Special Forces for each brigade," Harry recalled.

"I ran into Israelis all the time, who were still involved in training Mossad-type operatives, but they were limited in their numbers. The paltry group of 55 U.S. Special Forces military trainers could not accompany the El Salvador Army on combat ops. A lot of them were a hell of a lot more skilled than I was, but they were not allowed to do what I was doing. Even so, the Special Forces team was busy nation-building. They had to build an army down there. They did a wonderful job. Without these 55 advisers it wouldn't have happened. They were responsible for changing the war and bringing it to the end. They couldn't train much below the brigade level, so the platoon and squad levels did not have trainers at that time."

"Col. Steele, the MilGoup commander, made it clear that the group was to give me all assistance. The CIA furnished money and equipment for our training. The CIA and MilGoup were butting heads most of the time, staking out their own claims and homesteading. But the Agency helped. I was going to teach the Salvos how to be inserted behind enemy lines, set up a base of operations, and go about hunting the guerrillas down, and capture or kill them. We organized to hit high-value targets such as guerrilla hideouts," Harry said.

This was the beginning of the Goupos de Operationes Especiales (GOE) program in El Salvador.

"GOE teams were trained to operate clandestinely for extended periods deep in contested areas. A commander could employ the smaller GOE team without the necessity of committing larger units with their accompanying logistical requirements. A GOE team would be composed of 28 men organized into five groups—one command group and four action teams. The command group would consist of one lieutenant, one sergeant, one radio operator and one medic. Each of the four action teams would consist of a team leader, assistant team leader, a radio operator, a machine gunner, a grenadier and a sniper."

I asked Harry whether he had trained all of the GOE units.

"I trained four units and I went back to retrain them from time-to-time. In combat, you have attrition, new people come in, people get set in their ways, and you need to recall them back to go over the training to see what they are doing wrong, what they are doing right. Most of it was just hard work. I would go out with them on the first couple operations, then turn them loose. I was in the command and control, picked units and supplied equipment. I didn't do a lot of shooting. I couldn't have done it without the U.S. Army Special Forces advisers, the MilGroup, and the Brigade Operational Planning and Assistance Training Team (OPATT). Col. Rankin, the top U.S. Air Force advisor and Salvo Air Force liaison, was concerned that there were no forward air controllers in the Airborne battalion that had the capability of calling in air strikes. I worked out of his office. The MilGroup was overwhelmed, involved in getting brigades organized and operating," he responded. U.S. helicopter pilots were using helos, smoke grenades, and Zuni rockets to teach them how to call air strikes. The AC-47 gunships came down in 1985.

THE DAY HARRY BECAME FAMOUS, OR INFAMOUS

"After my picture, which was taken by RKB at the Contra base camp where an *SOF* team was training the Contras, came out on the cover of *Newsweek* in November 1986, I became a real Pariah," Harry said.

"I was there a couple weeks in El Salvador, after the earthquake and I go back to Santa Ana to start the next training cycle. I packed my gear up and went back to San Salvador for the weekend after a training session and checked into the Sheraton Hotel. One of the MilGroup said, 'Hey, Harry, have you seen *Newsweek* magazine? You're famous'! I said 'yea, right,' and he showed me *Newsweek*. The Operational Planning and Assistance Training Team (OPATT) guys thought this was too neat. The Ambassador and the MilGroup commander did not think this was neat at all.

"Stan Pickering had replaced Ambassador White. Col. Rankin, the ranking U.S. Air force with the MilGroup, informed me that Southern Air Transport, a CIA proprietary, had a seat for me on a C-130 flying back to McGill Air Force Base. I saw the article Sunday or Monday, and I was back on my way back to the States . They decided that I needed to take a vacation, as the top brass feared that some journalist would recognize me and the next cover of *Newsweek* would have the heading of 'American Mercenaries fighting in El Salvador.' That would compromise the MilGroup since I was involved in the thick of their training. I had to go, at least for a while till things cooled down. I was the only one on the plane other than the crew," Harry said. Our most important contact in El Salvador was banished.

SALVADORAN TET

It was 1989, and Harry was back and working directly for the Salvadorans. No one seemed to notice that the guerrillas were amassing huge stocks of weaponry, preparing for a final roll of the dice, refusing to give up on overthrowing the ARENA (National Republican Alliance) government that had been elected in an atmosphere of violence the previous March. I asked Harry whether the Salvadorian military had any indication as to how the guerrillas were able to move all the arms positioned in the city before the offensive?

"The guerrillas positioned the arms a little at a time. They had 24 months to bring this stuff in from Nicaragua," Harry replied. "Most of it came in through the remote areas on the Salvadoran-Honduran border. There was a large cache by the time it was all smuggled in."

On 11 November 1989, the FMLN launched a surprise offensive against military and civilian targets across the nation, especially in San Salvador,

San Miguel and Santa Ana. This was almost a re-make of the famous "Tet" offensive, undertaken by Viet Cong and North Vietnamese forces in South Vietnam, in 1968. The main similarities were the surprise factor and the real shock this large-scale attack caused. The ACIG described the offensive:

> ". . . The Ilopango AB was almost overrun during the initial onslaught, the rebels threatening to destroy up to 80 percent of FAS assets. In bitter fighting, the military incurred extensive losses, but the FMLN not only failed to gain its objective, it also sustained a bitter blow from which it would never recover, including 1,773 dead and 1,717 wounded. The FAS suffered one of its most unusual losses during this period of time, when on 18 November an A-37B was hit by a Dragunov rifle round in the cockpit area: the co-pilot was killed, while the pilot ejected safely."

Harry said, "The rebels remained active through the rest of 1989 and 1990, inflicting over 2,000 casualties on the Salvadoran armed forces and police per annum. Forty helicopters were shot down between 1988 and 1992."

The country was exhausted after a decade of civil war in which 70,000 had died. The Inter-American Commission on Human Rights focused on the brutality of the final surge in a vicious, bloody war.

"FMLN members used civilians as shields and obliged them to form corridors; on other occasions FMLN members obstructed the free movement of civilians and even obliged them to set up barricades. The Government reported that members of the FMLN took control of the Hospital Santa Teresa in the city of Zacatecoluca, using explosive to destroy one of the floors of the building and killing a sick soldier," Harry said.

THE BAD GUYS HAVE MISSILES

Harry was back in El Salvador when the missile crisis hit.

"One of the officers said, 'We need to go back to the base.' We flew with Gen. Bustillo, Capt. Castro and the Air Force XO. Bustillo was flaming hot; they had been waiting for us since midnight. They had found a 122mm Katusha rocket they thought was some kind of surface-to-air missile. The Salvadoran military breathed a sigh of relief. The FMLN did not have missiles that could take down the FAS planes. Until a couple weeks later, that is. The war was still hot, we were whipped, we went back, got some sleep until sunup, and went back out with the Airborne troops again," Harry continued.

"We had been at the base about two weeks when the Sandinistas tried to fly in a plane load of SA-7s from Nicaragua. They had hit a head wind and ran out of gas coming into El Salvador and crashed. The plane was overloaded with SA-7 missiles and four men. It just fell out of the sky. We got there just after it crashed. The bodies were still in the plane. One had lived but he ate his gun. He was busted up pretty good from the crash," Harry said.

"They had their flight plans from Managua to El Salvador in the plane. Before that, the FAS assets, other than helicopters, were safe from ground fire. But now the situation changed as the rebels obtained a weapon that could knock down even the AC-47s. After the plane crashed, everything was set in motion. The guerrillas had surface-to-air missiles! This was serious stuff. The Salvadoran government grounded all aircraft until we could figure out what was going on. I had some knowledge of this missile, but I needed training manuals to brief the pilots on how to evade it. It had been so long since I had done any work with the SA-7 and I had forgotten a lot. The MilGroup didn't have a copy of the manual," Harry said.

Harry called the *SOF* office on Captain Castro's phone to see if we could provide the manual. *SOF* shifted into quick action, rounded up a copy of the manual and faxed it to Captain Castro. (Nobody still with *SOF* recollects how we got a copy of this manual.) This caused some ruffled feathers with the American MilGroup because *SOF* was able to get a copy before they could get a copy through official channels. Without *SOF*, Harry and the others could not have obtained the tech manual for the Russian SA-7 surface-to-air missile.

"I'm the one that caught the heat on it. I didn't tell them where I had gotten it. They were just furious that I had. I still never got a real answer from the Air Force Liaison Officer as to why the Air Force dragged their feet," Harry said.

"It took *SOF* two hours to fax the manual. Once we got it, I wrote instructions on the SA-7 missile. Capt. Castro, the Air force Intelligence Officer and a 1977 U.S. Air Force Academy Graduate, watched as I wrote for four hours. Gen. Bustillo and every single pilot on that base went through that course, and when they came out of the class, they thoroughly understood the SA-7 missile, how it worked and how you could avoid it. After we briefed them, they started using their aircraft again. No aircraft was lost to an SA-7 until the next year."

So the Salvadorans would have been grounded for the next three weeks had they had to rely on the bureaucrats of the U.S. military. The Salvadorans developed a "U"-shaped piece of pipe that diverted the exhaust gases into the chopper's rotor blades to disperse the heat. Since the SA-7 was a heat-seeking missile, dispersing the heat meant that it could not lock onto the chopper. This missile system took four to six seconds for its heat-seeking mechanism to lock on, so you had to fly at ground level. That way the guy with the missile did not have time to lock on. If the chopper was at a higher altitude that gave him time to lock on and you were screwed.

The missiles didn't come in until the first phase of the offensive was over. Even once the offensive was over, the guerrillas still had SA-7s and in 1990 they knocked down an AC-47. A Hughes 500E was shot down on 2 February 1990, followed by Hughes 500D "35" on 18 May 1990 and an O-2A on 26 September. The FAS had an especially problematic November 1990, when the FMLN—despite ongoing negotiations with the government—launched another series of attacks against targets throughout El Salvador, reported ACIG.

On 2 January 1991, the FMLN shot down a UH-1H carrying three Americans en route from Honduras to provide intel to U.S. advisors in El Salvador. CWO Daniel Scott died in the crash. Lieutenant Colonel David Pickett and Private Ernest Dawson survived, but were brutally executed.

"Two or three of the planes were shot down with surface-to-air missiles that were more sophisticated than a SA-7," Harry said.

"The military was able to employ air assets all over the country. If *SOF* and RKB had not provided the SA-7 manual when they did, it would have given the guerrillas another three weeks without aircraft attacking them," Harry said.

In March 1989, Christiani was elected president of El Salvador and with the elections *SOF*'s involvement in that country was terminated, with the exception of several trips that "Machine Gun" Peter Kokalis made to train the Salvadoran police.

24

THE SOF *WILD BUNCH AND THE CONTRAS*

In 1985, my old friend and mentor, Major General Jack Singlaub, USA (Ret.), called my office.

"Brown, I want you to recruit a small team of Vietnam veterans to go down and train and assist the Contras. Congress has cut off aid to them. They need you to take over where the CIA left off when they were abruptly withdrawn. I'm told that the CIA agents didn't even teach the Contras how to operate the CIA-supplied communications vans which left them without commo."

First I called Harry Claflin, who was still advising and training in El Salvador. I contacted other *SOF*ers who I had worked with in numerous dark, nasty, places where we often encountered hot lead and cold steel.

"Harry can you handle commo and small units tactics with the Contras in Nicaragua, right next door to your stomping grounds?" I asked him. In his no bull manner, he said, "I'm in."

In addition to Harry, I recruited Lieutenant Colonel John Boykin, USA (Ret.), a strapping, tall Dennis Weaver look-alike, who could well have made some NFL team as a tight end.

"How would you like to be the *SOF* A-Team leader?" I gave Boykin an offer he could not resist. He had been the Deputy Commander of the El Salvador MilGroup, had made his bones in Special Forces in Nam and was a Commanding Officer in Ranger School.

Next, I called Phil Gonzalez, swarthy and movie-star handsome, a superb SF Medic whom I had met in Nam.

"I want you to conduct medical training and patch up any of us who happen to run into some errant lead." I gave him his marching orders without doubting that Gonzalez would take them. He was a dedicated professional medic, who always jumped at an opportunity for action and treating the wounded, be they the *SOF* team or the locals.

Jack Thompson, blue-eyed and muscular with a sturdy build and thinning hair, was a Marine embassy guard in Nam, Selous Scout Sergeant Major in Rhodesia and "small arms and sniper consultant" in Central America.

"I need you to handle the weapons instruction," I told him.

To round off the team, I still needed a demo expert.

"Can you go to Honduras and handle instruction in boom-boom?" I asked the soft-spoken, affable John "I.W." Harper, a slim man with jovial blue eyes who was a legendary, retired CIA demo expert. After he retired from the Agency, he got a contract with a rogue CIA agent, Ed Wilson, who was working for Qaddafi. Harper thought it was an off-the-books Agency operation, which was not the case. During his tour in Libya, a Russian helicopter blew up in the air, killing several Russian officers. Being the premier demo man, he was suspected of blowing the chopper up and was thrown in a quite unpleasant dungeon. The story goes that Harper, who had run an agent net in Libya when King Idress was in power, somehow reactivated his net and with its help escaped from the dungeon and the country! He will not confirm or deny this but it makes for a good tale.

The members of the heavy hitting team all said, "Count me in!" I flew them into Denver and put them up at the posh Brown Palace Hotel.

"Lay low," I told them.

Fat chance. The daunting group of tall, muscular, mean-looking, scruffy bearded guys with marauder eyes didn't have much chance of blending in with the dull, fatcat, suited-types booked into the prestigious hotel. I met them at the Brown Palace Hotel bar.

"General Singlaub is going to interview you for a special mission in Nicaragua. Not a word to anyone," I told them.

I arranged transport up to Singlaub's house in Fraser, Colorado, just to humor him, knowing good and well that he would accept my private little army at no cost to him.

"He brought us in one at a time up to his office, which was outfitted like a war room. Maps covered the walls. He grilled me about Force Recon, Spec Ops, how long I had been in El Salvador. We were interviewed and accepted and then found out what the big picture was," Harry recalled.

"Gentlemen," Singlaub growled, "you will leave here and travel to Tegucigalpa, Honduras, with your equipment and link up with members of the Fuerza Democrática Nicaragüense [FDN]. You will then be taken to Camp Las Vegas, the main Contra base on the Nicaraguan border. There you will train their elite commando unit for deep penetration operations into Nicaragua." Singlaub, upon retiring from the Army, had become one of the most effective, active civilian sector operators to oppose the communist menace worldwide.

"The length of training for the mission will be 90 days, starting from the time you get to Camp Las Vegas. Training sites have already been selected and the Contra units will be waiting for you. Each of you is an expert in your field, so you need not be told what to do. Thank you, and good luck," he said.

A CIVILIAN "GENERAL"

"We were going to train the Contra's elite commando unit," Harry remembered, "like we had trained the GOE [Groupos Operationes Especiales] in El Salvador. Singlaub implied that President Reagan was behind this. Don't forget that Singlaub had worked with CIA Director William Casey during World War II in the OSS, so we assumed that Casey had signed off on this," Harry said.

Singlaub had met Bill Casey while acting as an OSS member during World War II. He was involved in the formation of the CIA, had spook assignments in Manchuria after WWII and in Korea during the Korean War, and was commander of SOG, the secret, highly successful snoop-and-poop Special Forces operation which sent teams into Laos, Cambodia and North Vietnam to interdict the Ho Chi Minh Trail and gather intelligence. He served as Chief of Staff of the United Nations and U.S. Army Forces in South Korea in 1977. He retired that year after he publicly criticized President Jimmy Carter's attempt to withdraw U.S. troops from Korea, but he made the peanut farmer back down.

At the time, Singlaub was a freedom loving, anti-communist zealot and a prominent member of the World Anti-Communist League. He was going to fight the leftist Sandinistas that had taken over Nicaragua any way he could, and along with CIA head William Casey, Major General Richard Secord and Lt. Colonel Oliver North, was later charged with involvement in the conspiracy to provide arms to the Contras.

We were being asked to circumvent the U.S. Congress as he and Oliver North and others in the Reagan administration did in defiance of left-wingers who had cut off aid to the Contras in Nicaragua. To some degree, we were to fill in for our CIA predecessors.

By 1985, the Contras, composed of a sprinkling of former national guardsmen from the Somoza regime, and mostly poor peasant farmers from the highlands, were engaged in a life and death struggle with communist Sandinistas in Nicaragua. They violently rejected the communist practices of suppressing their religion and confiscating their land.

For years, beginning during the Carter Administration, the U.S. had armed and supported the Contras to such an extent that the Nicaraguan military considered them an American proxy fighting force. The Reagan administration ordered the CIA to support the Contras, but the Democrats cut funding.

Senator John Kerry had met with Sandinista Commandante Daniel Ortega. Even though the Sandinistas were known for their human rights violations, political oppression and support of the Salvadorian guerrillas, Kerry came back from Managua and pushed for ending U.S. support for the Contras. I would be lying if I said there were not abuses on both sides, including Contra atrocities, but the story was a self-serving, one-sided, pro-commie rant. The day after the House voted down a miserly $14 million aid package, Ortega boogied to Moscow and got $200 million in aid from the Soviets.

WHERE ARE THE CONTRAS?

The *SOF* team packed up gear and equipment and flew to Tegucigalpa with two tons of equipment and gear donated by anti-communist *SOF* advertisers. There they were to be met by a Contra reception party. Shortly after they arrived, I got a phone call from a very angry Harry.

"Nobody was here to meet us. Singlaub must think he is still a general in the U.S. Army and that everyone would jump to his command. Not so with the Contras," he fumed.

"The customs people were looking at us funny. We were there with illegal military supplies and bomb-making material."

Harry went back to the group who brainstormed, "Now what?"

Then Boykin contacted Mike Lima, a prominent Contra combat leader, who had lost a hand in a mortar accident.

"He welcomed us, 'Nice to see you. What are you doing here?'" Boykin made the intro.

"We have some gear here," the team said.

"We'll bring some trucks over," Lima replied.

"He brought one little Toyota pickup, which wouldn't put a dent in the load of medical supplies, training gear, uniforms and a mess of other equipment," Harry said.

"They go back and get more trucks and take us over to a 'safe' house which has no furniture in it. 'I.W.' and I bunk up together; Boykin is in the room with Gonzalez. We stay there for about a week twiddling our thumbs with nothing to eat but our C-rations, while the Contras are doing who knows what," Harry yelled in my ear.

Harry called me again a week later in Boulder.

"Brown, these Calero brothers, Mario, the logistics guy, and Adolpho, supposedly leader of the Contras who we had linked up with in Florida on our way down were supposed to coordinate our mission in Honduras. They never showed up to meet us!" Harry was hot.

I'd had it. I got down to Honduras in a few days and moved the team to a hotel. Enraged, I called Singlaub, who called Mario Calero the affable brother of the Contra political leader, Adolfo Calero and apparently chewed some ass as Calero sent someone to get us to Camp Las Vegas on the Nicaraguan border. It had been hacked out of the jungle and the last 100 miles of road was nothing but a bulldozed trail.

One hundred yards away from the camp was bad guy country so we were on alert for ambush on the brain-jarring ride. It took us 14 hours, bumping along in Toyota pickup trucks, to get to the base. It was 100 miles of nightmarish, rocky, miserable hell and endless checkpoints that took hours to clear.

We could see Sandinista bunkers on the hillsides maybe 300 meters away. We didn't have a good feeling when we arrived at the Contra camp. We crashed in a bamboo hut with a mud floor and awoke to the crowing of a damn rooster. Nobody offered us breakfast so we ate C-rations.

The commander of the Contra army, Colonel Enrique Bermudas, codenamed "Commander 380," came down to see us the next day.

"Hey how you doing? Good to see you. So why are you here?" he queried, without a clue as to what was going on. I shook my head in despair, again. The Contra logistical incompetence was overwhelming. How they did as well as they did against the Sandinistas still puzzles me.

"We're here to train your commando unit which was to make raids deep into Nicaragua," I told him since he was acting as if we were aliens. But 380 (we still don't know why he picked up the designation "380" as a nom de guerre) had never been advised we were coming! The Contra commando unit was already doing dirty deeds deep inside of Nicaragua.

We moved from the leaky bamboo huts to another area and put our tents up by ourselves on a hill. We probably had 200 supply kits. We thought, "Hell, we're here, so we'll train somebody. We'll start putting together some basic programs of instruction." And we did just that.

During the first weekend, on a bright clear Saturday afternoon, 380 came by and took us in his pickup down to a little country store 500 yards from the Nicaraguan border for a few hours of R&R. Cobbled together from bamboo and a roof of thatch, it had a dirt floor. Farm implements, cooking utensils and whatever one needed for subsistence farming were hanging from the walls and the ceiling. It also had beer, of questionable origin, for sale.

As we were unacquainted with Col. Bermudas, it took a few cervezas before things started to loosen up. Someone asked him, "Commandante, what's your plan?"

"PLON, PLON? We don't have no PLON," Bermudas said. We sat there in shock. It was like "Badges, badges? We don't need no stinkin' badges," from the Humphrey Bogart movie, *The Treasure of the Sierra Madre.*

There he was, possibly in the midst of some Sandinista spies, and he was sitting there saying, "The Sandinistas are always sending in spies to find out my PLONS. I have no PLONS."

I almost choked. We all got a pretty good buzz on to numb the dismay, then piled back into the truck. Pointing down a dirt road, 380 said, "By the way, there's Nicaragua over there and we have no guns with us." Not reassuring. However, he was the local so we hoped he knew what he was talking about.

They had assigned us an interpreter, who we all felt was also our "minder" with the mission of keeping 380 informed of what the crazy gringos were up to. With the nom de guerre of "Pecos Bill," he showed up on a mule, wearing a mixture of cowboy and combat gear and sunglasses. Inebriated to the brim, he stepped outside the tent and ripped off a 30-round magazine. Boykin did the same thing. Why? Only the Contras knew. Or did they? We went to sleep. The training with 380 and his team, the "Tigers," started the next day.

For the next four weeks we trained them in weapons maintenance, marksmanship, and basic small unit tactics. These people had no military training at all. Who knows what the CIA had been doing before we got there. Basic weapons training took up a lot of time. Until we got there, marksmanship consisted of spraying and praying. Aimed fire was a new concept for them. It was fortunate that the Sandinistas were no better marksman than they were.

Gonzalez spent the whole time teaching basic life-saving techniques to a number of the brighter ones: starting IVs, treating sucking chest wounds, keeping wounds clean and setting broken bones. He also had an unexpected problem to take care of as it turned out that about 95 percent of these young farmer-fighters from the mountains had some kind of VD. When discussing the training Harry recalled:

"I was up to my neck in rusted-out MGs, which consisted mainly of M-60s and Russian RPDs. The M-60s had frozen gas pistons. The overall condition of the guns was rubbish. The Tigers had not a clue about how to disassemble their weapons, let alone how to maintain them. We took care of that," he said.

"Rusty FN\FALs, Spanish CETMEs, AKs of all types and M-14s were in no better shape."

We were implementing our training program of small unit tactics and were finally accomplishing something, though not the mission we were initially tapped for. Until the Sandinista rocket attack slammed into our camp that is.

The first Katushka whizzed in on a Saturday morning, around 0900 hours. We had just sat down to our daily "feast" of rice and beans when suddenly the sound of Katushka rockets ripping the air apart hit about 200 yards from our tent. The next thing we knew, there were nine more missiles

SOLDIER OF FORTUNE
FDC 55096-11
$3.00
UK £1.75
NOV/1982
SOF FIRES UP RUSSIANS IN AFGHANISTAN
71658 55096
11

Above: SOF reporter, Jim Coyne, Vietnam Huey door gunner vet, exults after firing a burst from a Russian heavy machine gun at a Russian fort during *SOF*'s foray into Afghanistan in May 1982. RKB fired a British 1936 Stokes-Brandt mortar at the fort. *SOF archives*

Below: RKB, former Legionaire Paul Fanshaw and former Army Green Beret and Rhodesian Deputy Commander of the Gray Scouts inside Afghanistan in 1988. Came close to getting in a firefight with an Iranian contingent. *SOF archives*

Above: RKB, armed with a Russian Draganov sniper rifle poses with rebel Milan missile outside of Jalalabad in 1988. First photo proving the rebels had such sophisticated anti-tank systems to reach the West. *SOF archives*

Below: RKB loading round to fire at Afghan fort, May 1982. *SOF archives*

Left: SOF Demolitions Editor John Donovan poses with Hassan Gailani, a military commander of the moderate National Islamic Front, in Peshawar, Pakistan, in September 1980. A member of the *SOF* training team, Donovan explained to Gailani's troops that they had to put fuses in the anti-tank mines to make them explode. How many Russian tanks were subsequently blown up will remain a mystery. *SOF archives.*

Right: Doctor John Peters, *SOF* Paramedic Editor and General Practitioner, led many medical missions to countries fighting communism. His most challenging jump was over the Cordilla Blanca Mountains after the earthquake in Peru in 1970; his most challenging mission with *SOF* was keeping RKB calm as they smuggled 5,000 rounds of AK-74 ammo to the American embassy in Islamabad. *SOF archive*.

Left: Dick Swan, CEO of the innovative Atlantic Research Systems, with RKB on the left and former Marine Carlos Cuculan on the right, at the Central America booth at the first *SOF* convention in 1980. An outspoken anti-communist, Swan was a strong supporter of *SOF* operations in El Salvador. *SOF archives*

Hunting tigers and cows on the Ho Chi Minh Trail.

Left: Nate Thayer, former *SOF* author and presently Cambodian correspondent for *Far Eastern Economic Review*, organized "scientific" expedition to locate species of bovine, the Kouprey, thought extinct for 50 years. Thayer, aka Col. Kurtz, was so disorganized he made RKB look like role model for German General Staff.

Left: One of Thayer's more bizarre concepts was to place rubber masks, modeled here by "Col. Kurtz" himself, with lights behind them on trees facing away from camp to frighten tigers. Cooler heads determined it was unnecessary to implement this concept.

Top: Maj. Robert MacKenzie, 10-year veteran of Rhodesian SAS, and Robert K. Brown logged more "elephant time" than anyone could possibly want. Only access was by foot and elephant: Promised helicopters never materialized. MacKenzie carries Chinese Type 56-1 AK and Brown, whose mission was to summarily terminate any marauding tigers, is armed with Ruger .375 H&H Magnum with 1.5X-6X Bausch and Lomb scope.

CONVENTION '82

SOF Merry Men Meet In Magnolia Land

Gen. John Singlaub (above) and Gen. William Westmoreland (right) address 1,200 conventioneers at Saturday night's banquet. Photos: David Vine and Don Stuber

"The Vietnam War was immoral — because the U.S. didn't push to win," says G. Gordon Liddy (left) at the awards banquet. Liddy spent a day at the exhibit hall selling his book, *Will*, and was a guest of honor. Photo: Don Stuber

SOF convention speakers, bottom row from left-to-right: G. Gordon Liddy, Major General John Singlaub and General William Westmoreland. *SOF archives*

Above: Medal of Honor recipient Fred Zabitosky holds *SOF*'s Bull Simmons Memorial award at 1981 *SOF* convention in Scottsdale, Arizona. Zab played a major role in *SOF*'s POW search in S.E. Asia. *SOF archives*

Right: RKB congratulates Hmong General Vang Pao, who was a guest of honor at the first *SOF* convention held in Columbia, Missouri, September 1980. At the right is master of ceremonies, *SOF*'s Demolitions Editor, Major John Donovan. *SOF archives*

Left: Photo taken in *SOF*'s Sukhumvit Road apartment, summer 1982. From right, Bill Young, Bob Brown, "Col." Bounleut, and "Sam." *SOF archives*

SOLDIER OF FORTUNE

JAN.
1982

urnal Of Pr l Adventurers

FDC 55096-1
$2.75
UK £1.50

EXCLUSIVE!
SOF STAFF WITH LAOS' ANTI-COMMUNIST GUERRILLAS

Above: At the Small Arms Research Center of the People's Liberation Army (PLA) outside of Beijing; *from left to right:* the late Bob MacKenzie with a Type 81 light machine gun in caliber 7.62x39mm, Peter G. Kokalis, *SOF*'s Technical Editor, with a Type 67 light machine gun in caliber 7.62x54R, and LtCol Robert K. Brown, USAR (Ret.) with a Type 69 40mm grenade launcher (a copy of Soviet RPG-7) with its unique bipod. In the background is a Type 77 12.7mm anti-aircraft heavy machine gun. *SOF archives*

Below: SOF sent a team of veterans as advisors/trainers to Croatia in December 1992, the first of many. *Top row from left to right:* Colonel Mike Peck, highly decorated Vietnam veteran described by General Henry Emerson as ". . . the best combat officer I ever had," Colonel Alex McColl, two tour Viet vet, Major John Donovan, demolition expert, Peter Kokalis, one of the world's top experts on automatic weapons. *Bottom row;* RKB, Major Robert MacKenzie, Viet Nam vet, Rhodesian SAS 10 veteran subsequently KIA in Sierra Leone, and Nick Dodich, liaison between *SOF* and the Croatians. *SOF archives*

RKB at anti-communist Laotian United Liberation Front base camp inside communist Laos. At one time the camp held 125 armed Hmong who were to assist in search for American POW's. *SOF archives*

Former Marine Recon Nam vet, Harry Claflin, at left, served as an advisor to the Salvadoran Army for seven years. RKB is at the helm of a 76-foot Patrol Craft in the Gulf of Fonseca off the coast of Nicaragua. RKB and company took pleasure in firing a few bursts at the Nic coast. *SOF archives*

Brown had a custom sniper rifle built to take out guerrillas. At 11-1/2 lbs., it was too heavy to carry long distances. *SOF archives*

Right: RKB, left, Salvadoran Lt. Col. Jorge Cruz and Special Forces Vietnam veteran medic John Pagett play "winning the hearts and minds of the people in the Salvadoran countryside." *SOF archives*

Below: Phil Gonzalez, Vietnam vet and Special Forces medic, in Salvador. Gonzalez ran with *SOF* to hotspots worldwide, treating both military personnel and civilians. RKB noted, "It was comforting to have a couple of medical professionals with extensive combat trama experience in case one of us ate some lead." *SOF archives*

Doctor John Peters conducts a basic medic class for Salvadoran Army medics. Doc Peters participated in humanitarian relief efforts in Peru, Guatemala, Honduras, Dominican Republic as well as in hot spots like Burma, aiding the Karens and inside Communist Laos aiding the Hmong. Insert photo is of Salvo trooper Doc treated. One of the really, really good guys. *SOF archives*

Colonel Jose Bustillo, Salvadoran Air Force CO, accepts Hardcorps vests for chopper door-gunners and pilots from *SOF* Editor/Publisher Robert K. Brown. Vests were donated to Salvadoran cause by Richard Davis, President of Second Chance. *Photo: Alex McColl*

John "I.W." Harper, legendary CIA demo expert trains Contra's somewhere in Central America on basic demolition techiques. *SOF archives*

Above: RKB and Alaskan Brown Bear he took with one shot. Granted he was only about 10 feet away and the bear was just getting out of the Copper River. To the right is his guide, Jim West of Wild West Guns. *SOF archives*

Below: RKB hoists *SOF* flag at "Liberty City" base camp inside Communist Laos, August 1982. *SOF archives*

Above: Brown in Vietnam with his A-Team. Brown is in the center kneeling with his M-16. *SOF archives*

Below: *SOF* magazine's Robert K. Brown takes a moment to chat with Special Operations personnel during a break from the Persian Gulf War. *SOF archives*

Under the aegis of Major General Jack Singlaub, RKB recruited a team of Vietnam vets to train Contra's Spec Ops unit. *From left to right:* Former Recon Marine Harry Claflin on horse; in front of him "Jack Thompson," one of the best small arms instructors in the world; "Pecos Bill," our minder and translator; "I.W" Harper, CIA demo expert; nameless retired Army Lt. Col., and RKB on horse with UZI submachine gun. *Photo: Phil Gonzalez*

pounding down on us. The others dove into a deep ditch behind our tent before the next salvo landed. I sat on my cot in my underwear taking pictures of the rockets coming in.

"Get your ass down here," Harry yelled.

"Get lost," I told him.

We spent the night in the ditch. By this time we had replaced our rusty, worn out Swedish K submachine guns with brand spanking new Uzis. We were tempted to put them to use when six armed individuals shuffled by us at 0300 hours. Fortunately, we held our fire as we figured they might be Contras coming back from patrol, and they were. If we had lit them up, it would have been mucho embarrassing.

Harper, Gonzalez, Harry and I decided it was time to get off the bullseye to get a view of the action. There was a tall mountain at least one klick high to the west of us. Getting to the top was damn near as bad as when I climbed to our *SOF* Liberty City base in Laos in 1981.

The Contras had a relay station up on top and antiaircraft gunners. We thought, "If we are going to get attacked, let's go to top of hill so we can see it coming."

It took us until dark to get on top. We could see the war going on between the Contras and the Sandinistas from our panoramic view of the river, green tracers going one way and red tracers going another. Next morning we came back to camp. Nobody had told 380 where we had gone and he was in a tizzy because he thought that we were MIA. Around 450 rockets had hit in the base camp area.

He relocated us to a hospital area, such as it was, where all the commandos' wives came to have their babies. There's nothing like being billeted in a jungle maternity ward. We spend another week there thumb twiddling, and the biggest entertainment I had was spitting a stream of Skoal at roosters that were waking us up every fucking morning before sunup.

The next day, 380 told us we had best return to Tegucigalpa until a new training site could be located out of range of the rockets. There had been some KIAs at Camp Las Vegas and it was a bit difficult to conduct training in the midst of incoming rockets. No site was forthcoming so we packed our gear and headed home.

John Boykin and Harry went to El Salvador to pick up some mortar sights for the Contra mortars (and why hadn't the CIA provided them?)

and to get M-60 links and to bring back Jack Thompson, the team weapons specialist. Speaking of Thompson, while we were cooling our heels in Tegucigalpa, one afternoon he went into the hotel restaurant. He decided to sample something he was unfamiliar with, steak tartare, figuring it was some type of fancy Honduran hamburger. After the waiter had completed his elaborate preparations of mixing the raw meat, eggs and spices at his table, Thompson told him to take it back to the kitchen and cook it. It was probably the best hamburger ever cooked in that country.

Thompson, a rugged, good looking Viking type with a thick, light beard and steely sky blue eyes, had been operating as a security consultant for several years in Guatemala until we brought him to El Salvador. In Guatemala, he trained bodyguards and security units for large ranches, and gave shooting classes to those who could afford it. He also did some ops for the Guatemalan Army.

He recounted one incident: "I was doing some sniping . . . nothing really long range . . . maybe three or four hundred yards. I came up with a plan where I would locate a trail known to be traveled by guerrillas and then place a note, which said in Spanish, 'Take this to your leader.' The guerrilla point man, at the head of the column, would pick up the note and take it back to the leader at which time I would light him up. I did this a few times and the word got out because one time, the point man picked up the note, turned and walked back to give it to the leader who vigorously shook his head and thrust his palms of his hands toward the puzzled point man as he knew what was coming. And I chuckled as I whacked him too."

Our mission could hardly be called a resounding success. On the other hand, the four weeks of basic training we provided was better than the CIA bozos had given them, and we got one hell of a lot of the Contras' small arms up and running.

"I.W." Harper gave a week-long basic course in espionage trade craft to a handful of Contras who would be spies. After "graduation" they returned to Managua. However, the "students" were quickly compromised and executed when they returned home. They had not been assigned "war names," therefore they knew each other. Once one was compromised, he was interrogated and exposed the others. Their security mindset was non-existent.

Sometime later, Singlaub had "I.W." conduct another similar class in Tegucigalpa, using former Marine and longtime Miami soldier of fortune Marty Casey as translator. What happened to the second batch of would-be agents is unknown.

ANOTHER MISSION WITH THE CONTRAS

In 1986, four days before Easter, in the midst of Catholic Latin America's Holy Week, Nicaragua's Soviet-backed government kicked off a major offensive across the Honduran border, targeting the FDN's Las Vegas base where we had operated the year before. I immediately put together a small team focusing on providing medical support. The team included retired Special Forces medic John Padgett; the SF medic who was with me in '85, Phil Gonzalez, along with former Marine Marty Casey.

We laid up for a couple of days in Tegucigalpa waiting for transport to the battle zone. The hotel, allegedly one of the best in the city, was unique: the top floor of eight floors had been destroyed in a mortar attack during one of the periodic coups, and the hotel never rebuilt it. The main attraction in the central plaza was a magnificent statue of a warrior astride a rearing horse with sword drawn. Now, this type of sculpture is quite common throughout the world. However, what was amusing was how this particular statue got to Honduras. Don't hold me to precise dates, but apparently in the late 1800's, a politician was sent to Paris to commission and oversee the creation of a statue honoring a Honduran war hero. However, a problem arose. The politician became enchanted with Parisian wine, women and maybe song, in that order, and in a few weeks there was little money left for the sculpture. Being enterprising and probably fearing for his life upon his return to Honduras, he purchased a statue of a French notable that was, for unknown reasons, surplus, and shipped it to the capital. The problem was that on the side of the base, it had the name of a Frenchman! The Honduran establishment became aware of the fraud but decided to leave it standing as it added a bit of class to an otherwise pedestrian plaza.

Our medical mission was officially sponsored by *SOF*'s sister organization, Refugee Relief International (RRI). We brought down 500lbs of medical supplies, much of it donated by *SOF* readers, which included 600 doses of badly needed tetanus vaccine and anti-toxin. There was a problem in getting our goodies and us into the FDN's area of operation. Though the FDN was glad to see us, the Hondurans, who for diplomatic reasons could not acknowledge the presence of the FDN, were not enthusiastic about outsiders or the press visiting the area.

Our RRI credentials got us through the first Honduran checkpoints. At the third checkpoint, it was "Everybody out of the jeep!" We got through by bribing the Honduran sergeant with battle dressings and C-Rations. We arrived in a small valley, in which were located the administrative tent, hospital supply tent, sick call building and some living quarters. The FDN forward field hospital facility was well-dispersed with supply and administration in one location, outpatient, dental and student facilities in another, and surgery, X-ray (yes, X-ray!) and wards in another.

Although freedom fighter medical facilities are never long on supplies, they still helped nearby civilians in need. During our visit, hundreds of patients from both sides of the Nicaraguan-Honduran border presented themselves for treatment.

"Some of these people have been driven from their homes by the Sandinistas and have lost everything. They are the ones we are fighting for. We can't deny them what little we have."

When John Padget, Special Forces medic in Nam, was treating a FDN trooper's leg wound—he had been wounded in the left leg and both arms —he told him, "You know, when I was in Vietnam, if a man got wounded three times, he got a ticket home. No more fighting."

The wounded man responded, "You had a home to return to."

Padgett and Gonzalez provided 20 FDN combat medics with a week of intensive training. Padgett remembered, "These guys were pulled from the field and were going right back into harm's way. It was the only formal medical training many of them had. It mattered, and no doubt many lives were saved because of it. We researched what medical supplies were needed and sent many things after we returned to the U.S."

"These missions," Padgett recalled, "demonstrate that when friends of freedom are in desperate need of help, and our government will not or cannot act in a timely manner, the private sector and men of determination can make a difference. And even small efforts may be just enough to make the difference."

The war dragged on until 1992 when the U.N. came in and brokered a truce. Elections were held and, surprisingly enough, the Communists lost in 1989. Commander 380 wanted to be a player in Nicaraguan politics and was anxious to return to Managua. Hugo Hartenstein, a Cuban exile and close friend of mine, and I repeatedly told 380 that he should not go back; that he would be assassinated. Finally, against our adamant pleadings, he returned to Managua and was shot in the head within a few days of his arrival and killed. The hit men were never found.

25

SOF *TRIES BRIBERY; OR HOW I NEVER GOT RICH*

Soldier of Fortune was not just involved in the physical side of the war in Nicaragua; we also had dealings with the psychological side of the war. The following article was printed by the Boulder Daily Camera on 26 July 1987:

NORTH LIKED BOULDER PUBLISHER'S IDEA

Knight-Ridder Newspapers

As a secret network of covert military units was being formed, Lieutenant Colonel Oliver North displayed an impressive measure of independence within the White House.

For example, early in 1985 Robert K. Brown, publisher of the Boulder-based *Soldier of Fortune* magazine and a droll, tobacco-chewing former covert operator and showman, suggested a way to deal with the devastating effects of the Sandinistas' Soviet-built HIND helicopter gunships. Brown proposed in a meeting with North to offer a $100,000 reward to any HIND pilot willing to defect with his chopper.

"We didn't figure they'd defect," Bicknell [Ralph Bicknell, a former Marine captain, was *SOF*'s Marketing Director at the time] said in a recent interview. The hope, he explained, was to inhibit use of the HINDs near Nicaragua's borders where most Contras were operating. "Ollie thought it was a neat idea," Bicknell said.

> "But he added something. He said, 'Make the reward a million.'" Brown, embarrassed, confessed that he couldn't raise $1 million cash, Bicknell recalled. "'Don't worry,' Ollie told us, 'I'll handle that.'" Brown and Bicknell never knew where the money would come from and no HIND pilot ever defected, but in the summer of 1985, *Soldier of Fortune*'s reward notices, printed in Spanish, English and Russian, circulated widely inside Nicaragua. They said the $1 million reward would be paid by "publisher Bob Brown and several other loyal Americans."
>
> (Reprinted by permission of the *Boulder Daily Camera.*)

The headline of the Knight-Ridder story, "North Liked Boulder Publisher's Idea" (26 July 1987) was fairly straightforward. North, of course, was Lieutenant Colonel Oliver North, USMC, former member of the National Security Council staff, who gained notoriety during the Iran-Contra affair. The Boulder publisher was, of course, me.

The concept was simple. We would offer a reward for the first pilot or crewman to defect to a neutral country with an intact Soviet Mi-24 "Hind" attack helicopter. *SOF* readers first learned of the "idea" in February 1985, when the magazine announced a $100,000 reward for the first defecting pilot or air crewman to bring out a Russian Mi-24 helicopter gunship that had been provided to the Nicaraguan Sandanistas. The concept was nothing new. During the Korean conflict, U.S. military intelligence offered $50,000 to any North Korean pilot who would defect with his MIG-15 jet fighter. The objective, however, was not to obtain a MIG-15, but to sow suspicion amongst the powers that be to the extent that they would ground all North Korean air assets while their pilots were vetted. While all the MIG-15's were grounded, the American ground forces carried out a successful offensive.

Uncertain about the political reliability of their pilots, the Soviets and other communist countries had to go to extraordinary lengths to screen their squadrons for those who might be inclined to switch sides. In wartime, that meant aircraft sitting in their revetments instead of strafing friendlies. In Korea, enemy air strikes declined while the communist brass tried to find ways to keep their pilots from flying one-way missions south of the 38th parallel. Would the same concept work in Nicaragua?

Soviet-manufactured Mi-24s had arrived in Managua and were about to play hell with the Contras, who found themselves without any effective anti-aircraft defenses. I decided it was worth a try. I met North in his office in the Old Executive Building with Ralph Bicknell, in the course of attempting to sell the government Kevlar-hulled, high-speed attack boats. During the conversation, *SOF*'s reward for a defecting Mi-24 surfaced. Ollie chuckled and said, "Why don't you raise it to $1,000.000?" I gulped and replied, "Because, Ollie, I don't have a million bucks." He chuckled again and said, "Well, I'll make up the difference!" And who was I to argue with that?

What effect did the reward have on Sandinista air ops? Peter Collins, at that time a correspondent for ABC-TV in Central America, later told me that his contacts in the Sandanista military admitted the reward had the desired effects . . . the Nicaraguan crews were grounded and Cuban crews, who were deemed to be more reliable, were flown in. The death-dealing Mi-24s were kept out of action for three weeks. It was four and a half months before U.S. intelligence sources again reported hearing radio transmissions in Nicaraguan Spanish from the gunships, providing the Contras a brief respite from Sandinista air attacks.

Although no pilots defected, one high-ranking member of the Sandinista government did inquire if the reward was only for pilots, hoping to collect the reward himself. *SOF*'s efforts to encourage defections and buy time for the Contras worked as well as we could have hoped. Within the next year or two after the reward was offered, the air defense capability of the Contras improved dramatically and included ground-to-air missiles, so the Contras began taking down the Sandinista aircraft.

This would not be *SOF*'s only foray into psyops during the war. On Monday, 10 August 1987, the first news stories about the leaflet offering $25,000 in gold to the first Cuban or Nicaraguan security operative or intelligence agent who defected during the 10th Pan American Games appeared. *Soldier of Fortune* magazine's "Freedom Now Committee" and *SOF* were the source of the fliers and gold.

SOF's office became swamped by calls from the media: CBS, ABC, CNN, The New York Times, USA Today, Sports Illustrated, National Public Radio, Associated Press, United Press International and a host of other local and national news outlets wanted to know what was going on. Why were we offering the money? What was our purpose? A few of the reporters were sharp and they asked intelligent and concise questions. Most weren't, and didn't.

Why did *Soldier of Fortune* magazine offer $25,000 in gold for a Cuban or Russian intelligence or security defector? How did we pull the op together? It all started, as they say, when Colonel Alex McColl and I were out jogging in late July.

"What are we doing about the Cubans and Nicaraguans coming to the Pan Am Games?" I asked.

"To my knowledge, nothing, boss," came the reply. "Not good enough," I growled, and the planning session was underway.

With a timetable centered around the opening of the Games, barely 10 days away, gallons of spare midnight oil and quantities of Skoal were laid in. What was our mission? "We're gonna let people know those commie bastards come here to spy on the United States." The concept of the operation was about as simple as that. Execution, though, was a bit more difficult.

Our first major planning and idea throwing session took place on Monday, 3 August, less than a week before opening day. The main problem was how to most effectively get the word out that Cuban and Nicaraguan security and intelligence personnel would be accompanying their athletic delegations to the Games.

We knew they'd be there, of course. It was common knowledge within the intelligence community. Whenever any contingent traveled to the United States from a communist country, the heavies invariably came along. Their job was to provide security for their people. However, on a more insidious basis as any defector will tell you, they come to prevent defections to the United States. And they come to spy. Someone brought up the point that a few unseasoned reporters would no doubt query: What intelligence value could Indianapolis offer Havana or Managua? Another staffer with a long intel background summed it up: "Intelligence work is 99 percent information gathering. Bits of information here, bits of information there. How people dress; the kinds of things they're talking about; air, bus and rail schedules; prices; locations of federal, state and city offices; security at the entrance to Fort Ben Harrison; and personal contacts."

"It all adds up," he continued. "Ten or 20 agents report back; their information is analyzed, processed and transformed into an intelligence picture."

He jammed his cigarette out in an ashtray. "Next time an agent comes through, he or she has a good working knowledge about what to expect. Kind of like seeing the test before the exam."

Ideas for "getting the word out" bounced around like ping-pong balls. How about radio spots? We could rent a billboard . . . take out a full-page newspaper ad. Paul Fanshaw, our in-house former French Foreign legionnaire, volunteered to skydive into the stadium, dumping leaflets on the way down. I was leaning toward authorizing the project when someone observed, "Great idea, boss, but Fanshaw will probably get arrested." And that was the end of that.

Leaflets. That was the answer. English on one side, Spanish on the other. Pass them out at the Games. That'll get the message across. With the concept finalized, the office became bedlam. Who would we send back east? Could we print the leaflets in time and get them out there? How would we distribute once on-station?

By Saturday, 8 August, the answers had sorted themselves out. A staffer with connections in Indianapolis organized a distribution team. The leaflets themselves were rush-printed and sent overnight express. My scheduled trip to Central America went off as planned; I didn't even miss my flight.

Did we accomplish our mission? Undeniably, yes. Word of our $25,000 offer spread like wildfire. Even the Cuban delegation to the Games lodged an official protest. Did anyone defect? We never did have to pay.

MEANTIME, I TRY SHORTCUTS TO EASY STREET

I'm not much of a gambler so I can't explain why I have been suckered into so many schemes to get rich. First in grad school I invested in a failed Beryllium mine prospect that mined more money out of investors' pockets than it did the ground. Then a couple of dry oil wells. Then there was the altruistic purchase of stock in a corporation allegedly developing cutting edge technology to identify breast cancer, which went down the tube. I've often thought of starting a consulting business, in which for a significant sum of money, I would guarantee not to buy stock in my clients' firms.

NEW GUINEA GOLD

But some of the investments I made that never paid off were a kick in the ass. Most were just a kick in the bank account. Like trying to locate and recover gold a priest had allegedly horn-swoggled from natives in New Guinea before WWII and who, as the Japs approached, enlisted the aid of a young American medic to hide the treasure. He hid it so well that he could never find it again. Even my much more financially conservative brother, Alan Brown, with an ever-cheery demeanor set off with a blond brush cut and blue eyes over a long distance swimmer's body, was sucked in with the lure of gold. Peder Lund, tough, bushy eye-browed no bull guy, also fell in with us. So did Brigadier General Hiney "Heinie" Aderholt, who had somehow run into this "key" to hidden treasure. At the time, co-author Vann gave *SOF* readers a detached scoop on the scam.

"RKB, his brother Alan Brown, Peder Lund and a daffy, conniving old-timer called Posey had planned a rendezvous in one of the local hotels. The late General Heine Aderholdt, always up to some scheme if it involved money, had introduced the three to the old-time shyster who convinced the group that millions of dollars in gold bars were stashed in the walls of a parsonage in Papua, New Guinea. Mind you, this was early 2000 and this group's search for the New Guinea gold had been going on for nearly two decades.

"In what proved to be a most entertaining evening, I watched the three, with a crazed, lusty gleam in their eyes as they tried both right side up and upside down to read a probably phony, indecipherable map that was going to show exactly where the gold was stashed away over half a century ago behind the walls of an ancient parsonage. Venerable old Posey's eyes twinkled with glee, winking at me slyly, as he knew that I was on to his scheme.

"According to Alan Brown, the gold bars were worth over $3 million at the time the good pastor stashed it away to hide it from the approaching Japanese in WWII, and at least $34 million at the time of the meeting.

"Now it takes a great leap of faith to believe that the good pastor was paid that much for his selfless services in an impoverished country, even if he had lived several lifetimes. It takes an even greater leap of faith to believe that the good minister did not go back for his stash, unless he and all his ancestors had died, that is, and no one knew whether they had or not. This *SOF* group had taken that great leap and there was no going back. These guys, dead serious about the con, shot me withering glances, wishing me to evaporate, annoyed at my undisguised amusement. It's called gold fever and I got a firsthand taste of what drove the California Gold Rush. These investors had it bad. Or maybe to them it was another wild adventure that gave him an escape from publishing woes.

"Anyhow, after sending the conniving old timer on many free pleasure trips to his WWII stomping grounds, and a few expeditions with his patrons; and after the gold seekers invested in metal detectors, lots of airfares and hotel rooms and other extravagances, having spent a small fortune, the group finally gave up on the deal and the old timer died with his secrets."

I have dismissed from my mind the description of the devious old hoot that did the sucking.

THE PIPER AZTEC AND SMUGGLING INTO MEXICO

Then there was the twin-engine Piper Aztec with long-range fuel tanks that John Donovan and I bought through Ed Dearborne, a legendary Air America pilot in Southeast Asia. Dearborne, a fucking bum who still owes me $13,000, was the private sector advisor to the Contras meager airforce. We were going to smuggle electronics—TV's, Microwaves, etc., from the U.S. into Mexico. It was not against American law but was a violation of Mexican law, if they had any. Dearborne, a rugged, square-jawed pilot, got us a pilot, Rocky Newsome. Nothing happened; and then more nothing; then simply nothing. This went on for months—no Mexican customs busting—until the Mexicans figured out they could solve the problem by shooting down interlopers. So ended that not-so-clever smuggling venture, which we figured was even less clever when we found out good old boy pilot Newsome couldn't get a contract to haul the contraband because he had already crashed three planes. Donovan and I at least sold the plane, which we never saw, and only lost a few grand.

A NEAR KILLER KEVLAR BOAT

But the most intriguing and adventuresome venture was when John Donovan, Dr. John Peters and I invested in a Kevlar-hulled, fast attack boat built by the Harley Boat Company. I had been lured into the deal at a meeting during the 1982 *SOF* Convention with two former CIA agents and a former Brown River Navy man from Nam, Lt. Commander Karl Phaler.

Phaler's pitch was intriguing. Using this relatively new concept of using lightweight Kevlar in boat construction, we could save mucho weight and go mucho faster. Thus, ipso facto, the U.S. Navy, Customs, Coast Guard, and foreign navies would be our market.

Two boats, a 27-footer and a 42-footer, were built by Harley and shipped to Phaler who had an office and a slip at Marina Del Rey in San Diego. Phaler, anorexic thin, graying hair and piercing blue eyes that would wilt the fervor of a hangman, was wired to the gills 24/7 with nicotine and caffeine. A former lawyer, he was brilliant, though some would say raving mad. His IQ must have ranged up around 180.

He sold the Navy command in San Diego on the concept of hiring our fast attack boats to play the part of aggressors in naval exercises focusing on defending against attacks by small boats. This was before the Navy faced the threat of swarm attacks of small Iranian boats in the Persian Gulf.

Phaler was extremely opinionated and, even worse, extremely vocal. He ended up getting in a letter writing wrestling match with the Chief of Naval Operations (CNO), who got so irritated by Phaler's persistence that he ordered the Navy command in San Diego to refuse to pay Phaler and our company $1,000 for services rendered during the exercises. As my brother, Alan, a former Navy officer, said, "When you get in a pissing contest with the CNO to the extent that he gets down to the level of $1,000 issues, you know you are screwed."

Surprise—no sales to the Navy. Phaler's other problem was that he was insistent on browbeating potential purchasers, that he rather than they should decide what type of engines, transmissions, electronics and weapons systems should go along with the Kevlar-hulled boat. This didn't go over well. With his offensive, know-it-all attitude, he couldn't have even been a successful used car salesman. I kept telling him, "Karl, Karl, we don't give a shit what kind of engines they put in it. They can power it with rubber bands, or hamsters on a treadmill for all we care. All we want to do is sell hulls!" He wouldn't listen.

There was one unanticipated side benefit from this impending disaster. We hauled the boat back to the east coast for demonstrations to various government officials including the Director of Customs, Willie Von Rabb. We also had a meeting with Ollie North in his office to try and use his influence to obtain sales. (As mentioned earlier, it was during this meeting that we decided *SOF* should offer $1,000,000 for a defecting Sandinista Mi-24.)

Phaler came up with a concept to gain cheap publicity for our dead-in-the-water project. "Look, guys, we will take the 42-footer and break the world speed record on the sea of Cortez between San Filipe and Cabo San Lucas."

"Well," I said, "Why not. I haven't risked my life recently and I'm bored." Donovan and my bro, Alan, decided also, "Why not?"

Karl drove his pickup truck from San Diego to the Baja in Mexico. The sea was too choppy and rough for the first three days. The hotel we stayed in had no hot water and bad Mexican food. We were the only guests. "Let's get a beer," I told the guys the first night. Phaler and his mechanic opted out, but Donovan and I went wandering.

We ended up in the Perro Negro (the Black Dog). The tables and chairs were bolted to the floor, and the beer was served in plastic cups. We knew we had a problem. We were the only gringos in town, and the locals were hostile, to say the least. We downed our beers and got the hell out of Dodge before there was an international incident. So much for the nightlife.

On day four, Karl and Donovan went down to the beach, and swells were 5 feet high, but we figured that was good as we could get. Donavan remembered, "Karl felt that we could average 50 mph, breaking the speed record for the 350 mile run. We packed water and sandwiches from the hotel and departed. No radio. No flares. No extra gear. Into the sea we went, along with a mechanic."

My brother, with four years of Navy experience, suddenly decided that he had some urgent business and headed back to San Diego. We later found out that he decided this project was doomsday folly as there were no other boats at sea and the weather was kicking up heavy seas. His "business" he decided was not to drown.

We were going 50 mph as planned at first and bucking 5-foot swells, but it was not bad enough to keep Donovan, who enjoyed his chow, from eating. I told him he better quit inhaling all that food or he would run out on the long trip. I put rest of it in the back of the boat in a box.

The swells reached 15 feet high and were getting wilder. Within three hours of taking off, the deck started taking water. The food was floating in the sea water. An hour later, we were running five miles from the shore of the jungle with no other boats in sight. Karl was sick as a dog by then and the wild seas were reaching 20–30 feet high. The water pumps were running full time and the boat was beating around so violently that it was about to capsize. We started taking more water when the deck started to peel back from the hull.

"How much trouble are we in?" we asked Phaler.

"Don't talk about it," Phaler, who was by then green, said.

After six hours out, Karl told us to be on the lookout for a place to harbor up. Then a maverick wave shattered the windscreen. Karl finally got the message. No world record today or ever. We finally chugged into a small village and docked for the next six hours. Then we headed back to San Filipe. The lights weren't working but Phaler navigated us to shore by some miracle and docked the boat.

Donavan was seeing red. "I'm walking back to the hotel," he roared, jumping out of the boat, only to sink up to his waist. He told us to go ahead without him and meet him at the bar. An hour after we finally got to the hotel, Donovan came dragging in.

We ran out of money, sold no boats, and gave up on that very expensive get-rich-quick scheme.

26

HOSTAGE TO HOLLYWOOD

SOF DUO MAKES FILM DEBUT

"AYE SAY, old chaps, there will be no obscene or vulgar language in the studio or on location. A good movie does not have to have profanity, sex or violence," the Director announced.

John Donovan looked at me and I looked at him—the message passed at a glance: with this rude introduction, our movie careers were off to a rocky start.

Some weeks earlier in 1986, a Special Forces Reserve buddy of Donovan's, Michael Leighton, who made a fortune from computerizing the commodity market which he managed to piss away making "B" movies in Tinsel Town over a decade contacted me,

"Brown, how about playing a role in a movie I am going to film in South Africa? You play the commander of a group of mercenaries out to whack a bunch of Muslim terrorists who had kidnapped the grandson of a wealthy businessman. I also want you to be the technical advisor." he said.

I wasn't particularly enamored with the idea as I'd already had a walk-on role in the movie, *Stagecoach* which was filmed near Nederland, Colorado, in 1966. There was plenty of star power—Slim Pickens, Stephanie Powers, Bing Crosby, Ann Margaret, Robert Cummings—and a lot of waiting around. I was a stand in for Robert Cummings, which meant I rode in the stage coach and fired blanks at charging Indians. They weren't real Indians but Hollywood stunt men with make-up. The real Indians who had been brought on location, kept riding their horses down to the small hippie-infested mountain town of Nederland and getting drunk and they were eventually sent back to their reservation. And if you think anyone ever shot an Indian on a galloping horse out of a bouncing stage coach, you are smoking too many funny cigarettes.

Being on location was disillusioning as I got to see how phony Hollywood was. For instance, when the "Injuns" were chasing the stagecoach, the movie carpenters simply moved some rocks and trees around over a 50-yard stretch of ground, giving the impression that the action was going on over half-a-mile. The major lesson I learned was to bring lots of books to location.

However, although the money offered for this South Africa venture—$500 a week and expenses—was far from attractive, the fact that we would shoot for 10 days, be off 10 days and then shoot for 10 days would allow me to go hunting for a week and a half which would make it worth while.

"I will only do it if you bring over Donovan and write him into the movie," I insisted. I had no intention of being limited to associating with a bunch of fruity film personalities for the best part of a month.

Leighton flew me out to Hollywood to meet the director, a South African. I met with him in Leighton's office, and said, "I think you should let me get former Rhodesian SAS veterans to play the parts of my mercenary team, trying to play my role as technical advisor."

"I say," he whined, "We'll get the extras from central casting." Though Donovan and I were also to be the technical advisors, it was obvious this dork was going to listen to no one but his "inner-self."

In Africa, during the first day in the studio we found we had come all that way to play parts in a movie about mercenaries directed by a powder puff named Percival who didn't understand that soldiers don't talk, or act, like church deacons.

Leighton elected to film in South Africa where there were no labor unions and where the government was desperate for business. I sensed there was some kind of currency hanky-panky but never uncovered the details. Leighton brought over a bunch of fading movie stars from America, including Karen Black and Kevin McCarthy, who was a real pro, and Wings Hauser.

As I was leaving Leighton's office I ran into Karen Black, who played the part of a rundown, aging porno star, who, while waiting to be interviewed by Percival, started singing opera in a gurgling voice. While being driven to the airport by one of Leighton's foxy assistants, I asked her: "Is Karen Black crazy?" She responded smugly, and grimacing said, "All actresses are crazy."

After our initial meeting with Percival in Johannesburg, John and I went to the nearest bar to ponder whether we had been brought over to help make a "terrorists-take-hostages, *SOF*-led mercenaries-kill-terrorists-and-save hostages" movie, or the African version of Peter Pan.

Percival was chosen as director at the insistence of some of the investors. He obviously wasn't amused with the technical experts he'd been provided.

"He appears to be intimidated by our attitude, experience, background and earthy language," stated Donovan.

Early on, when we tactfully suggested to Percival that: "Americans would like a certain level of expertise and proper techniques in their shoot-'em-ups, Percival countered with,

"We're not making this movie for Americans."

In our dual roles as actors and technical advisers for *Hostage,* we should have been in Africa and involved with production weeks before filming began, not two weeks after it started. By the time we arrived in-country Percival had already made some bad technical decisions that could not be changed. For example, 22-year-old fuzzy-cheeked actors portrayed grizzled military veterans.

"We could use *Soldier of Fortune* magazine staffers," we suggested to the clueless producer. No go, perhaps justifiably, since the movie's meager budget couldn't handle the cost of airfares to Africa for a large group.

"Then how about fleshing out the mercenary force by drawing on an almost unlimited pool of former Rhodesian Selous Scouts and SAS types who were not only the right age but who also knew how to assemble, wear and handle their weapons and who are locally available."

No go again.

"Well then, how about if we procure uniforms and kit for the movie?" We were trying to salvage his show, but "Noooooo."

When we arrived on the set for the first day of shooting, we choked when we saw the moth-eaten, antique miscellany of packs, web gear and uniforms Percival had rounded up. Not to mention that we had to listen to Percival say, "OK sonny, here's how you wear your beret."

The casting, uniforms and kit were bad, but the weapons were worse. Some of the would-be mercs were to be armed with Armi Jager AP-74s, the Italian manufactured. 22-caliber M-16-lookalikes! We pleaded with the director, "PLEASE position these atrocities as far from the cameras as possible," but to no avail.

Prop master Mike Folly, a veteran of some 80 films worldwide, including *Zulu, Zulu Dawn, Charge of the Light Brigade, Shout at the Devil* and *The Wild Geese,* and who generally imported his weapons props from England, walked off the set when he got a taste of Percival's production standards. He didn't want to risk his credibility on the sub-par quality of the props.

Luckily, Donovan and I had enough sense to bring our own uniforms and web gear.

Four weeks into filming, producer Mike Leighton arrived, took one look at what was going on and told Percival to go back to filming church conventions. Folly replaced him, which helped, but with four weeks of film in the can we basically had to march on with what we had. From the time of Leighton's arrival, Donovan and I did have input, but that late in the game we weren't able to change much. Fortunately, all the merc scenes took place at night, so the errors that had me and John biting our nails and gnawing our knuckles would not be all that obvious to the average viewer.

Also, there were a lot of obvious implausibilities in the script, over which we had no control. For example the insertion of the male lead, Wings Hauser, into the AO by hang glider; using an acetylene torch to cut an entrance into the bottom of the plane where the hostages were being held while the main body of terrorist troops was only 50 yards away; a garrote scene and a cluster-fuck attack across an open runway. Also, against my better judgment I let them talk me into filming a scene where I pulled a grenade pin with my teeth. I busted the scene and on the retake I refused to bite out the pin and mess up my teeth as I knew Leighton would not pay the dental bill, so they just spliced the two segments together to get what they wanted.

The terrorist-villain lead, Tullio Monetta, found it all as amusing as we did. He had been a real-life merc in the Congo and later participated in the abortive Mike Hoare-led merc operation to take over the Seychelles islands.

The show had a lot of yelling, screaming, whining, crying, shooting, gurgling, smoke, deaths and stupidity. Also, to add insult to injury, Donavan and I got to go dove hunting only one day. Once we got behind schedule we had to work for 30 straight days. To hell with making movies.

AND TV'S NO BETTER

SOF's next exposure to the entertainment industry focused around a 1997–98 TV series, initially entitled, strangely enough, *Soldier of Fortune*. For several years I had been pursued to get involved in a *SOF* TV series by a Neil Livingston, a self-styled terrorism expert and author, along with Neil Russell, who I never did learn much about other than that he hosted some very expensive dinner parties for *SOF*ers and friends that easily ran to several thousands of dollars. Finally, they put together a deal for the *SOF* series to be funded by a Hollywood outfit named Riecher—to the tune of 45 million dollars!

From *SOF*'s point of view, it was a boondoggle from the beginning. The theme of the series was about a Special Forces operative who got deep-sixed by the army bureaucracy because he did what he thought was right but violated orders. Upon discharge, he was tasked to recruit a team to perform "non-authorized, deniable missions" for the U.S. government. The basic premise was reasonable but it all went downhill from the first episode.

Inept leadership ended up pissing away immense amounts of money. First they sent some yo-yo to travel around Eastern Europe looking for locations. Too expensive! Too Expensive! Then they were going to shoot it in South Beach, Miami, à la "Miami Vice." Finally, they decided to shoot in L.A. to save money.

Reicher decided to syndicate the show rather than go with a major network, as they did not want a network "sticking their fingers in the editorial pie." I could agree with this. However, it ended up that the series was aired with no consistency. It might show at 2:00 a.m. on Saturday in Chicago, 4:00 p.m. on Monday in Miami, 10:00 p.m. in Denver . . . you get the idea. Furthermore, they had blown all their PR budget on a couple of massive press parties to which neither I or any *SOF*ers were invited and had no funds available to promote the series in TV Guide, etc.

Of course, far be it for the Hollywood know-it-alls to consult with anyone at the *SOF* offices about a TV series titled *Soldier of Fortune*. At one point, I threatened to break Jerry Bruckheimer's legs; joking of course. He didn't find it amusing and that didn't help things. At a dinner thrown by the Hollywood pukes at the 1997 *SOF* convention in Vegas, being unhappy with the way things were playing out, I got a bit into my cups and allowed, stealing a line from Full Metal Jacket, that "*SOF* was getting fucked without a courtesy of a reach-a-round." That didn't help things either.

The only redeeming aspect of the show was that former SEAL Harry Humphries was the very competent technical advisor, and a very creditable Brad Johnson played the lead. The ratings weren't what the Hollywood pukes wanted so, without consulting *SOF*, they changed the name of the series to *Special Operations Force* and made one of the dumbest casting decisions I have ever seen. Some dunderhead decided they would raise the ratings if they cast Dennis Rodman as one of the covert team members. Talk about stupid! Inserting a six-foot-six pierced-up black guy with yellow hair into a team of covert operatives? Way to blend in. With such an incredible mistake, the show's ratings went lower than ever. They canceled the second season after shooting only 17 episodes, whereas they had shot 23 for the first season.

I'd love to meet up with the nutso that came up with the Denis Rodman idea.

27

SURINAM: SLOW BOAT TO A SLOW WAR

I was in the steamy hellhole of Surinam, the land that God did not forget, only because he was fortunate enough never to have been there in the first place.

BOOM! I opened one eye from my siesta and groggily speculated on what foolishness the guerrillas were up to. Another boom, and a third. No commie aircraft overhead, so it had to be the guerrillas. The hell with it, back to sleep.

"The booms you heard were when the guerrillas' leader, Ronny Brunswijk, was detonating homemade rockets we made for him to impress his followers," the British mercs in country told us when we asked what the hell was going on.

The "booming" was another example of the foolishness, fantasy and frustration we'd been threading our way through ever since we left *SOF* headquarters in Boulder the previous week to visit, write about and, if we were lucky, assist in an obscure, primitive anti-communist insurgency deep in the jungles of South America.

What started out as a straightforward reporting project slowly turned into an attempt to overthrow a corrupt president. I kick myself for not keeping a diary during all those years of running around the world. This was one of the rare times that I had enough self-discipline to keep one but only because I had to for the assignment.

This latest *SOF* adventure had started innocently enough. *SOF's* G.B. Crouse, a former Marine, had contacted the Sygma Photo Agency seeking photos to supplement a number of articles we had in inventory.

"Interested in a story on the war in Surinam?" the Sygma editor queried Crouse during the course of the conversation.

"'I'd like to look at it," replied Crouse.

"I'll send it out for your amusement," shot back the Sygma rep. A few days later we had a piece on a handful of Brit mercs and ill-equipped but intrepid anti-communist bush commandos, by the daredevil French military photojournalist Patrick Chauvel. Short, always wired, thin and totally fearless, Chauvel tore through the streets of Paris his motorcycle as if every destination was about to burst into war any second. Not as if just riding through Paris wasn't as dangerous as any battleground. The fact that he loved his booze no doubt enhanced his confidence.

We called Chauvel: "Can you get us in?"

"A piece of cake," Chauvel replied. Chauvel jetted into Boulder, where we debriefed him, and then phoned the leader of the Brit mercs, Karl Penta, who got our adrenaline pumping.

"If you get down here in the next three days, you can get in on something big," Karl hurriedly explained. We were on. How could we miss an anti-communist *coup de main*? We made calls to various manufacturers to round up miscellaneous equipment. Chauvel assured us that his connections could get us through French Customs in French Guiana. We had to infiltrate into Surinam from the neighboring French colony. with anything except guns and ammo. We were leaving in 48 hours. In a whirlwind two days, we Federal Expressed gear to Miami, and hastily got malaria pills, plane tickets and visas.

I took Derry Gallagher and Bob MacKenzie with me. Gallagher was a slim, blue-eyed blonde who was wound tighter than a watch spring. He was a Vietnam vet who was my *SOF* Assistant Director of Special Operations. MacKenzie, a Vietnam combat vet with many years in the Rhodesian SAS during their Bush War was a great one to watch your back and take out anyone trying to stick a knife in it. We headed to Cayenne, French Guiana, by way of Miami and Puerto Rico, or so I thought. We busted our ass and the bank when I decided to get a haircut. Rush was the name of the game. However, in Puerto Rico, we had sufficient lag-over time to get my not so golden locks, what was left of them, trimmed. As I relaxed in the barber chair, Gallagher stomped into the barbershop.

"Brown, you missed the flight," he grumped. I had failed to take into account the change in time zones from Miami. Panic time. I would miss the action. MacKenzie and Chauvel caught the flight to French Guiana while leaving Gallagher behind to round up my sorry ass. There were no more direct flights to Cayenne until the following week. What to do? Catch a flight to Caracas and overnight, a flight to Rio and overnight the next day, a flight to Belem, Brazil with a connecting flight to Cayenne. Right? Wrong. In Rio, pompous immigration officials said. "No. No. No. Have to leave the country tomorrow."

"But we just want to go to Belem and catch a connecting flight," we argued to no avail.

Gallagher and I got to watch the Rio Carnival on TV from the inside of the immigration office. The next day we flew to Lima, then to Bolivia, then to Cayenne. The coup would not wait! Or so I thought.

Cayenne, administrative capital of French Guiana, was a slow-paced tropical town, hot and humid, with the required amount of sea and sun. The only eyebrow raisers for the jaded *SOF*ers, until our guides finally showed up, were the bare-breasted French beauties lounging around the hotel pool. We had a week of impatient waiting before we were finally off to St. Laurent, at the head of the Maroni River across from Surinam, to link up with our guides to the guerrillas and the mercs. As mentioned, I kept a diary during our "sojourn":

4 MARCH 1987

After a sleepless night in a roach-filled $6.00 room located over the town's disco, which boasted a three-piece band and one chubby hooker with bad teeth, we overloaded our gear on a leaky pirogue and shoved off for guerrilla HQ.

"Government gunboat on the starboard," Chauvel muttered.

Our adrenaline levels rose slightly as the gunboat moved out into mid-channel. However, we lost her in a maze of jungle river channels in a few klicks. I took to thinking about what our course of action should be if we were ambushed at a narrow portion of the river. Over the side? Not to worry, we were assured. Piranhas don't attack unless there's blood in the water. Perhaps we should just point our cameras toward the ambush and hope the bad guys realize we're journalists?

16 MARCH 1987

I had a one-and-a-half-hour interview with Michel Van Rey, Ronny Brunswijk's military adviser, graduate sociologist and former Surinamese Army lieutenant. The mercs considered him a "snake" whom Karl had threatened to kill, apparently because Van Rey wanted to get rid of the mercs. Van Rey stated that the guerrilla headquarters had radio contact with five of 11 guerrilla commandos scattered throughout the northeast of Surinam. He also provided an estimate of the situation, which boiled down to the guerrillas having insufficient arms to overthrow the Marxist regime headed by Desi Bouterse, which had been in power since 1980.

Lunch consisted of a few cans of whatever got thrown in the pot—beans, carrots, peas, sausages. A young guerrilla in a red beret, with whom I traded badges, was making a voodoo charm out of metal cable. The kid said the charm would have more power if it was made in the presence of a white man.

Earlier in the day, the French pilot contracted to fly a captured Cessna 204 flew a practice-bombing run with homemade rockets. They did not explode, as they did not land on the detonator due to the crude firing pins and the lack of fin stabilization. A ground party could not find all of those rockets and apparently they are still there, armed.

Karl was disillusioned with Brunswijk's lack of aggression. He planned to move with 20 Hindus to the west, carry out an ambush and blow up a POL (petrol, oil, lubricants) facility. Karl said the Hindus spoke English and had a higher level of education. He envisioned organizing this group into a 200-man nucleus and seizing the predominantly Hindu western part of the country. The idea was to further shut the economy down. Karl planned to leave half the weapons captured in the ambush in a cache in the jungle; he would send two of Ronny's men back to the cache, and the rest of the captured weapons would go with Karl and his Hindu cadre to the west. The plan sounded interesting, as Ronny was inactive.

The Mercs sincerely appreciated the web gear and equipment we had brought as they had none and desperately needed that equipment in order to facilitate their move to the west. Good rapport was established since arrival. Charlie Mosley, a three-tour veteran of the U.K.'s Coldstream Guards and who served with the Grey's Scouts in Rhodesia, said Ronny had a "movie star" mentality. There were a number of reasons for him thinking this:

1. Ronny would replace the pilot of his plane and would taxi it down the tarmac after landing so his men would think he flew it.
2. His voodoo doctor, a Hindu, went into a trance and then said that Ronny should not go into battle.
3. A merc said Ronny fired bullets into a shirt, then had a man put it on to demonstrate that he is impervious to bullets and, therefore, Ronny had powerful voodoo.
4. Bush commandos believed that if they stood on one leg and put a leaf in their mouths they would be invisible to their enemies. Charlie told of four of them caught in the middle of the road by a government-armored vehicle. They utilized this technique and were all blown away. Perhaps they had the wrong type of leaf!
5. Ronny had blown up most of the rockets and bombs because he liked to make loud noises to impress his followers.
6. Karl captured a spy in St. Laurent and got him to confess to throwing grenades in Cayenne, which resulted in his control, the Surinamese consulate in Cayenne, being expelled. Ronny made the spy the jailer and storekeeper in his guerrilla headquarters.

The mercs were planning a homemade napalm air attack for Albina, located in Surinam, across the Marone river from St. Laurent, on Wednesday night. They planned on using an LPG canister with field-expedient drogue chute to stabilize the bomb into a nose-down attitude. They were to drop it on Albina, then they would strafe the Surinamese gunboat with the single guerrilla MAG out the door of the plane. The pilot didn't know about this phase of the mission and we weren't told how they were going to convince him to fly it. Perhaps with a pistol to the head?

The "plan" called for us to leave for St. Laurent by pirogue the day of the napalm attack so we could photograph the attack from across the river. We were then to link up with MacKenzie, who was going to be the gunner on the plane, after it landed at a small strip outside of St. Laurent. We were then to leave the shit hole and proceed to Cayenne. We needed to figure out commo with Karl so when we got back to Surinam at a later date, we could link up.

17 MARCH 1987

Guerrilla headquarters on the island was in a former Dutch administrative center for this isolated area. Admin HQ had a small dirt strip that would take a single-engine Cessna, a hospital, guest houses where the mercs were billeted, and a radio station.

A Cessna 204, taken by the guerrillas, operated on the small airfield at guerrilla headquarters. Sergeant Major Henk Van Rendwick, who was the OIC of Echo Battalion, Bouterse's version of Special Forces, had captured it. Van Rendwick had been captured during a guerrilla ambush in which three government troops were killed and had agreed to join the guerrillas. After three months, according to Charlie, Brunswijk gave him 300,000 guilders to buy weapons in Brazil. Instead, he split for the fleshpots of Holland.

"Brunswijk figured Van Rendwick had 'turned around,'" Charlie noted sarcastically. "He went the wrong way and became a crook."

At 1400 hours, we were at the airplane on the strip, photographing the mercs rigging the drogue chute with the homemade bomb. The chute was cobbled together from a shower curtain and shroud lines were made from heavy monofilament fishing line. The mercs were to kick the "bomb" out of the plane's door which would deploy the drogue chute and stabilize the bomb in a nose-down position which, with luck, would ensure that the firing device would hit the ground.

For the practice run, they filled the LPG cylinder with water to approximate the weight of the bomb when filled with napalm. The "plan" was to make an approach between 500 and 600 feet and kick the bomb out so we could observe chute deployment and confirm the nose-down position of the bomb upon impact.

The bomb was loaded, the chute rigged, the kicker boarded and the pilot took off. As the plane approached off course, the bomb was kicked out. The chute tore away and the bomb tumbled into the jungle, lost until searchers dug it up. Fortunately, the mercs were more adept at blowing up bridges than conducting air ops.

18 MARCH 1987

The previous night Karl said, "A guerrilla-initiated action killed 16 of Bouterse's men. Bouterse's man was burnt alive and the others were shot. No further details."

An anti-Bouterse Hindu businessman was very frustrated with Ronny as he had been asking for arms and uniforms for two months. The Hindu allegedly had 200 men but no weapons, near Nickerie, west of the capital of Paramaribo. This was a prosperous agricultural area where the majority of Surinam's farming was conducted. Karl was to use explosives that had been cached at jungle camps to attack the oil refinery.

"I don't know what happened to Ronny. He has lost all interest in the war. He is waiting for something, and we don't know what it is," Karl said.

About 1130 hours, we caught a canoe to a French outpost on Maroni River and spent the afternoon with the French commander talking mechanics and the finances of buying and selling gold nuggets/dust dredged from rivers. No boat to St. Laurent that day, "maybe" the next day.

20 MARCH 1987

After a 10-hour ride down the Maroni River, made interesting by our jovial boat crew, who were snorting and sniffing something, smoking pot and boozing it up the entire trip until we finally arrived in civilization. I'd take a Huey any day.

21 MARCH 1987

In St. Laurent, I interviewed Dr. Eddie Josefzoon, a political adviser, and Michel Van Rey:

Doctor Josefzoon was formerly an adviser to the Minister of Education. He was a representative of the Bush Negro groups: the largest group were the Creoles, second largest the Hindus, and third largest were the Javanese.

"Thirty-five percent of the population of Surinam was in the Netherlands, the majority of whom left in 1975 because of the uncertainty about their future once Surinam became independent," he said. There were about 180,000 exiles in the Netherlands from Surinam. The conflict was a "civil war" rather than a revolution to overthrow the government.

"When the war started the thought was it would take two to six months. We were too optimistic," Josefzoon stated. When it started the guerrillas were short of money and weapons, but we were convinced we were fighting for a good cause: democracy. We thought we could get help from France, the U.S., Brazil, Venezuela or Holland; Western democracies. We were obviously overly optimistic. All these countries opposed Bouterse. The Dutch government compared Bouterse with an animal. You hear that kind of statement and then you tend to believe you'll get help from these countries," he said.

"The Dutch say they are sympathetic and understand what is going on. They agree that we want to bring back democracy but they can't give anything more than moral support," he continued. After this disappointment, Van Rey said, "We decided to do things ourselves, to buy weapons; solve our own logistics problems."

"Ronny started with 40 men in July 1986, and at this moment he needed to have 1,500 men. Lack of weapons and ammunition is the main problem, and the problem is not being solved. In the last few months the guerrillas lost between one and two million guilders that had been ripped off by unscrupulous arms dealers or people alleging to be arms dealers," Van Rey said.

"I believe that additional pressures applied to Bouterse will cause the people to rise up against him, like in the Philippine situation where Aquino was successful. I believe they can be successful if they obtain $500,000. The government had 2,000 men but morale was bad; the troops were poorly trained. One U.S. pilot, a 63-year-old Vietnam veteran [name unknown], was flying one of their choppers. Bouterse had four other pilots, all foreigners," Van Rey said.

"There was no conflict between Ronny and the other guerrilla commanders," Josefzoon said. This contradicted the information that Patrick Chauvel received in a letter from an acquaintance. It stated that four bush commanders had told Ronny that they were no longer going to follow his orders unless he came to the front and showed up with weapons.

"10 well-trained officers were waiting to come from the Netherlands and a lot more were standing by," Van Rey said. "The above-mentioned individuals are not interested in fighting this type of war, whatever that meant. We apparently had a Catch-22 situation. The people in the Netherlands who were going to come had stated that they 'must have well trained soldiers and then we will help.'"

"Bouterse is more incompetent than Ronny. Josefzoon feels that military pressure was being kept on Bouterse and that Ronny commanded the loyalty of the men. He was not in favor of using mercs but needed personnel to conduct training," Van Rey continued.

"Foreign countries want us to get rid of the mercs but they do not provide any assistance," Josefzoon said. "There are 60 Libyan mercs and 14 blacks from Angola working for the Bouterse government. These were mercs but nobody said anything about them," he complained.

"One of the conditions for help from Western democracies would be unification of the various exile groups, but no similar provision or requirement is made of the Afghan rebels. It's unfair."

ESTIMATE OF THE SITUATION

Even though the ragtag rebels were outnumbered, poorly trained, ill-equipped and led by a charismatic but mercurial leader (one merc described Brunswijk as a 25-year-old with the brain of a nine-year-old), they still managed to force Bouterse's Marxist government into a military stalemate. Bouterse's 2,000-man army was also poorly trained, and had neither the stomach nor the strength to conduct effective counter-guerrilla operations in Surinam's dense jungle terrain. Government forces ceded control of the entire northeastern section of Surinam to the guerrillas, maintaining a single isolated outpost in Albina, located on the mouth of the Maroni River which borders French Guiana.

Guerrilla operations, haphazard and amateurish as they were, nonetheless almost brought the economy to a standstill. The guerrillas had forced closure of Alcoa's bauxite mine, which provided some 80 percent of the country's foreign exchange; cut power lines to the capital and rendered all but one of the major roads impassable. Raids on palm oil plantations, lumber operations and the aluminum industry cost Bouterse's regime at least $150 million. However, guerrilla forces were too unsophisticated to capitalize on the growing discontent in Paramaribo, which was been fueled by political oppression and import shortages.

Brunswijk's "Surinam Liberation Army" was aligned with an exile group in Holland led by Henk Chin-a-sen, who served as president under Bouterse. He met with U.S. State Department officials seeking support, but as one might expect, received no promises of assistance.

The wild card in this conflict was France, whose interests in Surinam were obvious. The French space station was located at Kourou, French Guiana, and the Libyan troublemakers who were tied into supporting an embryonic independence movement in French Guiana prompted the French to allow the Surinamese guerrillas freedom of movement in and out of St. Laurent for purposes of re-supply. Highly placed French sources suggested that if the Libyans were killed or captured in combat, the French might be willing to do more.

The tragedy of this obscure little war was that a primitive people who simply wished to return to democracy could not elicit $500,000-worth of arms and supplies from weak-willed Western democracies. Some years later, we found out from a former U.S. Army Delta Force officer that the U.S. had a contingency plan to invade Surinam after our invasion of Grenada. "Bouterse," he said, "however was smart enough to see the writing on the wall and kicked out all his Cuban military advisors. Therefore, the invasion plan was scrapped."

Gallagher, MacKenzie and I reviewed the Surinam situation when we returned to Boulder. We agreed that there was potential to overthrow a thuggish, pro-communist regime that was up to its ears in the dope business and counterfeiting U.S. dollars. I had MacKenzie recruit three of his buddies who were fellow veterans of the Rhodesian SAS to go back to Surinam and the bush guerrillas to determine if it was feasible to overthrow Bouterse.

Their report was positive. In short, a couple dozen mercs, all of whom would be ex-Rhodesian SAS personnel, and $500,000 for guns would get the job done. I sent Gallagher to Amsterdam to liaise with Suranamese exiles who were supporting the guerrillas. They were basically incompetent; full of promises but had squandered the funds they had raised. He returned to Boulder out of sorts and disgusted. I was in contact with one source who was seriously interested in the operation but he up and died on me.

For the want of half a million, a revolution was lost.

28

GUNS BEHIND THE GREAT WALL

SOF in communist China? What a bizarre thought. My teams and I had been to a lot of weird places prior to our invitation to China, but not one of us ever thought we would be jogging the Great Wall, firing the latest PRC small arms and eating weird, "I don't want to know" parts of plants, fish and fowl at the invitation of the Chinese communist government with a bunch of Chicom generals.

SOF's weapons guru, Peter Kokalis, was approached by contacts from the PRC in 1987, before the Berlin Wall came down, to test and evaluate a number of small arms never before seen outside the Bamboo Curtain. At the time, the People's Liberation Army (PLA) of China ground forces were upgrading their weaponry since much of it consisted of decades-old Soviet designs. Although the communist bloc was spearheaded by the two large communist powers, and the Soviet Union was supplying arms to the Chinese when the two were not having their own Cold War, the Chinese lusted after the advanced weapons technology of the West, and still do.

Numbering some 3,625,000 regulars at the time, the PLA was the largest army in the world. Largest in numbers that is, not in military strength during most of the Cold War, but things were changing. Under-mechanized and largely equipped with outdated weaponry at all levels, the PLA was primarily a foot-mobile army that would find itself at a severe disadvantage were it to engage the Soviet Union in a major military confrontation at that time.

However, the move in the late 1980s from a previously Leninist society to "market socialism" provided the PLA with the avenues to upgrade its military potential through importation of Western technology and the development of indigenous designs. Western authorities still regarded the Chinese defense industry as geared to the production of Soviet copies dating back to the 1950s. As we soon found out, this assessment no longer held true, at least in the area of military small arms.

SOF *SCOOPS THE CIA . . . AGAIN*

Adopted in 1984 by the PLA, the new Type 81 assault rifle and squad automatic weapon (SAW) gave Kokalis convincing proof that PRC designers were acutely tuned to the combat user's requirements and were fully capable of executing designs that incorporated time-proven concepts alongside numerous innovative features.

We were soon to find out how the superficially soft-spoken, polite Chinese military officers were very cleverly sucking experts into their web.

It was no secret that *SOF* had never been moderate about its anti-communist position, well actually, its anti-communist stance was rabid. "COMMUNISM STOPS HERE" posters, with me as the poster boy, hung all over our offices, were in the magazine and sold like hotcakes. Every chance it got, *SOF* bashed the PRC's form of government. We fought them in Korea and faced their fierce brutality at great cost. They backed the North Vietnamese and served them a perverted victory at an enormous cost to the United States. They had backed Robert Mugabe's terrorists in Rhodesia which gave them another mark in the "dark side" book.

However, times and governments change. The Chinese, avid readers of the outspoken, commie-hating *SOF*, took note of the sophisticated coverage of worldwide weapons by its experts and schemed to learn what *SOF*'s Peter Kokalis really knew.

SOF decided to adopt "the enemy of my enemy is my friend" concept, or at least that was the excuse for being seduced by the thought of what could prove to be a very dangerous mission. At the time the PRC was aiding the anti-communists in Cambodia and Laos and providing large quantities of Soviet killing items to the Afghan freedom fighters. (In April 1985, when *SOF* was training the Contras, we saw a half-million PRC-manufactured 7.62x39mm rounds in a Contra base camp. How they got there? We don't know.)

But why *SOF*? Why not International Defense Review, Jane's, Armed Forces Journal or any of a number of prestigious military trade magazines? Or, they could have invited a number of journalists from various publications if in fact the PRC's main objective was to gain maximum exposure for its line of small arms for military sales. We wouldn't get an answer to that mystery until we got to China.

I have been told that I have a superman-size ego, sometimes clouded by paranoia, which I admit to—but let those who have been on foreign leaders' hit lists and on the CIA watch list cast the first stone. Curious as to why we were chosen for this mission, I decided to call a number of foreign affairs experts. Taking that old adage, "two brains of those in high places are better than one" seriously had saved my ass numerous times.

One source speculated that the invitation was some "Byzantine Chinese plot" with unknown objectives. Lieutenant General Jack Singlaub, a long-time friend and accomplice, quoted an old Chinese proverb: "It is better to sit down across a table from an enemy you know than a friend you don't know." A well-known international defense consultant and military author agreed with Singlaub: "The PRC would rather sit down with a known, hard-core anti-communist than a wishy-washy liberal. If Carter had been president, no rapprochement would have been affected with the PRC . . . [although it was in 1979 that the U.S. and Chinese relations softened]. The Chinese knew where Nixon stood and therefore felt comfortable in dealing with him." So who was the common enemy for *SOF* and the Chinese? The Soviets were, with their nuclear weapons. The United States had played one against the other during President Reagan's tenure. To taunt the Soviets, it sold weapons to the PLA after the U.S. and China established diplomatic relations.

At the same time, the United States was selling weapons to Taiwan, feeding the explosive tensions between that island republic and the mainland. To China, with its non-negotiable "one China policy," Taiwan was simply a breakaway non-sovereign that would be brought into the fold, probably by force.

All of this intrigue added to the mystique of the unexpected invitation to *SOF*. There were questions to be answered, mysteries to be solved and weapons to fire. It was time to go. The *SOF* team consisted of: faithful Peter Kokalis; Major Bob MacKenzie (promoted to Lieutenant Colonel before being KIA in Sierra Leone), a merc extraordinaire, Rhodesia, South Africa and had worked for various governments training their troops; and Vann, who was studying Mandarin Chinese at the university in Hong Kong, although the official language in Hong Kong was Cantonese; and me. There is nothing that the Chinese did not know about any of us since we had to present documents that identified us before we were granted visas.

Peter Kokalis, an American Greek could obsess about anything. Tall, wiry, with prominent jagged features and shooting brown eyes, Kokalis had a sharp, sarcastic wit, was quick to improvise and was such a diehard commie hater that he wanted nothing more than to join any fight against them or learn any secrets they held. MacKenzie had a seething anger underneath his steely exterior, but no one would guess it, as he usually comported himself with utmost composure in dicey situations. Cold and hard as steel, to those who were weak and who became the conquered, he never gave another thought.

We had arrived at the airport in Beijing and, as usual, our signature camouflage-clad entourage drew a multitude of stares. Our hosts met us and took us to a rather splendid old hotel and assigned us rooms. Security lurked in the halls, trying to be invisible but not doing a very good job of it.

That first evening we had dinner with half-a-dozen of our hosts, including a couple of Chinese generals. We were honored with all sorts of weird animal, poultry and fish parts and, thank goodness, lots of plain white rice. The waiters kept bringing on more and more courses and, with each course, more rounds of their vile alcohol.

Although we were jet-lagged and ready to pass out after the endless flight halfway around the world, I called a strategy meeting in the room I was sharing with Kokalis. I mentioned something negative about the Chinese military officials, calling them communist "dickheads," or some such thing. Peter, very deep into his cups of white, tasteless Chinese moonshine, made of who knows what, that could knock an elephant off its feet, in full agreement with me, flipped the bird, "Fuck the Chinese!" We pointed to the cameras we had spotted in the room. That just got him going. This time he pointed his middle finger at the cameras and yelled even louder obscenities.

Mac didn't find much humor in Peter's antics, but we usually ignored the silent merc. That is until that first night in China, when we were listening to what soon became a Kokalis one-man show and Mac made his presence clear. Kokalis, one of those out-of-control drinkers, who was outspoken and feared no one even when he was sober, was not to be quieted, even by the formidable Mac. He cursed all "communist Chinamen" everywhere, even louder after Mac signaled vigorously for him to shut the hell up. I thought the two were going to come to blows. To inflame things even further, Vann, who had refused the Chinese moonshine, was sober and laughing, highly amused by the surreal scenario. Mac, annoyed because we were guests of military officials reputed to be the most ruthless on the planet, again ordered Kokalis to shut up. Mac pointed up to the cameras again, but Kokalis only got louder and cruder.

Eventually, Kokalis passed out without incident. I was amazed at how Mac kept his sober face, never finding for a moment any humor in the scene like one out of a half-star Cold War movie, with the main protagonists being a hard-core merc, a weapons expert and a semi-comatose publisher of a controversial military-style magazine.

Each day, the Chinese had the same tall, muscular, strongly chiseled featured chauffeur pick us up and take us out to the army bases, quite a way outside of Beijing. The soldiers were welcoming, no different from soldiers anywhere. They were curious, interested and very eager to learn English.

The days passed and we got plenty of trigger time with the Chinese weapons and rocket launchers. The Chinese were genuinely impressed with Kokalis' vast knowledge, as well as the extensive experience that MacKenzie had acquired on various battlefields. Vann found it a great thrill to be one of the first non-military Westerners to fire an RPG, and the Chinese got a big kick out of it as well. However, I did notice that the announcer gave loud warnings that probably reverberated to Beijing through his microphone when Vann approached the firing range. The laughing Chinese troops would then scramble to get out of the way.

The Chinese soldiers had let down their guard, warming to the free-spirited way of the Americans who were from a world with which they had no knowledge apart from what they gleaned from movies, if they were allowed to see them. The troops were learning English so much faster than they had in the classroom that one of the generals called Vann to his room and offered him a job helping them with their English. Vann politely declined. Without the conveniences and luxuries of the West, the invitation to this ancient land held absolutely no appeal for Vann. However, the gesture indicated that somehow, surprisingly, despite the first boisterous night, the shrewd general trusted our strange team.

We were in awe of the exotic Chinese architectural and archeological wonders, although all of us had spent considerable time in other parts of Asia. In Beijing, the chauffeur took us to all the famous Chinese sites and museums. Mac became especially animated when we visited the Revolutionary History Museum and mausoleums erected for dead heroes. Kokalis was delighted with an exotic weapons collection unknown to Westerners.

HEY, WE'RE NOT BEYOND BEING TOURISTS . . .

We were free to wander around the wide streets and did so although we knew we were being watched. However, without our passports, which were confiscated upon our arrival, we could not go far. As in most third world countries, we were shocked by the abject poverty we witnessed while our hosts were living in luxurious mansions with armies of servants and eating the world's delicacies, proudly showing off their rotund bellies. Peasants on bicycles were everywhere, cars drove in any direction, and carts pulled by donkeys, carrying a few meager goods, plodded down the roads. Mao would not have been happy.

The most spectacular Tiananmen Square, named after the Tiananmen Gate that was built during the Ming Dynasty in 1415 as an entrance to the Forbidden City, is the widest square in the world. Chairman Mao, the ruthless revolutionary/poet who founded the People's Republic of China and brought China into the industrial age, had expanded the square several times, planning to fit half-a-million people in it. The Great Hall of the People and other magnificent buildings and fortresses reflected the greatness of the Chinese Empire. Mac and I jogged a small portion of the expansive 2,000-year-old Great Wall of China, deservedly on the list of the Great Wonders of the World.

The first night before dinner, I took my normal daily run in the smog-saturated Beijing air, polluted by thousands of coal burning cooking fires and industries. The locals regarded me with as much amazement as they would a six-foot black Nubian clothed in a leopard skin with a spear. With my first breath, the sulfurous air hammered me. I knew I should not continue, but once again played stubborn/stupid and subsequently developed a dreadful, deep chest cough. That, however, did not prevent me jogging the Great Wall, a few days later.

Our chauffeur, a jovial man who had a ready smile once he got used to us, was enjoying his gig with the wacky Americans. But we realized that the class system was very much alive. He would sit on a stool in a different room with the other workers while we feasted with the Chinese officers. Being idealistic Americans, Vann asked the generals if he could dine with us and, much to their chagrin although they did not show it, they allowed it.

The generals I noticed, were beginning to show the signs of opulence, but were alert and cautious, and if anyone of us wandered a step away from where we should on the base, someone was there with lightning speed redirecting us back to the allowed areas.

The Chinese had a great sense of humor, and I am sure that the *SOF* delegation was the zaniest they had ever met. We had few inhibitions and provided them with two weeks of entertainment as well as expertise. The final banquet was one we would never forget and I am sure the generals didn't either. We were once again around a large table spread with white tablecloths and the usual feast. The exotic courses at mealtime just kept on coming. Their version of white lightening was once again flowing, everyone was relaxed and we all seemed to be friends.

A few years later, we met up some of the military officials we had worked with in China at the SHOT show in Vegas. They, and scores of other Chinese, became regulars. They infiltrated the U.S. weapons industry and exploited the technology and expertise they obtained. China is predicted to be as advanced as the United States in nuclear and other weapon craft by 2020. Economically, they are overtaking one continent after the other.

SOF was in China before the Cold War ended. At that time China, a poverty-struck, totalitarian country, was on the road to becoming the world's next superpower. In the following 25 years, China would advance by leaps and bounds, posing a threat to the other powers. Much, if not most, of their advancement was based on pirating U.S. technology, as

Soviet spies had done at Los Alamos during World War II, or because U.S. administrations handed nuclear secrets to the emerging superpower on a silver plate, or, more recently, because of the rampant cyber spying and hacking of U.S. government and industrial sites.

SOF published the results of our T&E's in the five issues following our Chinese adventure, something no other magazine had accomplished.

29

DESERT STORM DIARY

I landed in Saudi Arabia on 12 January 1991. For the next 40 days and nights I battled a military bureaucracy intent upon denying *SOF* access to front-line combat troops, or any troops for that matter. I also had to contend with the Banana Republic Brigade—scores of pseudo "war correspondents" whose closest brush with combat was filing expense account forms with the head office. Watching these would-be journalists making fools of themselves at the daily 1700 hrs U.S. military briefing was both sad and amusing. Typical question was

"Why did they bomb the bridge?"

"To destroy it."

One of the most egregious examples of the media phonies was a "talking head" who was doing a "standup" before the 1700 hrs briefing began. I was idly watching him when it suddenly hit me. He was holding a gas mask. I surveyed the room. No one else was! The phony bastard! I had left my camera in my room so I turned to Melinda Liu from *Newsweek* and asked her to get a photo of that dork with the gas mask." Unfortunately she couldn't get it out of her purse before the NBC dork quit babbling.

As I was quoted in the *Wall Street Journal* and *Newsweek*, "I thought I'd be riding the lead tank into Baghdad by now. Instead, I'm stuck in a briefing room with the biggest bunch of boobs and dorks I've ever met."

However, it was the lopsided treatment of the press corps that finally forced me to break all the rules and make my own way to the front. Media "barking dogs" the brass courted—the major television networks, newspapers and newsweeklies— while the rest, *SOF* included, were left out in the cold. I had had enough.

Packing up my cameras and trusty tape recorder I headed north, employing "smoke and mirrors" tactics to circumvent the rules and avoid roving military police anti-journalist patrols. The following is a diary of my infiltration into the war zone taken from my hours of taped notes.

21 FEBRUARY, 1745 HOURS

I find myself at a construction site near the Saudi Arabian National Guard (SANG) compound in the desert northeast of Hafar Al Batin. Bedouin troops here provide security for the oil pipeline lay in the early years of the Iran-Iraq War. There is also a U.S. Army compound, mission unknown, and an Egyptian compound, where I had lunch with Colonel Zagloul Mohammed Fathey, chief of staff of the Egyptian 3rd Mechanized Division and veteran of the '67 and '73 wars with Israel. In the background, outgoing 155mm rounds could be heard. There were also what appeared to be B-52 arc lights, or what the media now calls "carpet bombing."

It is interesting to see the way Fathey lives. He has a large tent, probably 30 feet long and 15 feet wide, which is carpeted and furnished with a full-size wooden desk, and chairs with upholstered pillows.

I am out here with Tim Lambon, a Rhodesian who used to work in a special intelligence unit. He drifted into TV work and met *Soldier of Fortune*'s African correspondent, Al Venter. The two worked on a project in Afghanistan. Since then, Lambon has been working for an independent British TV firm. He and I decided it was useless to stay in Riyadh as we were sick of being stonewalled by the joint information bureau (JIB). It was apparent that the only journalists who were getting access to the troops on the front lines were those with a lot of clout, i.e., the major "barking dogs" on major TV stations.

I met a young hotshot from the *Wall Street Journal* last week, Steve Horowitz, who contacted me regarding an interview. His intention was to interview people from the press for a *Journal* piece on press attitudes about the war. After spending some time with me and *SOF* associates Mike Williams and Paul Fanshaw, who were along with me, he decided that

SOF's trials and tribulations were of sufficient interest for a story.

He wanted something unusual, some color, and he wasn't particularly overjoyed with what he was finding on the walk from the Riyadh Hyatt Regency to the Riyadh Wendy's. He wanted to come out here to Hafar Al Batin, and I figured if we accompanied him it was more likely his story would make the front page of his paper. I rationalized that a large percentage of the cost of this so far unproductive trip could be justified by the P.R. value of a favorable article in the *Journal.* (Horowitz's article on *SOF*'s frustrations appeared on the front page of the *Journal* on 21 February, 1991.)

Mike Williams and I decided we would take Horowitz's car and drive back the next morning. I was expecting to get approval to interview some of the Marine recon troops that had been trapped in the battle for Khafji to supplement Mike's article.

It was Marine recon that called in Marine air and artillery support, significantly affecting the outcome of that battle. I had submitted a written request and subsequently discussed the request with Major Keith Oliver, the Marine Corps representative on the JIB. Oliver said he was enthusiastic about the concept, that the Riyadh JIB was enthusiastic and that he would be contacting his counterpart in Dhahran to see how my interview could be arranged. This was a unilateral request; in other words, it was a request that only I be allowed to conduct the specially arranged interview.

Upon our return, I contacted Oliver, who said he was now very pessimistic about the request after having contacted Dhahran. No explanation was forthcoming. It became clear that I was not going to get anything by going through normal channels or following the rules.

1804 HOURS

Our options were limited. We could continue to piss and moan in Riyadh or throw the dice and try and tag onto a column of somebody's troops during the confusion expected when the ground offensive kicked off. Lambon and I decided we had no choice but to exercise the latter option. The worst that the Saudis or U.S. forces could do would be to throw us out of the world's greatest kitty litter box.

Lambon, who is in his early 30s and slim, with a GI haircut, definitely had a good military appearance. He also had leased a brand new four-door Nissan Safari four-wheel-drive vehicle, which happened to be scarcer than pigs in Mecca. (Apparently, the U.S. military leased all the four-wheel-drive vehicles for staff and administrative types so that all the Humvees would be available for more vital tasks.)

Lambon painted the Nissan a desert tan, taped inverted "V" shapes on the doors (which all the Coalition vehicles were running around with), and slapped an orange panel on top. Our basic plan was to bamboozle our way through the Saudi checkpoints on the road from Riyadh to Hafar Al Batin by appearing as U.S. military.

When I pointed out that the rental agency might be upset about the new poly-vinyl acrylic paint job, which wouldn't wash off, Lambon said, "Ah, screw 'em. We'll deal with that when I turn it in. The mission comes first."

We put on outfits that could be mistaken for U.S. uniforms by the Saudis, who were as unfamiliar with our uniforms as we were with theirs. I wore desert cammie pants; desert boots, an olive drab "wooly pully" and a desert cammie boonie hat with jump wings. Lambon wore a crewcut and desert cammies.

We had found earlier that as long as we appeared to be military, the Saudis would wave us by without asking for I.D. Our disguises worked effectively to get us to Hafar Al Batin. Upon arriving, we reconned the Al Fao hotel to see if any journalists were inside.

My plan was to link up with a Saudi sheik, Mubarek, since I had established rapport with him on an earlier trip to Hafar, and see how he could help us. We met Mubarek and indicated we were having difficulty getting rooms—the hotel was booked. Mubarek offered to put us up in his suite, which meant we were in two drab, dingy rooms instead of one. But the price was right, so we accepted. Lambon decided to go on to Rafha. My gut feeling was that I should play my cards with Mubarek and see what might develop. I laid an Al Mar "Desert Shield" knife on him last night and he seemed to really appreciate it. A little low-key bribery often helps.

1818 HOURS

I find myself thinking about how this whole situation has developed. It has been a classic case of extreme frustration. Since the military and the Saudis work to make it impossible for the average reporter to cover this war, the only way anything can be achieved is by cheating, lying and violating the rules and regulations.

Certainly the stories that I need do not include going out and doing a piece on a combat support unit . . . no matter how important a part they play. I picked up a technique from an experienced magazine journalist, Malcom McConnell, who was representing *Readers Digest* as its Defense Correspondent for creating phony documents, which we utilized prior to our last trip up here. Using a Saudi Ministry of Information request sheet, we made up a line of bullshit saying that we were authorized to come up here to visit the Kuwaiti armored brigade. We simply typed in the minister of information's name and had an Arab friend sign it in Arabic. He then wrote an additional bullshit message at the bottom in Arabic. The idea was to confuse anyone we might run into, be they Saudi or American, who would give us a difficult time. It is important to always forge documents that are so vague they never can be traced back to anyone in the combat area.

Prior to our departure, the Saudi Minister of Information had published a directive denying all journalists travel to anywhere in the general AO where we have been operating. The memo also said no journalists were allowed to wear military uniforms. Of course, no one was following the minister's directives. There were about 40 correspondents in the area. When I came up there with Mike Williams a week ago, we ran into a journalist who said he had a contact in one of the military units who said that all journalists were going to be swept up and sent back. It hasn't happened yet.

We theorized that a number of journalists create rumors of this nature to serve their own purposes, for example to scare off other journalists. This certainly could be true. In any case, the old adage that all is fair in love and war could also be twisted to say all is fair in love and journalism. This was a "cut-throat, screw your buddy, look out for yourself" scenario. Rules are for suckers who will never get to where the action is.

1829 HOURS

The Sheik is on a trip where he is apparently arranging to move a lot of heavy equipment up to the Kuwaiti border. For whatever reason, he said he couldn't take me with him tonight, but would tomorrow. At least I'm slowly getting closer to where the action is. One of the reasons for my camping here in the desert is the hope that Mubarek can get me in with the Egyptians. If that happens, I can hook up with recon units and get across the border and perhaps observe some of the fighting. This is obviously the best shot I've had to date.

2016 HOURS

I have just come back from having tea and dates with the Bedouins. The city Arabs whom I met in Riyadh simply didn't do much for me. They seemed rather soft and effete. The Bedouins, however, are Saudi Arabia's cowboys or mountain men—down to earth and solid with a sense of humor. They were a pleasure to be around, even though communication was primitive.

I find myself reflecting on the "smoke and mirrors," tactics used to get here. Said tactics were used not only to bamboozle American and Saudi authorities, but also editors. Lambon, who got permission from his home office to drive up here on this op, did so only after he told his editor that he was coming up here with an American colonel. Now that wasn't a total lie, but certainly some omissions were made, e.g., that I was a Lieutenant Colonel and retired from the Reserves! Whatever gets the job done!

Another amusing scam I remember hearing about was pulled off by a group of British reporters. They drove up to a British installation with a military-looking vehicle where a young guard asked for the password. An authoritarian voice in the back of the vehicle responded with vigor and started chewing out the young trooper's ass, telling him that he wanted to see the general. The kid was quaking when the tirade finished. The Brit journalist then asked the trooper if he knew the password. The soldier told him not only the password, but also the response. The journalists proceeded on into headquarters. "Smoke and mirrors."

I still haven't completely figured out the story on Sheik Mubarek. He is apparently wealthy and claims to own a 100-square kilometer farm between Dhahran and Riyadh. He is not in the army, but is apparently in the construction business and is in charge of building support facilities and roads. He claims to be from one of the 10 most powerful tribes in Saudi Arabia and that his tribe supported whichever Arab king was responsible for unifying the country around 1920. Mubarek's aide, Faisel, told me that

Mubarek is highly regarded because he assumed his position to help the government for no salary, and that when the war is over he will assume a very significant position in the regime.

He also mentioned something I heard from two other Saudi sources: that this whole war has disturbed the Saudi psyche considerably. They're puzzled and upset that they've spent so much money on defense and yet in this time of crisis they have been so impotent and had to rely on infidels for their defense.

The feeling is that the Saudis are going to seriously reevaluate their military capabilities, which undoubtedly will result in a much more powerful military machine.

22 FEBRUARY, 0745 HOURS

An Egyptian mechanized unit has been moving past my tent for the last two hours, and another unit's coming in to the east now with a full brigade. The vehicles are well spaced so it's hard to get a count on how many there are. I'm by the side of the road looking like George Patton giving them the thumbs up. They appear to be in good spirits, with some motioning for me to get on.

1012 HOURS

It looks like most of the Egyptians have passed. The armored vehicles led the way followed by armored personnel carriers (APCs), self-propelled guns (SPs) and trucks. I can hear B-52 strikes in the background. We heard them thumping through most of last night. I was contemplating hitchhiking. However, if I did that, it might put Mubarek in the shits. Since he has been my host, I guess I'll be a nice guy and pass. It's hard to know what other correspondents are accessing so I decide to hang around and when Mubarek comes back, see if he can get me with the Egyptians on the way up front.

1100 HOURS

I just chatted with an Egyptian Lieutenant Colonel engineer who told me that he thought it's going to be about two days before the main Coalition thrust. What we've been seeing today is the movement of the 3rd Egyptian Mechanized Division to their attack positions.

1211 HOURS

I am now on a berm located a few klicks south of the Kuwaiti border. We saw a large explosion maybe 20 klicks away, a large black cloud rising into the sky. I have no way of determining what kind of ordnance made the hit. The Egyptians have been placed forward so we are moving along the route they apparently used this morning. We're now pulling into a construction area about 5 klicks from the border and 18 klicks from the main Iraqi defensive line. Apparently, this was as good a decision as I have made to date. Had the following conversation with Faisel:

> Faisel: This is a very dangerous area here.
> Brown: And, Faisel, why do you say that it is very dangerous?
> Faisel: Because we are within the range of the Iraqi artillery. There was one rocket that landed just up the road about a half an hour ago.
> Brown: Maybe the Iraqis will shoot some artillery and it will be very exciting. What do you think about that?
> Faisel: I don't think that it would be very exciting for me! (Laughter).

1313 HOURS

We are moving up with the dozer, directly to the berm. Now the question is whether or not they will let me drive the dozer to breach the berm, which will allow support vehicles to follow the tracked vehicles. That would truly be a magnificent accomplishment, and this is truly a high. The last 48 hours make it all worthwhile—the waiting, the B.S., the putting up with stupid people. Now it's all worthwhile.

1320 HOURS

Suddenly, it is all not worthwhile. There are some asshole journalists there, with a pool. So much for my visions of a great scoop.

The Egyptians have moved their armor up behind the berm. There are two APCs or trucks between each M-60 tank and their tanks are about 75 yards apart. I examine the interior of one of their M-113s. They are certainly well used but in very good condition. Things look neat and orderly; obviously a professional operation here.

Behind the line of vehicles and tanks are individual foxholes, which provide shelter from incoming. To the rear we have a number of tents spread out over at least 400 yards back from the berm. Trucks and support vehicles are dispersed in case of artillery attack. It appears from the way they're positioned that they'll make a linear frontal attack. Once they cross the berm that could well change depending on their op plans, which I am not privy to. We are following one of the bulldozers through a gap in the wall. Exciting! As we go through, we can see a large black cloud down range, probably 20 klicks away. Anyhow, we are through the berm.

23 FEBRUARY, 0823 HOURS

According to Hassan, one of Sheik Mubarek's workers, Bush has given Saddam until "noon today" to get out. I don't know whether that is our time or Washington time. More Egyptian troops have been moving through. It's difficult to determine what unit they're from, but obviously the one Egyptian brigade is not all that's been deployed.

Rain has brought up a fine coating of grass all over the desert. Looking at it from afar you would think you were looking at Kansas wheat fields in early spring. Coalition forces have sprinkled vehicle revetments all over the desert, which almost appear as sailing ships on a green sea from a distance. Flies are still everywhere, of course. I actually saw three or four dogs out here. Normally the Arabs, for reasons unbeknownst to me, don't like dogs.

It clears my mind staying out here in the desert. I could have gone into Hafar Al Batin last night, and maybe I should have, in order to contact Lambon and see what success he was having in accessing American units. I'm still hoping that I'll be able to tag along with Mubarek and the Egyptian troops.

The Egyptians are still moving. You can read in a military manual about an armored division's table of organization, but until you actually see it, it simply doesn't have an impact on you. They have been moving here now, off and on, since a little after 0700.

1004 HOURS

I have developed my amusement for the day: a field-expedient flytrap, consisting of a two-inch-high glass cylinder teacup, one-fourth full of tea heavily laced with sugar and milk. Flies occasionally fall into the mixture and I have found a way to accelerate the process. Heh, heh. When the flies walk on the inside of the cup, I slap my book down on the rim and the flies fall into the tea and drown. How satisfying. Right now there are about 15 casualties. This is a very gratifying experience and the most amusing thing I've done in the last five weeks.

To most effectively use this flytrap, one has to develop certain skills. Once the fly is on the inside of the cup, one brings the palm of the hand down firmly and jolts the fly down into the mass of other squirming and obnoxious sons-of-bitches. Another technique is to wait until there are four or five on the inside, then clamp your palm over the cup. Then you get the tea swirling around up along the sides and have them all fighting for their lives (evil laughter). Also, when you bring your palm down firmly on the top of the rim, the force will often shake the little creature loose from the side and plop him down into the gooey mass. In my experiments, not a single fly has escaped after becoming stuck in the tea. What a pleasure. Oh yes, it's teatime again. I do not care if I never see another cup of Lipton tea. The Bedouin serving the tea thinks I'm crazy. At this point, I wouldn't argue the point.

More B-52 strikes. The remainder of the Egyptian division keeps moving north, mostly all combat and combat support. Occasionally, a Black Hawk in desert cammie scuttles overhead. Faisel told me three Scuds were fired at the Bahrain airport last night, but doesn't know for certain whether or not Patriots shot them down. In the latest issue of *Newsweek,* it was suggested that a lot of Coalition flights had to be altered to deal with the Scud threat, so the Scuds are not only a psychological terror weapon, but are also having an impact on our air campaign.

A reporter from some paper based in Cairo just showed up in a flight suit, a leather vest and patent-leather shoes. God save us from news boobs! I asked him if he was going with the Egyptians if they made a ground attack, to which he replied he would if he could. I mentioned that I would like to go with them, too. He asked if I wanted to see Kuwait and of course, I said yes, so we will see if he could help arrange something. I believe one should develop new options whenever possible and pursue them all concurrently.

With the Egyptian APCs on line in attack position behind the berm and the movement of combat support this morning, I surmise the ground offensive will kick off tomorrow, on the 24th (unless political B.S. is thrown into the picture). I think I'll go into Hafar Al Batin tonight to see how the other journalists are doing. I will be talking to Mubarek later this afternoon, so can check to see if there is any way he can get me locked in with the Egyptians when they move. I should have made an effort yesterday when I was up on the front line B.S.-ing with the Egyptian M-113 squadron commander, but I didn't think of it at the time.

1643 HOURS

We've been heading down the road northeast of Ruqi, a border checkpoint between Iraq and Saudi. It has been eerie driving on this road with no other traffic, but now we're starting to encounter some Egyptian units. We just passed all the dug-in Egyptian 155mm SPs. I saw an American unit with them, but didn't have a chance to talk to them. I guess the Americans would be forward air controllers.

We've been watching the sun gradually sink in the west. There is an aura of excitement in the air that only war can bring. A desert sunset is pretty, but it is much more intriguing when there is a background of smoke from a B-52 strike rising into the air 20 klicks to the north.

24 FEBRUARY, 0853 HOURS

We are on our way to the front. Sheik Mubarek has just informed me that he has arranged for me to ride with the Egyptians. As we bounce along, I still have my fingers crossed. We moved from Hafar Al Batin to his construction base camp positioned near the SANG compound. We brought along Forrest Sawyer from ABC-TV News, with his crew. We left instructions that when the crew with the satellite and ancillary equipment showed up, they should be guided to a rendezvous point up near the front. The weather is overcast and a light rain is falling. Onward!

0913 HOURS

Mubarek just told me he's arranged for the ABC News crew to go on a tank with the Saudis and for me to go with the Egyptians. That makes me more than satisfied, as I think the Egyptians are combat tested and probably will see more action. Besides that, I would rather be with the combat-tested unit.

We're getting seriously close to the front. On the right, about 20 tanker trucks, both military and civilian, are moving toward the front. We can see rear echelon units under cammie netting, probably about 500 meters away.

Sawyer says that the military slapped a 48-hour embargo on all TV pool broadcasts. Being out here, Sawyer and his men will have a superb chance to scoop other TV networks if they can get their satellite dish to feed.

0940 HOURS

We are moving forward with rear echelon units, mostly ambulances and vehicle retrieval systems. Clouds are starting to part so it's clearing up, and visibility has increased. Out of the right window, I can see what appears to be smoke rising from the front lines. We're getting closer.

We just stopped where there was an American team attaching mine plows on four Saudi M-60s to explode mines. The Marine Lieutenant Colonel putting them on said that plows have to be used instead of line-exploding charges, as the Iraqis have Italian mines with three baffles. Contact will knock out the first baffle, but the other two baffles can only be exploded by actual pressure. The Egyptians have not moved out yet; their armor is still behind the berm, which incidentally was built some years ago as an anti-smuggling barrier.

I finally got a fix on our location. To our north is the Kuwaiti border, not the Iraqi border. We are barreling into the Egyptian rear now, apparently looking for the HQ so we can liaise with whoever is going to put who with who here. It is amazing the amount of equipment a division has—columns stretch out as far as the eye can see. We are hearing some explosions now, rather large stuff, as the blasts have to be at least 18 klicks away.

1210 HOURS

We are now trying to find the ABC News crew with the satellite dish, generator and ancillary items. More air strikes rumble in the distance. Above the length of the berm is this linear column of smoke, which comes from hundreds of fires in the Kuwaiti oil fields. Apparently, the attack is not going to kick off with the Egyptians until 0400, which means I'll have to wait around here for another 16 hours and get up early in the morning, which doesn't make me a happy camper. The adrenaline level has dropped way, way down and I'm getting bored.

I explained to Sawyer that I thought he'd be better off going with the Egyptians. It didn't seem likely that the untested Saudi units were going to play any major role in the ground offensive. He had an obligation to the Saudis, however, and his major objective was to beat out the competition. He now has about 36 hours to do that with the 48-hour news embargo in place. If he can't get a satellite feed set up, he'll still be able to get some footage of the Saudis and have the tape driven back to Riyadh.

1327 HOURS

We're still looking for the missing vehicle with the satellite dish. We have a problem with communication out here. The satellite crew and Saudi drivers were directed to go to the Bedouin compound; somebody else told them to go to the "water point." At any rate, they've disappeared . . . perhaps never to be seen again. Mubarek is most unhappy with the world at this point.

Egyptians are breaking ammo out of packing crates and stacking it around their long-range 122mm guns; troops are being issued web gear with ammo. The time grows near.

1527 HOURS

Helter-skelter, the ABC crew finally located their satellite equipment and vehicles. It seems there was some problem with one of the vehicles using contaminated fuel. Now they are trying to make a decision as to where to place the satellite station.

We have two stories at this time: One from the Saudis that the offensive is going to launch from this area and is going to kick off at 0400 tomorrow, another from Mubarek, who says the Egyptians are going to kick it off at 1600 this evening. What I am going to do remains to be seen. I'll continue to go with the flow.

After a couple of interesting adventures with Sawyer, I spent the night camped out with his ABC crew. Earlier in the evening, I was riding with him in his 4x4 trying to find the Saudi HQ. As we were driving through the Egyptian encampment, I remarked to Sawyer, "Smells like skunk. They got any skunks around here?" He didn't know. A hundred meters later, we were halted by a rather nervous group of young Egyptian troops wearing gas masks with AK-47s pointed directly at us. They wanted to know just who in the hell we were. It was "open the door verry slowly," "get out of the car verrry slowly" and "raise your hands verry slowly" time.

We convinced them we weren't terrorists, but decided since we weren't communicating real well, it would be best if we did an about face. Obviously the gas alert had been sounded, and recollecting the "skunk" smell, we put on our gas masks. We didn't die, however, so it was a false alarm.

25 FEBRUARY 0832 HOURS

I looked over the shoulder of the ABC News production chief as he read a note from Sawyer, who by this time was several klicks closer to the front. On the note, I found the phrase "lose Brown" somewhat disconcerting, but clear. I told the producer I saw the note, and would bow out with no hassles. He mumbled some shit about Sawyer having to suck up to the Saudis so much he was getting scabs on his lips.

Mubarek had disappeared and I was 70 miles out in the desert with no ride. Watching the last of the Arab forces move through the gap in the berm, I was faced with beginning the long and unpleasant hike back to Hafar Al Batin. Then the last Saudi jeep going through the berm stopped. A Saudi MP first lieutenant got out.

Saudi MP: Do you have a ride?

Brown: No.

Saudi MP: Would you like one?

Brown: Boy, howdy!

My fortunes had been radically reversed. I jumped in and we raced off. I was through the berm and on my way to Kuwait. We soon caught up with the column, which had halted for reasons unknown. The Saudi MP said we might be stopped here for six or seven hours, maybe less. Then he was talking to another Saudi. The paranoia set in. Was he talking to his commanding officer? Were they talking about the gringo with the *Soldier of Fortune* cap?

Fortunately, nothing came of the conversation. We were far enough to the rear of the column that no command elements could see me. The farther back, the better. The unidentified Saudi took off his glasses. He and the MP studied them. Apparently, they were talking about glasses. Great. Now one was laughing and the other wasn't. More paranoia began to build.

1214 HOURS

Every time a vehicle goes by, I lower my head. Every time the Saudi MP starts up our jeep, I wonder where we're going and who might see me. Getting closer to the command element, I'm hoping no one feels it their duty to let the generals know I'm around. Next thing I know, I've been dumped out of the jeep. The Saudi MP says he'll be back for me in about an hour. I hide behind a Nissan patrol vehicle. If he doesn't come back, I'll have some real fancy humping to do. At least I have a compass. The question now is do I attempt to get another ride, or sit here hoping he returns?

And then who magically appears? Mubarek, who says I'm a very impatient person. He adds I must not be able to fish, as I move around all the time. In any case, he says he has permission for me to go in any of the vehicles, as long as there is room, but he doesn't designate any specific vehicle.

The last few days have been some of the most unusual days I've had in a long time. My interest increases proportionally to my proximity to the front—my interest was way up when I was thinking of hiking the damned road through this miserable desert.

Three choppers just landed. Looks like American advisers on board.

1500 HOURS

I just finished chatting with an American major from one of the choppers. He's flying as an adviser to the Saudi scouts. They're screening the right flank. His associate told me they took fire from a couple of bunkers. They took them out, and the Iraqis who were left all surrendered—not in ones or twos, but 30 and 40 at a time. Then the major came back and said we would be moving out of here in about an hour.

I just met a Saudi prince. The major's associate said I ought to get him to see if he could get me a ride, but the conversation never quite developed that way. Maybe if I lay an *SOF* patch on him he might assist me. If he comes back, I'll make the request.

Finally, I'm in a vehicle. Out of nowhere, an American contractor I know shows up. He gets me a seat in a 4x4. The "contractor" was longtime acquaintance Don North, a TV producer who had a contract with the Saudi Defense Ministry to produce a documentary on the war. North was traveling with a Saudi Prince, name unknown, who he convinced to give me a ride to Kuwait City.

26 FEBRUARY, 0615 HOURS

Last night was tolerable. We borrowed a poncho, three stakes and some parachute cord from an American liaison, then rigged a lean-to on the side of our vehicle. I quickly found that sleeping with one's head under the frame of a vehicle doesn't work very well. Looks like we'll be deploying shortly.

0758 HOURS

We started moving at 0750. Heading north is a convoy of school buses, which I assume are going to pick up the many thousands of EPWs (enemy prisoners of war). As of this morning word is that there are 20,000 in hand, and there's trouble in moving them. We move on, hopefully farther than we went in the last displacement.

0809 HOURS

We've now caught up with the main body. Temporary hold here. The other column to our right is continuing to move forward. I've never seen so many military vehicles in my entire life. You get a good feel for the scope of this operation, because the land is flat and there's no undergrowth or any other type of vegetation.

0829 HOURS

North, who got me a ride, remarked, "I identify with your situation, so much because I've been a hitchhiker to wars so often . . . and damn it, anybody who wants to work as bad as you shouldn't have to cover the war with briefings in Riyadh." Amen. I will always owe this dude. I invited him to the *SOF* Convention in September. He accepted. Anyhow, we are finally inside Kuwait.

1011 HOURS

We are in the third defensive belt of the Iraqi position. We just finished looting some bunkers.

1015 HOURS

Approaching another Iraqi bunker. My goodness, what do we have here? A Russian radio would be a superb item to auction off for Refugee Relief at the *SOF* convention, but it's too heavy.

Iraqi defensive positions are not impressive. I wonder if they are representative of the vaunted Republican Guard fortifications. The bunker I'm looking at here has a light framework over it, maybe 6 or 8 inches of dirt or sand; another one with some logs across it, maybe three 8-inch logs, some galvanized iron and another 8 inches of sand on it.

Last night a source explained to me how Forrest Sawyer and ABC got permission to circumvent the press pool regulations and broadcast with the vanguard of the Saudi division. Sawyer sent personal letters to Lieutenant General Kalid bin Sultan, the Saudi commander-in-chief, and subsequently got an interview with him. Kalid was favorably disposed toward ABC and Sawyer because Kalid was on *Nightline* and apparently Sawyer does *Nightline* a fair number of times. Sawyer told me he couldn't tell me how he got the deal.

1115 HOURS

The battalion is moving out. We are following the command track. This is a most impressive sight. Being up on top of the vehicle gives you a far greater impression of the scope and magnitude of this whole operation. It is easy to envision oneself being with Rommel or Montgomery rumbling back and forth across the Libyan desert in '41 and '42. It is a truly awesome sight. The weather is cool, the sky overcast, a great day for a desert offensive. It's stopped raining, too. This is like going to a massive, motorized picnic. No enemy contact yet.

1142 HOURS

It is starting to drizzle as we continue to advance. My adrenaline pump roars right along with the growl of the scores of tanks and APCs barreling across the billiard table-like desert. Lawrence of Arabia, Attila the Hun, "Jeb" Stuart and George Patton must be smiling. I am.

1151 HOURS

We are again approaching the lead element of the vanguard of this column. Apparently, there is some action going on. We don't know what. Some of the people dismounted but there's no incoming.

We are going through another defensive position, we see occasional craters from CBUs (cluster bomb units). We are now in the Iraqi artillery positions. Some Saudi vehicles stop and look quickly through the artillery bunkers for loot. Looks like we are all racing along to hit the Iraqi command post about 500 meters up ahead. There seems to be neither rhyme nor reason as to why the Saudis are moving, but the tracks are moving fast.

1207 HOURS

We are now about 75 meters behind the lead tank and we want to get up about 50 feet behind it. We are approaching the lead tank from the left rear and the lead tank has stopped. The lead tank has just traversed his gun; maybe we will get some boom-booms. To the left of the lead tank, probably at 2,000 meters, it looks like there are some antennae, probably some kind of Iraqi commo position and/or headquarters.

This is not as gratifying as being a member of the U.S. armed forces, but on the other hand I have a greater opportunity to be at the sharp end of the sword. Splitting with ABC has been to my advantage, as had I stayed with them I would have had to stay with their support satellite unit.

We are now following about 18 Kuwaiti tanks that are on line. On the left is a column running for tens of klicks—supply vehicles and more armored vehicles and more supply vehicles. We are moving with the tanks. It is difficult to make an estimate of the situation; the fog of battle has enveloped us. Sawyer deserves a punch in the mouth for dumping me in the desert.

1231 HOURS

There's nobody between the bad guys and us, except for one tank. We are headed almost due north toward our ultimate objective, Kuwait City! Alright!

1254 HOURS

We stop. We're turning around? Going back? For prayers? These Muslims pray five times a day, and with a three-hour lunch they truly test one's patience.

1317 HOURS

Have turned around, again facing the front.

1450 HOURS

We are now linked up with a column of APCs, the same battalion we were with before. On our left we see a column of Kuwaiti APCs buzzing along, about 200 meters away. The compass shows we are going east.

1520 HOURS

We are now pulling onto an asphalt road, a high-speed route of approach. Now we are hearing the rattle of small arms; no one seems concerned because the troops are all giving us the victory sign as we go by the Kuwaiti units. Saudis and Kuwaitis are shooting their FNs and machine guns in the air. Everybody is a happy camper. Every time we drive by the Kuwaitis with a TV camera they think that it is fitting to sound off with their FALs on full auto. My God, there is a driver shooting without his hands on the wheel! Twenty-four hours ago this time, I was looking at playing Bedouin-in-the-desert by my lonesome.

1547 HOURS

We continue to explode through the desert. The question is how soon we will be in Kuwait City. Of course, I have no way of knowing what the intelligence picture is. We have heard no news since early this morning. No briefings for the troops, much less for an *SOF* journalist. The Iraqis are out there about 3,000 meters; they could pop one in our vehicle just as well as they could into one of these lead tanks. Another tank destroyed off to the left. We are making about 60 klicks an hour. Not too shabby. Once again the weather is overcast this morning. It's cool, a little bit of wind, a light smattering of rain. On the right we are passing a column of Kuwaiti Humvees, quarter-tons and deuce-and-a-halfs. We come to a road sign: Kuwait City, 49 kilometers. All right!

1616 HOURS

The route is like a thousand-lane highway with vehicles weaving in and out with no apparent order of march. These guys have been in too many camel charges. Most vehicles stay 200–300 meters behind the lead tank, but not us. No sir, we are right up there about 100 meters behind the lead echelon, which, of course, is gratifying. Isn't this fun! It's a very strange day and visibility is limited to 1,000 meters at best. No sun; it looks like we are going into very low cloud cover. Maybe the plan is to allow the Kuwaitis to enter the city first because, after all, it is their homeland.

At this point, I finally believe that I am going to get to Kuwait City.

Maybe not the first journalist but certainly sure as hell not the last, and I'm one of the few journalists with one of the attacking columns. I think that the observation Joe Galloway, senior editor from *U.S. News*, made is correct, that once the ground offensive began, control of the press would break down. This is certainly true of the Saudis.

27 FEBRUARY, 0710 HOURS

We are now starting to pass destroyed enemy vehicles: two or three tanks out there, a large transport truck, a tracked missile launcher.

0757 HOURS

Just talked to a trooper from the 2nd Armored Division, and when I was done, a Colonel Sylvester informed me that I just walked through a minefield. Subsequently, a sergeant told me that it was primarily anti-tank and not many anti-personnel mines. Little comfort. I had failed to follow the old dictum of walking where vehicles had tread. The sergeant major said the Abrams (tank) has proved its worth and had been taking out Iraqi tanks far beyond published maximum ranges. The 2nd Armored has not lost a tank yet.

0839 HOURS

We're getting ready to move out again: "Gentleman, start your engines."

1003 HOURS

We are on the move into the outskirts of Kuwait City again. Ernie Cox, photographer for the Chicago Tribune, told me that the plan was to let the American forces punch a hole through the Iraqis and then let Kuwaiti and Saudi forces make the triumphal entry into Kuwait City. 2nd Armored units are positioned on our left flank and Marines on the right flank as we move forward. This is a thoroughly amazing experience: honking horns, stopping, jumping out, taking pictures; everybody giving the "V for victory" sign, celebration time; and along the road a variety of burned out, shot up, bombed-out Iraqi vehicles. It's a good place to be, and the right time to be there.

1102 HOURS

I am sure that this is the first time in history that journalists in 4x4 commercial vehicles have accompanied an armored thrust into enemy territory.

Our new driver, whom I have unfondly named "Cowboy," likes to race with the tanks. It is a challenging sport, one that I would just as soon take a pass on.

What we have now is a parade, with jubilant Kuwaiti citizens tagging onto the tail of the military column as we try to work our way again up to the front of the column. Crowds are lining the street, shooting their guns, embracing each other and us journalists; cheering, flag waving, clasping hands; Arab women chanting "alalalala." I have arrived. I have beaten the system. What a buzz! It's not Baghdad, but it'll do.

30

ON THE SHARP EDGE WITH BOSNIA'S COUNTER-SNIPERS

WHERE HAVE ALL THE FIXERS GONE?

The 22-stories-high former Bosnia-Herzegovina parliament building in Sarajevo was almost gutted, riddled with gaping holes from high-explosive tank and artillery rounds. At one time it served as a seat of government; now it was being used as a key observation post and counter-sniping position by the besieged Bosnians as they defended their capital. Below, candles and lanterns provided dim illumination for homeless refugees who lived in dark rooms and corridors in the basement, taking refuge from enemy guns until thirst and hunger forced them up and out onto the treacherous streets that surrounded the Parliament building and the nearby Holiday Inn. The main drag was called "Sniper's Alley" and those few people with gas for their cars drove with pedal to the metal, swerving around shell craters and hurtling across intersections at manic speed to evade sniper fire. Some did not make it. Overturned and burned cars filled with bodies littered the road. For those (network or major press journalists, or U.N. personnel) who could afford them, armored vehicles were the transport of choice, but the local residents relied as much on luck as on driving skills.

A few weeks earlier, after the disintegration of Yugoslavia was turning quite bloody, I contacted my old friend and running partner, merc Bob

MacKenzie, to see if he was up for a quick trip to Sarajevo sniper land to play journalist and get an adrenaline fix.

"But of course," he replied and with that we were off to the charming tourist town of Split on the blue Adriatic, where we would link up with members of the Croatian Defense Council (HVO) Foreign Press Bureau, an organization set up by another Vietnam vet, J. P. Mackley, who I met during the Gulf War. The plan was that they would facilitate our movement to Sarajevo. Well, that was the plan. However, like with any military operation, plans change once the first round is fired. In this case, the plan went awry the minute we got off the plane in Split.

We found out that the only flights into Sarajevo from Split were those occasional ones flown by U.N. aircraft. They occasionally graciously allowed journalists to ride along. If they were in the mood, that is. So one day, two days, three days, four went by, and nothing. We were all used to the wait, wait and wait some more, but that did little to make it any more pleasant. Meanwhile, we picked the minds of other journalists as to how to best get stories and stay alive. The rules were simple:

"You need to check in to the well shot up Holiday Inn which, though on the front lines, had a bar in the basement. Preferably a room with glass in the windows. An opportunity to a get a free workout as the elevators didn't elevate. Sometimes the water ran . . . keep the bathtub full of water . . . sometimes the electricity was on . . . just make sure you insist on a room on the back side of the hotel. You will still hear plenty of gunfire to lull you to sleep," they collectively told us.

"Get a fixer," one added. "He will have a vehicle . . . will know who to see to get you access to the action. And, of course, he will translate. Ask the hotel desk for recommendations for fixers."

"Oh, and by the way, don't get shot," one smartass said.

Simple enough. Mac and I bummed a ride from the airport to the hotel, got a room on the opposite side from the gunfire and let it be known we were in the market for a "fixer." We then decided to recon the area. Going out the back of the hotel, we noticed a number of armored jeeps and SUVs. This was the only war I knew of where journalists went to the front in their own personal, or leased, armored cars. We saw a jeep of indeterminate age with "Washington Post" daintily painted on the driver's door with a couple of civilian males babbling about something nearby. I wasn't thrilled about asking somebody from the Post for anything, but what the hell.

"I am Robert Brown, publisher of *Soldier of Fortune* magazine and here is my fellow journalist, Bob MacKenzie."

I told Jim Rupert from the *Washington Post*, "We are looking for a fixer."

Fate smiled on us, or so we thought.

"Tell you what, I am leaving tomorrow," Rupert said. "You can hire my fixer."

"Sure, why not?" we figured, working on the not unreasonable assumption that if this dude was good enough for the prestigious D.C. mouthpiece of liberalism it should work for us. Wrong.

"One hundred dollars a day is what we can afford if you can get us where we want to go and to who we want to see," we told the fixer.

Three days later, we hadn't gone anywhere or seen anyone. Our mission was to do an inside story on the Sarajevo counter-sniper units and ascertain how effective they were. Our fixer couldn't fix anything. Maybe he couldn't score credentials for us or he may simply have not wanted to go there. Even in the relative safety of the backside of our hotel, the rattle of small-arms fire provided a fairly constant background melody. Explosions from incoming mortar, recoilless rifle and artillery fire echoed around the city every half-hour or so. The fixer had to live that shit 24/7 and couldn't be blamed if he didn't care to risk his life so a couple of nutso gringos could get a few photos and interviews while dodging rounds of various calibers, all of which were quite lethal.

MacKenzie and I, bored to tears, hung around the Holiday Inn waiting for our local fixer to arrange a visit to some of the defensive positions in Sarajevo. That night in the Holiday Inn bar we were picking the minds of other journalists. I was interviewing a French report about the Foreign Legion. Mac was a few yards away with several alleged reporters. He suddenly broke away, approached my table and with a disgusted look on his face growled,

"You are not going to believe this."

"What now?" I replied.

"See that good looking blonde at the table I just left? She must be all of 20. She is dumber than a fence post. When discussing the ruthlessness of the Serb Snipers, she became agitated and said, "Well, why don't they just throw land mines at the snipers. The editor at *Elle* should be strung up for the yardarm for sending her."

One positive thing came out of Mac's round table. A free lance journalist who had been in Sarajevo for a couple of months volunteered he could get us to the frontlines. It wasn't 'til we hired him did we find out he had a case of tourrette syndrome. We had almost given up because only a suicidal maniac would try to dodge the unending incoming fire, despite the supposed ceasefire in effect, just to escort a couple of journalists trying to get a story.

SNIPER'S ALLEY

That is when I first met Mark Milstein, a fanatic of a journalist who had figured out the ropes of how to get the necessary papers after several months in Sarajevo. He was relieved that professional soldier MacKenzie would join him interviewing a unit tasked with suppressing snipers in a Serbian-held suburb on a hillside overlooking part of Sarajevo. Since I was able to get an appointment with the French Foreign Legion unit securing the Sarajevo airport, MacKenzie and Milstein headed out for the front lines.

The following is MacKenzie's report: "We didn't have to go far to find the front; it was about a block away from the Holiday Inn. We first crept around the sides of the hotel, trying to make ourselves invisible to gunmen on the hillside above. On reaching the edge of the dreaded Sniper's Alley (the dread was real enough—a civilian had been shot in front of our hotel the previous afternoon), we firmly grasped our camera bags, tightened up our rear apertures and sprinted across a hundred meters of empty boulevard and center divider. It was almost an anti-climax when we got to the cover of some shell-pocked buildings on the other side of the street without drawing a single round of small-arms fire.

"As Milstein had been there before, he led the way around parking lots and pedestrian concourses to the local command post. There we presented his paperwork and spoke to a succession of increasingly senior Bosnian Army soldiers until finally the area commander, Ante, appeared. We must have impressed him, or maybe it was a slow day, because he decided to show us around himself.

"Ante's unit was responsible for 800 meters of front along the 10-meter-wide Miljacka River, which runs through the middle of Sarajevo.

Ruined factories, burned out skyscrapers and scarred apartment buildings (still occupied!) provided his men with excellent cover and observation of similar Serbian positions, which in some places were only 20 meters away across the river. As my friend and I followed Ante through the rubble, we asked him about his troops. He prudently wouldn't tell us their strength, except to say that he could get as many men as he had arms to issue.

"Some of his troops were members of the Bosnian Army and some were from a police counter-terrorist unit formed to provide security for the 1984 Winter Olympics. Some had served in the Yugoslav Army and some had no previous military experience. However, all were fiercely determined to defend their city from the "Serbian invaders." The few camouflage-clad female combatants in the group, some of whom were reported to be counter-snipers, were in obvious agreement. A platoon leader told me that of his 37 men, seven were Orthodox Serbs, five were Catholic Croats and 25 were Muslim Bosnians. He said they were fighting together because they had always lived together and wanted to do so in the future, without interference from politicians in Belgrade, Zagreb, the United Nations or their own city hall. That attitude, widespread among all ethnic groups living in Sarajevo, denied the Serbs the easy victory they hoped for when they started fighting there in April 1992."

MAUSERS AND .50 CALS

The unit was armed with a variety of weapons, which provided them with good counter-sniping capability and included scoped German K98k Mauser rifles and Yugoslav copies; Russian Dragunovs and Yugo M76 sniping rifles; and the M72AB 1 N-PN Yugo FAZ weapons-family light machine gun variant with a folding metal stock, which was also fitted with bases for telescopic sights. At one position I noticed a small, neat pyramid of .50-caliber shells which, when I asked, were said to have come from a .50-caliber bolt-action rifle.

The unit's several machine guns had also been used with some success by responding to muzzle flashes at night with short bursts. Rounding out the unit's weaponry were Yugoslav AKs, a scattering of hand grenades, some anti-tank rockets and, as always in Bosnia, a variety of civilian shotguns and hunting rifles.

Whatever the weapon in use, after months of practice the Bosnian counter-snipers knew their jobs. Their hides were always well back from windows or shell holes and they had easy routes to dozens of alternates.

Since Serbian counterfire often took the form of a tank round, "shoot and scoot" was one of their most closely followed operating principles. With every two or three shooters was an observer equipped with binoculars or 40x42 spotting scopes, who also carried maps and sketches of scores of known Serbian positions and bunkers.

As I climbed many, many stories up the parliament building, I had a firsthand look at the Bosnians' biggest problem in trying to suppress enemy snipers. On the hillside opposite were literally thousands of empty windows and thousands more trees, bushes, and piles of debris, each one a potential firing position. One of the worst areas was an overgrown cemetery, about 300 meters away, where each crypt and tombstone could hide a rifleman. Clearly, the Serbs were proficient in their tactics and use of ground.

These phantom shooters seldom were highly skilled military technicians with specialized equipment, selectively taking out justifiable military targets at ranges of up to 1,000 meters. More often than not, it was a Chetnik taking potshots at baby carriages from 200 meters with an AK. It was simply the callous, terrorist assassination of innocents. Most journalists and U.N. observers agreed that the sniping of civilians was premeditated—the objective being to force civilians to leave the city.

Ironically, some of the Serbian sharpshooters had served in the same police counter-terrorist unit as their Bosnian counterparts and they were all known by name to each other. Perhaps the most discussed was a former shooting instructor who had trained some of the same people trying to shoot him. An Olympic-medalist marksman, he was reputed to be very capricious in his choice of targets. The first week only women, the next week only journalists, the following week firemen, etc. His former students were very much in dread of his cross hairs, as he reportedly never, ever missed. If he dropped the hammer on you, you got more than your ticket punched. Why this former policeman, once dedicated to law enforcement and who specialized in anti-terrorism, had now become virtually a terrorist himself, was the subject of a good deal of conjecture. As with many things during the war in Bosnia, there were no obvious answers.

Unable to take Sarajevo by storm, the Serbs resorted to murder-by-rifle-fire and indiscriminate shelling to force the surrender of the city. Since the battle had started the previous year, some 10,000 people had been killed and 60,000 wounded, the vast majority civilians. Serb troops cut off the electricity and water and were trying to prevent food from getting in, hoping to break the resistance of the inhabitants. The populace was now being forced to boil sewage for drinking water. The Serbs made a mockery of U.N. forces, closing the airport and stopping convoys whenever they felt like it. All this happened while American and European political leaders bickered over whose fault and whose responsibility the war was, and issued statements condemning the actions of just about everyone. It was enough to make a grown man weep with frustration—or maybe take a rifle and go shoot a Chetnik.

31

HARD ROAD TO SARAJEVO

UNDER MACHINE GUN FIRE

Most of the artillery explosions and white-hot arcs of large caliber tracer bullets were a few kilometers behind us on the Sarajevo skyline. We had been cramped in the truck bed for many hours, stuck in the suburbs of the city. We were miserably bound in flak jackets, in a sandbagged truck bed and were numb to the much closer AK-47 fire.

As long as no bullets pinged into the steel of our truck, no one in our party seemed too concerned about the random rounds. Basically, all 12 of us in the truck were tired and wet enough that we could give a damn about who got greased as long as it wasn't us. Then suddenly, a Serbian 12.7mm heavy machine gun opened up on us, coming at us in what seemed like football-sized orange tracers.

The hot rounds came screaming toward our soft-skinned truck and softer-skinned bodies. Silently and instinctively, we scrambled to shove ourselves deeper into the truck bed to protect our heads and arms from the killer rounds. Moments before, I had been amusing myself by dictating a play-by-play of the action into a tape recorder. I have been told that I record everything and that my tapes could fill dump trucks. But now we had nothing to do but count the malevolent tracers swishing overhead as the huge machine gun roared in the background. My tape recorder was a welcome distraction.

"I figure that the gun position is about 500 meters out and the only reason we aren't exposed is because we are hidden by that ridge of dirt," John Jordan, a big, blustery, hot-headed Marine vet said.

We had left our Springfield Armory Super Match M1A behind in Sarajevo or we might have gone into the night looking for the Russian machine gun. Jordan let out one of his booming laughs of nervous relief that shattered our silence, "The SOB knows we are here but he can't depress his gun quite get low enough to get us. His gun is mounted in a concrete bunker and unless he takes it off the mount and moves out of the bunker, he can't get us."

I glanced at the column of trucks in the rain. Who knows what the Serb was thinking as he glared at our white United Nations white truck. We seriously doubted that he knew that the dozen men in the truck were Americans and Canadians who had just smuggled in some critical items right under his very nose, or that John Jordan, who had killed some Serb snipers, was in our group. At that moment Jordan was no more popular with us than he was with the Serbs. He was the one who had gotten us into this mess that had reduced us to sitting ducks at the base of Mount Igman, some 10 klicks from Sarajevo.

Jordan, then 38, a giant of a man at 6'4" and 250 pounds, had served seven years in the U.S. Marines and looked the part. An Irish American boxer, who worked heavy construction in Rhode Island, he had packed up to lead a group of volunteer firefighters, under the name Global Operation Fire and Rescue Services (GOFRS), who wanted to save lives in the blown-up and bullet-riddled streets of Sarajevo.

Since the beginning of the war, he had received permission from the Bosnian mission to the United Nations to haul men and equipment into Sarajevo to help the Bosnian fire department. He helped save the lives of a number of civilians and U.N. workers. For a time he and his volunteer firefighters and paramedics enjoyed the protection and help of the United Nations but, according to Jordan, after U.N. forces failed one too many times to protect him and his people, he went rogue and began shooting back at the Serbs, killing six snipers, which made the muck-a-mucks at U.N. headquarters very unhappy indeed.

SOF *TEAMS SMUGGLE IN AIR-PAKS*

I had been supporting Jordan's G.O.F.R.S. for some time. When he found out that I was bringing a crew to Bosnia and Croatia, he asked me to help get some equipment to firefighters in Sarajevo. Scott Air, the company that manufactured the backpack breathing apparatus used by firefighters while they were inside burning buildings, agreed to donate 20 Air-Paks to the Sarajevo Fire Department, and Jordan was looking for a way to get them in. I agreed to pay the cost of freighting the Air-Paks on DHL and Jordan's airfare into Zagreb, Croatia. Jordan was to bring along enough U.S. volunteer firemen, who paid their own way, to help hump the Air-Paks over the mountain and into Sarajevo.

We landed at the Zagreb airport and all went as planned until a nitwit Zagreb DHL manager, named Milan Percic, told Jordan that the $45,000 worth of Air-Paks in their custody would not be released.

"This is not America, this is our country. In Croatia you must follow our procedures. If you fill out papers and pay customs duties, maybe you can have your shipment in two or three weeks."

Jordan produced his documentation proving that it was humanitarian aid merely being transported across Croatia to Bosnia and then on to Sarajevo. However, Mr. Percic, full of himself and his authority and, according to Jordan, not willing to be intimidated by America or Americans, wouldn't budge. In fact, he became even nastier, blocking the delivery.

Jordan and company didn't have two or three days, let alone weeks. After taking Srebrnica and Zepa, the Serbs would probably increase pressure on Sarajevo, and we might not even be able to get the Air-Paks in. Jordan notified me of the hangups when I was waiting in Split, the designated assembly point for the Bosnian war. One of my party, J. P. Mackley, who had excellent connections, flew up to Zagreb. After he and an old friend, who was highly placed in the Croatian equivalent of the CIA, shared coffee with Jordan, both DHL and Croatian customs got a call notifying them that it would be a good idea if they arranged for Jordan to take immediate delivery of the Air-Paks and screw Mr. Percic. The dimwit Percic was suddenly anxious to expedite the mission.

"This guy," commented Jordan, "acts like somebody really rang his bell." No doubt.

The Air-Paks were released, but then there was the problem of how to transport them, along with eight firemen, to the bus station in downtown Zagreb. Then we still had to figure out how to get the Air-Paks from

Split to the jump-off point on the forward slope of Mount Igman above Sarajevo.

Bob Barrett, a firefighter with the Essex, England, Fire Department, ran an international aid organization called Fireman's Relief Aid in his off hours. He was reckless. In late 1992, although every place in Bosnia was dangerous and difficult to get to, his organization got the aid into places where others feared to go. By 1994, many organizations were filling warehouses in the tamer areas of Bosnia, but not many were going into Sarajevo. The city, left with perhaps 150,000 inhabitants, was wholly dependent on airlifted aid, and nothing came in over the road or through the Serb-sieged airport. Barrett personally repeatedly drove tons of supplies down Mount Igman and into Sarajevo. On one trip down the mountain, a 20mm round passed between Barrett and his assistant driver and destroyed the engine block of his truck.

WE SCORE A LELAND TRUCK

As soon as Barrett met up with us, he was able to borrow a beast of an ex-British Army Leland-manufactured 2½-ton truck from one of the NGOs hauling shampoo and soap up to the refugee centers in Tuzla. It was painted white just like those of the British Army, and equipped with left-side steering for use outside the United Kingdom. It had a hole in the roof for access to a long-absent machine-gun mount and for good measure there was a large British Union Jack decal pasted on the middle of the dashboard. The tires were still bullet free.

That evening we packed the bare essentials we would need in the unlucky event that we got caught on the mountain or got delayed in Sarajevo. The meager supplies included two canteens, poncho and poncho liner, spare socks and skivvies, flashlight, lots of batteries, plenty of rope to lash on the items we might have to hump, and a variety of aged U.S. government rations we called "Ham and Motherfuckers," all stuffed into a medium Alice rucksack.

Around 0900 hours the next morning, 13 men dressed in blue GOFRS uniforms loaded the Scott Air-Paks, one medium Alice rucksack per man, plus web gear and four large plastic boxes of $10,000-worth of medicine on board the big white Leyland. Phil Gonzales, a Special Forces medic who specialized in field anesthesiology, and I had worked together off and on since I had him at my Special Forces team camp A-334 at Tong Le Chon in 1969. We had joined up later in Asia, as well as in Central and South America. And now we were in the hellhole of Bosnia.

"I can put you out in a shell hole," said Doc, "fast enough for the surgeon to filet you and then bring you out of it fast enough to catch the medevac. I have enough medicine to completely treat 40 gunshot wounds and enough IV solutions to keep you alive until I can get to you." He handed out plastic bottles of Saline or Ringers solution to most of us along with the appropriate IV lines and needles. "In case you need to start an IV on yourselves or someone else, in case the whole truckload of us get a direct hit," Gonzales said.

We passed into Bosnia. The Croatian border police waved the big Leyland through. The identically dressed Bosnian-Croatian border police, who pretended to be unrelated, waved the big Leyland through on the other side. Although that part of Bosnia was controlled by the Croatian government in Zagreb, for reasons known only to them they pretend to be controlled by the Bosnian Muslim government in Sarajevo.

The Croatians controlled the prosperous region of Herzegovina that appeared to be mostly untouched by war at that point, since most of the damage had been repaired. New gas stations, convenience stores and hotels, probably funded by war profiteering or official corruption, had sprung up. The dividing line between Croatian Bosnia and Muslim Bosnia (and in fact between Western Civilization and Eastern) was the Neretva River passing through the center of the city of Mostar. West Mostar, the Croatian part, was intact, but the Muslim-inhabited eastern side was firebombed after the Serbs first rained artillery on it, and later the Croatians bombarded East Mostar for about nine months, forcing the Muslims underground.

THE WAR STARTS FOR US

The war started for us as soon as we crossed the American Bailey Bridge over the river. The people we encountered were gaunt and gray, and the Austro-Hungarian architecture had been riddled with artillery holes. The Muslims had blown up every bridge north toward Sarajevo over the Neretva River to try to keep the Serbs and Croatians from crossing to attack East Mostar. The road detoured over makeshift bridges and at one point we waited for traffic to clear on a single-lane bridge protected by a lone

Malaysian U.N. soldier. A civilian car slowed down to a crawl and the driver, face scowled with hatred, spat at us and flipped us the bird, thinking we were with the United Nations. The U.N. Dutch Army contingent had walked away from their "safe havens," abandoning thousands of the driver's countrymen, women and children to be slaughtered in ditches along the roads leading from Zepa and Srebrnica. A number of the young women were reported to have committed suicide rather than be captured. More than 8,000 Bosnians were murdered by Serb Army troops under the command of General Ratko Mladic.

At Jablenica, a ragged Muslim in civilian clothes armed with an RPD squad automatic weapon, jumped into a banged-up Fiat police car and followed us through the city. At first we were on alert, but let down our guard a little when we figured he was just protecting himself, wanting to make sure that the U.N. people were not murdered in his jurisdiction.

As we neared Sarejavo, we saw a few houses that showed hits from heavy machine guns and from a main tank gun. Every town and village had skinny men of all ages outfitted in well-worn camouflage scattered about, appearing to be going somewhere.

Barrett's organization maintained a transfer point at Tarcin on the reverse slope of Mount Igman, some 30 kilometers from Sarajevo. A team of Sarajevo firemen was supposed to be waiting at Tarcin to help carry the medicine and Air-Paks over the mountain. Both for reasons of operational security and flexibility, Jordan had given the Sarajevo fire chief a fairly broad window, between 1300 and 1800, when he and his men were supposed to show up each day for three consecutive days. It was day two and they had failed to show up on either day. We no longer had the third day to play with.

It was Thursday. Mackley had been warned that the Croatians intended to kick off a major offensive the next Monday. We believed the low-grade intel, because if the offensive did happen, the Serbs would be certain to make things tougher on Sarajevo, which might include increasing their barrage on the city and laying in some concentrated artillery on Mount Igman. We could be trapped in Sarajevo for a few weeks or perhaps even a few months, not good for Mamma Brown's boy.

We were deciding whether to scrap the mission and go home, or try to get in and get out of Sarajevo by Monday. Jordan decided that attempting the harrowing mission on foot was a no-go and that we should drive the big white Leyland down the mountain and take our chances with everything that could go wrong, including being hit by the infamous Serb 20mm that had nearly killed Barrett.

We tightened the velcro closures on our flak vests and strapped on helmets if we had them, just in case. Doc Gonzales double-checked the paramedics and gave us our marching orders: "Remember, the main objective is to stop the bleeding and start the IV to replace the lost blood until and if such time that you can get to a hospital."

The guys at the next few checkpoints controlling access to the Mount Igman road held us up for a few minutes, pretending to make an official document check, figuring that our hapless bunch of gringos was on a death march straight into the arms of the gringo-hating, gun-toting Serbs.

We traveled over the typical torn-up old Yugoslav road, which was too narrow to let large vehicles cross more than in single file, forcing us to stop off and on to let a French VAB armored vehicle or a Bosnian truck going in the other direction to pass. At one point, we surprised three French Foreign Legionnaires on sentry duty at the start of a rough path cut in the bank of the main road. Our French speakers dismounted and asked them if we were going the right way. The Frenchmen shifted back and forth and one of them reached for the hand grenade he carried in his load bearing harness.

"Serbs pretending to be legionnaires had killed two French officers only a few days before, prompting the French to send a Mirage-dropped smart bomb to Serb HQ in Pale," Mackley warned. He looked over the side of the truck for an escape route. The Frenchman with the hand grenade turned his back on us so we couldn't see what he was doing, but instead of pulling the pin and throwing the grenade, he simply hung it on the harness of one of his comrades.

Shortly after dark, we hit the top of Mount Igman and started down the other side. Barrett was speeding up, switching his lights off and on, mostly off. He only lit them up for seconds, so Serb gunners would have difficulty spotting us. We began to get a few glimpses of the lights in the Serbian positions. We came to a sudden halt and detected some excitable chattering going on in the dark.

"Be quiet!" Jordan warned. "No English!" as he pulled out his big K-Bar knife and slipped over the side of the truck into the night. The compulsive talker of our group, Fenshaw, fully capable of carrying on both sides of a conversation, dropped his voice a few decibels, but continued to ramble on.

SHUT UP OR DIE

"Shut Up!!" Doc Gonzales ordered him. When he did not, Mackley unsheathed a Fairbairn-Sykes dagger and prepared to shut both of them up permanently. Tension filled the truck. Jordan came back and broke the tension with a breathless warning.

"I thought we'd taken a wrong turn and it was the Serbs up there," he said with great relief. "If something happens and we have to run for it, run uphill. They will be shooting downhill as that is the direction they expect you to run." The holdup was caused because two trucks had just been shot up ahead of us with a 20mm gun about an hour earlier on a stretch of the road called Breakdown Ridge. Six people had died and the wrecks were still burning.

"The French claimed to have knocked that gun position out as part of their mandate to protect convoys, but that same gun had been responsible for knocking as many as 20 trucks off the mountain in the past two months. No one even bothered to take the bodies out. The first French or British U.N. vehicle that was large enough for the task simply pushed the shot-up vehicles over the edge of the road. If the road was blocked, they said, more people would die if they could not pass that stretch at maximum speed," Jordan said.

Jordan tried to convince the commander of the French VAB armored vehicle that he should allow our white truck to get in between his two white U.N. armored vehicles to travel the most dangerous stretch down the mountain. He told us where to go in the French equivalent of "tough shit, there isn't enough armor here even for me if the Serbs start firing."

Bob Barrett, a taxpaying subject of Her Majesty, had earlier made the same request to a pair of British armored vehicles going down the mountain and was told to bugger off. As soon as the next French VAB came past us on the way down, Barrett yelled back to us, "We are on the way!!"

THE VALLEY OF HELL

Jordan stood up in the bed of the truck so he could see where the tracers were coming from if they opened up on us. Obviously nervous about having us so close on his tail, the French armored vehicle driver tried to outrun us. But Barrett was the better driver and kept the big white truck close enough to the back of the VAB for us to note that the Protection Force part of the black-lettered U.N. license plate was painted white. To our right and down the hill we spotted the two trucks that had been shoved over the side of Breakdown Ridge.

It was pitch black and after midnight when we finally found our way to a firehouse in the Sarajevo suburbs. We obtained clearance to carry our medicines and Air-Paks through a tunnel that the Bosnians had dug under the tarmac of the Sarajevo International Airport. The French, who controlled the airport, were in bed with the Serbs and refused to let the Bosnians go over the airport tarmac and into Sarajevo so they had to go under it. The Bosnians took in food, weapons, fuel and ammo not allowed in by the French through what had become a very lively tunnel.

As Jordan phoned for permission for us to pass through the tunnel, he was told that he needed to head to Sarajevo immediately. A police car waited to take him to the tunnel entrance. We bedded down for the night. Former legionnaire Paul Fanshaw found a place to sleep inside piles of truck tires erected as an artillery barrier in front of the firehouse doors. Mackley and I unrolled our ponchos outside in the rain, refusing to get caught inside a building if the Serbs put in some artillery.

Early on Friday morning, Jordan phoned from Sarajevo: "We have been denied permission to use the tunnel. It is in such bad shape that it took me five hours to navigate the 1,000-meter, 3-foot, 7-inch-high route. It would be almost impassable for 13 people carrying heavy loads to navigate."

We decided to go for broke. Barrett charged ahead, planning to present us at the airstrip checkpoint. We swerved through the suburbs of Sarajevo during broad daylight as we approached the road across the airstrip. Houses were largely abandoned and most were badly shot up from the constant incoming artillery and mortar fire. The entry to the tunnel, the only supply route, was devastated with signs of recent Serb shelling and was still in flames.

A French soldier waved us through the first checkpoint and we pulled onto the tarmac where we were protected by a high earthen berm. However, as soon as we cleared it, we would be out in the open and vulnerable to anything the Serbs wanted to throw at us for about 200 meters. We all hugged the bottom of the truck for the fast dash, past the wreckage of a shot-up jet transport plane and into the open. The wind whistled over the truck. We easily passed the second French checkpoint on the outside of the strip and breezed through the Bosnian checkpoint as we entered a city of wasted buildings jumbled by a three-year volley of large caliber, high-velocity projectiles. We passed some civilians walking down the famous Sniper Alley, then pulled into the headquarters of the Sarajevo Fire Department where we offloaded the medicine and the 20 Scott Air-Paks. John Jordan was there to meet us, covered in mud from his trip through the tunnel and carrying his M1A.

By some miracle, we had passed through the valley of death unscathed! The *SOF* GOFERS team was the first to break the Serb blockade of Sarajevo in six months and the Sarajevo firemen were thrilled that we had pulled off bringing in the breathing equipment that would allow them to save a good number of lives.

Barrett decided to take the truck back across to the other side to get the food and clothes destined for the firemen and their hungry families. He loaded everything he could into the Leyland and decided that since it had been so easy on the first crossing, he would tow across a non-functional large, red fire truck that was nonetheless badly needed in Sarajevo. Todd Bayless, a Canadian firefighter, was steering the big, red fire truck as Peter Dietz, another Canadian firefighter, rode in the Leyland with Barrett driving. They must have been quite a sight to the bystanders as they drove with breakneck speed into the killing zone of the airport tarmac. Certainly, no one tried to stop them and there was probably more than one bet about whether they would make it.

A SNIPER AMBUSH

Almost as soon as they left the protection of the berms and drove into the killing zone, a Serb sniper opened up on them from nearby with a Yugoslav SVD semi-automatic sniper rifle. Seven boat-tailed 7.9-mm bullets had penetrated the soft-skinned trucks.

Four bullets hit the white truck and three were found in the red one. Shortly before driving past the protective berm, Peter Dietz, just for the hell of it, held an extra protective vest with a steel trauma plate up alongside his face. It was a good thing that he did and it was a good thing that he didn't move much after he held it up. One of the bullets struck the edge of the armor plate on the front of the British-made flak vest. Had he coughed at the wrong moment or had Dietz scratched his scrotum, the sniper's bullets would have missed the edge of the plate and passed easily through the Kevlar fabric. The result would have been Peter's head looking something like a watermelon that had been dropped on the sidewalk. Both Dietz and Barrett were wounded by fragments of the bullet, which had broken up on the edge of the steel trauma plate.

The bullets all entered the cab from slightly above. One of the others passed through the thin metal of the Leyland's cab. One of those bullets shattered as it passed through the cab and one of the fragments entered Bob Barrett's leg. The third and fourth bullets passed through the bed of the truck, one of them entering about center, and the other hitting an accessory box in the rear and going on to neatly sever the wires from the rear taillight.

Todd Bayless was totally helpless. He saw it coming at him, but he couldn't speed up or slow down or even swerve as he watched the sniper's bullets hit the white truck towing him. He heard window glass shattering all around him, but when he looked up he was uninjured. Clearly the sniper had been waiting for them, having been probably tipped off by French Army sentries. They were regular French Army, not legionnaires.

When the truck pulled into the Sarajevo Fire Department yard, the U.N. white paint of the Leyland was flecked silver around ragged holes made by sniper bullets. The side windows in the red pumper truck were completely shot out and one well-aimed round had gone through the windshield, barely missing Todd Bayless' head. He would have been toast had he not ducked.

"Lucky, lucky, lucky," observed Doc as he examined the trucks and their occupants, all in miraculously acceptable condition. In three years of driving in and out of the city, Bob Barrett was targeted by direct fire "10 or 11 times depending on how you count them." In Bosnia, indirect fire such as mortars, rockets and artillery did not count unless you got hit or it came close; it was usually a random act and if you caught one, it was just bad luck. Direct fire becomes a highly personal matter when someone tries to inflict harm on your very own warm body.

"I don't know much about guns, and I don't like them but I certainly take an interest in them when they are pointed in my direction," Barrett said as he pointed to each bullet hole and noted the approximate order they came in. The main cluster of shots hit the cab of the white truck. Then the sniper moved back toward the red fire truck and placed another cluster in the cab all around Bayless. It was just a miracle that the sniper didn't actually hit anybody since the trucks had to drive through the killing zone at 10mph.

Bayless had an explanation: "We were a ridiculous sight. When that sniper saw that red fire truck packed with boxes of old clothes being towed across the airport by that big white truck he probably thought that only idiots would try that kind of crap and he laughed his ass off and missed."

"It was obvious," said Barrett, "they were waiting for us. One of their spotters probably got on the radio to Serb HQ at Lukavica Barracks and they sent the sniper out."

The Serbs knew well of John Jordan and the volunteer firefighters. "I used to be on decent terms with them," he told us. "Hey, we are firemen trying to help anyone who needs it. We used to cross Serb lines and put out their fires too, but it started to go sour one day when a couple of U.N. Civil Police were trapped in a car wreck. I couldn't get a truck in close enough because Serb snipers were very active, and I couldn't get any help from the U.N. It was amazing, one of their own trapped in a vehicle with an engine in his lap and a sniper is trying to finish him off.

"We watched one of them die and the other one would have too if we didn't neutralize the sniper. I had seen the muzzle flash and Bosnians who were there also identified the window; they'd been shot at quite a bit from there. So I started laying some rounds in slow-fire with the M1A from about 400 yards out. Anyway, the sniper was drunk or something, he was hanging out the window and I got him. Two days later, we were fighting a fire on the hill above the stadium and the Serbs put mortars on us and their snipers shot up the fire truck. I returned the sniper fire. It became a major firefight. Relations weren't good, and two days later U.S. jets led the NATO air strikes against Serb positions. American relations with the Serbs were not good from there on," Jordan continued,

UN: THE ENEMY?

"We've neutralized a lot of Serb snipers since then and they would definitely like to have our ass. And you know what the U.N. did for us for saving their guy when they couldn't? They screamed like hell and said we had no right to defend ourselves while we are fighting their fires and saving their people, and they sent armed U.N. troops over to take back the equipment they lent us. If I told someone in a bar back home about that, they wouldn't believe it. They would say nothing could be that screwed up. But the U.N. is really that screwed up!" Jordan said.

Every Serb in the world knew of our trip into Sarajevo because the previous day an interview that had been filmed the week before with me doing a standup had been prematurely aired by Fox News network in Los Angeles and other markets. Perhaps the largest Serb community outside of Belgrade lived in Los Angeles, and probably an L.A. Serb had been on the phone asking his relatives if the American firemen had yet smuggled the Air-Paks into Sarajevo. I had laid out the plan for Fox News on the understanding that they wouldn't use it until the job was over and everyone had returned to the United States. Breaking their word not to broadcast until it was all over had seriously jeopardized our mission. We did not know this at the time and didn't become aware of it until much later. However, we figured something was up.

What we did know was that if the Serbs were waiting for us at the killing zone on our way out, they probably would be better prepared. If there were 13 of us tightly packed in the bed of the soft-skinned truck, the probability was high that someone would be perforated. The worst part was that the randomness of bullets flying through the air guaranteed that all of us had a pretty even chance of catching the bad news.

There were only three ways out of Sarajevo: drive out the way we came in across the killing zone on the airport tarmac; leave the truck behind and try to get permission from the Bosnian government to go through the crowded tunnel under the tarmac; or try walking out at night through the sniper firing lanes and booby traps that lay among the grave markers at the Jewish Cemetery on the hillside.

We had to get out, now. Jordan had gotten word through the Bosnian government that the impending Croatian offensive would kick off in the next 48 to 72 hours; it would be likely that the Serbs would respond by laying plenty of artillery on Sarajevo to keep the Bosnians occupied. If things heated up just a little bit more, we could be stuck in Sarajevo for quite some time and that would be ugly.

As Jordan and I began working on the route and method of our exfil, Doc Gonzales went out to distribute the medicines we'd smuggled in to Sarajevo's hospitals and clinics. The neighborhood clinics that first received trauma cases were largely without the medicines and implements they needed to treat gunshot wounds. Gonzales found the single greatest threat to public health in Sarajevo was Serb snipers when he checked the logs of the incoming cases. Cases that would have made the news nationally if they had happened in Seattle or Richmond seemed pretty ordinary in Sarajevo.

A seven-year-old girl was shot down while playing in her backyard, as was an old woman who was too slow crossing a street. Others, clearly not male military types, were shot down in cold blood. Snipers on the Serb side of Sarajevo were not necessarily Serbs. According to the Bosnian military, there were also a few Russians, a few Americans and even a Japanese national who carried journalist's credentials. They used Yugoslav-made SVD knockoffs and 98 Mausers, but the most common sniper weapon was a belt-fed RPD in 7.62x39mm, mounting a 4X scope. The common technique was to locate a target at any range and fire bursts, adjusting fire up or down as it went.

"On balance," said Gonzales, "shooting little girls in their own backyard is a pretty chicken shit way to operate. Somebody would be doing planet earth a favor if they took out some of those guys."

Unfortunately, the counter-sniping was limited on the Bosnian government side. According to Jordan, the expertise, let alone equipment, just wasn't there. In fairness to the Bosnian Army, even the highly touted counter-sniper radar deployed more than a year previously by French U.N. forces had done little to check the sniper problem.

Shortly before curfew, I decided that we would go to the Holiday Inn for a beer so all 13 of us, including half the off-duty firemen, loaded into a VW bus, a truck and several cars. Mackley and I were unlucky enough to get into the lead VW driven by Jordan. Mackley asked one of the G.O.F.R. Firemen, sitting in the middle, holding both Jordan's Springfield M1-AA and an AR-15, if he wanted to sit on the outside. "Nah, we aren't going to stop to shoot it out. If we take any fire it will be near the Holiday Inn."

The streets of the government-held sections of Sarajevo were not lit, and clouds blocked the sky, making it black on the bleak streets of Sarajevo. Jordan had his nose to the windshield and the accelerator to the floor running 60 miles an hour with no lights. With little gasoline in the city there wasn't much traffic, but several times we swerved to narrowly avoid head-on collisions with other speeding and lightless vehicles. The nearest miss, however, was with a dumpster Jordan didn't see in the darkened street. Every so often Jordan turned on the lights just to adjust his course. Navigating the darkened streets of Sarajevo gave a new meaning to the term "dead reckoning."

A BLACK AND WHITE HITCHCOCK MOVIE

Stepping from the dark of a blacked-out city into the lobby of the Holiday Inn was like stepping onto the set of a black-and-white Hitchcock movie. One of the first things people noticed was that the place looked pretty run down. There weren't many lights, and the dimly lit marble floors and high ceilings felt like Egyptian tombs.

Most of the occupants of the Holiday Inn were on expense accounts paid by television networks, humanitarian organizations and the United Nations. For enough money the best to be had in Sarajevo was found in the basement-level bar and dining room. TV crews, plus a few U.N. types and a jungle-camouflaged British Army captain, having gourmet meals by candlelight, occupied the booths along the wall. The same piano player who for three years had been playing Balkanized versions of "New York, New York" and "Sunday Kind of Love," was hard at work, his black suit only slightly fraying at the cuffs.

Everyone appeared remarkably well fed, compared to folks outside who suffered visibly from malnutrition. There was an abundance of black-market food in Sarajevo, but the prices were in German marks and too high for ordinary people. We watched a fat Italian TV reporter cut into a steak that likely cost $100. "What a remarkable sight," Doc Gonzales noted, "considering that the meat ration in Sarajevo had been one can per person per month."

After about 30 Bosnian and American firemen sat down, I said to the waiter, "Please give us several rounds of beer and soft drinks for everyone." At that moment, I did not care that the cost was $5 each. Fortunately, a wire-service reporter on an expense account ended up paying the $485 tab.

SOF photographer Mark Milstein and Mackley went up to the sixth floor to have a look at the war. We guessed that some people would no doubt live through the night because of the bad weather. Then suddenly, an armored Land Rover of the type favored by journalists from the television networks started out of the front driveway and was immediately engaged. Trying it once again, the Land Rover fell in behind a French light armored car and ventured out. The result was the same, but the firing seemed more intense, as if it were coming from both the Serb and the Bosnian sides.

The U.N.'s prestige had sunk to a new low when it gave the Serbs back the artillery surrounding Sarajevo in June and then abandoned to the Serbs the safe areas of Zepa and Srebrenica in July. It was the Srebrenica example that worried Sarajevans the most. According to the survivors' accounts and information collected by intelligence services, there were mass murders and rapes after the fall of Srebrenica. A number of refugees were coaxed out of the woods and murdered by Serbs wearing U.N. helmets.

Early on Sunday we pondered the information crucial to our exfil.

"The tunnel is absolutely out," I said. Although the Bosnians certainly appreciated the Scott Air-Paks and all of the great work done by Jordan and his firemen, they could not allow us to clog the tunnel. They were just being practical about preserving their only lifeline into the city to build up supplies, which could now be moved down Mount Igman but might be cut off if fighting intensified due to Serb anger over an unrelated Croatian offensive."

"The only viable possibility was driving across the tarmac of Sarajevo's Butmir airport and back up Mount Igman, and that route was also overloaded with what-ifs. The first was, what if the French simply refused to let us pass? We all knew that the French were only allowed by the Serbs to control the airport if they cooperated. In fact there was a French military liaison officer sitting in Lukavica Barracks who reported nearly everything he heard on the radio to his French-speaking Serbian counterpart. All that had to happen would be the Serbs telling the French to hold up that truck long enough to call in coordinates and dump a few four-deuce mortar rounds on it," Mackley said.

Mackley had been one of the conspirators when some official and unofficial Americans tried to smuggle donated telephone equipment into

Sarajevo to connect its lines to the world. The French repeatedly stopped them by informing the Serbs. The equipment eventually got through mainly due to the direct involvement of U.S. Ambassador Vic Jackovic. The French simply could not be trusted because they had their own agenda, which didn't have much to do with doing the right thing.

"Assuming the French did let us through their checkpoint, they might keep us long enough for that sniper with the SVD to get set up, or maybe the guy was already sitting out there waiting for us," I mused.

On Saturday afternoon, television interviews regarding the operation were given to both CNN and BBC reporters and they were likely to run the interviews on Sunday evening, which meant we had better be across the tarmac before that. We had smuggled a helluva lot of difficult-to-smuggle items, including the 20 Scott Air-Paks, $10,000 worth of medicines and a red fire truck into Sarajevo right in front of the Serbs' noses. Jordan and me on television, rubbing said noses in it would make for bad public relations with the Serbs, who might well dedicate some resources to try to kill us for it.

"We have no choice but to use the same route back. Even if we make it across the tarmac and onto the other side, four semi-trucks were destroyed by Serb artillery at the Hrasnica Bridge a couple hours after we passed through. We had made it through, but that was then. Beyond, there was Mount Igman and high exposure to the Serb 20mm aimed along Breakdown Ridge," I recorded Mackley and Jordan's concerns.

"There is no way in hell that anyone is that damned lucky," interjected Doc Gonzales, who immediately went to work sorting out the implements and supplies he would need to clamp off bleeders and start IVs into those of us who would need it. The benefits of driving the white truck were clearly outweighed by the disadvantages. Being mistaken for the United Nations might give us some official advantage with French privates, but it might also cause us some grief with the Bosnians, and being shot by your friends kills you just as dead. Also, the high-visibility white was no deterrent to the Serbs.

CORNERED

"When we go through, somebody is going to take a shot at us," said Jordan as we interlocked sandbags along the front and sides of the truck bed.

"They see a dozen guys in blue uniforms hunkered down in the bed of this truck and they will shoot. The question is how accurate and how sustained that fire will be. As we move along we will be looking for places to hide if the engine is shot out."

Mackley had insisted on the sandbags, but they were very heavy and too many would slow down the old Leyland, so we had to put them on the side where we were most likely to get hit, which for most of the route would be the driver's side. We interlocked the sandbags as best we could along the front corner of the truck bed and along the side to the rear. If the Serb sitting on that 20mm so much as twitched his finger, those 20mm rounds would sail through the tailgate, the sandbags, everyone in the back and into the cab before they broke the engine and exited out the radiator.

We barreled down Sniper Alley, where there was nothing but shot-out buildings and burned-out shells of buildings, no other traffic on the street. We lay low and could not tell whether anyone was out walking or not. It was 1649 hours and we were stopped at a checkpoint. We didn't know whether it was Bosnian or French.

"It is French. A couple of young men just leaned over the truck bed and asked for our passports, which gives the Serbs . . . how did you put it Mackley?" I asked him.

"It gives them time to know exactly where to shoot," Mackley said. I spoke into my tape recorder again as the two French privates went away with our passports. 1700 hours and we were cutting it close because in another hour CNN would come onto every Serb television set in Sarajevo.

We had been sitting at the French checkpoint for 20 minutes—plenty of time for the French to notify the Serbs at Lukavica Barracks—when Jordan came back and stuck his head over the side to let us know what was going on.

"Do you think the Frogs would shoot an American," asked Jordan, "for lifting the gate? Yeah, maybe so. I asked if they would let us into the bunker if the shit started coming in and they said 'yes.' Yeah, damn right they would."

"There are only two of them," Mackley noted. "The first mortar round comes in, we'll just run over their asses and go on in their bunker."

"By the way," said Jordan, "these guys say they are familiar with the sniper who shot up the trucks yesterday. They say he is here all the time and that he is at 100 meters out." The minutes dragged on and it began to drizzle. A large-caliber machine gun opened up in the distance. Just then Jordan reappeared. "We got another problem. The Frogs were about to let us through and this Land Rover pulled up. Don't stick your heads up to look, we don't want them to know how many of us are here, it might make the situation worse."

Jordan continued to give a play-by-play to those of us lying flat in the truck bed. "OK, in the Land Rover we have a Bosnian Brigadier and his wife and kid, a Bosnian Colonel and a British Major or Captain. They are arguing now. The Brigadier is telling the Frog that this is his country and he can go wherever he wants and they have no right to stop him. Guys, we may have to ram the gate and get the hell out of here. If the Serbs know this guy is here they are liable to send some bad guys in after him."

Mackley interrupted, "Jordan, where are the passports? Get the damn passports right now and we'll crash the gate."

"Oh shit," Jordan said. "The brigadier is reaching for his holster. Shit. They may shoot it out right here."

"Get the passports!" I yelled to Jordan as he dropped off the side of the truck. We had been sitting for nearly an hour by then and that was almost enough time to get 20 snipers in position. Sarajevo was starting to look like not such a bad place to be stuck after all. Then the pipe gate was lifted and Barrett drove forward. Everyone was suddenly silent and the tension was heavy in anticipation when the truck engine was suddenly turned off. Jordan's head popped over the side of the truck again.

"We're through the gate now so to hell with 'em, but we don't have the passports back yet and I'm getting sick of this shit. They let the Bosnian go through, but they are holding us back because they say one of their armored personnel carriers got in an accident or something up ahead. They still have our passports."

For the first time, Jordan's voice sounded a little concerned, which didn't do much for the confidence of the rest of us. "I'm trying to be nice with these guys. I'm not being an asshole, but I gotta get out of here. My mortgage company doesn't give a shit that French troops won't let me out of Sarajevo. We delivered humanitarian aid and it is time to leave now. By now the Serbs have had a chance to rag their French friends about yesterday and, who knows, maybe they have gotten the word to start some shit.

Maybe that is what they are waiting for. Whatever happens they have no right to hold me hostage in Sarajevo. They can hold the truck but they can't hold me and I will start walking across this tarmac very soon and take my chances with the Serbs."

Hoofing it across the tarmac was not good—there were too many of us and we would be strung out in a nice pattern for machine gunners or mortar crews. We would be better off either taking our passports away from this guy or forgetting about them and driving on ahead. Another long minute or two passed and Mackley and I had just about decided to take our passports off this French private's dead body when he handed them to Jordan, who threw himself into the back of the truck and suddenly we were speeding off across the tarmac and into harm's way.

Doc Gonzales, who was wearing a flak vest, lay across Mackley's body to give him a little protection since my vest was protecting the driver. We expected to hear the report of a sniper's rifle and his rounds cracking into the truck, but the only noises were from the truck's engine and gears. It was still daylight when we arrived at the last Bosnian checkpoint before the Mount Igman road. The guards refused to let us pass and several other trucks were pulled off to the side of the road.

IT'S A SETUP

Barrett told us, "What the Bosnians are telling us is that we were being set up for the Serbs back at the French checkpoint. A French VAB had fallen off the road and tumbled down the mountain. Three French troops had been killed and they were holding up traffic while the French tried to do a recovery."

"Get the hell out of here," the Bosnian trooper at the guard post yelled when we pulled the big, white truck to the side. "The convoy won't get underway over Igman until around 2300. You are going to draw fire. You are a prime target that jeopardizes all of us, so get lost."

As we started down the road, an AK-47 opened up on us from close range. We all went down as the rounds buzzed over us. Barrett put the pedal to the metal.

"It's the Bosnians shooting at us this time," Jordan yelled. "It's just a warning. They don't want us parked near their houses drawing Serb mortar fire.

We went back to the Hrasnica firehouse and waited for nightfall. As we waited, Mark Milstein wandered off in a cammo poncho. He was standing in front of the grocery store, his arms full of chocolate and sodas. A lot of starving people were watching from the surrounding apartment buildings when someone shot at him. The round landed between his feet, and the chocolate and soda went flying. Milstein's foot had just begun working well again after the last time he was wounded. He was in a bad humor when he came back to the fire house but Mackley had a great, long laugh and told him he damn well deserved it. (Mackley and Milstein almost got into a knife fight in the hotel dining room in Pristina, Kosovo a few years later. I had to intervene to preclude soiling the ratty carpet with blood and one of them ending up in a rat-infested KLA prison.)

About 2200, we returned to the checkpoint at the base of the Igman road. It was raining and black and we were grateful. After a few hours most of us settled down and snoozed fitfully as the skyline periodically lit up with explosions.

It was about 0400 the next morning when Barrett started the engine and we began moving up the mountain. We were about the seventh truck back as we wound around to the start of the road and put our big white tail toward the Serb with the 20mm gun. I got bored and started to doze off. Mackley rudely woke me up after a few minutes and pointed down the mountain. It was almost daylight and we could see. The weather had held for us; it was still raining and the cloud cover was low. The Serb gunners couldn't see us anymore. We were home free.

Further down the road we were held up in Mostar while a motorcade went by. It was the Bosnian president being followed by the Iranian ambassador. The Iranians were supplying him arms and all we had brought were $45,000-worth of Scott Air-Paks and $10,000 worth of medicine. About the only real help that Sarajevo was getting from the Americans thus far was coming from *SOF*, Doc Gonzales, John Jordan and the volunteer firemen. Eight years later Mackley visited the Sarajevo Fire House and found the Scott Air-Pacs. They were all the worse from repeated use and the firemen still remembered John Jordan, that giant of a man with brass balls whom we could never forget.

I swore I would never go back to that Godforsaken land. Until Clinton bombed it in 1999, that is.

32

HELL ON THE HO CHI MINH TRAIL: THE HUNT FOR AN EXTINCT COW

Lurch, jolt, lurch, jolt. Riding elephants for 12 hours a day at three klicks an hour was proving to be a mind- and butt-numbing experience as Robert Mackenzie and I moved through the desolate, savanna-type Cambodian jungle. Ant-covered bamboo slapped our faces in rhythm to the lurching gait of the elephants. Thank God and Gargoyle sunglasses we still had our eyes.

It was becoming another pointless, painful adventure. There had been a point to it all, but at this juncture, after hours on the back of an elephant, we found the purpose growing less and less noble.

Like most adventures, it initially sounded more intriguing and glamorous than it was turning out to be—like jumping from a perfectly good airplane, when, while shuffling to the door, the bile trying to claw its way up your throat, you ask yourself once again, "Why am I doing this?"

It all started in the spring of 1993, when Nate Thayer, a young journalist whose career *SOF* helped launch a few years before, called the *SOF* office.

"Brown, how ya doin'? How'd you like to go on a scientific expedition . . . to locate a species of cow that was thought to be extinct for 50 years?" He was talking about a creature called the "Kouprey," native to Southeast Asia.

Well, we always thought cows were for eating or, if wild, e.g. Cape buffalo, for shooting and then eating. A scientific expedition? Ho-hum.

Thayer, an American son of some diplomatic or upper crust family, was a daredevil, a handsome ladies man who had forsaken a normal lifestyle and gone native in Thailand. Ever resourceful, and some would say a certifiable mad hatter, he had been pushing the envelope for years. He'd had malaria 16 times, and kept a motorbike hidden on the Thailand-Cambodia border to periodically make unannounced drives into Khmer Rouge (KR) country. He also managed to get blown up when the truck he was riding in hit a land mine, killing ten of the other 12 passengers, and when he positioned himself to the right-rear of a recoilless rifle shooting Burmese from a Karen bunker, instead of a Pulitzer-winning photo he got a snap of the bunker ceiling and lost 95% hearing in one ear.

Vann and I had met Thayer in an ex-pat hangout in Pat Pong, the notorious red light district in Bangkok, a few years earlier. He was getting over some illness or other and was haggard and down and out. The fevered eyes enhanced his tall good looks. He had been risking his ass putt-putting on a motor bike into KR country, which was both stupid and foolhardy, so I put him on the *SOF* payroll for $400 a month. I was throwing the dice again, gambling on an unknown quantity. It wasn't the first time and wouldn't be the last.

He started turning in some good copy so I introduced him to one of the few AP journalists I respected, Denis Gray, the longtime AP bureau chief in Bangkok. Thayer, starting out as a freelancer, started selling more and more good copy to Gray and, was promoted by Gray to AP Bureau Chief in Phnom Penh, Cambodia, shortly before the '93 elections. He had nobody to "Chief" as he was a one-man show, but he made his bones. Because of his connections with the KR (nobody ever figured out why they didn't just shoot him when he showed up) he managed to orchestrate the surrender to the U.N. of some 400 Montagnard tribesmen from Vietnam who had been fighting the Vietnamese in the eastern part of Cambodia ever since the fall of South Vietnam in April 1975. The Yards, their numbers depleted over the years because of continuous combat, had been fighting along with the KR for years. A classic case of the "enemy of my enemy is my friend". He also played a part in getting the Montagnards resettled in the U.S.

A MADMAN ADVENTURER STRIKES GOLD

He later had an exclusive during the highly politicized trial of the genocidal murderer Pol Pot. Pol Pot, who was supported by the United States at first, ordered the slaughter of a million Cambodians. A newscaster I won't name, stole the scoop. Thayer sued him and received a bundle.

Thayer must have sensed I was less than enthusiastic about his cow idea, so he started upping the ante.

"Brown, we'll chopper into the base camp; use elephants to recon." On an interest level of one to 10, that was at about a two.

"We're going into KR country in eastern Cambodia, near the Vietnamese border, along the Ho Chi Minh trail." My interest level was now at five.

"We'll all be carrying AKs and whatever else is necessary." Interest level six.

"Our tracker/scouts will be former FULRO [United Front for the Struggle of Oppressed Races] Montagnards who fought the NVA for 17 years after Saigon fell whom I helped resettled in the States," he continued. "If we find that 'extinct' cow, we'll all be famous!"

Thayer, a very seasoned wheeler-dealer sensed me wavering. He hesitated and then sank the harpoon of adventure deep in my psyche.

"And there are marauding tigers in the AO. We'll need someone to deal with that threat. An AK, even on full auto, won't do the job quickly enough. We need a big-caliber gun and someone who knows how to use it."

Bingo! Interest level 10.5. I was hooked but good. I had hunted dangerous game in Africa but never thought I would have a chance at a tiger. Now, as our elephantine convoy continued to lurch and jolt through the bamboo like a sailor on leave, we wished I had spit Thayer's hook out.

After losing several thousand dollars' worth of camera gear to thieves who work the pricey Sukhothai Hotel in Bangkok, we arrived in Phnom Penh to be greeted by Tim Page, a crazy British film shooter who made his bones big time as a combat photographer in Nam, and Thayer, whom we quickly labeled "Colonel Kurtz."

Thayer, speaking fluent Cambodian, bamboozled my stainless steel Ruger .375 H&H through customs, prattling about being a friend of the king; close friend of the prime minister, yada, yada. Whatever works.

In the capital, we were headquartered on the second floor of an old, mildewy French villa that served as an office for the only English-language daily, the Phnom Penh Post. As we dumped our gear on floor, Thayer popped beers and said, "Welcome to the freest country in the world!"

Our puzzled glances prompted him to open a large cabinet containing an old French MAT-49 submachine gun, a selective-fire Chinese M-14, several AKs, an M79 grenade launcher and cases of ammo. Obviously, no 4473s required here. As if to reinforce his assertion, Thayer rolled and lit up a joint, continuing: "Anything you want. You can get a 50-kilo bale of pot at the market; there's an opium den down the street and you can pick up a case of AIDS without much difficulty." Hmmm. One might define freedom that way; all in the light of what you're smoking. The arsenal was intriguing, but we passed on the offer of dope and communicable disease.

Thayer's prior planning primarily consisted of drinking, smoking and banging the local bimbos. Even though Tim Page had assumed S-4 responsibility and acquired a fair amount of equipment, there would be considerable delay. Food, weapons, communications and air transport were among "minor details" not resolved for our 25-man foray into the KR-controlled, tiger-infested jungle.

Over the next days we cleaned weapons, scrounged equipment in Phnom Penh markets and met other expedition members. An experienced Italian veterinarian and author of the definitive book on camels, Maurizio "Mo" Dioli, was the scientific member.

Mo, Phnom Penh Post publisher Mike Hayes, his reporter and a Thai TV cameraman were ready to go. We awaited the four-man team of FULRO Montagnards with their American escort from Stateside.

We marked time visiting the battle zone at Pailin where the last remnants of the KR were battling for survival with the armed forces of the Cambodian government and aside from that just caught some rays. As we tanned, the plan evolved into final form. Alternative transportation had to be organized; the three Cambodian choppers Thayer had promised were not to be—turned out the Cambodian Army only had three choppers. Scrounging had us at operational status by the time the Montagnards arrived. Master wheeler dealer Thayer had convinced Cambodia's prime minister of the expedition's merit, so we had use of his personal twin-engine turboprop.

A RENDEZVOUS WITH ELEPHANTS

The first staging point was Sen Monoram in Mondol Kiri province, where the governor organized a truck for the next leg and provided a 12-man detachment of Cambodian para-military police because of Khmer Rouge in the area. The governor issued the Montagnards AK-47s to increase expedition firepower. The *SOF* team members brought their own. Next morning, our party with our supplies boarded a clapped-out truck and headed north on a dirt road. Most Cambodian roads boasted only dirt and potholes; this one ran more to potholes than dirt. The plan was to drive until we ran out of road, where we were to link up with elephants arranged by the provincial governor.

Of course, there were no elephants. By the time some they showed up, we'd lost another day. We hung out at the trailhead in hammocks, impressing local villagers. They were so enthralled that the headman invited us for rice wine (as third world vintages go it could have been worse, but not much) and a pitch for American aid, lest his village vanish. The chief had three wives and the village was knee deep in children and pregnant women, so vanishing didn't seem imminent. At daybreak we continued north.

KUOMINGTANG, ELEPHANTS AND FROGS; ALAS NO COW

All walked except the overweight American who escorted the Montagnards. By mid-afternoon it approached a stifling, heat-stroking 100 degrees. We had become separated into two groups, since elephants walk more slowly than men. The command element, English-speaking Montagnards and Thayer, were two hours behind.

"There is a river a couple of hours out," Thayer had promised. By 1400 there was still no river, so we stopped and waited for the "leaders." When they appeared at 1600 the priority was water, so we moved west toward the nearest watercourse. An hour of bush-bashing brought us to the blue line on their map, huge pools of water. Soon elephants were in one pool, Cambodian soldiers in another and the expedition was drawing water from a third. A third world car wash was underway in the elephant pool with much splashing and frolicking as the mahouts scrubbed their charges.

We reached the proposed base site the next day and pitched camp. The following day we split into two groups to search for the cow. Both groups saw herds of Banteng, another wild ox with which the legendary Kouprey often cohabits. One group also saw packs of wild dogs and wild boar but no cow, yet. The next morning as we were getting ready to leave our overnight site, Thayer's walkie-talkie crackled with the words we didn't want to hear. A sentry had spotted a Khmer Rouge soldier, who had also spotted him. The sentry returned to camp firmly convinced the soldier was not alone and that this did not bode well for our mission.

Despite Thayer's assurance from the KR representative that the area commander was aware of and approved our mission, there was no certainty all local KR guerrillas had gotten the word. On return, we had a hurried conference to discuss options. We could continue stumbling through the bush seeking the Kouprey, we could try to talk to the KR and assess the situation, or we could haul-ass back to Phnom Phen. The *SOF* contingent opted for the second choice since the KR surely knew we were there and showed no hostile intent. Prevailing sentiment, however, was that no one wanted to get killed looking for a cow, so everyone upped sticks and returned to base camp. The KR's reputation for ferocity and unpredictability was enough to tip the scales in favor of withdrawal. Things were not going well back at camp, however. Suffering from the heat, Page, a real prissy, sniveling Brit whined, "I am dying here. Please get me a helicopter medevac."

Right. On the Ho Chi Min Trail! News of KR in the area corroborated his premonition of bad things happening and reinforced his demand to go home. The American Montagnards' adviser was also down with heat and excess poundage—another candidate for medevac. With no radios to call the non-existent helicopter, we sent them out by elephant the next day. The TV cameraman, with several hours of footage already, and the Post reporter with a deadline, also returned with three of the elephants and four of the Cambodians.

The remaining crew spent the next several days looking for Kouprey in an area clearly devoid of any animal life (but far from the KR), as there was neither hoof print nor cow pie anywhere in the barren landscape. However, as we could not convince the semi-intrepid Montagnards' leader to go back to where we had seen herds of cows and the lone rifleman, we ended the futile search and returned to base. We broke camp in the evening in order to get an early start back to Sen Monoram.

Late that night, the dry season ended and in the next hour more than three inches of rain inundated our campsite, which was devoid of tarps. Amid curses and mutterings around the camp, our hammocks took on water at a slow but constant rate and did not let it out. The noise of the storm faded, replaced by a din such as we had never heard during many campaigns on many continents: The first monsoon rain was reveille to all the frogs in Cambodia, who had been waiting underground for it for months. Hundreds of thousands of frog voices in varying tones, timbres, pitches and strengths joined in a vast jungle cacophony loud enough to elicit empathetic vibrations in the intrepid expeditionaries' chest cavities. It was an incredible, surreal experience—National Geographic should have been there to record it.

Musing on the phenomenon, MacKenzie tipped more water from his hammock and wrapped himself in a sodden but still effective poncho liner, finally drifting off into a broken sleep in order to dream of giant frogs. Finally, back in Phnom Penh, Thayer gave MacKenzie and me a gracious invitation: "Let's do this again soon,"

"Go to hell! Once was once too much."

Just before 9-11, Vann and I met up with Thayer in Washington D.C. He had not changed. By then he had gained fame with his interview of dictator Pol Pot and was a sought-out journalist. He was restless, completely out of place in the city of pompous suits, and just waiting for the next adventure that could provide adrenalin rushes and a lawless freewheeling, devil-may-care lifestyle. 9-11 and the invasion of Iraq provided the opportunity.

■ CONCLUSION

AS LONG AS TYRANTS AND LIBERALS EXIST AND I AM STILL KICKING . . .

The preceding pages have described just a few highlights of what drove *Soldier of Fortune* and its teams to some of their global exploits while tackling the Evil Empire and other tyrannies. At first it seemed like a mission impossible to sift through the mounds of archives piled up over nearly four decades to try to get a book written. We were almost right; a mission nearly impossible. The project has taken several years and miraculously Vann and I survived the ordeal without severely maiming each other. Many of the players in the book were of enormous help, granting interviews and providing their input. Thirty-eight years on the go and ten times that many trips to over 60 countries, many of which included humping a camera in one hand and a gun in the other, racked up a lot of adventure and practically as many misadventures.

So much has occurred since the Cold War ended that those events would fill another book. *SOF* achieved what I believe was the most penetrating on-site coverage of the Oklahoma City bombing at the time, and took on the hostile homegrown militias in its reports. *SOF* has become a strong opponent of terrorism, has joined DEA operators and native SWAT teams in Colombia, Brazil, Argentina, Albania, Kosovo and other festering hell holes that keep the global drug war and war on terror fed and escalating. We were on the cutting edge of exposing the sex slave trade in early

2000 when the media was unaware of or shying away from the subject. A sellout issue included an interview with the French General who broke the back of the terrorist effort in Algiers by the use of torture. Americans were so traumatized after 9-11 that all reason had vanished in the wind and vengeance was the name of the game. *SOF* is a strong defender of the 2nd Amendment, which is constantly being challenged by left-wing control freaks. I have been elected to the NRA Board of Directors for 30 years. I even scored the Fascist Mayor Bloomberg of New York's NRA movers and shakers list. He can kiss my ass.

I am proud of the fact that the emergence of *SOF* offered Vietnam vets the recognition they deserved, a home in a sense, a meeting place for their souls. We valued their sacrifices, and Vietnam continues to be featured in *SOF*'s pages. We maintained from the beginning that the blood of our warriors shed in Nam was just as red as that of that shed in WWI, WWII or Korea.

Now we also cover the sacrifices of those who have gallantly fought the long and seemingly endless War on Terror. A difference is that with the onset of the age of cyber intel, many of our reports are from our troops exactly while the action is happening.

SOF defined and put the face on "participatory journalism." The distinction between us and other news organizations is that we embedded with local rebels, tribes and insurgents by invitation and carry guns, not just tag on with U.S. troops with a truckload of restrictions and official clearances. By the time the bureaucrats were going to get us approved to embed with troops as they were preparing to attack Iraq in 2003 the action could have been over, so I packed my bags and headed for Kuwait to meet up with the troops as they prepared to invade.

And I can make the case that we were the first private military "contractors," as we trained and fought with the Salvadoran Army, although there we have another distinction because we basically did it without pay.

I personally led groups of seasoned SpecOps or sent them independently into Afghanistan, the Sudan, El Salvador, Uganda, Rhodesia, Angola, the Congo, Lebanon, Mozambique, Burma, Laos, Chad, Nicaragua, Sierra Leone, Israel, Croatia, Bosnia and a good few others that I haven't written about. Many of those professionals of all sorts of different nationalities remain friends. Some died during some very dark days at *SOF*, including Lance Motley, whose body I had to accompany home from Burma; Bob MacKenzie who was killed and reportedly eaten by guerrilla cannibals in Sierra Leone; George Bacon, former Green Beret medic and CIA case officer, who was KIA by Cuban troops in Angola; and iconic martial artist Mike Echanis, who died under mysterious circumstances in Nicaragua. *SOF* staffers Craig Nunn and Alex McColl were killed in tragic traffic accidents. Bob Poos lost a battle to throat cancer. Rest in peace, warriors.

SOF doesn't shy away from taking a strong stand against the Pentagon, whether Republican or Democrat administrations are at the helm, nor point out the missteps which U.S. forces have gotten involved in.. Most of the intel we get is from the troops themselves who still rate *SOF* as the leading military-related journal in their arenas.

Because of *SOF*'s finger-in-the-eye style of journalism, I have been loved, hated and ridiculed by those wimps who lacked the cojones to do it to my face. They know where to find me. But ultimately, all that never mattered. I figured it was a sign of achievement that *SOF* became a KGB and later a terrorist's nemesis. As a matter of fact, I derived just as much pleasure by being a pain in the CIA's butt. And screw the liberals or "progressives," especially members of the press whose reporters had no concept of military affairs and who became "experts" after a few days in a five-star hotel with an entourage of security and cameras. That is a dangerous game they play because their propaganda has led down the path to misguided wars and other foreign disasters.

A case in point was the abysmal coverage of the Gulf War. Very few of those who had been accredited as correspondents had the faintest clue of the fundamentals of modern-day conflict. Another is the ongoing misjudgment of rebels we are supporting in Egypt, Iraq, Syria and other current hot spots. That misjudgment is going to come back to bite us in the ass as many of those rebels are terrorist-affiliated and will use us and spit us out just as the Taliban who we trained in the first Afghan war have done.

The mainstream media has been a vicious foe to us, but some of its members have also proven to be valuable allies. Joseph Goulden, a former deputy-director at Accuracy In Media, a conservative watchdog organization, admitted that he regularly read the magazine. "They report on events at a depth you don't find anywhere else . . . and I can't see myself spending a comparable amount of time with Time just to see what [its chief political correspondent] happens to think. I just don't care that much," he stated in an interview in the publishing trade magazine Folio.

Then there was the *Detroit Free Press*, which gave us kudos for blasting right-wing militias for their extremist views in an article titled "Leading the Charge": "Lately, in columns and articles, Brown's magazine has been attacking domestic terrorist; as enemies of liberty (and as a director of the NRA) of law-abiding gun owners." *Soldier of Fortune*, it said, had devoted long articles to debunking two widespread myths that were then being promulgated by militia-type conspiracy theorists. The first of these was that a fleet of black helicopters had been readied for use as part of a crazy New World Order by UN storm troopers or American soldiers under UN command. The other was that a train of flatbed cars carrying UN tanks and armored cars had been sighted in Montana.

I found it highly amusing that many of the members of the main stream media paraded through my office as we were about to attack Iraq and Afghanistan to pick my brain for what I knew about the players and terrain we were about to face. That could only mean that they had been reading *SOF* from the get-go. I was glad to oblige and have actually made some fine friends as well as enemies in the media.

I have met dozens of generals, a king, enough con artists, crooks, thugs and shysters to fill a large island where they should all be exiled together. I have been welcomed to the most exotic and forbidden war zones and met some of the world's toughest and most effective operators and officials, plus a fair share of just plain killers.

I have lived long enough to see the nemesis of most Vietnam vets, that ANTI-WAR traitor turned warmonger of convenience, John Kerry, become Secretary of State in a twist of fate I would have never imagined and can barely swallow.

But the enduring rewards have come from interacting with those hundreds of fine young men who grew up on *SOF* and whose decision to serve our country came from reading the adventures and non-stop action that we provided. Heroes-turned-authors like the late Chris Kyle, author of *American Sniper*, Major Rusty Bradley, author of *The Lions of Kandahar*, just to name a couple, told me that *SOF* was a primary motive in their decision to join the military. Hollywood action figures like Governor Schwarzenegger, Don Johnson, Sylvester Stallone, Clint Eastwood, Lee Marvin graced the covers of *SOF*. Sly even based one of his Rambo movies on a theme *SOF* gave him when he called the office.

For the last nearly four decades, I've been humping a rifle and a camera around the world's combat zones. I've hunted terrorists with the Rhodesian African Rifles and fired up a Russian fort in Afghanistan with the Mujahideen. I've searched for POWs in Southeast Asia and survived a Sandinista rocket barrage alongside Nicaraguan contras. In between firefights, takeovers and insurgencies, I've managed to put out a magazine. I've been doing it for 38 years, and I'll keep doing it until my luck runs out.

It's been a hell of a ride and as long as tyrants continue to pollute the environment, and I am still kicking, I march on with my mission. I have a few regrets and made a lot of mistakes but make no apologies. And I will continue to follow my long time motto; "Slay Dragons, Do Noble Deeds, and Never, Never, Never, Never Give Up."

■ APPENDIX A: *MY WAR IN EL SALVADOR*

BY PETER G. KOKALIS

The below article, which appeared in the November 2000 issue of SOF, provides an intensive insight into the type of training that SOF volunteers provided to various units of the Salvadoran Army.

I went to El Salvador to fight the Evil Empire twenty one times, more than any other member of the *SOF* staff. It became personal, very personal. My first trip was in 1983. My last occurred in 1992; just before the peace accord was signed. My decade in El Salvador was the seminal experience of my life. I wrote about my experiences fifteen times in *Soldier Of Fortune*. Although nothing I wrote could ever convey the emotions and memories I hold so close to my heart, what follows is a brief more or less chronological summary of my training missions, including the issue of *SOF* in which my account appeared.

SEPTEMBER 1983

The first and last words of the first article I ever wrote about El Salvador bear repeating as they eerily set the tone for my entire decade in that tormented land.

"Four companies of men pile out of new, tan-colored Ford, three-ton trucks and fall into formation in front of the headquarters building at Ilopango Airport, El Salvador. The usual grunting and straining is accompanied by the clatter and banging of field equipment and infantry weapons.

"My attention is drawn first to their cammies, a pattern I do not recognize.

My eyes sweep upward and lock on their faces—regal Mayan features, covered by death masks applied with black face paint.

"Who are they?" I ask, turning to the Mil Group adviser standing next to me. "The Atlacatl Battalion," he replies. "Bad asses, the toughest unit in El Salvador—an immediate-reaction battalion. They really kick ass. When they move in, the Gees [guerrillas] move out or die."

". . .While forever attracted to its implements, God, how I loathe war. And yet . . . no wine gives fiercer intoxication, no drug more vivid exaltation."

My first full day in country I trained the antiaircraft/perimeter-defense battery at Ilopango Airport on the disassembly-assembly/cleaning and maintenance of the M16A1 rifle. The following day I worked with the doorgunners of the helicopter squadron and their M60-D guns. Afterwards, I walked over to where the company from the Atlacatl Battalion was assembled and began to examine and work on their badly abused M60s. That evening 1st Lt. David Koch of the Atlacatl Battalion stopped by the hotel and asked if I could help them with *Las Cincuentas,* as they called the .50-caliber Browning M2 HB. The next day I did and the day following I worked with the Atlacatl M60 gunners. It was the beginning of my long association with the Atlacatl Battalion. Under the command of Lt. Col. Domingo Monterrosa Barrios and their executive officer Major Jose Armando Azmitia Melara they were without doubt the finest combat unit in El Salvador.

JANUARY 1984

I conduct an intensive three-week retraining cycle for the elite Atlacatl Battalion. Since its inception on 1 March 1982, the battalion has seen more combat than any unit in El Salvador. I trained the battalion armorers, conducted a section weapons seminar for all the officers and NCOs, trained the M60 GPMG and .50 caliber Browning M2 HB crews in depth, and conducted intensive ambush/counter-ambush drills.

MARCH 1984

Assignment to Salvadoran Cavalry Regiment—work with French AAT 7.62 NF1 GPMG, coaxial gun on the Panhard AML (*Automittrailleuse Legere*) Armored Car, and the earliest version of Heckler and Koch's HK21 GPMG, as well as the Argentine FMK 9mm submachine gun.

DECEMBER 1984

I had spent two weeks prior conducting weapons research and repair with the Atlacatl battalion. I also conducted trials comparing the M79 and M203 40mm grenade launcher. While the M203 when mounted on an M16A1 returns a rifleman to the platoon, its principal sighting system is a plastic quadrant sight that mounts to the left side of the M16A1 carrying handle. It's entirely too fragile and would return from 90 days in the bush in a paper bag. It was my recommendation to Major Azmitia that they decline the replacement of their M79s with the M203. He concurred.

MARCH 1986

Flying combat missions aboard the ancient AC-47 with three AN-M3 .50 caliber Browning machine guns mounted in the two windows adjacent to the left cargo door. Circling in "pylon turns" and blasting communist guerrillas to pieces was a rewarding experience, but after firing no more than 2,300 rounds all three of our original guns had failed and we were forced to call upon the spares. The mean rounds between failure was less than 700. There were also more than one dozen feed stoppages—cleared almost immediately by manual cocking. Why all these problems with the usually incredibly reliable Browning?

After the mission I spent a day in the air force armory inspecting maintenance, repair and calibration techniques used on these weapons. Not instructed otherwise, the Salvadoran armorers submerged the back plate assembly, without disassembly, into the cleaning solvent. Solvent seeped into the buffer housing and got trapped between the Belleville washers that then acted as a solid wall during the gun's recoil cycle, robbing the system of all buffering action. The consequent stress overload on the reciprocating components caused parts to break with alarming frequency. The immediate fix was to disassemble the back plate with the correct spanner, remove the solvent, dry and lubricate the washers and all reciprocating parts in the bolt and feed assemblies with the proper lubricant. As a consequence, the number of failures were reduced to acceptable levels.

AUGUST 1986

Training the Salvadoran Airborne Battalion I am afforded a rare opportunity to examine and study captured small arms.

MAY 1988

Working with the "PRAL" a highly secret clandestine infiltration group funded by the CIA and based at Ilopango, I study a wide range of land mines, anti-personnel and vehicular, but mostly improvised. They range from the *Mina Atlacatl* (named after the Atlacatl Battalion which first encountered it), *Mina Anti-Transporte Arce-1* (named after the Arce Immediate Reaction Battalion), *Rayo de la Muerte* (Ray of Death), *Papa* (Pope or potato), to the *Mina Caza-Yanqui* (Yankee-Chasing Mine).

While the U.S. left-wing press never ceased its cacophonous chant about the so-called human rights abuses of the Nicaraguan contras, they remained totally silent about the thousands of innocent *campesinos* maimed and murdered by Marxist mines in El Salvador.

NOVEMBER 1990

I designed an intensive five-day course for the *Equipo de Reaccion Especial* (Special Reaction Team or ERE) of El Salvador's *Policia Nacional* (PN), which would provide training in the handgun, MP5 submachine gun, combat shotgun, and M16A1.

SEPTEMBER 1991

Consisting of 50 enlisted personnel and one officer, ERE's mission included sniper incidents, barricaded terrorists with hostages, VIP protection and counterterrorist operations in general. In addition, the ERE continued to raid Farabundo Marti Liberation Front (FMLN) safe houses on an almost daily basis, capturing terrorists and large caches of weapons, munitions and explosives. All of these scenarios provided potential applications for highly skilled marksmen with scoped rifles. A three-day course was developed for the ERE that would offer Level 1 training in basic marksmanship, maintenance and the urban tactics required of police countersnipers.

MARCH 1992

Back in country to provide Level II countersniper training to the ERE, we participate in a house search that included 26 ERE members. No war that I participated in before or since, including Afghanistan, Angola/Southwest Africa or Bosnia-Herzegovina came even close to the total commitment I gave to El Salvador and its people. It was my war. *Siempre Atlacatl.* God, how I loved them!

POSTSCRIPT—Several years subsequent to the above events, the *Director General* of the newly formed *Policia Nacional Civil* (PNC), Rodrigo Avila, who I had met during the war, asked me if I would be willing to come to El Salvador again and help him with the several different SWAT teams of the PNC. They were in the midst of fighting the deadly street gangs, collectively known as *Mara Salvatrucha Trece* (aka *Las Maras*) and desperately needed training. Assembling a team of volunteer professionals, I accepted his invitation and went down numerous times until The FMLN candidate, Mauricio Funes became president of El Salvador on 15 March 2009. At that time I left another country whose war we had won only to lose the peace.

APPENDIX B: *CORRESPONDENCE*

DEPARTMENT OF THE ARMY
US ARMY ARMAMENT RESEARCH AND DEVELOPMENT COMMAND
DOVER, NEW JERSEY 07801

REPLY TO ATTENTION OF:

DRDAR-RAR 16 April 1981

Mr. Robert K. Brown
Editor
Soldier of Fortune Magazine
PO Box 693
Boulder, CO 80306

Dear Mr. Brown:

This thank you letter is long overdue. Your organization's contribution to our knowledge of Soviet weapons has ended years of sometimes rather wild speculation about the latest Russian small arms.

By bringing back the first AK74 5.45mm ammunition to be seen and tested by the Dept. of Defense, you helped immensely in adding to our knowledge of Soviet small arms developments.

As a small token of our appreciation, I am confirming my personal invitation to you for a future visit to the Army's Armament Research and Development Command; and home to the Joint Service Small Arms program.

As the project officer who headed the study efforts that have led to the military services decisions to discard the Cal .45 M1911 and Cal .38 revolver in favor of the 9mm, I am sure we will have some interesting discussions.

I see your staff needs to do some checking on the XM-18 assault weapon referred to in the article "Dogs of War" (Jun 81, SOF). Tom Swearingen in his excellent book, "The World's Fighting Shotguns", has a chapter devoted to the series of weapons now called the MM-1. However, for your edification, the series is not a new development, but the resurrection of the Manville guns of the 1930's.

DRDAR-RAR 16 April 1981
Mr. Robert K. Brown

It appears that all the drawings, tooling, and working fixtures, etc., were destroyed by Mr. Manville in 1943. The current private development of the weapon is based on a gun located in a museum. My intent is to clarify any misconceptions on the origin of this development and not to cast any disparaging remarks at whoever is presently working on the gun. Many excellent weapons, now in museums, have never been adopted for many reasons other than design. Additionally, this explanation was presented to give credit where credit is due; to the original inventor, Mr. Charles Manville.

Keep up the good work!.

Sincerely,

William J Bielauskas

for DAVID E. BASKETT
MAJ, IN
C, JSSAP Technical Working Group

EMBASSY OF THE
UNITED STATES OF AMERICA
Defense Attache Office, Islamabad, Pakistan
Department of State, Pouch Room
Washington, D.C. 20520

U-035-81

22 January 1981

TO: Lt Col Robert K. Brown, 315-30-9054
U.S. Army Reserve
P.O. Box 693
Boulder, Colorado 80306

SUBJECT: Letter of Appreciation

1. I would like to express appreciation for your outstanding service to the United States of America. Through your efforts, the U.S. Government has gained significant insights and better understands the militar capabilities of potential adversaries. Your efforts are greatly appreciated.

2. Your aggressiveness and steadfast determination in the face of considerable obstacles exemplify the characteristics essential for officers and leaders. You can be proud of the contributions you have made.

3. Again, please accept my thanks and appreciation for your efforts.

4. Request a copy of this letter be inserted in your personnel folder to document the significant contributions you have made.

Harold A Mauger, Jr

HAROLD A. MAUGER, JR.
Colonel, U. S. Air Force
Defense and Air Attache

THE LAW ENFORCEMENT ALLIANCE OF AMERICA

Lt. Col. Robert K. Brown
Founder and Publisher
Soldier of Fortune, Inc.
5735 Arapahoe Ave., Suite A-5
Boulder, CO 80303

September 15, 2005

Dear Bob,

On behalf of the more than 75,000 Members and Supporters of the Law Enforcement Alliance of America (LEAA), I am pleased to write you this letter of congratulations on the occasion of the 30th anniversary of Soldier of Fortune Magazine.

In three decades, the pages of your magazine have paid witness to the frontlines of the fight for freedom around the globe and even here at home. As a voice for those who know all too well the price of freedom, your magazine has served as a reminder to all Americans that the precious liberties granted by the efforts of our founding fathers came at a terrible but worthy price and their preservation over the centuries has been paid for by the lives of equally dedicated patriots in service to their country.

As a soldier, you've risked your life to defend our freedoms and as a publisher you've helped keep Americans aware of the ever present need for vigilance in preserving those freedoms. As such, I am pleased to award you the **Law Enforcement Alliance of America's *'Freedom Fighter Lifetime Achievement Award'*** on this the occasion of the 30th anniversary of SOF Magazine. The citation for your award is as follows:

Robert K. Brown (2005) For a lifetime of conspicuous gallantry and intrepid service in defense of freedom and liberty. Lt. Col Brown has served his country in uniform and in the private sector - A soldier, a scholar and a journalist. Lt. Col. Brown's service in the United States Army reflects his commitment to the defense of the American ideal of liberty and freedom the world over. As a journalist, Brown used the First Amendment to defend the Second Amendment here in the United States as well as the cause of liberty worldwide. As a scholar, Brown bucked the trend of academia to promote the important victory of liberty and democracy over the oppression of communism and tyranny.

I am honored to present you with this award, privileged to have you as a Life Member of the Law Enforcement Alliance of America, and proud to call you my friend.

Sincerely,

James J. Fotis
Executive Director

FEBRUARY 2006 SOLDIER OF FORTUNE • www.sofmag.com • SUPPORT OUR TROOPS! 59

THE NATIONAL RIFLE ASSOCIATION OF AMERICA

Resolution

WHEREAS, *SOLDIER OF FORTUNE magazine is celebrating its 30th anniversary; and*

WHEREAS, *From its inception, SOLDIER OF FORTUNE magazine has been uncompromising in its support of those who have fought against terror around the world; and*

WHEREAS, *SOLDIER OF FORTUNE magazine has been a champion of the men and women of the Armed Forces; and*

WHEREAS, *From its inception, SOLDIER OF FORTUNE magazine has been uncompromising in supporting freedom and the Second Amendment through its right-to-keep-and-bear-arms editorial policy and public appearances; and*

WHEREAS, *SOLDIER OF FORTUNE magazine has played a prominent role in electing pro-gun political leaders and defeating antigun politicians as candidates for various State Legislatures, the U.S. House of Representatives, and the U.S. Senate; and*

WHEREAS, *SOLDIER OF FORTUNE magazine originated in 1980 the concept of a rifle, pistol, and shotgun tactical match; and in the course of 21 years hosted a total of more than 10,000 individual competitors; and*

WHEREAS, *SOLDIER OF FORTUNE magazine, since its inception in 1975, has consistently offered Viet Nam Veterans recognition and support they so richly deserved; now, therefore, be it*

RESOLVED, *That the Board of Directors of the National Rifle Association of America, in meeting assembled in Anchorage, Alaska, October 1, 2005, recognizes and commends SOLDIER OF FORTUNE magazine on its 30th anniversary and for support of the National Rifle Association of America, the Second Amendment, and the fight for freedom; and, be it further*

RESOLVED, *That the text of this resolution be spread upon the minutes of the meeting, and that a copy, suitably engrossed, be presented to Lt. Col. Robert K. Brown.*

Attest: Edward J Land *On this* 20th *day of* October 2005

Edward J. Land, Jr.

SPECIAL OPERATIONS ASSOCIATION

PROCLAMATION

The Special Operations Association wishes to congratulate SOLDIER OF FORTUNE MAGAZINE (SOF) on its 30th Anniversary.

Whereas, The Soldier of Fortune Magazine has consistently supported the United States Special Operations community, and

Whereas, The Soldier of Fortune Magazine, since its inception in 1975, was the first publication to offer all United States Vietnam military veterans the recognition and support they so richly deserved.

Be It Therefore Resolved, That in this year of 2005 the members of the Special Operations Association are honored to recognize through this Proclamation its appreciation to Soldier of Fortune Magazine for thirty years of outstanding service in support of our Nation's Armed Forces.

Signed this 28th Day of September 2005 during the conduct of the Special Operations Association Reunion in Las Vegas, Nevada.

Fraternally,

JAMES F. HETRICK
President, SOA

FEBRUARY 2006 SOLDIER OF FORTUNE • www.sofmag.com • SUPPORT OUR TROOPS!

ACKNOWLEDGMENTS

Where to start? There are so many who have made this happen. First and foremost are the legions of readers and faithful advertisers who have supported *SOF* from the beginning and continue to do so, without which we would have never been able to continue our journal over the last four decades. And those amongst our readers and advertisers who supported our Afghan Freedom Fighters Fund, El Salvador/Nicaraguan Defense Fund and our First Amendment Defense Fund.

Vann and I would like to thank those who gave us input, guidance, suggestions and clarification and all of those who gave us interviews, some lasting hours or days in the last few years. Our thanks to Mark Berent, Robert "Bac si" Bernard, Alan Brown, Marty Casey (deceased), Harry Claflin, Jim Coyne, John "Boom-Boom" Donavan, Derry Gallagher, James Gebhardt, Galen Geer, Phil Gonzales, Bill Guthrie, Gerry Merceria, Hugo Hartenstein, Harry Humphries, Harold Hutchison, Lynn Kartchner, Sheldon Kelly, Jim Lyons (deceased), Peder Lund, Peter Kokalis, Jay Mallin, Pat Mackley, Malcolm McConnell, Jim Monaghan (deceased), Jim Morris, Jerry O'Brien, John Padgett, Michael Pierce, Colonel Mike Peck, USA (Ret.), Dr. John Peters, Mark Pixler, Columbus Smith, Dick Swan, David Truby, Steve Schriener, Steve Sherman, Major General John Singlaub, USA (Ret.), and Richard Venola, Darrell Winkler and others who I may have inadvertently missed who helped in this project.

I especially thank Lt. Col. Michael Lanter, who assigned me to my A-Team, and my sainted mother who kicked my ass to work harder, harder and harder.

Special mention goes to Vann Spencer who twisted my arms, not one but both, to focus on completing this too-many year project. Spencer's objective restraint, insight and vast knowledge of world events, familiarity with the world of soldiers of fortune and mercs were invaluable. Without Spencer's persistence and years of doggedly listening to my stories over and over again, interviewing, recording and writing and rewriting and rewriting again, the project would not have happened.

Casemate publisher David Farnsworth and editors Steve Smith and Libby Braden deserve high praise.

A last minute note: Quoted conversation by no means are to be construed to be precise. They simply reflect the flavor of words spoken decades ago. As anyone that knows me knows, I do not have precise recall.

INDEX